The Portable Mentor

Expert Guide to a Successful Career in Psychology

The Portable Mentor

Expert Guide to a Successful Career in Psychology

Edited by

Mitchell J. Prinstein
Yale University
New Haven, Connecticut

and

Marcus D. Patterson
Boston University
Boston, Massachusetts

Kluwer Academic / Plenum Publishers
New York Boston Dordrecht London Moscow

Library of Congress Cataloging-in-Publication Data

The portable mentor : expert guide to a successful career in psychology / edited by
Mitchell J. Prinstein and Marcus D. Patterson.
p. cm.
Includes bibliographical references and index.
ISBN 0-306-47457-3
1. Psychology—Vocational guidance. 2. Career development. I. Prinstein, Mitchell J., 1970–
II. Patterson, Marcus D.

BF76.P67 2003
150′.23–dc21 2003051301

ISBN 0-306-47457-3

233 Spring Street, New York, New York 10013

http://www.wkap.nl

10 9 8 7 6 5 4 3 2

A C.I.P Catalogue record for this book is available from the Library of Congress.

Printed in the United States of America.

To teachers and trainees in psychology,
and to all who inspire us to keep learning.
—mjp

To my Grandfather, Donald Manlove,
my mentor in life.
—mdp

Contributors

Mitchell J. Prinstein, Ph.D. is Associate Professor and Director of Clinical Training in the Department of Psychology at Yale University and an Adjunct Assistant Professor (Research) at Brown Medical School. The emphasis of Dr. Prinstein's published work in developmental psychopathology examines interpersonal models of internalizing symptoms and health risk behaviors. His research has been funded by grants from the National Institute of Mental Health and several private foundations. Apart from his research, Dr. Prinstein has had a long standing interest in the professional development of psychologists, beginning with his development of a survival guide in graduate school that served as a conceptual blueprint for this volume. As the elected Chair of the American Psychological Association of Graduate Students, Dr. Prinstein has had numerous opportunities to represent graduate student training interests to governance groups in psychology internationally, such as the Psychology Executives Roundtable, APPIC, the APA Board of Educational Affairs, and APA Council of Representatives. Dr. Prinstein was the first student representative to serve as a member of the APA Board of Directors, and he is currently the Chair of the APA ad hoc Committee on Early Career Psychologists. He created and currently is the instructor of a Professional Development Workshop Series offered to doctoral students in psychology at Yale University.

Marcus D. Patterson is currently a doctoral (Ph.D.) candidate at Boston University and an Adjunct Professor at the University of Massachusetts at Boston. As a student, Mr. Patterson was a member of the APA Committee on Accreditation and a member of the international Psychology Executives Roundtable. He served on the APA Advocacy Coordinating Team from 1996–1998, and has been an invited attendee at the State Leadership Conference for over five years. Mr. Patterson has also served as a liaison to the APA Council of Representatives, the Association of State and Provincial Psychology Boards (ASPPB), the American Board of Professional Psychology (ABPP), the Presidential Commission on Education and Training Leading to Licensure and on the APA Education Leadership Conference. He received the President's award for contribution and service to the profession of psychology from the National Association of Graduate and Professional Students (NAGPS) in 1998. He was the 1997–98 Rosenblum Fellow in Political Advocacy for the Massachusetts Psychological Association (MPA) and founded the MPA Doctoral Student Group. He was Chair of the American Psychological Association's Graduate Students (APAGS) from 2000–2001 and continues to serve on the APAGS executive committee. Mr. Patterson has written a number of articles and given numerous presentations on training issues impacting students.

Kathleen Barker, Ph.D. is Professor of Psychology at Medgar Evers College/City University of New York. Dr. Barker has combined social psychology with labor economics in her research on nonstandard work, higher education, social justice and methodological issues. She co-edited a collection published by ILR/Cornell University Press, *Contingent Work: American Employment Relations in Transition* (1998), selected as one of the year's noteworthy books in industrial relations and labor economics by Princeton University's Firestone Library. Her current research is in the area of nonstandard work and the erosion of tenure in higher education.

Jeffrey E. Barnett, Psy.D. is a frequent author and presenter on professional practice issues, ethics, and training issues in psychology. A Fellow of the American Psychological Association, Dr. Barnett serves on the APA Council of Representatives, is a member of the Board of Directors of APA's Division 42 (Independent Practice) and is the President of APA's Division 31(State and Provincial Psychological Association Affairs).

Roy F. Baumeister, Ph.D. has held the E. Smith professorship at Case Western Reserve University and will soon accept an Eppes Professorship at Florida State University. He received his Ph.D. in social psychology from Princeton University in 1978. He has over 250 scientific publications, including 15 books.

Nicholas M. Berens is currently a doctoral student at the University of Nevada, Reno. He has served as the Assistant Director of the University of Nevada, Reno Early Childhood Autism Program and the Assistant Director of the Center for Advanced Learning.

Paula J. Caplan, Ph.D. is a clinical and research psychologist, an Adjunct Professor (Research) at Brown University, and former Full Professor of Applied Psychology and Head of the Women's Center, Ontario Institute for Studies in Education, University of Toronto. She is the author of nine nonfiction books, including *Lifting a Ton of Feathers: A Woman's Guide to Surviving in the Academic World.* She is also a consultant on court-related matters and an actor, playwright, and director.

Lindsey L. Cohen, Ph.D. is Assistant Professor in the Department of Psychology at West Virginia University, and was previously on faculty at Washington State University. Dr. Cohen is the recipient of the Association for Advancement of Behavior Therapy President's New Researcher Award for his work in the field of pediatric psychology. In addition to his published work in this area, Dr. Cohen has authored, co-authored, and served as a mentor for over 70 oral and poster presentations.

Jill M. Cyranowski, Ph.D. is Assistant Professor of Psychiatry in the Department of Psychiatry, University of Pittsburgh School of Medicine. She has received postdoctoral support through NIMH-funded institutional training (T32) and mental health education (R25) grants. She has served as Co-Investigator on NIMH-funded R01 and R21 research awards, and she is currently Principal Investigator of a K01 career development award examining biobehavioral mechanisms of depression in women.

Daniel Dodgen, Ph.D. is Special Assistant to the CEO of the American Psychological Association (APA), Director of the APA Congressional Fellowship Program, and Senior Legislative and Federal Affairs Officer in APA's Public Policy Office. Dr. Dodgen has served on multiple federal advisory groups and executive committees of national organizations. He received his Ph.D. in clinical psychology from the University of Houston.

Rhea K. Farberman, APR is the Executive Director for Public and Member Communications at the American Psychological Association. In her position she directs the association's public education and media relations programs, serves as the Association's national spokesperson, runs its in-house publications department and is the Executive Editor of The Monitor on Psychology, APA's monthly newsmagazine.

Raymond D. Fowler, Ph.D. served from 1989 to 2002 as Executive Vice President and Chief Executive Officer (CEO) of the American Psychological Association (APA), the primary scientific and professional association for psychologists in the United States. As CEO, he was responsible for overseeing both the corporate and professional management of the 155,000-member association, for supervising a staff of 500, and for APA's continuing relationships with other national and international organizations. He received his PhD from Pennsylvania State University in 1957 and is Professor Emeritus of the University of Alabama. He is currently the Treasuer of the International Association of Applied Psychology.

Laurie A. Greco, M.A. is earning a doctoral degree in Psychology from West Virginia University, and currently is completing an internship specializing in Child Clinical and Pediatric Psychology at Cincinnati Children's Hospital Medical Center. As a student, she has been an author or co-author of over 20 presentations.

Corey J. Habben, Psy.D. has been highly involved as a psychologist and advocate for the unique issues of new psychologists. He has written and presented extensively on new psychologist and student issues and has represented new psychologists in several capacities within the American Psychological Association (APA). Dr. Habben is currently the President of Division 51 of APA. He has worked in private practice and currently works in Washington, DC at Walter Reed Army Medical Center.

Steven C. Hayes, Ph.D. is Professor of Psychology at the University of Nevada. An author of 23 books and 300 articles, he was among the 30th highest citation impact psychologists in the world during the late 1980's. Dr. Hayes has been President of Division 25 of APA, AAAPP and AABT and was Secretary-Treasurer of APS. He received the 2000 Hake Award from Division 25 for the applied impact of his research.

Elizabeth Henshaw, M.S. received the Master of Science degree in Clinical Psychology from Loyola College in 2001. She is presently continuing her graduate studies in the Department of Psychology at Loyola College while working in the mental health field.

Alan D. Katell, Ph.D. Earning his Ph.D. from West Virginia University, Dr. Katell joined the faculty of Nova Southeastern University. Advancing his interests in teaching, research, and supervision, he has studied eating disorders, exercise and fitness compliance, stress in the workplace, and clinical interviewing. He has served as the Director of Clinical Training for 10 years, and has maintained a part-time private practice for 20 years.

Alan E. Kazdin, Ph.D. is Professor and Director of the Child Study Center and John M. Musser Professor of Psychology at Yale University School of Medicine. He is also Director of the Yale Child Conduct Clinic, an outpatient treatment service for children and their families. He has served as the Editor of the *Journal of Consulting and Clinical Psychology*, *Clinical Psychology: Science and Practice*, *Psychological Assessment*, *Behavior Therapy*, and *Current Directions in Psychological Science*. Dr. Kazdin has published 35 books and over 500 articles and chapters since his Ph.D. in 1970.

W. Gregory Keilin, Ph.D. is a staff psychologist and former internship Training Director at the Counseling and Mental Health Center at The University of Texas at Austin. He led the effort to implement the computer matching system for psychology internships. He is currently the Vice-Chair of the APPIC Board of Directors and serves as the APPIC Match and Clearinghouse Coordinator.

Jessica Kohout, Ph.D. is Director of the Research Office of the APA The mission of this office, with its focus on the collection, analysis and dissemination of data on the demographics, employment and education of psychologists, dovetails perfectly with the focus of the chapter she coauthored with Dr. Barker. Her contacts with federal agencies and her counterparts at other professional associations have provided many opportunities to become familiar with outside sources of data and to keep an eye on the big picture.

Ronald F. Levant, Ed.D., ABPP. Since earning his doctorate from Harvard, Ronald F. Levant has been a clinician in independent practice, clinical supervisor, clinical and academic administrator, and academic faculty member. He has served on the faculties of Boston, Rutgers, and Harvard Universities. He is currently Dean and Professor of Psychology, Nova Southeastern University. He is currently serving his second term as Recording Secretary of APA.

Shane J. Lopez, Ph.D. received his Ph.D. in counseling psychology from the University of Kansas in 1998. Currently, Dr. Lopez is an assistant professor at KU and is serving as junior editor of the Handbook of Positive Psychology (Oxford) and co-editor of the Handbook of Positive Psychological Assessment (APA). Research foci include examining the effectiveness of hope training programs in the schools (under the auspices of the Making Hope Happen Program) and refining his model of and measure of psychological courage. He continues to advocate for improvements in the psychology training system.

Ann S. Loonstra, M.S. is a Ph.D. candidate in Clinical Psychology at Nova Southeastern University. She is currently completing her pre-doctoral psychology internship at Kaiser Permanente in San Diego, California. Throughout her training, she has avidly pursued both research and clinical interests in assessing and treating trauma and dissociative disorders, Dialectic Behavior Therapy, clinical neuropsychology, and marital adjustment in older adults.

Kathleen Malley-Morrison, Ed.D. is Professor of Psychology at Boston University. At this institution, she has served as a former acting Department Chair, Director of the Personality Psychology program, and the former director of a training grant to assist the development of students' research. She has been a committee member on over 100 doctoral dissertations, and is the author of many books, book chapters, instructor's manuals and articles—including several focusing specifically on the teaching of psychology.

Susan Allstetter Neufeldt, Ph.D. is lecturer and clinic director at the University of California, Santa Barbara, where she runs the training clinic, teaches basic counseling and supervision, and supervises practicum and supervision. Author of numerous articles and chapters on supervision, she has also written the first supervision manual, *Supervision Strategies for the First Practicum*, published by ACA press. Previously in private practice for 19 years, she was also Associate Professor of Psychology at Lewis-Clark State College in Idaho.

Ted Packard, Ph.D. is a Professor at the University of Utah. In addition to being a board certified counseling psychologist, Dr. Packard is immediate past president of the American Board of Professional Psychology. He has also served on the Utah psychology licensing board, the Association of State and Provincial Psychology Boards, APA's Ethics Committee, and, currently, with the APA Committee on Accreditation. He writes and lectures regularly on credentialing and regulatory topics relevant to professional psychology.

Paul A. Pilkonis, Ph.D. is Professor of Psychiatry and Psychology in the Department of Psychiatry, University of Pittsburgh School of Medicine. He serves as Associate Director of Research Administration and Development at Western Psychiatric Institute and Clinic. He has participated in all parts of the NIH grants process—as a funded investigator, as a member of NIH review committees, and as a program officer for two years at the National Institute of Mental Health.

Kenneth S. Pope, Ph.D., ABPP. in independent practice, chaired the APA and ABPP ethics committees. His publications include 10 articles in *American Psychologist* and 10 books, many on ethics and malpractice. An APS and APA fellow, he received the APA Division 12 Award for Distinguished Professional Contributions to Clinical Psychology, the APA Division 42 Presidential Citation, and the APA Award for Distinguished Contributions to Public Service.

William C. Rando, Ph.D. founding Director of the McDougal Graduate Teaching Center at Yale University, is a leader in the field of faculty and instructional development. He has authored or contributed to numerous publications in the field, including a book, *Learning From Students, Teaching on Solid Ground Techniques and Strategies for Interpreting Student Evaluations*. As a practitioner with nearly 20 years of teaching and consulting experience, he specializes in helping teachers transform passive, lecture-based recitation into dynamic, activity-centered learning.

Heather N. Rasmussen. M.S. is a doctoral candidate in the counseling psychology program at the University of Kansas. She received a B.A. from the University of Iowa and an M.S. from the University of Kansas. During the 2002–2003 academic year, she will be applying for the predoctoral internship in psychology. Research interests include coping, positive psychology, and multicultural issues. She hopes to pursue a career in academia.

Carla J. Reyes, Ph.D. graduated from the University of California, Santa Barbara in Counseling/Clinical/School Psychology in 1996. Her first academic position took her to Logan, Utah were she was introduced to leading the Psi Chi chapter. There she received the Outstanding Regional Advisor Award and recently was elected as the Vice President for Psi Chi for the Rocky Mountain Region. Currently Dr. Reyes is an assistant professor in the Counseling Psychology program at the University of Utah.

Leonid Rozenblit, J.D., M.S. coordinates the peer consultation program at the Yale University McDougal Graduate Teaching Center. He served as a teaching consultant at the same office, his emphasis on information technology in teaching. Leonid earned a J.D. from Louisiana State University in 1996, and expects to receive a Ph.D. from the Yale University Department of Psychology in 2003.

Valerie A. Simon, Ph.D. Assistant Professor of Psychology in the Clinical Psychology Program at Bowling Green State University in Ohio. She completed her postdoctoral training at Brown University Clinical Psychology Training Consortium.

Anthony Spirito, Ph.D. is Professor of Psychiatry and Human Behavior in the Brown Medical School. He has served as both a clinical supervisor for both predoctoral interns and postdoctoral fellows for 18 years. He also has served as a research supervisor for postdoctoral fellows for 15 years. He is currently the Director of the Clinical Psychology Training Consortium at Brown.

Robert J. Sternberg, Ph.D. is IBM Professor of Psychology and Education at Yale University and Director of the Yale Center for the Psychology of Abilities, Competencies, and Expertise. Dr. Sternberg is currently the President of the American Psychological Association.

Joseph E. Trimble, Ph.D. formerly a Fellow at Harvard University's Radcliffe Institute for Advanced Study, is Professor of Psychology at Western Washington University and a Senior Scholar at the Tri-Ethnic Center for Prevention Research at Colorado State University. He has held offices in the International Association for Cross-Cultural Psychology and the American Psychological Association. Dr. Trimble has generated over 130 publications on cross-cultural topics in psychology and received numerous teaching and mentoring awards for his work in this area, including the Division 45 Lifetime Achievement Award and the Janet E. Helms Award for Mentoring and Scholarship in Professional Psychology at Teachers College, Columbia University.

Carol Williams-Nickelson, Psy.D. is the Associate Executive Director for the American Psychological Association of Graduate Students (APAGS) and a former elected Chair of APAGS.

She is a spokesperson, representative, and advocate for APAGS and psychology graduate students to various credentialing, accrediting and governing boards and committees, as well as membership organizations, both internal and external to the APA.

Liang Yap, Ph.D. is currently the coordinator of the Massachusetts Alzheimer's Disease Research Center at the Massachusetts General Hospital (MGH) in Boston. Her past academic experiences include a Research Fellowship at the Laboratory of Developmental Psychology and Developmental Psychopathology at McLean Hospital in Belmont MA., and research experiences at the Behavior Therapy Unit at the Department of Psychiatry at MGH.

Philip G. Zimbardo, Ph.D. has been a Professor of Psychology at Stanford University since 1968, after having taught previously at Yale University, New York University and Columbia University. He has authored more than 250 professional articles and chapters, and four-dozen books, including his popular introductory psychology text, *Psychology and Life*—now in its 16th edition, it is currently the oldest, continuously selling textbook in U.S. psychology. Dr. Zimbardo designed, wrote, and hosted the award-winning PBS television series, *Discovering Psychology*, shown in colleges and high schools internationally. He was recently the President of the American Psychological Association.

Preface

Although graduate training in psychology typically offers students opportunities to develop an extraordinary number of skills and to be exposed to the enormous breadth and history of our field, training on how to develop a successful career in psychology is sometimes more difficult to obtain. The idea for this volume was borne from each of our experiences as Chair of the American Psychological Association of Graduate Students (APAGS). Through interactions with psychology departments across the nation, and with over 60,000 APAGS constituents, we learned that students and early career psychologists often express a need for additional information on practical career issues, such as how to write a grant, teach a class, publish a research manuscript, apply for a postdoctoral fellowship, or acquire skills necessary to begin a clinical practice, for instance. Students might acquire some of these skills through interactions with their mentor, however not all mentors have had experiences with each of these professional tasks.

The aim of this book is to provide graduate students and early career psychologists with a comprehensive and practical resource text on professional development issues in psychology. To accomplish this task, we have selected "expert" contributors who have demonstrated a strong commitment to training in psychology each to serve as the "field's mentor" in a particular domain of professional development. Thus, with this volume, it was our goal to offer students the best possible professional development training from the most successful leaders in psychology.

In designing this volume, we wished to create a resource that would be comprehensive in scope, and practical in use. The book is divided into five sections that cover professional development issues relevant to each stage of early career development in psychology. Chapters review topics relevant to both science- and practice-oriented psychologists, with a specific focus on universal hurdles and professional tasks that are not ordinarily included in typical graduate curricula. We requested that authors provide bullet-pointed lists, and illustrative examples whenever possible, as well as lists of additional resources for each topic. We also asked that each contributor provide the kind of specific instruction and suggestions that they would offer their own mentees.

Section One of the book reviews general, overarching issues that apply to graduate students and to young professionals beginning their careers. The book begins with a discussion of the scientist-practitioner model and guiding principles for developing a career that will have maximal impact on our evolving field. Chapters on cultural competence and ethics offer excellent discussions of topics that can serve as a foundation for decisions made throughout a career in psychology. Each of these chapters reviews issues specifically relevant to students and early career psychologists. This section concludes with a review of difficult challenges and helpful suggestions relevant to the balance between personal and professional lives.

Section Two includes chapters pertaining to career development in research and academic domains. Each chapter addresses a task that is crucial to a successful scientific career, but often not discussed explicitly during graduate training. Chapters on research offer specific steps for reviewing scientific literature and disseminating research findings, in both presentation and publication formats. This section also includes a chapter outlining the tasks involved in completing the dissertation, and a chapter with recommendations for preparing and teaching a course on psychology.

Section Three addresses professional development in the practice domain. An introductory chapter reviews opportunities to gain clinical experience at each stage of training, and offers ideas for the competencies that should be obtained following the completion of each clinical experience. This section also includes a chapter with specific strategies for beginning a successful private practice, including considerations for selecting a specific type of practice and business skills that are needed to manage it. In our experience, students most frequently have questions regarding application processes relevant to training hurdles in professional psychology. Four chapters are therefore included with concrete suggestions regarding the internship and licensure application processes, and information regarding board certification (ABPP) in psychology. Because many early career psychologists are also clinical supervisors, this section offers a useful discussion of models to guide the development of clinical supervision skills.

Not all psychologists are involved in professional service, but those who are often cite strong mentorship and excellent role models as leading reasons for their involvement. For this reason, Section Four is dedicated to the development of a professional service career, with chapters that help to explain the importance of professional service within psychology. This section begins with a chapter on the roles served by professional organizations in psychology, and the range of options for students and early career psychologists to become active in these groups, either as members or governance leaders. This section also includes a discussion of advocacy in psychology with specific ideas on how students and young psychologists can become involved with efforts to solicit support for the needs of our field. Two chapters address the promotion of psychology in the media, offering a vision and example for the successful public education of psychology, and specific guidelines to follow when interacting with a media source.

Section Five addresses professional development issues that are most relevant to the end of formal graduate training. This section begins with a comprehensive discussion of postdoctoral fellowships in psychology, including different types of positions and practical strategies for the post-doc application process. This section also includes a review of the NIH grant application process and funding mechanisms most relevant to early career psychologists. Two chapters addressing employment issues in psychology are also included in this section. One of these chapters reviews the application process for academic positions, and the other reviews recent data regarding employment trends in psychology and among graduates in psychology.

Overall, we hope that this volume will serve as a helpful resource for students, early career psychologists, and teachers of psychology. We have structured the book so that it might be used as a text in a professional development workshop series and/or a resource volume that psychologists can refer to throughout their careers. To all who are beginning their careers in psychology, we wish you luck and success.

MITCHELL J. PRINSTEIN
MARCUS D. PATTERSON

Acknowledgements

With a special debt of gratitude, I wish to acknowledge the hard work, cooperation, and generosity of the contributors to this volume, all of whom are devoted and deeply committed to the training of psychologists.

Thanks to Peter Salovey, Kelly Brownell, and Alan Kazdin for their support and guidance with this project. Also, thanks to Sharon Panulla and Sarah Williams at Kluwer for their assistance in the preparation of this volume, and to Erica Foster and Carrie Hommel for their clerical assistance.

Most importantly, thanks to my mentors, Annette La Greca and Tony Spirito, whose dedicated and selfless mentorship throughout my training served as inspirational examples, and helped me earn the opportunity to share just a little of what I learned from them in this volume.

Thanks to my family and friends for everything, always.

—Mitch Prinstein

This book would not have been conceivable without the influence, support and encouragement of my own mentors, supervisors, colleagues, and trainers. I want to thank the faculty and my colleagues in training at Boston University, within APA, and at the Boston Consortium. In particular, I would like to thank Bob Harrison and Dave Barlow for their personal and professional support around this project. Also, I would like to express my gratitude to Jessica Henderson Daniel, Kamala Greene, Liz Donovan, Wanda Grant-Knight, Terry Cline, Jerry Koocher, Marty Seligman, Jeanne Fama, and Kathie Malley-Morrison for their advice and support concerning this undertaking. The book would also not have been possible without the Job-like patience of my parents, Judith Hazelton and Trent Patterson, and stepparents, Phillip Hazelton and Mary-Beth Patterson, during this process and throughout my graduate career.

—Marcus Patterson

Contents

IV. YOUR PROFESSIONAL SERVICE CAREER

SECTION I

BEGINNING YOUR CAREER

CHAPTER 1

Taking the Scientific Path

A Road Map for Applied Psychology Students

STEVEN C. HAYES AND NICHOLAS M. BERENS

If the average applied psychology student is asked confidentially why they are pursuing a career in their field, the most likely answer is "to help people." Although this answer is such a cliché that it sometimes causes graduate admissions committee members to wrinkle their noses, in fact it is perfectly appropriate. The ultimate purpose of applied psychology is to alleviate human suffering and promote human health and happiness. Unfortunately, good will does not necessarily imply good outcomes. If mere intentionality were enough, there would never have been a reason for psychology in the first place, since human beings have always desired a happy life. It is not enough for psychology students to *want* to help: one must also know *how* to help.

In most areas of human skill and competence, "know how" comes in two forms, and psychology is no exception. Sometimes knowledge is acquired by actually doing a task, perhaps with guidance and shaping from others, and with a great deal of trial and error. This approach is especially helpful when the outcomes of action are immediate, clear, and limited to a specific range of events. Motor skills such as walking or shooting a basketball are actions of that kind. The person trying to learn to walk, stands or falls. The basketball goes through the hoop or it does not. In such areas, "practice will make perfect," or at least adequate. Sometimes, however, knowledge is best is acquired through rules that are carefully tested and systematized based on the verifiable experience of many people and then passed on to a learner. This approach is especially helpful when the task is complex and the outcomes are probabilistic, delayed, subtle, and multifaceted. Sending a rocket to the moon, or learning what practices protect a person from cancer are events of that kind, and human "know how" did not advance greatly in such areas until the maturation of scientific methods of knowledge acquisition over the last few centuries.

The problem faced by students of applied psychology is that the desire to be of immediately assistance pushes in the direction of "learning by doing" even though many aspects of applied psychology are not associated with outcomes that are immediate, clear, and occurring within a

---

STEVEN C. HAYES AND NICHOLAS M. BERENS • Department of Psychology, University of Nevada, Reno, NV 89557-0062

narrow and known range of options. A clinician in psychotherapy can do an infinite numbers of things. The delayed, probabilistic, subtle, and multifaceted reactions that may occur over time in a client, such as possible changes in attitudes, emotion, or behavior in others settings, are a weak guide to the direct acquisition of clinical know how.

This would be admitted by all were it not for two things. First, some aspects of the clinical situation *are* responsive to directed shaping and trial and error learning. Experience alone may teach clinicians how to behave in role, for example, because the parallel role-related reactions of patients (e.g., the belief that they may be helped; the decision to return for the next session) *are* relatively immediate and clear and students of professional psychology usually quickly learn how to produce these reactions. As the role is acquired, the confidence of clinicians will almost always increase, because these role-related actions from the patient reinforce the clinician's role. The clinician seemingly "knows what to do." Unfortunately, this type of know how does not necessarily mean an increase in the ability to actually produce desired clinical outcomes. That brings us to the second feature of the situation that can encourage students in professional psychology to to rely heavily on direct experience. Clients change for many reasons and what practitioners cannot see, without specific attempts to do so, is what would have happened if the practitioner had done something different. Many medical practices (e.g., blood letting; mud packs) survived for centuries due to the judgmental bias produced by this process.

These two features help explain how practitioners have often responded to the tormenting facts that clinical judgment is generally an extremely poor guide to clinical action (Dawes, Faust, & Meehl, 1989), and that general experience and training does not increase clinical effectiveness (Christensen & Jacobson, 1994). Many applied psychologists resolve the tension created by these facts by turning away from science itself, embracing instead the processes produced by direct experience: increased confidence and the biasing effects of the absence of proper control conditions. Change in the lives of clients is obvious to clinicians in practice, and the relationship between the clinical work and this change seems equally obvious. Relying on clinical experience is soothing and seductive, and if science values can be put aside, the tension of not knowing if one is really helping disappears.

In one sense, scientist-practitioners are simply those who have deliberately taken the harder road of retaining scientific values even though they too have entered into a career that is about helping others, whether it be in the clinic or in the research laboratory. Fortunately, due to the past efforts of others, it is a road that now does have some comforts. There is a vast literature showing that the use of specific empirically-based procedures with specific populations increases positive outcomes (Chambless et al., 1996; Hayes, Follette, Dawes, & Grady, 1995), for example. The applied psychologist can thus serve the immediate desire to help through the acquisition of scientifically guided know how. Even then, however, the road is not easy. For the applied researcher, what drives an interest in research is often the possibility of doing a greater amount of good for a larger number of people than could be reached directly, through the production of scientifically filtered know how that will be used by others. Unfortunately, this dream is surprisingly hard to realize. It is difficult to produce research that will be consumed by others and that will make a difference in their applied work. For the practitioner, a reliance on scientifically-based procedures will not fully remove the tension between clinical experience and scientific forms of knowing, because virtually no technologies exist that are fully curative, and only a fraction of clients will respond fully and adequately based on what is now known.

This chapter is for students who are considering taking "the scientific path" in their applied careers. We will discuss how to be effective within the scientist-practitioner model, whether in the clinic or in the research laboratory. We will briefly examine its history, and then will consider how to produce and consume research in a way that makes a difference.

HISTORY OF THE SCIENTIST PRACTITIONER MODEL

Despite its difficulties in linking science to practice the scientist-practitioner model of training in professional psychology is one of the most highly revered and (at least nominally) adopted training models in North America (Kanfer, 1990; Philips, 1989; Shakow, 1976; Stricker, 1992). From the early inceptions of applied psychology, science and practice were thought of by many as inseparable. This is exemplified by Lightmer Witmer's claim that:

> The pure and the applied sciences advance in a single front. What retards the progress of one, retards the progress of the other; what fosters one, fosters the other. But in the final analysis the progress of psychology, as of every other science, will be determined by the value and amount of its contributions to the advancement of the human race. (Witmer, 1907/1996, p. 249)

This vision began to be formalized in 1947 (Shakow, Hilgard, Kelly, Luckey, Sanford, & Shaffer, 1947) when the American Psychological Association adopted as standard policy the idea that professional psychology graduate students would be trained both as scientists and as practitioners. In August of 1948 a collection of professionals representing the spectrum of behavioral health care providers met in Boulder, Colorado with the intent of defining the content of graduate training in clinical psychology. One important outcome of this two-weeklong conference was the unanimous recommendation for the adoption of the scientist-practitioner model of training. At the onset of the conference not all attendees were in agreement on this issue. Some doubted that a true realization of this model was even possible. Nevertheless, there were at least five general reasons for the unanimous decision.

The first reason was the understanding that specialization in one area versus the other tended to produce a narrowness of thinking, thus necessitating the need for training programs that promoted flexibility in thinking and action. It was believed that such flexibility could be established when "... persons within the same general field specialize in different aspects, as inevitably happens, cross-fertilization and breadth of approach are likely to characterize such a profession" (Raimy, 1950, p. 81).

The second reason for the unanimous decision was the belief that training in both practice and research could begin to circumvent the lack of useful scientific information regarding effective practice that was then available. It was hoped that research conducted by those interested in practice would yield information useful in the guidance of applied decisions.

The third reason for the adoption of the scientist-practitioner model was the generally held belief that there would be no problem finding students capable of fulfilling the prescribed training. The final two reasons why the model was ultimately adopted is the cooperative potential for the merger of these two roles. It was believed that a scientist who held at hand many clinical questions would be able to set forth a research agenda adequate for answering these questions, and could expect economic support for research agendas that could be funded by clinical endeavors.

Despite the vision from the Boulder Conference, its earnest implementation was still very much in question. The sentiment was exemplified by Raimy (1950):

> Too often, however, clinical psychologists have been trained in rigorous thinking about nonclinical subject matter and clinical problems have been dismissed as lacking in "scientific respectability."

> As a result, many clinicians have been unable to bridge the gap between their formal training and scientific thinking on the one hand, and the demands of practice on the other. As time passes and their skills become more satisfying to themselves and to others, the task of thinking systematically and impartially becomes more difficult. (p. 86)

The scientist-practitioner model was revisited in conference form quite frequently in the years that followed. While these conferences tended to reaffirm the belief in the strength of the model they also revealed an undercurrent of dissatisfaction and disillusionment with the model as it was applied in actual. The scientist-practitioner split feared by the original participants in the Boulder Conference gradually became more and more of a reality. In 1961 a report was published by the Joint Commission on Mental Health voiced concerns regarding this split. In 1965 a conference was held in Chicago where the participants displayed open disgruntlement about the process of adopting and applying the model (Hoch, Ross, & Winder, 1966).

The late 1960's and 1970's brought a profound change in the degree of support for the scientist practitioner model. Professional schools were created, at first within the University setting and then in free-standing form (Peterson, 1968, 1976). The Vail Conference went far beyond previous conferences in explicitly endorsing the creation of doctor of psychology degrees and downplaying the scientist-practitioner model as the appropriate model for professional training in psychology (Korman, 1976). The federal government, however, began to fund well-controlled and large scale psychosocial research studies, providing a growing impetus for the creation of a research base relevant to practice.

The 1980's and 1990's saw contradictory trends. The split of the American Psychological Society from the American Psychological Association, a process largely led by scientist practitioners, reflecting the growing discontent of scientist practitioners in professional psychology disconnected from science (Hayes, 1987). Professional schools, few of which adopted a scientist-practitioner model, proliferated but began to run into economic problems as the managed care revolution undermined the dominance of psychology as a form of independent practice (Hayes et al., 1999). The federal government began to actively promote evidence-based practice, though a wide variety of funded initiatives in dissemination, diffusion, and research/practice collaboration. Research-based clinical practice guidelines began to appear (Hayes & Gregg, 2001), and the field of psychology began to launch formal efforts to summarize a maturing clinical research literature, such as the Division 12 initiative in developing a list of empirically-supported treatments (Chambless et al., 1996).

As the new millennium begins, professional psychology is more diverse than ever. A substantial body of evidence about what practices work best is now available, and governmental bodies are turning to that evidence for guidance in policy with growing frequency. New, more vigorous forms of science-based clinical training are available across the country (see, for example, the rise of the "clinical scientist" programs, McFall, 2000). At the same time, professional training programs that eschew the importance of science for day to day professional practice continue to grow as well.

The student of professional psychology needs to think through these issues and consider their implications for professional values. Professionals of tomorrow will face considerable pressures to adopt evidence-based practices. We would argue that this can be a good thing, if psychological professionals embrace their role in the future world of scientifically-based professional psychology. Doing so requires learning how to do research that will inform practice, how to assimilate the research evidence as it emerges, and how to empiricize practice itself. It is to those topics that we now turn.

DOING RESEARCH THAT MAKES A DIFFERENCE

The vast majority of psychological research makes little impact. The modal number of citations of published psychological research is zero. Most psychology faculty and researchers are little known outside of their immediate circle of students and colleagues. From this situation we can conclude the following: If a psychology student does what usually comes to mind in psychological research based on the typical research models, he or she will make only a limited impact, since that is precisely what others have done who have come to that end. A more unusual approach is needed to do research that makes a difference. The approach we will advocate here has been consciously followed by the senior author and has resulted in a citation impact of some note for that research.

Making a difference in psychological research can be facilitated by clarity about a) the nature of science, and b) the information needs of practitioners.

The Nature of Science

Science is a rule-generating enterprise that has as its goal the development of increasingly organized statements of relations among events that allow analytic goals to be met with precision, scope, and depth, and based on verifiable experience. There are two key aspects to this definition. First, the product of science is verbal rules based on experiences that can be shared with others. Agreements about scientific method within particular research paradigms tell us how and when certain things can be said: for example, conclusions can be reached when adequate controls are in place, or when adequate statistical analyses have been done. A great deal of emphasis is placed on these issues in psychology education (e.g., issues of "internal validity" and "scientific method") and we have little additional to offer in this chapter on those topics.

Second, these rules have five specific properties of importance: organization, analytic utility, precision, scope, and depth. Scientific products can be useful even when they are not organized (e.g., when a specific fact is discovered that is of considerable importance) but the ultimate goal is to organize these verbal products over time. That is why theories and models are so central to mature sciences.

The verbal products of science are meant to be useful in accomplishing analytic ends. These ends vary from domain to domain and from paradigm to paradigm. In applied psychology, however, the most important analytic ends are implied by the practical goal of the enterprise itself, namely, the prediction and influence of psychological events of practical importance. Not all research practices are equal in producing particular analytic ends. For example, understanding or prediction are of little utility in actually influencing target phenomena if the important components of the theory cannot be manipulated directly. For that reason, it helps to start with the end goal and work backward to the scientific practices that could reach that goal. We will do so shortly by considering the research needs of practitioners.

Finally, we want theories that apply in highly specified ways to given phenomena (i.e., they are precise); apply to a broad range of phenomena (i.e., they have scope); and are coherent across different levels of analysis in science, such as across biology and psychology (i.e., they have depth). Of these, the easiest to achieve is precision, and perhaps for this reason the most emphasis in the early days of clinical science was the development of manuals and technical descriptions that are precise and replicable. Perhaps the hardest dimension to achieve, however, is scope and as we will argue in a moment, that is the property most missing in our current approaches to applied psychology.

The Knowledge Needed by Practitioners

Over 30 years ago, Gordon Paul eloquently summarized the empirical question that arises for the practitioner: "what treatment, by whom, is most effective for this individual with that specific problem, and under which set of circumstances does that come about." (Paul, 1969). Clients have unique needs, and unique problems. For that reason, practitioners need scientific knowledge that tells them what to do to be effective with the specific people with who they work. It must explain how to change things that are accessible to the practitioner so that better outcomes are obtained. Practitioners also need scientifically established know how that is broadly applicable to the practical situation, and can be learned and flexibly applied with a reasonable amount of effort and in a fashion that is respectful of their professional role.

Clinical manuals have been a major step forward in developing scientific knowledge that can focuses on things the clinician can manipulate directly in the practical situation, but not enough work has gone into how to develop manuals that are easy to master and capable of being flexibly applied to clients with unique combinations of needs. With the proliferation of empirically-supported manuals, more needs to be done to come up with processes that can allow the field to synthesize and distill down the essence of disparate technologies, and combined essential features of various technologies into coherent treatment plans for individuals with mixed needs.

One way that can be done is through models and theories. It is often said that practitioners avoid theory and philosophy in favor of actual clinical techniques, but an examination of popular psychology books read by practitioners shows that this is false. Practitioners need knowledge with scope, because they often face novel situations with unusual combinations of features. Popular books take advantage of this need by presenting fairly simplified models, often ones that can be expressed in a few acronyms, that claim to have broad applicability.

Broad models and theories are needed in the practice environment because they provide a basis for the use of knowledge when confronted with a new problem or situation, and suggest how to develop new kinds of practical techniques. In addition, because teaching based purely on techniques can become disorganized and incoherent as techniques proliferate, theory and models make scientific knowledge more teachable.

Book publishers, workshop organizers, and others in a position to know how practitioners usually react often cringe if researchers try to get too theoretical, but this makes sense given the kind of theories often promulgated by researchers, which are typically complicated, narrow, limited and arcane. Worse, many theories do not tell clinicians what to do because they do not focus primarily on how to change external variables. Clinical theory is not an end in itself, and thus should not be concerned primarily about "understanding" separated from prediction and influence, nor primarily with the unobservable or unmanipulable.

To be practically useful, psychological theories and models must also be progressive, meaning that they evolve over time to raise new, interesting, and empirically productive questions that generate coherent data. It is especially useful if the model can be developed and modified to fit a variety of applied and basic issues.

Finally, to be truly useful applied research must fit the practical and personal realities of the practice environment. It does no good to create technologies that no one will pay for, that are too complicated for systems of care to adopt, that do not connect with the personal experiences of practitioners, that are focused on methods of delivery that cannot be mounted, or that focus on targets of change that are not of importance. For that reason, applied psychology researchers must be intimately aware of what is happening in the world of practice (e.g., what is managed care; how are practitioners paid; what problems are most costly to systems of care; and so on).

Research of Importance

Putting all of these factors together, applied research programs that make a difference tend to *reach the practitioner with a combination both of a technology and an underlying theory or model that is progressive, fits with the practical realities of applied work, and is learnable, flexible, appealing, effective, broadly applicable, and important.* This is a challenging formula, because it demands a wide range of skills from psychological researchers who hope to make an applied impact. Anyone can create a treatment and try to test it. Anyone can develop a narrow "model" and examine a few empirical implications. What is more difficult is figuring out how to develop broadly applicable models that are conceptually simple and interesting and that have clear and unexpected technological implications. Doing so requires living in both worlds: science and practice. The need for this breadth of focus also helps makes sense of the need for broad knowledge of psychological science that is often pursued in more scientifically based clinical programs.

THE PRACTICAL ROLE OF THE SCIENTIST-PRACTITIONER

In the practical environment, the scientist-practitioner is an individual who performs three primary roles. First, the scientist-practitioner is a consumer of research, able to identify, acquire, and apply empirically supported treatments and assessments to those in need. This requires well-developed practical skills, but it also requires substantial empirical skills. The purpose of this consumption is too put empirically based procedures into actual practice.

Second, the scientist-practitioner evaluates his or her own program and practices. The modern day scientist-practitioner "... must not only be a superb clinician capable of supervising interventions, and intervening directly on difficult cases, but must also be intimately familiar with the process of evaluating the effectiveness of interventions ... and must adapt the scientific method to practical settings ... " (Hayes et al., 1999, p. 1). This requires knowledge of time series or "single case" research designs, clinical replications series, and effectiveness research approaches, among others. Additive model group research methods, which use existing programs as a kind of baseline and thus raise far fewer ethical issues that group research protocols with no treatment control groups, are also gaining in popularity in applied settings.

Third, the scientist-practitioner reports advances to applied and scientific communities, contributing both to greater understanding of applied problems and to the evolution of effective systems of care. In today's landscape, a wide variety of contributions are possible from practical sites.

For example, clinical replications series in applied settings are highly valued in the empirical clinical literature (e.g., Persons, Bostrom, & Bertagbolli, 1999; Wade, Treat, & Stuart, 1998; Brown & Barlow, 1995). Clinical replication series are large collections of single case experimental designs and empirical case studies using well defined treatment approaches and intensive measurement. Their purpose is to determine rates of successes and failures, and factors that contribute to these outcomes, in a defined patient group.

These kinds of contributions are essential to the overall goal of developing scientific known how that will help alleviate human suffering. Clinical replication series provide an excellent example. For clinical research to be useful to practitioners it must be known what kinds of client are most likely to respond to what kinds of treatments. This question cannot be adequately answered purely based on data from major research centers because the number and variety of clients needed to address such questions is much too large. Only practitioners have the client flow and practical interest that formal clinical replication series demand.

The Scientist Practitioner in Organized Healthcare Delivery Systems

The combination of roles embraced by scientist-practitioners give them a special place in the healthcare marketplace as organized systems of care become more dominant. No one else is better prepared to help triage clients into efficient methods of intervention, to train and supervise others in the delivery of cost effective and empirically-based approaches, to deliver these approaches themselves, to work with complicated or unresponsive cases to learn how to innovate new approaches, and to evaluate these delivery systems. Unfortunately, with some exceptions (e.g., the pioneering work of Nicholas Cummings, see Cummings, 1991; Cummings & Hayes, 1996) psychologists have largely resisted cooperation with organized systems of care, so the contributions to be made by scientist-practitioners are more limited.

LOOKING AHEAD

The history of science suggests that, in the long run, society will ultimately embrace scientific knowing over know how that emerges from trial and error whenever substantial scientific evidence exists. That has happened in architectural and structural design, public health, physical medicine, food safety, and myriad other areas, presumably because scientific know how is a better guide to effective practices. The same shift is beginning to occur in mental health and substance abuse areas. But while progress has been made in the identification of techniques that are effective with specific problems (e.g., Barlow, 1994; Chambless et al., 1996; Roth & Fognay, 1995) it is clear that we still have a long way to go. Today's students will help decide how fast the transition to a empirically-based professional will be.

If the trends seen in other fields are a good guide, ultimately applied psychology will be required to adopt an evidence-based model. In the present day, however, professional trends continue to pull the field in both directions. Some in the practice leadership (e.g., Fox, 2000) have argued against embracing the movement toward empirically supported treatments, preferring instead the adoption of new forms of professional training (e.g., pharmacotherapy training).

Meanwhile, changes in the field itself make the scientist-practitioner model more viable. For example, the skills needed to add value to organized behavioral healthcare delivery systems are precisely those emphasized by the scientist-practitioner model. The scientist-practitioner model may yet provide the common ground upon which psychology as discipline relevant to human suffering will flourish. "When we agree among ourselves on fundamentals, we begin to take on the character of an authentic profession, capable of articulating itself to itself and to the rest of society." (Ghezzi, 1995, p. 261). Students of professional psychology will have a large role in determining how these struggles for identity will ultimately work themselves out. The scientific path is not an easy one, but for the sake of suffering humanity, it seems to be the one worth taking.

REFERENCES

Adler, P. T. (1972). Will the Ph.D. be the death of professional psychology? *Professional Psychology, 3*, 69–72.

Albee, G. W. (1970). The uncertain future of clinical psychology. *American Psychologist, 225*, 1071–1080.

Barlow, D. H. (1994). Psychological interventions in the era of managed competition. *Clinical Psychology: Science and Practice, 1*, 109–122.

Bergin, A., & Strupp, H. (1972). *Changing frontiers in the science of psychotherapy*. Chicago: Aldine.

Brown, T. A., & Barlow, D. H. (1995). Long-term outcome in cognitive-behavioral treatment of panic disorder: Clinical predictors and alternative strategies for assessment. *Journal of Consulting and Clinical Psychology, 63*, 754–765.

Chambless, D. L., Sanderson, W. C., Shoham, V., Johnson, S. B., Pope, K. S., Crits-Christoph, P., Baker, M., Johnson, B., Woody, S. R., Sue, S., Beutler, L., Williams, D. A., & McCurry, S. (1996). An update on empirically validated therapies. *The Clinical Psychologist, 49*, 5–18.

Christensen, A., & Jacobson, N. S. (1994). Who (or what) can do psychotherapy: The status and challenge of nonprofessional therapies. *Psychological Science, 5*, 8–14.

Cummings, N. A. (1991). Arguments for the financial efficacy of psychological services in health care settings. In J. J. Sweet, R. H. Rozensky, S. M. Tovian (Eds.), *Handbook of clinical psychology in medical settings* (pp. 113–126). New York: Plenum.

Cummings, N. A., & Hayes, S. C. (1996). Now we are facing the consequences: A conversation with Nick Cummings. *The Scientist Practitioner, 6*(1), 9–13.

Dawes, R. M., Faust, D., & Meehl, P. E. (1989). Clinical versus actuarial judgment. *Science, 243*, 1668–1674.

Fox, R. E. (2000). The dark side of evidence-based treatment. *Practitioner, 12*(2), 5.

Ghezzi, P. M. (1995). Science, theory, and practice. In S. C. Hayes, V. M. Follette, R. M. Dawes, and K. E. Grady (Eds.), *Scientific standards of psychological practice: Issues and recommendations*. Reno, NV: Context Press.

Hayes, S. C. (1987). The gathering storm. *Behavior Analysis, 22*, 41–47.

Hayes, S. C., & Gregg, J. (2001). Factors promoting and inhibiting the development and use of clinical practice guidelines. *Behavior Therapy, 32*, 211–217.

Hayes, S. C., Barlow, D. H., & Nelson-Gray, R. O. (1999). *The scientist-practitioner: Research and accountability in the age of managed care*. Boston: Allyn and Bacon.

Hayes, S. C., Follette, V. M., Dawes, R. M., & Grady, K. E. (Eds.). (1995). *Scientific standards of psychological practice: Issues and recommendations*. Reno, NV: Context Press.

Hoch, E. L., Ross, A. O., & Winder, C. L. (Eds.) (1966). *Professional education of clinical psychologists*. Washington, DC: American Psychological Association.

Kanfer, F. H. (1990). The scientist-practitioner connection: A bridge in need of constant attention. *Professional Psychology: Research and Practice, 21*, 264–270.

Korman, M. (Ed.) (1976). *Levels and patterns of professional training in psychology*. Washington, DC: American Psychological Association.

McFall, R. M. (2000). Elaborate reflections on a simple manifesto. *Applied and Preventive Psychology, 9*, 5–21.

Paul, G. L. (1969). Behavior modification research: Design and tactics. In C. M. Franks (Ed.), *Behavior therapy: Appraisal and status*. New York: McGraw Hill.

Persons, J. B.; Bostrom, A., & Bertagbolli, A. (1999). Results of randomized controlled trials of cognitive therapy for depression generalize to private practice. *Cognitive Therapy & Research, 23*, 535–548.

Peterson, D. R. (1976). Is psychology a profession? *American Psychologist, 31*, 572–581.

Peterson, D. R. (1968). *The clinical study of social behavior*. New York: Appleton-Century-Crofts.

Phillips, B. N. (1989). Role of the practitioner in applying science to practice. Professional Psychology: *Research and Practice, 20*, 3–8.

Raimy, V. C. (Ed.) (1950). *Training in clinical psychology (Boulder Conference)*. New York: Prentice-Hall.

Roth, A., & Fonagy, P. (1995, February). *Research on the efficacy and effectiveness of the psychotherapies (National Health Service Report)*. Report to the Department of Health.

Shakow, D. (1976). What is clinical psychology? *American Psychologist, 31*, 553–560.

Shakow, D., Hilgard, E. R., Kelly, E. L., Luckey, B., Sanford, R. N., & Shaffer, L. F. (1947). Recommended graduate training program in clinical psychology. *American Psychologist, 2*, 539–558.

Stricker, G. (1992). The relationship of research to clinical practice. *American Psychologist, 47*, 543–549.

Wade, W. A., Treat, T. A., & Stuart, G. L. (1998). Transporting an empirically supported treatment for panic disorder to a service clinic setting: A benchmarking strategy. *Journal of Consulting & Clinical Psychology, 66*, 231–239.

Witmer, L. (1907/1996). Clinical psychology. *American Psychologist*, 248–251. [Original article from *The Psychological Clinic*, 1907, 1, 1–9.]

CHAPTER 2

Cultural Sensitivity and Cultural Competence

JOSEPH E. TRIMBLE

> "Never look for a psychological explanation unless every effort to find a *cultural* one has been exhausted." Margaret Mead quoting William Fielding Ogburn, one of her mentors at Columbia University (1959, p. 16).

> "This was my first night in Lesu alone. As I sat on the veranda of my thatched-roofed, two-room house in the early evening I felt uncertain and scared not of anything in particular, but just of being alone in a native village. I asked myself, 'What on earth am I doing here, all alone and at the edge of the world?'" Hortense Powdermaker (1966, p. 51).

The two quotations from the well-known cultural anthropologists capture a part of the experience of what it means when one chooses to study and work with people from different cultural and ethnic groups. In her quote, the esteemed anthropologist, Margaret Mead referred to the "psychological" as innate, generic characteristics of the mind while the "cultural" referred to the behavior that one learned in her or his culture. Mead's quote refers to her experiences as a student with Columbia University's cultural anthropologist William Fielding Ogburn. In the 1920s, Ogburn maintained that the study of human kind lacked any useful comprehensive psychological theory. Then, and up to recently, psychologists were not at all interested in cultural explanations or explorations of human affect, behavior, and cognition. In fact, most psychologists then firmly believed that "all humans were alike" hence the need to identify and study cultural correlates exceeded what was sufficient to understand the sum total of the conscious and unconscious events that make up an individual's life. Although many behavioral social scientists would disagree with Ogburn's contention I take the position that before anyone can begin to apply conventional psychological principles and theories to an ethnic or cultural group, they must understand their unique lifeways and thoughtways.

JOSEPH E. TRIMBLE • Center for Cross-Cultural Research, Department of Psychology, Western Washington University, Bellingham, WA, 98225-9089

OVERVIEW

The two quotations serve to set the tone for this chapter on cultural sensitivity and cultural competence. By way of summary, one must exhaust cultural explanations for affect, behavior, and cognition before they attempt to apply conventional psychological theory and principles and to do so one will be intellectually, psychologically, and physically challenged. At first blush, why should any one be reminded that they must be culturally sensitive and culturally competent when conducting psychological research or providing mental health services for culturally different groups? Moreover, why should psychologists be interested in different cultural groups? "Of course they should," is the obvious reply to both questions. Although the answer to the questions is straightforward, there is considerable anecdotal and empirical evidence to suggest that historically psychologists in the main have not been sensitive to the lifeways and thoughtways of people from different cultural and ethnic groups. Accusations of imperialism, cultural encapsulation, ethnocentrism, parochialism, and, in some circles of dissent, "scientifically racist," run the gamut of criticisms hurled at the field of psychology in the past three decades. Robert Guthrie (1976), for example, writing in his strongly worded critique of psychology, *Even the Rate was White*, argues that culture and context were not taken seriously in the history of psychological research. Psychology's preoccupation with tightly controlled experiments through use of laboratory animals left little room for studies with people in their natural settings. Although the field has expanded its acceptance of various research methods and procedures, the full acceptance of culture and ethnicity into the fabric of psychological inquiry has not occurred.

Achieving true cultural competence and cultural sensitivity is complex and daunting. Putting the constructs into action in a research or clinical setting compounds their complexities. However, achieving a state of competence and sensitivity can be accomplished at some level of proficiency to the point where it does not sap our courage and subdue our fears and anxieties. Therefore, the intent of this chapter is to provide a framework for achieving and maintaining cultural competence and cultural sensitivity. To achieve the goal, the chapter is organized along several points where cultural competence and sensitivity are salient and prerequisites for conducting research and providing psychological services. Definitions and guidelines are provided for the two constructs followed by a brief discussion of the terms, ethnicity, ethnic group, and culture. Suggestions are provided for achieving competence as a counselor, clinician, researcher, and at a personal level. Since the achievement of cultural competence and sensitivity requires common skills and psychological perspectives, emphasis will be placed on the research setting. Thus, the chapter's last section focuses on cross-cultural methodological and procedural concerns including gaining entry to the field, cultural measurement equivalence, and collecting data and reporting the findings.

CULTURE, CULTURAL COMPETENCE, AND CULTURAL SENSITIVITY SPECIFICATIONS

Why should any student of psychology or psychologist be interested in and concerned about achieving cultural competence and cultural sensitivity? In spite of conditions to the contrary, psychology has all but ignored the surface and deep level meanings and implications of culture and ethnicity for the past 100 years. First, the mission statement of the American Psychological Association (APA) provides a partial explanation. Simply stated, the APA maintains that the object of the American Psychological Association shall be to advance psychology as a science and profession and as a means of promoting health and human welfare. Until about 30 years ago, the mission appeared to be restricted to a limited population as references to African Americans, Asian Americans, American Indians and Alaska Natives, Hispanics, Pacific Islanders, and Puerto Ricans were almost absent from the psychological literature; in fact, the words *culture* and *ethnic* were rarely used in psychological textbooks. The long absence of culture in the web of psychological inquiry did not go unnoticed. About 30 years ago, ethnic minority and international psychologists began questioning what APA meant about *human* and to whom the vast body of psychological knowledge applied. America's ethnic minority psychologists and those from other countries as well as a small handful of North American psychologists argued that American psychology was not inclusive of what constitutes the world's population—they claimed that findings were biased, limited to studies involving college and university students and laboratory animals, and therefore not generalizable to all humans. Comprehensive literature reviews reinforced their accusations and observations. Another response to the question concerns the growth of ethnic minority groups in the United States. America never was and likely will not be a melting pot of different nationalities and ethnic groups for another century or two. Consider the population projections offered by the U.S. Bureau of the Census. By 2050 the U.S. population will reach over 400 million, about 47% larger than in the year 2000 (U.S. Bureau of the Census, 2001). The primary ethnic minority groups specifically, Hispanics, African Americans, Asian Americans, and American Indians and Alaska Natives will constitute almost 50% of the population in 2050. About 57% of the population under the age of 18 and 34% over the age of 65 will be ethnic minorities. Currently, Hispanics number 35.3 million persons, about 12.5% of the U.S. population and are comprised of a diversity of races and countries of origin. Projections for the year 2010 suggest that Hispanics will be the largest ethnic group, second only to White Americans, and followed by African Americans. The 2000 U.S. census estimates that African Americans number about 35 million. There are distinct group differences in terms of socioeconomic levels, urban or rural residential distributions, and within group cultural variation. Asian-Americans and Pacific Islanders number 10.6 million in the United States. There are 32 different cultural groups with unique ethnic or national identities, different religions, histories, languages, and traditions that are included within the category of Asian American and Pacific Islander. The most numerous Asian groups in the United States are Filipinos, Chinese, Koreans, Japanese, Vietnamese, and Asian Indians. Moreover, the 2000 Census declared that 2,475,956 citizens are American Indians and Alaska Natives—a 26.4% difference from the 1990 Census, when the figure was 1,959,234.

In the 2000 U.S. Census individuals had the option of marking more than one "race" category, and so were able to declare identification with more than one group. For example, whereas less than 3% of the total U.S. population chose to do so, more than 4,119,000 individuals who chose to mark multiple categories marked *American Indian and Alaska Native* along with one or more "others." The *race alone or in combination* count is much higher for this ethnic group then the *race alone* count of 2,475,956. The discrepancy raises the question about which count is more accurate or representative of the *true* Indian population, 2,475,956 or 4,119,000. Similar findings occur for the other ethnic groups (see Pedersen, Draguns, Lonner, & Trimble, 2002).

The changing demographic context calls into question the relevance of a psychology that historically has not been inclusive of ethnic and racial groups and that fostered a research agenda that is ethnocentric and bound by time and place. How well prepared will practitioners be in the delivery of quality mental health services to ethnic and language minorities—to conduct research that is culturally resonant with the lifeways and thoughtways of culturally unique populations? The changing demographics will move the field toward the full consideration of diversity in ways that are inclusive and truly reflect diversity of our changing demographic context.

The third response to the question has to do with the concepts of *culture* and *ethnic group*. While there are over 150 definitions of culture, cultural and ethnic advocates in psychology generally agree with Brown's definition of culture that appeared in his 1991 book, *Human Universals*. "Culture," Brown argues, "consists of the conventional patterns of thought, activity, and artifact that are passed on from generation to generation in a manner that is generally assumed to involve learning rather than specific genetic programming. Besides being transmitted 'vertically' from generation to generation, culture may also be transmitted 'horizontally' between individuals and collectivities" (p. 40). Culture is transmitted through groups often referred to as *racial* or *ethnic* groups. Feagin (1978) defines a racial group as one in which "persons inside or outside the group have decided what is important to single out as inferior or superior, typically on the basis of real or alleged physical characteristics subjectively selected" (p. 7). An ethnic group, maintains Feagin (1978) is one "which is socially distinguished or set apart, by others and/or by itself, primarily on the basis of cultural or nationality characteristics".

Culture, ethnicity, and race are socially constructed abstractions and thus hypothetical constructs. Segall, Dasen, Berry, and Poortinga (1990) for example argue for an ecological approach to culture where the forces are the movers and shapers that shape behaviors hence "it becomes possible to define it as simply the totality of whatever all persons learn from all other persons" (p. 26).

Culture provides complex settings in which affect, behavior, and cognition occur and, therefore, at best may be viewed as overarching moderating variables. All cultures and ethnic groups contain identifiable values, attitudes, beliefs, languages, and corresponding behaviors that are often considerably unique and distinctive. Cultural lifeways and thoughtways emerge as adaptations to particular geographic and climatic conditions. Ecological conditions even influence what ethnocultural groups agree to ascribe to them. Given these considerations, psychologists can no longer ignore culture's contributions to the human condition and the extraordinary variability that spans population distributions. To understand and appreciate a cultural group's contribution to variability we must learn to be culturally competent and sensitive.

CULTURAL COMPETENCE AND CULTURAL SENSITIVITY DEFINED

There are numerous definitions and explanations of the terms, cultural competence and cultural sensitivity. At a general level, competence is a state where one is being psychologically and physically adequate and having sufficient knowledge, judgment, skill, or strength. Sensitivity is the capacity of a person to respond psychologically to changes in his/her interpersonal or social relationships. The component parts of the terms are embedded in definitions and uses of the terms when *cultural* is added. Orlandi (1992) defines cultural competence as "a set of academic and interpersonal skills that allow individuals to increase their understanding and appreciation of cultural differences and similarities within, among, and between groups" (p. vi). He continues by drawing attention to ones "willingness and ability to draw on community-based values, traditions, and customs and to work with knowledgeable persons of and from the community in developing focused interventions, communications, and other supports" (p. vi). The key words in his definition are *skills*, *understanding*, *appreciation*, *willingness*, and *ability*; perhaps the most salient of these is *willingness* for without a conscious intent and desire the achievement and realization of *cultural competence* is not likely to occur.

Moritsugu (1999) offers a more general definition where he maintains that it is "the knowledge and understanding of a specific culture that enables an individual to effectively communicate and function within that culture. This usually entails details regarding language and metalanguage, values, and customs, symbols and worldviews" (p. 62). The emphasis here is on *knowledge* and *understanding*. Emphasizing *skills* and *knowledge* in the context of counseling, Constantine and Ladany (2001) define multicultural counseling competence as "counselors' attitudes/beliefs, knowledge, and skills in working with individuals from a variety of cultural (e.g., racial, ethnic, gender, social class, and sexual orientation) groups" (p. 482).

A few definitions expand the construct to include stages of competence development. Ballenger (1994) identified six stages that include: (1) *cultural destructiveness*. This is the most negative end of the continuum and is represented by attitudes, policies, and practices that are destructive to cultures, and to individuals within cultures; (2) *cultural incapacity*. This stage represents systems or individuals with extreme biases, who believe in racial superiority of the dominant group and assume a paternalistic posture towards the *lesser* groups; (3) *cultural blindness*. The beliefs that color or culture make no difference and that all people are the same. Values and behaviors of the dominant culture are presumed to be universally applicable and beneficial. It is also assumed that members of the nondominant culture do not meet the dominant group's cultural expectations because of some cultural deficiency or lack of desire to achieve, rather than the fact that the system works only for the most assimilated; (4) *cultural pre-competence*. This stage occurs when there is an awareness of one's limitations in cross-cultural communication and outreach. However, there is a desire to provide fair and equitable treatment with appropriate cultural sensitivity. There may be a level of frustration because the person does not know exactly what is possible or how to proceed; (5) *cultural competence*. This is the stage represented by the acceptance and respect for differences, continuing self-assessment regarding culture, careful attention to the dynamics of differences, continuous expansion of cultural knowledge and resources, and a variety of adaptations to belief systems, policies and practices; and (6) *cultural proficiency*. This stage occurs when one holds culture in high esteem and seeks to add to their own knowledge by reading, studying, conducting research, and developing new approaches for culturally competent practice. Thus, a sensitive person can progress from a cultural destructiveness stage to a proficient stage of competence by actively engaging in the study and expression of respect for others regardless of their cultural or ethnic background.

In recent years especially in the subfields of ethnic minority psychology and multicultural counseling the term, *multiculturalism*, has replaced the term *competence* although the terms often are used synonymously. While the core meanings of *competence* and *sensitivity* are retained, *multiculturalism* is a more inclusive construct as its embraces multiple aspects and facets of what it means to value cultural pluralism. Because of the additive nature of the construct, definitions of *multiculturalism* are lengthy. For example, ten counseling psychologists compiled a 150 page ten chapter monograph dealing with an assortment of topics for the term (Sue et al., 1998). The authors define *multiculturalism* in four parts that encourage the exploration, study, and internalization of cultural pluralism. In a related text, Pope-Davis and Coleman (1997) explore the complexities of multicultural counseling competencies; their definition of the construct extends for several pages and takes up the better part of one of their chapters.

Culture and all that it means and implies is explicit and implicit to *multiculturalism*. Instead of asking whether or not one is culturally competent perhaps it would be better to ask if one is *multiculturally competent* as this captures the direction of the field and the interest. Interest in the field has accelerated to the point where it is now influencing psychology at all levels. Pedersen (1999) emphasizes that *multiculturalism* is "a new perspective in mainstream psychology complementing the three other major theoretical orientations in psychology; psychodynamic theory, existential-humanistic theory, and cognitive-behavioral theory addressing the needs of culturally diverse client populations" (p. 113).

BECOMING CULTURALLY COMPETENT AND SENSITIVE

Whether one is a student of psychology or a practicing psychologist attainment of cultural competence is not a linear path where one reaches some level of acknowledged proficiency and skill and in the process receives some sort of written verification of the attainment. Attainment of cultural competence and sensitivity is a life long journey that involves considerable self-reflection, a critical examination and study of one's cultural and ethnic heritage including those factors that influence maturation and enculturation, and a willingness to learn about the intricacies and subtleties of other enthnocultural groups with an open mind coupled with an adventuresome spirit. The journey begins with self-exploration and self-reflection. Self-reflection is a journey that is never over if one is faithful to the conviction that self-understanding never ends as long as one is open to change. Exploring all facets of multiculturalism involve change and flux. In psychology, a critical and thorough examination of the vicissitudes and essential character or constitution of multiculturalism are critical in the areas of mental health services delivery and research. The remainder of the chapter describes various suggestions and directions for achieving cultural competence and sensitivity cast in the framework of multiculturalism.

Self-Reflection and Ethnocultural Influences

Achievement of cultural competence begins with an intense interest and willingness to learn about one's cultural and ethnic background. All of us are a part of and linked to a culturally unique lifestyle; some of us benefit from multiple cultural orientations and influences, as our ancestral lineage may be a mix of relatives representing different nationalities, religious orientations, and ethnocultural groups. Thus, all people exist within a cultural milieu that wittingly and unwittingly influences who, what we are, and what we become. For full and active cultural competence to occur one must know the origins and nature of the factors that influence her or his uniqueness as cultural beings. The search and the eventual knowledge involves learning much more then why certain foods, languages, dress styles, ceremonial and religious celebrations, and music are preferred as it also requires we know the source and nature of our prejudices, attitudes, beliefs, values, mannerisms, gestures, affective styles, and idiosyncratic behaviors. All of these have a cultural base.

The search begins with asking questions of our relatives about our ancestral heritage and punctuating the questions with "why did we do that, or believe, or act that way?" These are daunting questions but no less daunting then the questions the cultural anthropologist, Margaret Mead, asks about Americans. She asks rather pointedly, "What are Americans ... How does one become an American ... Why are Americans as they are?" (1942, p. 80). Answers to these probes are extraordinarily difficult as most Americans rarely if ever reflect on them. Expanding on her questions, and to achieve more specificity, we can replace the noun, *American*, in the questions with such nationalities as Canadian, Mexican, or Australian or with place names such as New York, Toronto, Tijuana, or Sydney, or with the names of ethnic groups such as American Indian, African American, Asian American, Mexican American, or Puerto Rican. We can further break down the ethnic group labels into tribe, linguistic group, or region of the world where a variant of the group lives (e.g., Jamaica, Brazil, Japan, Papua, or the Yukon Territory). In all instances, each is a cultural unit or *cultunit* ("cultural bearing unit") rich with all of those elements that constitute a cultural group and thus rich with deep cultural information for one to explore (see Berry, Poortinga, Segall, & Dasen, 1992, pp. 176–177). What, how and why therefore are practical beginnings towards achieving understanding of one's origins and sociocultural influences. A list of sources for developing and achieving *cultural self-empathy* is included at the end of this chapter.

Cultural self-reflection activities and explorations bring the unconscious, often subtle factors to the forefront of our conscious hopefully providing enlightenment and *deep-cultural self-empathy* (Ridley & Udipi, 2002). Sodowsky, Kuo-Jackson, and Loya (1997) remind us that "through continuous self-focus and deep introspection, counselors (and other psychologists) can become more sensitive to their cultural-self. Such deep-cultural self-empathy or sensitive understanding of one's cultural-self will, in turn facilitate accurate empathy with clients (and others) who are culturally different" (p. 12).

Achieving Multicultural Counseling Competence

Before 1976, close to 25 articles and chapters were written on the subject of culture and counseling. Now in 2002 and since 1976 close to 500 books, chapters, and journal articles have been written expressing a variety of perspectives on the topic ranging from theory to research findings. The accelerated rate of interest and concern generated on the topic in the past 25 years or so is extraordinary but not surprising. The argument and justification for the increased interest rest on the contention that conventional counseling and mental health service delivery approaches are incompatible with the lifeways and thoughtways of ethnocultural groups. Since all thoughts and behaviors are culturally based accurate assessment, meaningful understanding, and culturally appropriate interventions are required for the understanding of each context for counseling to effectively occur.

Multicultural counselors and mental health practitioners assert that one must demonstrate multicultural competence and sensitivity to work with culturally different clients. A seminal paper written for the *Counseling Psychologist* journal by Sue, Bernier, Durran, Feinberg, Pedersen, Smith and Vasquez-Nuttal (1982) stimulated interest in this area. The authors present a series of explicit multicultural counseling competencies that since have been modified in various forms. In essence, the central themes of the competency guidelines include: "knowledge about diversity; psychological client-counselor policies; client's collective culture; client's religion and beliefs; client's language; client's experience with racism; psychologist's advocacy role; psychologist's client notes address cultural factors; client's economic and political conditions; client's cultural identity; and client variables' interventions" (Sodowsky, Kuo-Jackson, & Loya, 1997, pp. 6–7). Detailed presentations of the guidelines can be found on the following internet web sites: http://www.counseling.org/multi_diversity/competencies.htm; and http://www.apa.org/divisions/div45/resources.html.

Interest in multicultural counseling is not uniform and consistent. Some critics see the domain as another example of "political correctness" while others comment that it is a passing fancy and will dwindle in influence in time. Within the field, a few psychologists are challenging the meaning of multiculturalism and the extent to which it truly captures interpersonal dynamics and the influence of race and ethnicity in society. Helms and Richardson (1997) argue the position that multicultural competence requires a philosophical orientation grounded on the sociopolitical principles of race and enculturation. From their perspective, solely emphasizing development of multicultural competency skills is insufficient, as counselors must be knowledgeable and sensitive to the sociopolitical and historical backgrounds of their clients. From their perspective, multiculturalism "should refer to the integration of dimensions of client cultures into pertinent counseling theories, techniques, and practices with the specific intent of providing clients of all sociodemographic and psychodynamic variations with effective mental health services" (p.70). Put more succinctly, the authors maintain that counselors should tailor their approaches "to react to each of the various dynamics of clients in a manner that best suits the clients' mental health needs" (p. 70).

Developing and acquiring multicultural counseling competencies is extraordinarily complicated and engaging, especially if one aspires to work with clients from a myriad of cultural backgrounds and levels of acculturation. It can be difficult, too, when one strives to work with clients from their own ethnic group and assumes they know the depth of their clients' ethnocultural backgrounds. Becoming multiculturally competent can occur through reading, participating in intensive workshops, attending conference presentations. However, the acquisition of competency skills and knowledge through didactic approaches is incomplete. One must experience a culture in all of its moods and settings to fully understand the potential applicability of counseling skills and techniques within a cultural milieu.

As interest in the field of multicultural counseling has grown more and more, counselors and students are asking questions on how one should provide counseling services for culturally different clients, that is, clients who are from ethnocultural groups different from one's own. In addition and invariably, the inquisitive persons want to know where they can obtain the skills to be multiculturally competent in mental health settings. Even a straightforward answer is complicated, involved, daunting, and conditional.

For the sake of illustration let us focus on the first part of the inquiry. As discussed earlier cultural differences are varied and pervasive. To understand the extent and pervasiveness of culture and the counseling relationship consider the following: (1) the cultural orientation of the counselor and the extent to which he or she is continuously involved in self-focus and deep cultural introspection of their cultural-selves; (2) the culture of the client and the extent to which they are self-aware and involved in the cultural or ethnic group with which they identify if they do at all; (3) the negative assumptions related to the counseling process which may be quite different from the cultural orientation of the counselor and the client; and (4) the culture of the environment in which the counseling occurs (Pedersen, Lonner, & Draguns, 1976). We can roll these four together and find "ourselves working with a client from another culture, on a problem relating to a third culture, in the environment of a fourth culture where each participating culture presents its own demands" (Pedersen et al., 1976, p. vii). While extreme, nonetheless the scenario represents the extraordinary complexities associated with providing counseling to culturally unique clients.

Many students and practitioners wonder what counseling styles or theoretical orientations would be most effective and useful with cultural and ethnic clients. Unfortunately, there is no simple, straightforward recommendation here, too. On the one hand, if a counselor shows evidence of being warm and empathetic, establishes trust and rapport, shows respect for cultural values and beliefs, and expresses flexibility in meeting the client's expectations, then it would make sense that any counseling style would work. Yet a number of writers in the field suggest that certain styles are likely to be more effective than others, even though there is at this point little empirical evidence to support their claims.

Throughout the writings on the topic of multicultural counseling, one theme surfaces repeatedly: Counselors of culturally ethnically different clients must be adaptive and flexible in their personal orientation and use of conventional counseling techniques. Commitment to understanding the cultural context and unique cultural characteristics of clients also is essential. This often requires counselors to extend their efforts beyond what is typical in a conventional office. Thus, in general, when faced with a culturally different client one should be mindful of the following recommendations offered by Miller (1982): (1) a counselor's personal identification with the culture of a client is hardly sufficient for a thorough understanding of the impact of a cultural lifestyle on a client; (2) a client's personal history contains information that focuses on certain strengths, and this can be useful in promoting positive counseling expectations; (3) counselors should be aware of their own personal biases and stereotypes about cultural pluralism; (4) counselors should encourage clients to become active in identifying and learning the various thoughts and behaviors that promote positive growth and development; and (5) the most important yet basic counseling approaches involve empathy, caring, and a sense of the importance of the human potential.

The answer to the second part of the question requires careful study and participation in programs that emphasize multicultural counseling education. Indeed, numerous books have been written on the subject and more are becoming available. Similarly, the topic has become a major focal point of professional psychological conferences and meetings. Taken together these are rich sources of information. Unfortunately, not all counseling psychology graduate and professional schools in psychology embrace multiculturalism and thus do not fully endorse multicultural counseling guidelines. Avoid these institutions if you aspire to work in the multicultural counseling or clinical fields. Counseling and clinical psychology programs should be accredited primarily by the American Psychological Association (APA) and if they are then one can be assured that culture and ethnicity are included in the curriculum and field and internship experiences. The APA has a cultural competence standard in its accreditation protocol. Fortunately, there is a growing list of institutions where one can receive culturally appropriate and sensitive graduate education in counseling; that was not the case ten years ago. Currently, the American Psychological Association provides a list of such institutions through its Office of Ethnic Minority Affairs (see www.apa.org/pi/oema). Among these, the APA selects specific colleges and universities whose programs demonstrate excellence in the recruitment and retention of ethnic minority to receive the APA Suinn Minority Achievement Award; one of the selection criteria centers on the presence and emphasis of multicultural competence in teaching, practice, and research.

Achieving Multicultural Competence in Research

The standards and criteria for achieving multicultural counseling competence and sensitivity also apply to conducting research with ethnocultural groups although the themes and approaches vary to accommodate the methodological rigors attached to the research venture. Both fields require that one gather, interpret, and analyze information however methods and procedures will vary depending on the research question. The counselor is interested primarily in the client's background and the diagnosis of the presenting problem while the researcher typically is interested in testing hypotheses and components of a theory where something about the sample population's culture is of prime interest. To an extent, the similarities end there as the research venture is filled with numerous theoretical, procedural, and methodological considerations one is not likely to encounter in the multicultural counseling field.

Given the current interest in cross-cultural and ethnic psychology, it would be safe to conclude that more and more studies will be directed to culturally different populations, not only in North America but probably for other nation states, too. Consequently, social scientists face a multitude of theoretical and methodological concerns quite often presented by ethnocultural groups whose cultures are unique in contrast to the dominant groups in North America. Predictably, the ongoing and increasingly significant work of cross-cultural psychologists will be a source for guidance and direction. For example, the official publication of the International Association for Cross-Cultural Psychology (http://www.iaccp.org/), the *Journal of Cross-Cultural Psychology*, is an excellent resource as it now contains over 30 years worth of excellent research findings and commentary on the subject.

To build one's research cultural competence requires researchers to examine the methodologies of cross-cultural psychologists, cultural and ethnic psychologists, and cultural anthropologists especially those directed to the conduct of field based research. One should be aware that cross-cultural psychology is defined more by methodology than by findings (Berry, Poortinga, Segall, & Dasen, 1992). Knowledge of the empirical findings in both fields may prove useful, but not nearly as useful as the methods. Building research cultural competence requires that researchers place an emphasis on what cross-cultural psychologists refer to as *universals* not universal psychological constructs or similarities in behavior, but universally acceptable methods of generating empirical data. A discussion of universal psychological processes has itself received a good deal of attention and criticism (Jahoda, 1980).

The basic challenge for a field approach to cross-cultural psychology is to identify useful and appropriate *methodological etics*—research technologies that are both sensitive and appropriate for use in all cultural groups. It would be naive for one to assume that a *methodological etic* is sufficient to collect data from different cultural folks—other intercultural nuances may exist that could affect data collection and use of results. In an attempt to highlight issues and problems, the remaining sections of the chapter focus on major and selected methodological concerns, the influence of researchers as agents of sociopolitical change, and the ethical and social responsibilities of applied researchers.

In conducting culturally distinct research with ethnocultural groups, the would-be researcher sets a process in motion that of necessity must take into consideration the *ethos* and *eidos* of the groups in question. Not to do so could lead to an early death of the project and likely alienate the research team from future work with the community. In turn, as has happened far too often, community members receive further substantiation for their levels of distrust toward research and its progenitors. Lack of cultural sensitivity and awareness of community dynamics sets up a difficult situation and science receives a bad reputation (often much deserved), and the community problem continues to go unsolved.

What can one do to minimize cross-cultural conflicts accruing from the researcher-community interface? Fortunately, owing to the growing body of research in cross-cultural settings, a good deal can be learned from successful efforts. Before one prepares a research plan involving one or more ethnocultural groups, they should be mindful of the *comparability phenomena* as it remains as a daunting and perplexing problem for researchers. *Comparability* or *cultural equivalence* is a methodological problem for cross-cultural researchers because one must decide when and if the intended measures, techniques, procedures, representative of one ethnocultural group are equivalent to the lifeways and thoughtways of another ethnocultural group. Some cross-cultural researchers argue that achieving cultural equivalence is impossible while others argue that one can approach equivalence through use of carefully designed studies (see Berry et al., 1992).

The problem often is referred to as the *Malinowskian Dilemma* where the distinguished cultural anthropologist Bronislaw Malinowski "was most insistent that every culture be understood in its own terms, that every institution be seen as a product of the culture within which it developed. It follows from this that a cross-cultural comparison of institutions is essentially a false enterprise, for we are comparing incomparables" (Goldschmidt, 1966, p.12). If we align ourselves with Malinowski's position we should stay with the study of one culture and not engage in the comparison of one ethnocultural group with another or many others as we run the risk of functional, conceptual, and metric inequivalence. Considerable debate abounds in the literature on the approaches advocated by *cultural psychology* and *cross-cultural psychology*; the former advocates study of one culture alone and the latter studies for comparison purposes.

DESCRIBING THE ETHNOCULTURAL GROUP. In the design of cultural or ethnic intended research, attention must be given to the manner in which one specifies and describes ethnic and culturally distinct populations. In the cross-cultural literature, studies abound in which researchers purport to be studying such groups as the Japanese, Israeli Jews, Hong Kong Chinese, Canadians, Australian aborigines, Greek Australians, Nigerians—this list could continue, comprising a multitude of nationalistic and hyphenated ethnic and nationalistic populations. Occasionally, researchers provide greater specificity concerning their respondents in their titles and abstracts by giving reference to a geographic region or city in the United States. Others will distinguish their respondents along urban and rural lines while others, when referring to an American Indian group, will specify the tribe and the location on a reservation where the study occurred; this in itself can present problems as many tribes don't want to be identified in published reports. For a vast majority of the studies in the ethnic minority and cross-cultural literature, descriptions of ethnocultural groups tend to rely on use of broad *ethnic glosses*, superficial, almost vacuous, categories which serve only to separate one group from another (Trimble, 1991).

Use of such *glosses* provides little or no information on the richness and cultural variation within these groups, much less the existence of numerous subgroups characterized by distinct lifeways and thoughtways. Furthermore, use of broad *ethnic glosses* to describe a cultural or ethnic group in a research venture may be poor science. Apart from the fact that such sweeping references to ethnic groups are gross misrepresentations, their use can violate certain tenets concerning external validity, the ability to generalize findings across subgroups within an ethnic category, and erode any likelihood of an accurate and efficient replication of research results.

Use of *ethnic glosses* as subject and respondent descriptions has generated many concerns in recent years. Critics point to the fact that ethnic minority groups—specifically American Indians and Alaska Natives, Asian American, Pacific Islanders, Blacks, and Hispanics, the major ethnic minority groups in the United States—represent varied sociocultural and subgroup categories. American Indians (often Native American), a widely used and abused *ethnic gloss*, actually represent an extremely diverse and complicated ethnic group from well over 500 identifiable tribal units where individual members represent varying degrees of mixtures resulting from intermarriages and reflect varying acculturative orientations that effect ethnic identity. There are at least 32 distinct Asian American ethnic and cultural groups that can be meaningfully listed under this designation—the differences among and between these groups are extraordinarily complex. Given the diversity of languages, norms, mores and immigrant status, it is evident that to label these peoples as Asian American implies a homogeneity which is lacking." The Hispanic *ethnic gloss* is a term used to designate those individuals who reside in the United States and whose cultural origins are from Mexico, Puerto Rico, Cuba, and other Latin American countries. Blacks in America are people who can trace the origins of their ancestors to Africa. Blacks, as a race, is an illusion if one means by it a homogeneous group with common anatomical and psychological characteristics. Moreover, Blacks in America are as culturally heterogeneous as the other three groups as reflected in social class characteristics, progeny from mixed ethnic marriages and American Blacks who are descendants or are originally from the Caribbean Basin (e.g., Bahamas, Dominican Republic, Haiti, and Jamaica) and Central and South America.

In North America an ethnic minority group may be defined as: "(1) subordinate segments of complex state societies; (2) (having) special physical or cultural traits which are held in low esteem by the dominant segments of the society; (3) self-conscious units bound together by the special traits which their members have and by the special disabilities they bring; (4) (one where) membership is transmitted by a rule of descent which is capable of affiliating succeeding generations even in the absence of readily apparent special cultural or physical traits; and (5) (people who) by choice or necessity tend to marry within the group" (Wayley & Harris, 1958, p. 10). These factors must be taken into consideration when defining research samples and populations.

In selecting ethnic samples for social and behavioral science studies researchers almost tacitly assume that the respondents share a common understanding of their own ethnicity and nationalistic identification. It is as though the researcher believes that American Indians, Blacks, and others share some modal characteristic that at one level sets them apart from another comparative sample such as "whites" (Trimble, 1991). The assumption may be invalid. Heath (1978) argues that "categories of people such as those compared under the rubric of "ethnic groups" are often not really meaningful units in any sociocultural sense" and "that the ways in which people define and maintain the 'social boundaries' between or among self-identified categories are often far more important and revealing of sociocultural dynamics" (p. 60).

At an individual level, the researcher can use labels to describe one's ethnic affiliation and thus one's identity but this approach is incomplete and insufficient to adequately capture the full range of one's identity. Use of the label, often obtained by having the respondent fill in a list of ethnic categories, is a small part of one's ethnic identification. One must consider gathering information on natal background, acculturation status, attitudes toward their own and other groups, preferences such as language use, friendship affiliations, music, foods, and participation in cultural and religious events. The variables are closely aligned to the four-part ethnic identification measurement model advocated by Trimble (2000) and related ethnic and racial identification scales (see Trimble, Helms, & Root, 2002).

Ethnic self-identification is a unique psychological construct and "refers to the description of oneself in terms of a critical ethnic attribute; that is, an attribute that defines more then merely describes the ethnic group" (Aboud, 1987, p. 33). If a researcher intends to isolate and discover the extent to which deep-cultural variables influence outcome variables it is imperative that attention be given to the extent to which respondents identify themselves. Thus, cultural and ethnic studies involving nationalistic or ethnocultural groups must provide respondents the opportunity to define themselves in terms that far exceed what is captured by a label or an *ethnic gloss*.

GAINING ENTRY TO THE FIELD AND THE COMMUNITY. All researchers should know exactly what kind of relationship they want with their respondents because the nature of that relationship will determine the depth and quality of the information and data. I often refer to this as *relational methodology*. Approaching a community setting as though it was a laboratory where respondents were treated as subjects to be manipulated according to strict scientific principles likely would generate a certain set of results. Psychology's over emphasis on variable control at all levels belies the fact that people live in social contexts and these contexts profoundly influence our actions, thoughts, and feelings. Thus, the laboratory-based findings might be quite different from those where the researcher approached the community as a participant observer and viewed the informants and respondents as collaborators in the research enterprise. In the first scene, respondents may tell you what they believe you want to hear and nothing more. In the second scene, respondents may tell you what they really believe and know more so because they know that they are collaborators in the venture. In this scene, the investigator focuses on the community as the context in which individual behavior occurs. The meaning of one's actions and thoughts are contextual and situational and thus the context and situation become a source of information. The scene and perspective have been referred to as an *Ecology of Lives* approach to field based research where the emphasis is placed on how lives are lived and influenced by the context in which affect, behavior, and cognition occur (Trickett & Birman, 1989). For the approach to work effectively, the researcher must firmly establish trust and rapport; that will never occur in *one shot* approaches to research as trust and rapport require a long term commitment to the people and community.

The presence of social scientists in ethnocultural communities, especially certain ethnic minority communities in North America, is cause for considerable suspicion. Even the mere suggestion that one is an academic is enough to spark controversy. Often, this is the case for researchers who share the same ethnicity as members of the host community. Origins of the suspicions derive from two primary sources: a community's lack of experience with the research process, and previous relationships with former researchers.

Many ethnic minority and ethnocultural communities have little or no understanding or appreciation for academic-grounded research. Scientism and all its trimmings often are foreign to the residents. Researchers, too, often are viewed by themselves and community residents as socially and culturally marginal to the society they intend to study. Consequently, "no matter how skilled he is in the native tongue, how nimble in handling strange social relationships, how artistic in performing social and religious rituals, and how attached he is to local beliefs, goals, and values, (the researcher) rarely deludes himself to thinking that many community members really regard him as one of them" (Freilich, 1970, p. 2).

Field based researchers often stand to be accused as some kind of government agent or interloper. "He is not what he pretends to be and that he is gathering information for some purpose harmful to the community (Freilich, 1970, p. 3), an outsider looking for a place to establish permanent residence, a missionary sent in to convert the residents, or another social scientist whose prime interest may be to gain prestige and promotion. Because of the recent concern about the presence of researchers, a number of indigenous and aboriginal communities in the United States, Canada, and countries in Central and South America have issued edicts prohibiting and restricting any form of research in their respective communities (see Tierney, 2001).

Most Native American Indian reservation communities in the continental United States require all outside researchers to present a prospectus to the tribal council for review and sanction. If sanctioned, researchers are granted what is equivalent to a solicitor's license that carries with it a number of contingencies, that typically include (1) the assignment of a knowledgeable tribal member to monitor all research activities, (2) restrictions on the nature and composition of potential respondents (this restriction makes random sampling almost an impossibility), (3) the right to review all original and completed research questionnaires, interview schedules, and field notes, (4) the right to review any documents submitted for publication with the understanding that the tribe has the right to reject such documents, and (5) the right to review, comment, and pass judgment on any final reports. Add to these contingencies the procedures for receiving informed consent and protecting the rights of all respondents and one could readily surmise that conducting field research is much more complex than randomly pooling college students in quasi-laboratory settings.

Gaining entry into the field, whether invited by the host culture or not, carries an enormous responsibility. This responsibility not only extends to the residents and respondents, but also to the maintenance of one's scientific integrity. More important, the researcher should recognize that mistakes, errors in protocol, and violations of cultural norms, beliefs, and values are not easily forgiven by members of the host and scientific communities. Impetuously and boldly rushing into a community for the sheer sake of advancing one's pet theory and hopefully promoting science is unconscionable, intolerable, and indeed disrespectful.

Before setting foot into a culturally different community for the purposes of conducting research, researchers would do well to heed the recommendations of those who have been there before. After spending some five years conducting research on the aging process in numerous ethnic minority communities in the United States, Bengston, Grigsby, Corry, and Hruby (1977) drew up the following considerations for researchers, as follows:

- Research should be multidisciplinary. If not possible, the solitary researcher should seek the consultation of other social scientists and persons who have some working knowledge of the community in question;
- Conventional laboratory grounded research strategies are not easily translated to field research. The scientific community will be concerned with methodological soundness and the lay community will want to be assured that they are not getting ripped off, that their collective voices will be heard, and that they will share in monetary remuneration if its available.
- Because of the number of the community members involved, the potential for conflict is considerable. Bengtson et al. (1977) argue that the conflict between the lay community and professional researchers may demand that strategies for conflict resolution be given consideration equal to that directed toward design criteria and methodological procedures.
- Above all the considerations, filed researchers must be prepared to adapt to many changes that could occur in the course of the effort. They must be prepared to revise strategies and tactics to accommodate the changing concerns of community life.

CULTURAL EQUIVALENCE OF RESEARCH TOOLS. Field based researchers typically rely on use of survey and structured interview formats to collect information. In addition, some researchers make use of case study approaches, meta-analytic procedures, secondary data analytic methods, and, to a very limited extent, quasi-experimental approaches. These research approaches could be referred to as *methodological etics*, for it is assumed that the techniques could be used with any group, regardless of its cultural background.

Methodological etics are akin to what cross-cultural psychologists refer to as *cultural equivalence phenomena* that are consistent across all human beings and all human groups. Berry et al. (1992) argue that essentially three kinds of equivalences can exist: (1) Functional equivalence exists when behaviors emitted by people from different cultures occur in response to similar problems; (2) conceptual equivalence exists when people from different cultures share a common meaning about specific stimuli; and (3) metric equivalence exists when the psychometric properties of one's data obtained from different cultures reveals a comparable pattern. The nature of functional and conceptual equivalences present real problems for cultural and ethnic researchers as exclusive reliance on *methodological etics* without regard for these concepts could invalidate an entire research venture.

To understand conceptual equivalence, one must recognize that every culture has developed ways of looking at the world that make sense to them. Their worldview, much of which is reflected in the language of the culture, has been shaped by environmental, historical, biological, and other factors that have marked that people's evolution as a unique group. While there may be commonalities in all worldviews, depending to some extent on the proximity of groups, there are also usually areas of significant differences. For instance, many American Indians differ from White people in their view of what constitutes mental illness. For some tribes, mental illness is the result of having in some way transgressed the rules of right living, and until this can be rectified through ceremony, the illness will continue; thus, it is perceived as a spiritual issue whose resolution is in the hands of a medicine person or shaman. This contrasts with the White view that the person has been subjected to a pathological process that can be relieved through medication combined with the individual's efforts to change his or her behavior.

One way to ensure equivalence involves the prudent use of local people as part of the research team. It is important that these people be deeply involved with the planning and that their views be given full consideration. Too often, local people are hired as program staff, but their ideas are not sought and they are not included in planning sessions. Therefore, researchers must be aware that many ethnic minorities interact and communicate with one another in unique ways. In meetings where ideas are being shared and plans are being made, it is common for indigenous tribal people, for example, to withhold their comments until everyone else has spoken. It often happens that meetings are ended before those in attendance have had an opportunity to present their views, and an important source of information is lost.

We now turn our attention to measurement issues and begin with the concept of *metric equivalence*. This concept refers to the possibility that survey and questionnaire items or scales often operate differently across cultures. Another *metric equivalence* problem occurs when the relationship between variables is not the same across cultures. Although it is often ignored, establishing *metric equivalence* should be a standard task for researchers. It is not enough to identify measures that have been used in other studies to measure a concept under consideration. It must be demonstrated that the selected instrumentation is both valid and reliable for the population on which it will be used. In addition to the usual reliability and validity studies, it is useful to analyze the factor structure of the measures and constructs being used. Besides establishing *metric equivalence*, use of factor structure analysis, item response theory, and Rasch modeling algorithms can help in examining problems that may also exist with functional and conceptual equivalence.

The question is often raised as to whether it is best to use *off-the-shelf* measures or to construct new measures when doing research in a cross-cultural milieu. There is no one answer to this question, given that problems can be encountered with each approach. Unless there is evidence that an existing measure has already worked in the population being evaluated, it is usually necessary to establish reliability and validity with that group. This is not to say, however, that all measures are inherently culturally biased and cannot be used, either in part or in whole, with other populations.

Construction of new items and scales is not a task that should be taken lightly. Many researchers underestimate the difficulty of scale construction, and this difficulty is multiplied when the new scales are applied across cultures. One of the most common errors is not to test the scale before using it for evaluation. Pilot testing is an absolute requirement and should involve a debriefing procedure in which potential subjects can talk about their interpretation of the items.

There is one final set of points to be made in this section. Over the years, researchers working with different cultures have resorted to the use of measurement tools that are based on norms and the testing orientation of those with a Western perspective. All too often, these researchers encounter problems in administration, scoring, and, assuredly, interpretation. Critics abound, though, and a number of cross-cultural researchers have commented on the cultural inappropriateness of measurement approaches (see Irvine & Berry 1983). Many of us in the field of cross-cultural and ethnic psychology wonder why some investigators, almost blindly and with utmost diligence, continue using conventional measurement and psychometric traditions in cultural and ethnic research.

Here are seven common pitfalls in cross-cultural testing:

- Psychological constructs are viewed as synonymous with locally derivable criteria, which may or may not be consistent with the implied intent of the construct.
- The establishment of several types of equivalence is not considered essential.
- It is assumed that once tests are purged of verbal material, leaving only nonverbal stimuli, they are more *culture-fair*.
- Norms gathered in one culture are used to evaluate the performance of individuals in other cultures.
- People from around the world may have variable and different modes of responding to test items.
- Such testing generally tends to infer deficits based on test score differences.
- Nearly all psychological tests are culturally isomorphic to the West, which can be characterized as sophisticated and test-wise.

REPORT WRITING AND DISSEMINATION OF FINDINGS. Ordinarily, emphasis on report writing and dissemination of results is not included in articles and books dealing with the conduct of cross-cultural and ethnic research. In recent years, however, many of us have become aware that numerous research studies have had a negative impact on the reputation of ethnocultural communities due in large part to the way in which reports and articles are written and publicized. Applied social research programs, for example, are designed to address social ills; therefore, written descriptions often focus heavily on the negative aspects of communities. When ethnic minority communities are involved, this type of reporting—over time—reinforces negative stereotypes. Consequently many ethnic minority communities especially American Indian and Alaska Native ones require that they have a right to review the results, how the data will be analyzed, and how the results will be written and disseminated. If the investigator does not agree with the conditions community and tribal sanctions will not be granted.

In the worst case, study results can be blatantly used to denigrate a community. Some years back, a local border town newspaper obtained the results of a survey of alcohol and other drug use that was given on an American Indian reservation in the U.S, and it sensationalized the results. Although there were no overt racial statements, the intent was clear and the Indian community experienced a great deal of shame. Social problems do exist in ethnic minority communities; however, it is necessary to place them in context, and any research report should reflect that context. For example, alcohol and drug use problems in most American Indian communities largely reflect socioeconomic conditions and are not related to any inherent cultural characteristics. Many American Indians are becoming increasingly impatient with the litany of social ills that are ascribed to them, and a research report that presents a balanced picture will get a much better reception and is more likely to be used. In a word, the report should be written and presented respectfully.

Community based research may have two purposes. At the local level, people need to know whether the research has value for them, that is, is it culturally congruent, well received by the community, and consistent with local values and norms? There is also a need for technical data that support the report's conclusions and may be used to answer more specific questions. These two purposes suggest the need for two types of reports. It often happens that technical reports are never used at the local level because they are too complex and do not respond directly to the need to make decisions. In the absence of a more comprehensible document, the community may be left with the feeling that the research was a wasted effort, and it may develop a negative attitude toward research in general. Thus, a report written in non-technical language specifically to address the local need is appropriate.

The release and dissemination of a research report often will have to be handled carefully, particularly if the report contains sensitive information. In one sense, this is a question of who owns the data; many American Indian communities will claim they do since they were the ones who provided the information. Given this, the community or its representatives would have the final decision about the dissemination of results. There must also be a recognition, however, that the information can be useful in other communities and therefore needs to be published in some form.

Several approaches can be used to reduce controversy over publication. First, negotiations should occur very early in the research process, and some general agreement should be reached. In some cases, even if prior agreement has been reached, there may be some unanticipated results that community people find sensitive and would not like to see publicized. Usually, a compromise can be reached through negotiation, whereby some information may be deleted or left in a report for internal purposes only. It is also useful to allow local people to preview the report to determine whether there are any conclusions that could be more accurately interpreted in light of local culture, values, or beliefs.

Whenever there is concern over report content, the manner in which the report is released can be extremely important. In 1980, a very sensitive report on alcoholism in a Native Alaska village was released to the general media (see Manson, 1989). In addition to a number of other serious errors in protocol, the information from the study was presented at a press conference thousands of miles away from the village where the study was conducted. This precluded any participation by local people and allowed the whole situation to be presented out of context. Once again, a Native Alaska community experienced a great deal of shame because the information released implied that nearly all of the Native adults in the community were alcoholic. Although the actual situation was quite different, there was no way to moderate what was presented.

It is wise and prudent to have local people involved in any release of research information, either in person or through a cover letter signed by an agency representative. This once again demonstrates the need for community people to be intimately involved with any research effort. It not only ensures that the most accurate information is presented, but also precludes the perception that the community is once again the subject of outside research and is not capable of resolving local issues and understanding the implications of the findings.

SUMMARY AND CONCLUSION

The chapter begins with two related quotations concerning the importance of cultural explanations and the experiences of a researcher studying another ethnocultural group. The quotes form the chapter's theme that takes us from definitions about cultural competence and cultural sensitivity to conducting research in culturally appropriate and sensitive ways. Mixed in are discussions about self-reflection and learning about one's cultural self and multicultural counseling and how one can attain competency in this rapidly emerging field of inquiry. Care has been taken in the selection and use of relevant references describing important concepts, techniques, and information related to the overarching chapter theme; the references serve as a tool for the reader to use to explore the depth and richness of the chapter's topics.

For decades psychology has been selective in the study and characterization of people. Critics argue that most of the early findings generated from psychological researchers occurred in a cultural vacuum and were limited to North America. The more harsh and cynical critics point out that the findings could only be generalized to Whites or Euro-Americans, as they were the major source of researcher's data. Robert Guthrie's (976) small book, *Even the Rate was White*, tells a good part of the reason why early psychology was *scientifically racist*. Similarly, beginning in the late 1960s, counseling and clinical psychologists were accused of being *culturally encapsulated* because their theories and approaches were limited to certain ethnocultural groups—ones who valued talking about their problems with professionals with the hope that the problems could be solved or cured. At that time and continuing to the present many international, ethnic minority, and cross-cultural psychologists argued that culture and ethnicity should be central to the psychology rather than an outlier or an object for exotic study.

Cross-cultural and ethnic psychologists have discovered that cultural differences make a difference in the way people act, perceive, think, and feel so much so that major theories have to be revised to accommodate the new and contradictory results. Counseling and clinical psychology approaches also have undergone revision and change. Mental health and how one achieves and maintains it vary from one ethnocultural group to another and counselors are discovering that an approach that works for one may not work for another. Culture and all that it means and represents is challenging psychology but the field, too, is challenging culture in reciprocal ways. Psychologists in the main keep asking us to define what we mean by culture, ethnicity, and the processes and mechanisms that mediate and influence thoughtways and lifeways. Becoming culturally competent and culturally sensitive does not imply that one discard the contributions of past and present psychologists. The challenge for the reader is to recognize that we cannot fully understand the human condition without viewing it from a cross-cultural and ethnic perspective. What was learned about the human condition in the past can be reframed and tested with a new set of approaches and procedures in contexts not considered in the past. Similarly, we may find that specific thoughtways and lifeways of certain ethnocultural groups may have some extraordinary value for psychology as a whole and thus assist in improving our understanding of humans and the settings we live in.

ACKNOWLEDGEMENT: I want to extend my deepest gratitude to the administration and research staff at the Radcliffe Institute for Advanced Study, Harvard University for providing me with the time, resources, and support that allowed me to conduct research for the preparation and writing of this chapter. Additionally, I want to extend my warm appreciation to my former Radcliffe Research Junior Partners, Harvard College seniors, Peggy Ting Lim and Maiga Miranda who conducted research and provide me with wonderful thought provoking commentary and advice for many topics covered in this chapter.

ADDITIONAL RESOURCES

Pedersen, P. (1988). *A handbook for developing multicultural awareness*. Alexandria, VA: American Counseling Association.

Brislin, R., & Yoshida, T. (1994). *Improving intercultural interactions: Modules for cross-cultural training programs*. Thousand Oaks, CA: Sage.

Brislin, R., Cushner, K., Cherrie, C., & Yong, M. (1986). *Intercultural interactions: A practical guide*. Thousand Oaks, CA: Sage.

REFERENCES

Aboud, F. E. (1987). The development of ethnic self-identification and attitudes. In J. S. Phinney, & M. J. Rotheram (Eds.), *Children's ethnic socialization: pluralism and development*, (pp. 32–55). Newbury Park, CA: Sage.
Ballenger, W. (1994). *Developing cultural competence*. Training materials developed for the Los Angeles County Department of Children's Services. Los Angeles: University of California, Los Angeles.
Bengsten, V., Grigsby, E., Corry, E., & Hruby, M. (1977). Relating academic research to community concerns: A case in collaborative effort. *Journal of Social Issues, 33*(4), 75–92.
Berry, J., Poortinga, Y., Segall, M., & Dasen, P. (1992). *Cross-cultural psychology: Research and applications*. Cambridge: Cambridge University Press.
Brown, D. E. (1991). *Human universals*. Philadelphia: Temple University.
Constantine, M., & Ladany, N. (2001). New visions for defining and assessing multicultural counseling competence. In J. Ponterotto, J. M. Casas, L. Suzaki, & C. Alexander (Eds.), *Handbook of multicultural counseling*, (2nd ed., pp. 482–498). Thousand Oaks, CA: Sage.
Feagin, J. R. (1978). *Racial and ethnic relations*. Englewood Cliffs, NJ: Prentice-Hall.
Freilich, M. (Ed.) (1970). *Marginal natives: Anthropologists at work*. New York: Harper & Row.
Goldschmidt, W. (1966). *Comparative functionalism*. Berkeley: University of California.
Guthrie, R. (1976). *Even the rate was white: A historical view of psychology*. New York: Harper & Row.
Heath, D. B. (1978). Foreword. *Medical Anthropology, 2*(4), 3–8.
Helms, J., & Richardson, T. (1997). How 'multiculturalism' obscures race and culture as differential aspects of counseling competency. In D. Pope-Davis & H. Coleman (Eds.), *Multicultural counseling competencies: Assessment, education and training, and supervision* (pp. 60–79). Thousand Oaks, CA: Sage.
Irvine, S., & Berry, J. (Eds.) (1983). *Human assessment and cultural factors*. New York: Plenum.
Jahoda, G. (1980). Theoretical and systematic approaches in cross-cultural psychology. In H. Triandis & W. Lambert (Eds.), *Handbook of cross-cultural psychology: Vol. 1. Perspectives* (pp. 69–142). Boston: Allyn & Bacon.
Manson, S. (1989). *The Journal of the National Center, 2*(3), 7–90.
Mead, M. (1942). *And keep your powder dry: An anthropologist looks at America*. New York: Morrow.
Mead, M. (1959). *An anthropologist at work: Writings of Ruth Benedict*. Boston: Houghlin-Mifflin.
Miller, N. B. (1982). Social work services to urban Indians. In J. W. Green (Ed.), *Cultural awareness in the human services* (pp. 157–183). Englewood Cliffs, NJ: Prentice Hall.
Moritsugu, J. (1999). Cultural competence. In J. Mio, J. Trimble, P. Arredondo, H. Cheatham, & D. Sue (Eds.), *Keywords in multicultural interventions: A dictionary* (pp. 62–63). Westport, CT: Greenwood.
Orlandi, M. (Ed.) (1992). *Cultural competence for evaluators working with ethnic minority communities: A guide for alcohol and other drug abuse prevention practitioners*. Rockville, MD: Office for Substance Abuse Prevention, Cultural Competence Series 1.
Pedersen, P. (Ed.) (1999). *Multiculturalism as a fourth force*. Philadelphia: Brunner/Mazel.
Pedersen, P., Draguns, J., & Lonner, W. (Eds.) (1976). *Counseling across cultures*. Honolulu, HI: University Press of Hawaii.
Pedersen, P., Draguns, J., Lonner, W., & Trimble, J. (Eds.) (2002). *Counseling across cultures, fifth edition*. Thousand Oaks, CA: Sage.
Pope-Davis, D., & Coleman, H. (Eds.) (1997). *Multicultural counseling competencies: Assessment, education and training, and supervision*. Thousand Oaks, CA: Sage.
Powdermaker, H. (1966). *Stranger and friend: The way of the anthropologist*. New York: Norton.
Ridley, C., & Udipi, S. (2002). Putting cultural empathy into practice. In P. Pedersen, J. Draguns, W. Lonner, & J. Trimble (Eds.), *Counseling across cultures*, (5th ed., pp. 317–333). Thousand Oaks, CA: Sage.
Segall, M., Dasen, P., Berry, J., & Poortinga, Y. (1990). *Human behavior in global perspective: An introduction to cross-cultural psychology*. New York: Pergamon.
Sodowsky, G., Kuo-Jackson, P., & Loya, G. (1997). Outcomes in the philosophy of assessment. In D. Pope-Davis & H. Coleman (Eds.), *Multicultural counseling competencies: Assessment, education and training, and supervision* (pp. 3–42). Thousand Oaks, CA: Sage.
Sue, D., Bernier, J., Durran, A., Feinberg, L., Pedersen, P., Smith, E., & Vasquez-Nutall, E. (1982). Position paper: Cross-cultural counseling competencies. *The Counseling Psychologist, 10*, 45–52.

Sue, D., Carter, R., Casas, J. M., Fouad, N., Ivey, A., Jensen, M., LaFromboise, T., Manese, J., Ponterotto, J., & Vazquez,-Nutall, E. (1998). *Multicultural counseling competencies: Individual and organizational development.* Thousand Oaks, CA: Sage.

Tierney, P. (2001). *Darkness in El Dorado: How scientists and journalists devastated the Amazon.* New York: Norton.

Trickett, E., & Birman, D. (1989). Taking ecology seriously: A community development approach to individually based preventive interventions in schools. In L. Bond, & B. Compas (Eds.), *Primary prevention and promotion in the schools. Primary prevention of psychopathology: Vol. 12* (pp. 361–390). Thousands Oaks, CA: Sage.

Trimble, J. E. (1991). Ethnic specification, validation prospects and future of drug abuse research. *International Journal of the Addictions, 25*(2), 149–169.

Trimble, J. E. (2000). Social psychological perspectives on changing self-identification among American Indians and Alaska Natives. In R. H. Dana (Ed.), *Handbook of Cross-Cultural/Multicultural Personality Assessment* (pp. 197–222). Mahwah, NJ: Lawrence Erlbaum Associates.

Trimble, J., Helms, J., & Root, M. (2002). Social and psychological perspectives on ethnic and racial identity. In G. Bernal, J. Trimble, K. Burlew, & F. Leong (Eds.), *Handbook on Racial and Ethnic Psychology* (pp. 239–275). Thousands Oaks, CA: Sage.

U.S. Bureau of the Census. (2001). Census of the population: General population characteristics, 2000. Washington, DC: Government Printing Office.

Wayley, C., & Harris, M. (1958). *Minorities in the new world: Six case studies.* New York: Columbia University Press.

CHAPTER 3

Developing and Practicing Ethics

KENNETH S. POPE

We bring our personal ethics to graduate school and begin to create our professional ethics. We read about professional ethics, we discuss them in our courses, and we see the individual differences in how they are reflected in our professors' lives and work.

We begin to face questions: How central will professional ethics be to who we are and what we do? Are the professional ethics we begin developing for ourselves consistent with our own deepest values that we lived by before we entered graduate school, with the formal ethical standards affirmed by the profession, and with the realities of graduate school?

Graduate school often presents us with intriguing situations, prompting us to evaluate the ethics of research and publication, faculty-student interactions, psychological assessment and intervention, and the other aspects of what we do as psychologists. Consider the following scenarios:

1) As a research assistant for one of the department's most respected and influential professors, you compute the inferential statistics on a large data set. The findings are not statistically significant, and the professor's new theory is not supported. The professor then throws out the data from 20% of the participants. When you re-run the stats, the tests are significant and the theory is supported. You receive your first authorship credit when the results are published in a prestigious scientific journal and you're listed as co-author. The article, however, makes no mention of the initial tests or excluded participants.
2) Your dissertation is on how children ages 8–10 think about their own creative processes. You obtain written informed consent from the custodial parent or guardian, assuring them that your contact with the child will be limited to only a one-hour session, that the session will be completely confidential, and that when writing up your dissertation and at all other times, you will never provide any information to anyone that would allow identification of any child or family. In each session, the child makes up a story during the first half-hour, then you ask questions about how he or she thought up the theme, characters, plot, and details. One girl, whose father is a famous attorney who has won multimillion dollar judgments in defamation cases, makes up a story about how a little girl is terrified of her father, an attorney, because he comes into her room almost every night and has sex with her. He has told her that if she ever tells anyone

KENNETH S. POPE • Independent Practice, Norwalk, CT 06856

their secret, he will stomp her dog to death and that no one would believe her anyway. When you ask her how she thought up the story about the little girl, your research participant says, "Well, she's almost exactly like me in a lot of ways." When you ask her what she means, she says she is afraid to talk any more and remains silent until the hour is up.

3) You and your best friend are talking about how much you're both looking forward to graduating next spring. Your friend confides: "I had no idea how I'd ever get my dissertation done but luckily I had enough money to hire a consultant to design the study and analyze the data. And I was so relieved to find a good professional author who could write it up for me."

Such events pose a tangle of questions to a graduate student: Are there ethical issues involved and if so, what are they? If you're considering these scenarios as part of a course, workshop, or supervision group, to what extent do you agree or disagree with others about what the issues are and what the student in each scenario should do? What options are available for the student to attempt to understand, address, accept, or turn away from the situation? To what degree do you believe that the APA ethics code clearly and adequately addresses the issues you've identified in each scenario? To what extent does your graduate school set forth and implement clear and adequate standards that address these scenarios? If the scenarios seem to you to involve conflicting values, responsibilities, or loyalties, how do you sort through the conflicts and arrive at a decision about what to do? What are the costs, risks, and possible outcomes of the different approaches the student could take? How we work our way through such complex situations helps shape the professional ethics we begin developing in graduate school.

Ethical development is, for most, a career-long process. Ethical development that stops at graduate school can be a little like the professor relying on the same yellowing lecture notes decade after decade, never bothering to update, rethink, or renew.

The purpose of this chapter is first to discuss steps that seem important to the development of professional ethics, and then to look at some of our shared vulnerabilities that can lead us to rationalize unethical behavior.

DEVELOPING PROFESSIONAL ETHICS

Starting With What We Do

Professional ethics are meaningless unless they fit well with what we actually do. We're not in a good position to consider the ethical implications of our acts unless we clearly understand what we do as psychologists. Teaching, research, supervision, mentoring, assessment, and intervention are abstractions until we understand what they mean in specific terms. This is not always easy. In 1947, APA president Carl Rogers appointed David Shakow to chair a committee on defining and teaching psychotherapy. Shakow's report resulted in the influential Boulder Conference and the "Boulder Model" (i.e., the scientist-practitioner model) of clinical psychology. On August 28, 1949, the recorder for the Boulder task force attempting to define therapy and establish criteria for adequate training wrote the following summary: "We have left therapy as an undefined technique which is applied to unspecified problems with a nonpredictable outcome. For this technique we recommend rigorous training."

The psychologists who created APA's first ethics code developed an ingenious way to fit the code to the work psychologists do in their day-to-day lives and to psychology's empirical roots. As committee chair Nicholas Hobbs wrote in 1948, this approach would produce "a code of ethics truly indigenous to psychology, a code that could be lived." To develop the code, a critical incident study was conducted in which all APA members were sent a letter asking them to share personal "experiences in solving ethical problems by describing the specific circumstances in which someone made a decision that was ethically critical."

It is important to ask ourselves from time to time: Do our own individual professional ethics fit what we actually do in our day-to-day work as psychologists? Do they take account of the pressures, conflicting needs, ambiguities, subtleties, gray areas, and other realities we—and our students, supervisees, research participants, therapy clients, and others—face? Professional ethics that are unrealistic are unlikely to be much help to psychologists in the real world.

Seeking Information

Few psychologists would try to design research without first reading about the topic, looking at the research already conducted in that area, becoming knowledgeable about what is already understood about the phenomenon. This kind of active searching for information can be crucial in approaching ethical issues as well. For virtually any aspect of our work as psychologists, there is a framework of formal ethical standards, laws (both legislation and case law), and published research. It can be fundamentally important to know what organizations, agencies, and committees set forth and enforce the ethical, professional, legal, and other standards relevant to our work and settings, to find out their policies and procedures, not only what they do but how they do it. To what degree does your graduate school set forth standards for faculty and students, and how are these standards implemented? Which of your local, state, or national psychology associations have ethics codes and ethics committees, and how do they function? What standards does your state psychology licensing board enforce, and how are they enforced? The reference section presents resources on the web and in the published literature that may be helpful in locating some of this information.

Thinking

Finding the relevant ethics codes, legal standards, policies, procedures, and research doesn't tell us the most ethical approach to a specific situation any more than reading prior research studies tells us how to design the best research for that topic. In both cases, finding the information does not mark the end of the process, but rather the beginning of informed thinking about the specific instance at hand.

> "Awareness of the ethics codes is crucial to competence in the area of ethics, but the formal standards are not a substitute for an active, deliberative, and creative approach to fulfilling our ethical responsibilities. They prompt, guide, and inform our ethical consideration; they do not preclude or serve as a substitute for it. There is no way that the codes and principles can be effectively followed or applied in a rote, thoughtless manner. Each new client, whatever his or her similarities to previous clients, is a unique individual. Each situation also is unique and is likely to change significantly over time. The explicit codes and principles may designate many possible approaches as clearly unethical. They may identify with greater or lesser degrees of clarity the types of ethical concerns that are likely to be especially significant, but they cannot tell us how these

concerns will manifest themselves in a particular clinical situation. They may set forth essential tasks that we must fulfill, but they cannot tell us how we can accomplish these tasks with a unique client facing unique problems.... There is no legitimate way to avoid these struggles." (Pope & Vasquez, 1998)

Acknowledging Complexity: Dual Relationships as an Example

One of the most difficult challenges in developing professional ethics is acknowledging the sometimes overwhelming complexity. The situation that a psychologist encounters may have layer upon layer of complexity; moreover, the ethical standards, laws, and research relevant to that situation may form a complex tangle. The concept of dual relationships (aka multiple or overlapping relationships) exemplifies this lack of simplicity.

During the last decade or so, few topics in the area of clinical ethics sparked such intense consideration as dual relationships and related phenomena, with numerous articles and books offering thoughtful explorations of virtually every possible view. Not every author uses terms in a way that is exactly the same as every other author, but generally the context, if not an explicit definition, makes it clear whether a term like dual relationship is used in its broadest possible sense or to examine only a subset of meanings (e.g., only dual professional roles; only blending a professional role with a social, financial, or romantic relationship; or only dual relationships that seem to place clients at undue risk for harm).

A 1989 article not only demonstrated the diverse beliefs and behaviors in regard to dual relationships but also illustrated how many variables were significantly associated with this diversity. This national survey of 4,800 psychologists, psychiatrists, and social workers (with a 49% return rate) examined how both views and practices tended to vary in regard to 10 factors: therapist gender, profession, age, experience, marital status, region of residence, client gender, practice setting, theoretical orientation, and practice locale.

The patterns in regard to these 10 factors are fascinating. For example, male therapists are more likely than female therapists not only to endorse but also to engage in various nonsexual dual relationships. (Other studies have shown that the same gender pattern holds for sexual dual relationships.) Psychiatrists are less likely than psychologists or social workers to view social or financial involvements with patients as ethical. The article concludes with 10 recommendations, such as suggesting that training programs need to present students with researched-based literature and other readings so that they may evaluate for themselves the full range of views, evidence, and approaches in this area.

A 1992 study used the method that had been the basis of developing APA's original ethics code mentioned in a previous section (i.e., asking psychologists to describe the dilemmas they encountered in their day-to-day practice) collected additional data about the dual relationships encountered by psychologists. Based on the findings, the authors called for changes in the ethical principles, so that the ethics code would, for example, (1) define dual relationships more carefully and specify clearly the conditions under which they might be therapeutically indicated or acceptable, (2) address clearly and realistically the situations of those who practice in small towns, rural communities, remote locales, and similar contexts (emphasizing that neither the current code in place at the time nor the draft revision under consideration at that time fully acknowledged or adequately addressed such contexts), and (3) address realistically the entanglements into which even the most careful therapist can fall.

For psychologists seeking resources in approaching dual relationships, fortunately there have been countless guides published in articles and books, helping clinicians carefully weigh the factors, values, and possibilities in trying to arrive at the best possible decision about whether entering into various kinds of relationships with a client makes clinical and ethical sense (for examples of such guides, see the section "Dual Relationships: Trends, Stats, Guides, and Resources" at http://kspope.com/dual/dual.php). In addition to the more general decision-making aids, there are resources for virtually every kind of specialty practice and context (e.g., a 3-level model for family therapists involved with religious communities to negotiate dual relationships; a decision-making model for social dual-role relationships during internships).

Knowing Actuarial Data about Challenging and High-Risk Topics

It can be helpful to know the areas of psychology that psychologists find most ethically challenging. A prior section described how APA used a critical incident study as the unique basis for its first ethics code. Half a century after that first study, another critical incident study asked a random sample of APA members what major ethical dilemmas they encountered in their day-to-day work. The most frequently cited dilemmas fell into the following categories, listed in descending order:

1) confidentiality
2) blurred, dual, or conflictual relationships
3) payment issues
4) academic and training issues
5) forensic issues
6) research issues
7) the conduct of colleagues
8) sexual issues
9) assessment issues
10) harmful interventions
11) competence
12) ethics codes and committees
13) school psychology
14) publishing issues
15) helping the financially stricken
16) supervision issues
17) advertising and (mis)representation
18) industrial-organizational psychology
19) medical issues
20) termination issues
21) ethnicity issues
22) records and documentation

Ethics in Psychotherapy and Counseling, 2nd Edition discusses in detail actuarial data about licensing board complaints and malpractice suits against psychologists, from which the following lists are abstracted. Data from psychology licensing boards over a 14 year period show that the most frequent disciplinary actions involved violations in the following areas, in descending order of frequency:

1) dual relationships (sexual and/or nonsexual)
2) unprofessional or negligent practice

3) fraud
4) conviction of crimes
5) inadequate or improper supervision
6) impairment
7) confidentiality
8) records and documentation
9) using false information in applying for a license

Data from malpractice suits against psychologists over a 15 year period shows that claims most often fall into the following areas, in descending order of frequency:

1) sexual violations
2) incompetence in developing or implementing a treatment plan
3) loss from evaluation
4) breech of confidentiality or privacy
5) improper diagnosis
6) other (a mysterious category of individual claims not falling into any other category)
7) suicide
8) defamation (e.g., slander or libel)
9) countersuit for fee collection
10) violation of civil rights
11) loss of child custody or visitation
12) failure to supervise properly
13) improper death of patient or third party
14) violation of legal regulations
15) licensing or peer review issues
16) breach of contract

A national study found that about 12% of those who practice clinical or counseling psychology were the object of at least one formal complaint (i.e., ethics, licensing, malpractice). Male psychologists (17%) were significantly more likely than female psychologists (6%) to encounter formal complaints, and aspects of practice were significantly related to the probability of a formal complaint. Knowing the actuarial data about challenging and high-risk aspects of practice can help ensure that psychologists approach these areas with adequate care and thoughtfulness.

Consulting

In a national study, psychologists reported that consultation with colleagues was their most valuable resource for acting ethically. The degree to which we are honest and open with our colleagues in this area can be a source of useful information. One can always ask: "How would I feel if all of my colleagues knew my *actual* ethical values and the ways in which I evaluate what I do from an ethical perspective?" If considering that scenario makes us uneasy in some way, it's worth reflecting on why it makes us uneasy and what, if anything, we might want to do about it. Routine consultation with colleagues can not only help us identify—and not act on—blind-spots, momentary lapses, and misjudgments—but also strengthen the sense of community among psychologists, a community in which ethics are an important value, thoughtfully examined and frequently discussed. If, in arriving at a decision about a troublesome situation, we find ourselves reluctant to consult, more comfortable keeping the dilemma or our decision completely to ourselves, it may be a red flag, marking one of those instances in which consultation with trusted colleagues can save us from a terrible misstep.

It's worth paying attention also to those times we consult but not with complete honestly, openness, and readiness to learn. In such times we choose our consultants carefully because of what we believe they will or won't say. We spin the situation in a way that downplays or conceals entirely certain aspects, and that pulls for a particular response (i.e., the one we are subtly guiding the consultant to give us). This form of talking to colleagues is not really consultation so much as it is extracting permission to do what we've already decided to do or trying to gather protection should we get caught ("But Dr. X said it was OK!!!").

When confronting especially difficult ethical decisions, we can consult not only with individual colleagues but also with relevant committees. The American Psychological Association has worked hard to ensure that its ethics code is not simply window-dressing in a public relations campaign but a practical statement of principles to which all members agree to be held genuinely accountable. The ethics committee hears and adjudicates formal complaints based on this code. Consulting with the members of this committee can often be exceptionally useful. Many state psychological associations also have ethics committees that can provide consultation. Universities have committees serving similar purposes—ethics committees, grievance boards, Institutional Review Boards addressing research standards, etc. It makes sense for every graduate student to find out what committees monitor and enforce standards, to learn how they work and what standards they uphold, and to consult with them when the need arises.

Assessing Costs and Taking Risks

The ethical implications of our choices in some situations may lead us to act against our own financial or similar self-interests. Part of developing professional ethics is assessing just what our ethics are worth—how much money, how much time, how much trouble—and what risks we are willing to take to practice our ethics. Our ethical values may bring us into serious conflict with our professors, supervisors, employers, colleagues, or friends. Under what circumstances, if any, are we willing to risk a good grade, an important letter of recommendation, a fellowship, a promotion, or a job because to "go along" with what we ourselves believe to be an unethical situation seems wrong?

Simon's classic article "The psychologist as whistle blower: A case study" documents what can happen when a psychologist tries to do what he or she considers ethically right. Simon describes the dilemmas faced by psychologists who "find that their professional responsibilities to their clients are in conflict with the demands of their organization. This problem is illustrated in the firing of a VA psychologist who objected, first internally and then publicly, to VA policies that he believed jeopardized the health and well-being of his patients. The responses of the VA, the Civil Service Commission, professional associations, and others to this incident show a series of threats to the integrity of professional practice in institutional settings."

When the costs appear too steep, it is always tempting, of course, to reason that remaining silent or participating in what we think is an unethical act is justified. We allow ourselves to be convinced that silence or participation will also enable us—by making more money, keeping our jobs, not rocking the boat, showing our loyalty to those around us—to do far more good and address much more important ethical issues than we could by a Quixotic and self-destructive attempt to "stand on principle" with regard to the current inconsequential issue. This is the great vulnerability of any psychologist's professional ethics, no matter how well-developed:

the sophisticated cognitive maneuvers through which any unethical act can be transformed into acceptable legitimacy. Awareness of this slight-of-mind magic can head off—or at least give us a fighting chance against—it's charms and is the topic of the following section.

Rationalizing Unethical Behavior

However well-developed our individual professional ethics, there may be times when the temptation is just too great and we need to justify behaving unethically. The following rationalizations—adapted from those originally suggested by Pope and Vasquez—can make even hurtful and reprehensible behaviors seem ethical, or at least insignificant. All of us, at one time or another, probably have endorsed at least some of them. If some excuses seem absurd and humorous to us, it is likely that we have not yet had to resort to using those particular rationalizations. At some future moment of great stress or exceptional temptation, those absurdities may gain considerable plausibility if not a comforting certitude.

1) It's not unethical as long as the topic of ethics never comes up. If no one says anything about ethics, all can breathe a sigh of relief and concentrate on the important matters. As long as the only language of ethics is silence, no choices or acts can be identified as unethical.
2) It's not unethical if there's no ethics code, legislation, case law, or professional standard specifically prohibiting it that you didn't already know about. Two basic rules are at work here: specific ignorance and specific literalization. "Specific ignorance" means that if you don't know about, for example, a prohibition against making a custody recommendation without actually meeting with the people involved, then the prohibition doesn't really exist in a way that applies to you. As long as you weren't aware of certain ethical standards in advance, then you cannot be considered ethically accountable for your actions. The rule of "specific literalization" allows you declare any act that is not *specifically* mentioned in the formal standards to be ethical. Interestingly, this rule can be called into play even when the psychologist knows in advance about a specific prohibition, if the psychologist also invokes the rule known as "insufficient qualification." Consider, for example, a psychologist who knows that there is an ethical standard prohibiting sexual involvement with a therapy client. The psychologist can call attention to the fact that the sex occurred outside of the consulting room and that the standards made no mention of sex occurring outside the consulting room, or that the psychologist's theoretical orientation is cognitive-behavioral, psychoanalytic, or humanistic, and that the standards do not explicitly mention and therefore presumably are not relevant for his or her specific theoretical orientation.
3) It's not unethical if you know at least 3 other psychologists who have done the same thing. After all, if there were anything wrong with it, do you really think others would be doing it so openly that you would have heard about it?
4) It's not unethical if none of your students, research participants, supervisees, or therapy clients has ever complained about it. If one or more did complain about it, it is crucial to determine whether they constitute a large representative sample of those you encounter in your work, or are only a few atypical, statistically insignificant outliers.
5) It's not unethical if a student, research participant, supervisee, or therapy client wanted you to do it.

6) It's not unethical as long as the student's/research participant's/supervisee's/therapy client's condition made them so awful to be around that their behavior evoked (that is to say: *caused*) whatever it was you did, and they must own responsibility for it. Which is not, of course, an admission that you actually did something.
7) It's not unethical if you have a disorder or condition (psychological, medical, or just being tired and cranky), and that disorder or condition is willing to assume responsibility for your choices and behavior.
8) It's not unethical if you are pretty sure that legal, ethical, and professional standards were created by those who cause harm to countless thousands because of their closed-minded, simplistic approaches; or by those who are not involved in teaching, supervision, research, therapy, or other aspects of what psychologists do and so don't comprehend the hard realities that those doing the real work of psychology confront; or by those who do the real work of psychology and have as a consequence become so entrenched in their own ways of doing things that they want to require everyone else to live by their idiosyncratic rules.
9) It's not unethical if you've heard that the people involved in enforcing standards (e.g., licensing boards, administrative law judges) are dishonest, stupid, extremist, unlike you in some significant way, or—however well-meaning they may be—are conspiring against you.
10) It's not unethical if you're basically a good person and have upheld most of the other ethical standards. This "majority rule" gives you time off (from ethics) for good behavior. This means that all of us can safely ignore a few of the ethical standards as long as we scrupulously observe the other, far more important ones. In tight circumstances, we need observe only a majority of the standards. In a genuine crisis, we need only have observed one of the standards at some time in our lives. Or at least given it serious consideration.
11) It's not unethical if you don't mean to hurt anybody. If anyone happens to get hurt it was clearly an accident because you didn't intend it, and no one should be held responsible for something that is a chance, accidental happenstance.
12) It's not unethical if there is no set of peer-reviewed, adequately replicated, universally-accepted set of scientific research findings demonstrating, without qualification or doubt, that exactly what you did was the sole cause of harm to the student, supervisee, research participant, or therapy client. Few have articulated this principle with more compelling eloquence than a member of the Texas pesticide regulatory board charged with protecting Texas citizens against undue risks from pesticides. Discussing Chlordane, a chemical used to kill termites, he said, "Sure, it's going to kill a lot of people, but they may be dying of something else anyway."
13) It's not unethical if it's a one-time-only exception to your customary approach. Really. This is it. Never again. Don't even ask.
14) It's not unethical if you're an important figure in the field. Many psychologists have defined importance using such criteria as well-known, extensively published, popular with students, popular with granting agencies, holding some appointive or elective office, being rich, having a large practice, having what you think of as a "following" of like-minded people, etc. But many of us find such ill-considered criteria to be far to vulnerable to Type II error. In deciding whether we are an important figure in the field, who, after all, knows us better than ourselves?

15) It's not unethical if you're really pressed for time. In light of your unbelievable schedule and responsibilities, who after all could really expect you to attend to every little ethical detail?

It is likely that most, if not all of us could extend this list. Our abilities to think creatively and respond ethically to even the most daunting challenges seem mirrored by the strategies available to rationalize even the most unethical approaches.

CONCLUSION

Developing and practicing ethics is an active process continuing from graduate school throughout our careers. The psychologist who remains unaware of recent research, changes in the law, or other emerging information relevant to ethical decision-making is as limited as a professor teaching a course who hasn't read any literature on the topic for the last decade. Gathering the relevant information enables informed consideration. Drawing on help from our colleagues and wherever else we can find it, we attempt to see the implications of the information for the ethical aspects of the situation at hand and evaluate options to see which makes the most ethical sense. Just as when we design an experiment we try to search out the many sources of potential error—investigator paradigm effect, unintentional expectancy effect, demand characteristics, Hawthorne effect, spurious correlations, etc.—through which our persistent efforts to understand a phenomenon can end up misleading us, ethical considerations require constant, active awareness of our human vulnerabilities to rationalize unethical choices and to fall prey to inductive and deductive fallacies. With ethical development and practice, as with so many other aspects of what we do as psychologists, we never escape the need to seek new information, think critically, remain aware of our vulnerabilities, and always question.

REFERENCES AND ADDITIONAL RESOURCES

Websites

http://www.apa.org/ethics At this site the American Psychological Association Ethics Office presents ethics information and resources.

http://www.asppb.org This site, maintained by the Association of State & Provincial Psychology Boards, is a good source of information on licensing laws and standards, providing contact information (and links where available) to state and provincial licensing boards.

http//www.firstgov.gov A good place to start searches for government regulations, laws, etc. Search engine searches every word of every U.S. government document in a quarter of a second. Provides links, where available, to state and local government sites.

http://www.nlm.nih.gov/pubs/cbm/hum_exp.html This site presents an extensive bibliography of books, audiovisuals, and journal article citations on "Ethical Issues in Research Involving Human Participants."

http://kspope.com This site provides full-text articles on ethics, malpractice, and professional standards from such journals as *American Psychologist*, *Journal of Consulting & Clinical Psychology*, and *Psychology, Public Policy, & Law*; the ethics codes of APA and over 40 other organizations in the areas of therapy, counseling, and forensics; a guide to dual relationships; a guide to the security of clinical records on computers; links to psychology laws and licensing boards in Canada and the U.S.; and other free resources.

http://ori.hhs.gov The Office of Research Integrity "promotes integrity in biomedical and behavioral research" and "monitors institutional investigations of research misconduct and facilitates the responsible conduct of research through educational, preventive, and regulatory activities." The site provides numerous resources and has created "three listserves to foster discussion and networking among institutional officials and others interested in preventing research misconduct, teaching the responsible conduct of research, or conducting research on research integrity."

Publications

American Psychological Association. (1992). Ethical principles for psychologists and code of conduct. *American Psychologist, 47*, 1597–1611.

American Psychological Association. (1993). Record keeping guidelines. *American Psychologist, 48*, 984–986.

American Psychological Association, Committee for the Protection of Human Participants in Research. (1982). *Ethical principles in the conduct of research with human participants.* Washington, DC: Author.

American Psychological Association, Ethics Committee. (1996). Rules and procedures. *American Psychologist, 51*, 529–548.

Canadian Psychological Association. (1991). *Canadian Code of Ethics for Psychologists.* Ottawa: Author.

Chastain, G., & Landrum, R. E. (Eds.) (1999). *Protecting human subjects: Departmental subject pools and IRBs.* Washington, DC: American Psychological Association.

Fisher, C. B., & Tryon, W. W. (Eds.) (1990). *Ethics in applied developmental psychology.* Norwood, NJ: Ablex.

Gates, J. J., & Arons, B. S. (Eds.) (2000). *Privacy and confidentiality in mental health care.* Baltimore: Paul H. Brookes.

Hadjistavropoulos, T., & Bieling, P. J. (2000). When reviews attack: Ethics, free speech, and the peer review process. *Canadian Psychology, 41*, 152–159.

Kalichman, S. C. (1999). *Mandated reporting of suspected child abuse: Ethics, law, & policy, Second Edition.* Washington, DC: American Psychological Association.

Keith-Spiegel, P., & Koocher, G. P. (1998). How to confront and unethical colleague. In G. P. Koocher, J. C. Norcross, & S. S. Hill (Eds.), *Psychologist's desk reference* (pp. 469–473). New York: Oxford University Press.

Koocher, G. P., & Keith-Spiegel, P. (1998). *Ethics in Psychology: Professional Standards and Cases.* New York: Oxford University Press.

Payton, C. R. (1994). Implications of the 1992 ethics code for diverse groups. *Professional Psychology: Research & Practice, 25*, 317–320.

Pope, K. S. (1994). *Sexual involvement with therapists: Patient assessment, subsequent therapy, forensics.* Washington, DC: American Psychological Association.

Pope, K. S., Tabachnick, B. G., & Keith-Spiegel, P. (1987). Ethics of practice: The beliefs and behaviors of psychologists as therapists. *American Psychologist, 42*, 993–1006.

Pope, K. S., & Vasquez, M. J. T. (1998). *Ethics in Therapy & Counseling, Second Edition.* San Francisco: Jossey-Bass.

Pope, K. S., & Vetter, V. A. (1992). Ethical dilemmas encountered by members of the American Psychological Association: A national survey. *American Psychologist, 47*, 397–411.

Shidlo, A., & Schroeder, M. (2002). *Conversion therapy: Ethical, clinical, and research perspectives.* Binghamton, NY: Haworth Press.

Sieber, J. E. (1992). *Planning ethically responsible research.* Newbury Park, CA: Sage.

Simon, G. C. (1978). Psychologist as whistle blower: A case study. *Professional Psychology: Research & Practice, 9*, 322–340.

Tabachnick, B. G., Keith-Spiegel, P., & Pope, K. S. (1991). Ethics of teaching: Beliefs and behaviors of psychologists as educators. *American Psychologist,* 1991, *46*, 506–515.

Whitley, B. E., & Keith-Spiegel, P. (2002). *Academic Dishonesty: An Educator's Guide.* Mahwah, NJ: Lawrence Erlbaum.

CHAPTER 4

Balancing Career and Family

PAULA J. CAPLAN

Even the most experienced psychologists have trouble balancing paid work and family, whether their work is in academia or in clinical practice, so undergraduates, graduate students, and interns have no reason to feel incompetent and inadequate if they have trouble doing the balancing act. We feel we are shortchanging our loved ones when we spend time on our studies or work, and we feel we are being insufficiently productive as students or workers because of spending time meeting family responsibilities—and even more when we notice that we are actually having fun with our partners, parents, or children. Spending any time meeting our other needs, such as going for a swim or reading a book of poetry or just sitting quietly and thinking, often makes us feel we are shirking both of our other sets of duties. This is the case for people of both sexes but is more common for women and for men who are not white, heterosexual, able-bodied, or doing what is considered to be "mainstream" work (Caplan, 1994).

It is even more pressing to be aware of the balancing difficulties and to find ways to deal with them when we consider the increasing proportions of women among students and faculty in psychology, as well as in the profession outside of academia (Enns, 1997; Snyder, McDermott, Leibowitz, & Cheavens, 2000). For example, according to an American Psychological Association report (APA/Pate, 2001) based on the association's 1999–2000 study of graduate departments of psychology, women represent 34% of fulltime faculty in traditional academic settings and 43% of fulltime faculty in professional schools for psychologists; and according to Gehlmann, Wicherski, & Kohout (1995), the percentage of women among fulltime faculty in graduate departments of psychology in the United States was only 22% in 1984. Furthermore, in 1984 racialized people and members of ethnic minority faculty accounted for about 6% of all fulltime faculty, and that number had increased to 11% in 1999–2000 (APA/Pate, 2001; Gehlmann et al., 1995), but although Canadian staffing patterns were similar with respect to sex distribution, racialized people and members of ethnic minorities represented only 2% of their Canadian fulltime faculty in graduate programs of psychology (APA/Pate, 2001). On their own, these percentages suggest the special pressures that come from being in the minority as a faculty member or, as a graduate student who is a woman or a member of a racialized group or ethnic minority, from seeing few people from one's own group-assignments on the faculty. But what makes the pressures and membership in devalued groups even

PAULA J. CAPLAN • Pembroke Center for Teaching and Research on Women, Brown University, Providence RI 02912 clearer is the following: women in the U.S. currently represent between 70 and 75 percent of first-year, fulltime students in doctoral and master's programs in psychology, respectively; those numbers have been steadily increasing for many years; the 18% of first-year enrollees who are members of racialized or ethnic minority groups also represent a steady increase; a similar pattern is seen in Canada (although racialized people and members of ethnic minority groups account for only 5% of first-year psychology graduate students there: APA/Pate, 2001). The fact that these increases have filled the pipeline with members of marginalized groups who are highly qualified to teach in graduate programs, and yet all of these groups still account for a minority of psychology faculty in such programs, testifies powerfully to the continued presence of intense bias and oppression in academia (and see Caplan, 1994). It is clear, therefore, that the workplace part of the double load includes the necessity of coping with this bias and oppression.

The Second Wave of the feminist movement beginning in the late 1960s and early 1970s called attention to the difficulty of the balancing act, but social changes to make it easier both for women and for men have been exceedingly slow in coming. Women have been expected to be Superwomen, to balance career and family with ease and aplomb, not complaining, not asking for help and certainly not expecting it from any quarter, and feeling grateful for the opportunity to obtain university degrees and to work as psychologists (Caplan, 2000, 2001). Media stories about "Mr. Moms" or even about men shouldering more of the household and family responsibilities have given a false picture of reality, for recent research shows that the percentage of housework and childcare done by men has increased very little over the past thirty years (Pleck, 1997, 1986). What has been difficult for men has been confronting the conflicting forces, a pull from their families (and progressive elements of society) to spend more time with them and do more of the caretaking, a push from traditional elements to consider themselves masculine for doing paid work and less than manly when feeding babies or vacuuming carpets at home.

Increasing the burden for parents has been the crazy-making pair of messages our society gives:

(A) One is that the welfare of children matters desperately and is overwhelmingly the responsibility of parents, especially mothers (Caplan, 2000).
(B) The other is that children's welfare is not important enough for our governments to spend much energy or money on it.

This leaves parents, especially mothers, working frantically and tirelessly to meet all of their children's needs while knowing that that work is shockingly undervalued.

Despite the changed expectations about both women and men, there has been no let-up in pressure, not the pressure on graduate students to do well in courses, the pressure on early- and mid-career faculty to publish and to take on committee work and advising duties, the pressure on clinicians to maintain heavy case loads (in private practice, in order to earn a living, and in hospitals and clinics, in order to be seen as a team player who does one's share of the work), or the pressure on parents to produce perfect children (Caplan, 2000). In fact, if anything, all of these pressures have increased and show little sign of abating. To do good work as a graduate student, a therapist, or a teacher requires focus, concentration, energy, and persistence. Furthermore, being a graduate student can be emotionally draining because you have far less power than the people who grade you and write (might refuse to write) letters of recommendation, as well as because it can be hard to find out when the work you've done on a thesis or dissertation is enough, so time and energy are spent in trying to divine the wishes of your supervisor. Being a conscientious therapist is draining because of the demands placed on one's time, energy, and patience by suffering or difficult clients. Being a good, caring teacher is draining because of the energy and time that go into responding to students' learning, emotional, and mentoring needs and because of the worry about how much publishing will be enough to obtain tenure or promotions. Canadian feminist psychologist Cannie Stark has wisely pointed out that, in jobs in which one is supposed to think creatively, one doesn't just stop thinking—whether about teaching, research, or therapy patients—just because one arrives back at home, and these thoughts are likely to pop up or continue while one is changing diapers, cooking, or doing other household tasks (Stark-Adamec, 1995). Based on her own research about women in academia, Stark reports that women bring home an average of 71.6 hours of workplace work per month, partly because of their love for work but partly because of the enormous numbers of demands to which women have to respond while at work and partly because, unlike some 9-to-5 work, it is never clear when work is done (Stark-Adamec, 1995). Stark also reports that at home, women spend more than 102 hours a month taking care of household activities assigned to women and, as a result of all of the above, women get an average of only 210 of the 240 hours of sleep per month they feel they need.

In the early 1970s, I had my first post-Ph.D. job, a fulltime position as a psychologist in a clinic. I spent 40 hours a week there and often took work home as well, and at home I had a husband, two biological children, and two stepchildren. I tried to work efficiently in order to make everyone happy. One day, a clinic administrator took me to task because I did not "seem available to the staff." I replied that I was bewildered, because I always attended every meeting, finished my work on time, and quickly carried out psychological assessments when they were requested by nonpsychologists in the clinic. The reply was, "Well, but, um, you don't... hang around in the hallways or the coffee room." I didn't know whether to laugh or cry at that, but that was the moment I learned that every workplace has unwritten rules that employees and students are supposed to figure out and follow.

WHAT MAKES IT SO DIFFICULT

Standards and expectations make finding the right balance impossible for people of both sexes. For women, the standards are simply unmeetable. At home, you are supposed to do the lion's share of the work. As a student or employee, you are supposed to do as much as or even more work than the men; if you do not, you will be perceived as doing *less* (this has happened to me). And as a student or employee, you will be expected to do not only what is defined as "work" but also the very real work of nurturing, such as listening to troubled people, maintaining a sunny, supportive demeanor. If you fail to do the latter, you risk being disliked because you are insufficiently womanly, but if you *do* the latter, you risk acquiring an image of "motherly person" rather than "good student or worker." Even today, the two are often considered mutually exclusive. A senior psychologist in a research institution who was married and had four children told me this: She worked diligently until 5:00 every day, and one day as she was leaving the office, a male colleague called out, "Could you help me? My grant application has to be postmarked before midnight tonight, and I need to pick your brain." Obligingly, she spent the next hour trying to help him, and near 6:00 he looked at his watch and said, seriously and judgmentally, "You should be home cooking dinner now!"

For men who are committed to doing their fair share of household work, the standards are somewhat different. In spite of the women's movement, our society has not yet decided either how much housework and childcare a man *should* do or how much he can do and still be considered a real man (whatever that is) who is presumably also doing conscientious work as a student, instructor, researcher, or therapist.

Due to increases in the numbers of women, racialized people, and openly gay, lesbian, and bisexual people among graduate students, faculty, and practitioners in psychology combined with the increasing preponderance of women on campuses and in the workplace, one might expect these sites to be welcoming for people who are not white, straight, mainstream males. However, women account for the majority of undergraduates, support staff, cleaning and food service staff, and faculty in low-level and part-time positions, and members of other marginalized groups are more commonly found in those positions as well. Harvard University, for instance, continues to have a disturbingly low percentage of women in tenured positions. The "academic funnel" is the term based on the findings of fewer women as status and salary increase (Caplan, 1994).The university campus was never intended to educate women or hire women faculty (Sheinin, 1987), and many of their organizational aspects still reflect this. For instance, junior faculty aiming to publish enough to get tenure typically need to do this during the very period in their lives when women are of childbearing age; and early attempts to allow for this, such as programs granting an extra year to apply for tenure because of having a new child, have been of limited use. Reasons they have not been more useful include: the fact that it takes far more than one year to care for a baby and young child; the irony that expectations about women's publishing productivity are often increased because "they've had a whole extra year to write"; the tendency of administrators and peers to look down on men who ask for that extra year so they can co-parent; and the criticism and marginalization of anyone who uses flextime, does workplace tasks at home, or works part-time.

Other reasons the balancing act is so difficult include:

- the rarity with which those at the top in academic and clinical settings have altered values and norms to reflect the extensive documentation from our own field that the "double load" (e.g.,Greenglass, 1985) occasions enormous stress, even desperation
- the difficulty of finding women mentors to help show the way, because mentors for both sexes are rare—women mentors because they are overburdened by their own balancing attempts within the workplace (e.g., meeting expectations that women will carry the lion's share of advising about personal problems, and serving on many committees because without you, they will be all-white and all-male)
- the difficulty of finding male mentors who have made sustained attempts to share equally with women the household and childcare tasks
- the scarcity of affordable, high-quality daycare
- the socialization of people of both sexes, for somewhat different reasons, to be reluctant to ask for help
- the tendency for part-time students to receive less financial aid, even proportionally

In addition, many factors make the balancing act more difficult for women, including:

- the tendency for more part-time employees to be women, who are sometimes working part-time by choice because of their family responsibilities, although they virtually never receive benefits such as health insurance. This is a dramatically increasing concern, since in the mid-1970s part-timers accounted for 22 percent of undergraduate teachers but in 1995, 47 percent (Donnis, 2001)
- the tendency of students and employees to evaluate female faculty and supervisors more harshly than males (Caplan, 1994; 2000); thus, for instance, women are expected to do more household work but are then criticized for not publishing enough

Together, the many impediments to finding ways to balance career and family benefit a status quo in which the most powerful people keep the less powerful scrambling, overworking to try to meet the impossible standards for mothers to do virtually all the childrearing on their own (the philosophy in Hilary Clinton's *It Takes a Village to Raise a Child* remains outside the mainstream), and keep paid workers striving to produce nonstop (Caplan, 2000).

WHAT CAN HELP (CAN, NOT WILL)

In Your Head and With Others

Start by realizing this: It is almost certain that you will never *feel* that you are successfully balancing family and work. So what can you do? (see Table 1) you can assume community, or at least commonality. Know that, no matter how calm and secure other people may appear, *anyone* doing that balancing act is struggling. Long ago, I presented at a conference a paper about what I considered bizarre, unique problems at work that I figured were somehow probably my fault. I was so ashamed that I introduced each example by saying, "One psychologist had the following experience" or "Another psychologist told this story." I was so astounded to see people sitting up in their chairs and nodding vigorously that by the time I got to the third example, I took a deep breath and said, "Here is what happened to me." As a teenager, I had the typical adolescent's belief that my feelings and experiences were weird and probably proof

TABLE 1. Strategies That Can Help Balancing Career and Family

- Assume community, or at least commonality.
- Try to find work that you love, an aim whose importance cannot be overestimated.
- Assume, and help create, community with people from various levels and in various realms.
- Talk and talk and talk about the obstacles to finding balance between career and family.
- Guard against blaming or pathologizing yourself.
- Ask senior people for "clarity" about what is expected of you on the job.
- Try to clarify with other adults, as well as older children, in your household the way you will distribute household responsibilites, time for work, and leisure time with each other and alone.
- Keep in mind this apparent paradox: *Give yourself permission* to take more time to do things in any realm, so that you don't feel so pressured, *but* aim to do them more quickly than you can imagine doing them once you get started.
- Never forget that, in an ideal world, changes that make balancing between family and career a task of human scale would come from the top down, through policies *initiated, implemented, and evaluated* at the highest levels of administration. So maintain the perspective that the people with the greatest power should be doing this work by keeping in mind that no less a body than the American Psychological Association has said that "administrators, especially department chairs and deans, must be held accountable for gender equality and climate in their units. Those who fail to make the corrections necessary for gender equity should be given feedback, and their effectiveness in correcting these problems should be reflected in compensation. If necessary, ineffective administrators should be replaced (APA, 2000, p.1)."
- Create initiatives for change if you want to, or can afford to, take the risks that such initiatives would involve; but if you do this, try to maintain low expectations about the speed and magnitude of change.
- Begin initiatives for change by choosing strategically which ones are most important to you or seem most doable, first making or finding a list of policies and practices that have been helpful at other universities or workplaces for psychologists.
- Remember that the best, time-tested antidotes for burnout are ongoing contact with people who share your dilemmas and aims; an ability to remember that every step in a long struggle is important; and a whopping appreciation for irony and sense of humor.

that I was abnormal. Later, I came to understand that any feelings and thoughts I have are invariably shared by at least a few, carefully chosen people. And finally, I realized that I come closest to guessing the truth if I assume that my feelings are virtually universal. My taking the plunge and being the first one to express confusion, fear, or a particular perspective has nearly always elicited sighs of relief from others who had considered themselves strange, stupid, or both. Simply acknowledging feelings of puzzlement and vulnerability can create a community as you speak about them.

Try to find work that you love, an aim whose importance cannot be overestimated:

- Graduate students can choose paper and dissertation topics they find compelling rather than routine, and if they fear that their committees will regard their preferred topics as unacceptable, they can brainstorm with other students or trusted faculty members about ways to design research that is likely to be approved by committee members while retaining their fascination for the students.
- Faculty members can design or modify courses in ways that suit students' needs but are interesting and enjoyable to teach (e.g., if you're told your department needs you to teach the introductory developmental psychology course and you find the textbook to be rather dry, you can teach it from a critical thinking perspective).
- After reaching a more secure employment level, such as a tenured position, you can design new courses based on what you most love to read, think, and talk about, then see if they can be added to the list of your department's course offerings.
- If you are a clinician and have any say over what patients you see, try to refer to other people any prospective patients with whom you are unlikely to make a good, human connection, to be a solid, working "fit." This is both good practice as a therapist and a way to maximize the interest factor in your work life.

Assume, and help create, community with people from various levels and in various realms—graduate students connecting with secretaries, faculty with cleaning or food service staff, psychology faculty with faculty from other departments or with psychology professors in other institutions. Breaking through these kinds of class barriers increases opportunities for everyone to present their different perspectives, offer different kinds of useful information about how the department or workplace is really run, and provide support for each other. It also brings members of different groups down or up to human scale, making distance and stereotyping of group members harder to maintain and humanizing the campus and other workplaces.

Related to the above, talk and talk and talk about the obstacles to finding balance between career and family. Know that by bringing up dilemmas and fears in conversation, you will help to free others to do so, but you will also make some people exceedingly uncomfortable, even belligerent. The latter is all the more reason you need to reach out to others, give and receive support (see Caplan, 1994, for specific suggestions).

Guard against blaming or pathologizing yourself if you are not balancing work and family with grace and aplomb. Make a mental note that you'd be unlikely to blame or pathologize others who are having that trouble. Keep coming back to the current systemic ills (see previous section) that make balancing so hard. This, too, is easier, the more you discuss it with other people.

Ask senior people for "clarity" about what is expected of you as a student or employee, a crucial practice in light of the power and number of unwritten rules, as mentioned earlier. The relevance of this point to the balancing dilemma is that, in the face of unclear expectations, many of us strive mightily to do far more than is acceptable. Since asking for clarity can make one feel extremely vulnerable, this is another instance in which it can be terrifically helpful to brainstorm with other people, whether in your field or outside of it, about how to word requests or suggestions in ways that reduce that feeling of vulnerability and help you maintain your dignity. It's often good to include script-writing in the brainstorming because, when one is very worried and/or angry, one can get mental blocks, finding it impossible to think of anything to say other than making requests that sound like demands, threats, complaints or intense anger.

Try to clarify with other adults, as well as older children, in your household the way you will distribute household responsibilities; time to do paid work, coursework, or dissertation work; time for fun together; and leisure time on one's own or with others. Be aware, however, that these advance plans are often jettisoned, due to several factors:

- Most women and men have been subjected to intense social pressures to divide family responsibilities along traditional sex-typed lines.
- The continuing disparity in women's and men's salaries helps shape the decision in heterosexual families that, if only one adult will maintain fulltime paid work while the children are young or any family member is chronically ill or disabled, it's the man who will keep his job, because his income will probably be higher than hers would be, so it makes economic sense for the woman to stay home and do the caretaking there.
- Men's intelligence and achievements tend to be assumed to be greater than those of women.

Keep in mind this apparent paradox: (A) *Give yourself permission* to take more time to do things in any realm, so that you don't feel so pressured, *but* (B)aim to do them more quickly than you can imagine doing them once you get started. These two suggestions may seem to work at cross-purposes, but in fact they don't, because both are ways to minimize pressure that comes from the impossible standards imposed on us from all around. This is reflected, for instance, in the raising of the bar in recent years: workers spend significantly increasing amounts of time at work, hence the constantly-heard complaint, "I am *so* busy, never have a moment to myself or relax with my partner." To explain part (B) a bit, in more than twenty years of teaching, I have found that students and colleagues tend to overestimate the amount of time many tasks will take... and even assume they are *supposed to* spend extensive periods of time doing such things as writing dissertations or grant proposals. When I suggest to anyone that they try to do such projects in a single day or even one hour, they initially tell me that that is absurd and impossible. I then explain that, of course, they cannot finish the project in that time, but that they will undoubtedly be amazed by how much they can accomplish if they take seriously the suggestion to finish in a day or an hour. They invariably report back to me that this experiment showed them that they can work much more efficiently than they had realized. I also explain that they will have plenty of time to go over their work and fill in gaps, make alterations, or reorganize the material but that all of that is easier once the most important material and the bulk of the structure is written or sketched out in that short period of time. The other function served by this advice is to remove some of the heavy emotional load that "writing a dissertation" or "writing a grant application" tends to carry, a load that significantly impedes the process of completing the task. Once you discover that you *can* do some parts of your work in less time than before without losing its quality, you will know that you don't have to work constantly under intense time pressure (see A above).

Change from the Top Down... Or from You

Never forget that, in an ideal world, changes that make balancing between family and career a task of human scale would come from the top down, through policies *initiated, implemented, and evaluated* at the highest levels of administration. *You* should not have to make this happen. Top administrators should set a tone of respect for all and warn that reprisals against those who take parental leave or use flextime or job-sharing will not be tolerated. Administrators should sponsor seminars for management, other employees, and students about difficulties of the balancing act, and they should set a tone of compassion and support for those who are attempting it. Top administrators should initiate and fund studies of steps their universities or clinics could take to decrease these difficulties, such as pushing for adequate maternity and paternity leave for all. In fact, an American Psychological Association report holds that "administrators, especially department chairs and deans, must be held accountable for gender equality and climate in their units. Those who fail to make the corrections necessary for gender equity should be given feedback, and their effectiveness in correcting these problems should be reflected in compensation. If necessary, ineffective administrators should be replaced (APA, 2000, p.1)." Despite this strong statement, however, few colleges and universities have yet taken steps to make this kind of thing happen.

Although change should come from the top, so that those who are burdened and oppressed need not take on the additional, onerous tasks of initiating and campaigning for change, some of you will feel you want to, perhaps can afford to, take risks by creating initiatives for change. Ideally, you would take such action working with your peers and possibly more senior, supportive people. Trying to make change happen can be empowering precisely because it involves taking action rather than waiting passively, hoping needed changes will take place but feeling powerless. One example of such an initiative would be for graduate students who are becoming increasingly anxious about forthcoming comprehensive examinations to form a group and ask the faculty to make available examples of questions from past comprehensives. They may refuse you, but they may not, and making the request as a group will minimize the risk to each student insofar as that is possible.

If you choose to work for change, expect powerful resistance from those at the top or in middle management, and know that you may suddenly feel even more powerless than before. I cannot emphasize enough how much it helps to be prepared for resistance, setbacks, and even reprisals; it is crucial to consider what risks you may be taking. Similarly, assume that change for the better may come slowly. Of course, if you ask for change, you may be accused of being belligerent, demanding, or—an increased danger in an arena populated by psychologists—needy, immature, or oppositional. It is important to try to gauge the risk versus benefit situation and to make sure you document everything you have done, so that there will be an accurate record in case you are accused of wrongdoing. Furthermore, be aware that change for the worse may come abruptly and unexpectedly, perhaps due to the visibility of your activism, such as a sudden reduction in the number of hours for which an assistant is signed to you or the announcement that a promised salary increase will not be forthcoming. Awareness of the risks can not only minimize the disappointment you may feel if change comes slowly but also keep you from setting a standard for change that is so high that you don't notice small steps toward your goal along the way.

If you choose to push for changes, begin by choosing strategically which changes are most important to you or seem most doable, first making or finding a list of policies and practices that have been helpful at other universities or workplaces for psychologists (Caplan, 1994, includes such a list, pp. 161–72). Actions can range from being on the lookout for discouragement of cooperative work and encouragement of malicious competitiveness, to establishing study groups for students and support groups at work for people struggling with the double load, to systematic gathering of questionnaire data in order to identify and document the struggles and wishes of those who are juggling family and career. Other examples of specific actions include pushing for benefits for part-time workers such as health insurance, reasonable workloads, and clearly-specified expectations would be helpful, as would fair and proportional financial aid for part-time students.

Above all, remember that for the major institutions of universities and mental health settings it is simply not a priority to help ease the double load for women or for men, and because the struggle for change will be long and exhausting, it will be tempting to give up. The best, time-tested antidotes for burnout are ongoing contact with people who share your dilemmas and aims; an ability to remember that every step in a long struggle is important; and a whopping appreciation for irony and sense of humor.

ACKNOWLEDGEMENTS: Many thanks to Professors Kathryn Morgan and Sandra Pyke for getting me involved in writing about women in academia in the first place.

ADDITIONAL RESOURCES[1]

Bell-Scott, P., & Sheftall, B. G. (1987). *Black women in higher education: Struggling to gain visibility*. New York: Garland.

Chrisler, J. (1998). Teacher vs. scholar: Role conflict for women? In L. Collins, J. Chrisler, & K. Quina (Eds.), *Career strategies for women academics: Arming Athena* (pp. 107–27). Thousand Oaks, CA: Sage Publications.

Committee on the Status of Women (1991). *Non-regular instructional personnel in Ontario universities*. Toronto: Council of Ontario Universities.

Committee on Women in Psychology, American Psychological Association (1992). *Survival guide to academe for women and ethnic minorities*. Washington: American Psychological Association.

Haley, E. (1989). Support systems for women in graduate school. In C. Filteau (Ed.), *Proceedings of a conference on women in graduate studies in Ontario* (pp. 32–41). Toronto: Ontario Council on Graduate Studies.

Hensel, N. (1991). *Realizing gender equality in higher education: The need to integrate work/family issues*. (Report No. 2). Washington: George Washington School of Education and Human Development (ASHE-ERIC Higher Education).

Kitzinger, C. (1990). Heterosexism in psychology. *The Psychologist*, 391–2.

Levstik, L. S. (1982). The impossible dream: The Ph.D., marriage, and family. In S. Vartuli (Ed.), *The Ph.D. experience: A woman's point of view* (pp. 93–104). New York: Praeger.

Pyke, S. (1990). *A message to council*. Council of Ontario universities, annual report 1989–90. Committee on the Status of Women. Toronto: Council of Ontario Universities.

Roby, P. (1973). Institutional barriers to women students in higher education. In A. S. Rossi, & A. Calderwood (Eds.), *Academic women on the move* (pp. 37–56). New York: Russell Sage Foundation.

Rose, S. (Ed.) (1986). *Career guide for women scholars*. New York: Springer.

Task Force on Women in Academe (2000). *Women in academe: Two steps forward, one step back. Report of the Task Force on Women in Academe*. Washington, DC: American Psychological Association.

Trofimenkoff, S. M. (1989). A woman administrator looks at life and love in the graduate school. In C. Filteau (Ed.), *Proceedings of a conference on women in graduate studies in Ontario*. (pp. 114–18). Toronto: Ontario Council on Graduate Studies.

Williams, R. (1982). In and out of relationships: A serious game for the woman doctoral student. In S. Vartuli (Ed.), *The Ph.D. experience: A woman's point of view* (79–82). New York: Praeger.

[1] Many of these references were published in the 1970s, 1980s, or early 1990s; they are included here because, unfortunately, the issues to which they are addressed and the patterns of data reported therein still apply. Also, please see references in Section A of the Bibliography in Caplan (1994).

REFERENCES

American Psychological Association (2000). Report of the Task Force on Women in Academe. *Women in academe: Two steps forward, one step back.* Retrieved July 18, 2002, from http://www.apa.org/pi/wpo/academe.

Caplan, P. J. (1994). *Lifting a Ton of Feathers: A Woman's Guide to Surviving in the Academic World.* Toronto: University of Toronto Press.

Caplan, P. J. (2000). *THE NEW Don't Blame Mother: Mending the Mother-Daughter Relationship.* New York: Routledge.

Caplan, P. J. (2001). Motherhood: Its changing face. In *Encyclopedia of women and gender* (Vol. 2, pp. 783–794). San Diego, CA: Academic Press.

Donnis, I. (2001, December 14). Illiberal education. *Providence Phoenix, 1*, 8–9.

Enns, C. Z. (1997). *Feminist theories and feminist psychotherapies: Origins, themes, and variations.* New York: The Haworth Press.

Gehlmann, S., Wicherski, M., & Kohout, J. (1995). *Characteristics of graduate departments in psychology: 1993–94.* Washington, D.C.: American Psychological Association.

Greenglass, E. (1985). A social-psychological view of marriage for women. *International Journal of Women's Studies, 8*, 24–31.

Pate, W. E. II. (2001). *Analyses of data from graduate study in psychology.* Retrieved July 18, 2002 from http://research.apa.org/grad00contents.html

Pleck, J. (1986). Employment and fatherhood: Issues and innovative policies. In M. Lamb (Ed.), *The father's role: Applied perspectives* (pp. 385–412). New York: John Wiley and Sons.

Pleck, J. (1997). Paternal involvement: Levels, sources, and consequences. In M. Lamb (Ed.), *The Role of the Father in Child Development* (pp. 66–103). New York: Wiley.

Sheinin, R. (1987, June). The monastic origins of the university. Presented to Canadian Association of University Teachers' Status of Women workshop, Fredericton, NB.

Snyder, C. R., McDermott, D. S., Leibowitz, R. Q., & Cheavens, J. (2000). The roles of female clinical psychologists in changing the field of psychotherapy. In C. R. Snyder, & R. E. Ingram (Eds.), *Handbook of psychological change: Psychotherapy processes and practices for the 21st century* (pp. 640–659). Toronto, ON: John Wiley & Sons.

Stark-Adamec, C. (1995). Women's ways of working: Rocking the boat and the cradle in academia. Research-based policy recommendations. Women, work, and stress: Developing mechanisms for change by bridging the gap between research and policy [Special Issue]. *The WINning edge*, December, 1–29.

SECTION II

YOUR RESEARCH/ACADEMIC CAREER

CHAPTER 5

Writing a Literature Review

ROY F. BAUMEISTER

Literature reviews occupy an important corner of the world of scientific activity, yet most scientists do not receive training in how to write them. In the early days of psychological research, many people did their research based on intuitions and personal insights, and one did not have to spend much time in background reading simply because there was not much to read. As our field's knowledge base expands month by month, however, it becomes increasingly important to be able to master the amount of information already published. New ideas increasingly have to build on previously published works.

In many cases, psychologists can now test their theories without collecting data at all—they can simply rely on works already published. Many literature reviews represent empirical tests of hypotheses. There is already so much published information that you can probably find some information on almost any broad question about human behavior. To be sure, collecting new data will continue to represent the vital core of scientific activity, but literature reviews will be an increasingly important and common part of scientific activity.

Literature reviews are special for a couple reasons. First, they combine results of many different studies, and that gives them power and value that no single study can have. The results of any one study might be tainted by experimenter bias, random fluctuations in the data, methodological errors, and other such problems. Hence it is always risky to draw too firm a conclusion based on a single study. In contrast, literature reviews often combine data from dozens or even hundreds of studies. When so many findings point toward the same conclusion, one can have high confidence in the correctness of that conclusion. It is unlikely that many different studies will yield similar results because of experimenter bias or other such problems.

Second, literature reviews permit researchers to address broad questions. Researchers may start with broad questions like "Does money bring happiness?" or "Are religious people healthier than others?" or "Are men more ambitious than women?" But a single investigation is limited to its sample, procedures, and measures, and so it will not usually permit the researcher to furnish a strong answer. For example, happiness can be measured in many different ways, and even money could be assessed in terms of salary, wealth, savings, or change in any of the above, and so unless one study has used all the different possible measures, it cannot justify a broad conclusion. In contrast, a literature review can draw on studies that used all different methods and measures, and so a sweeping conclusion can be justified.

ROY F. BAUMEISTER • Department of Psychology, Case Western Reserve University, Cleveland, OH 44106

To put this another way: The research journals are full of findings that are necessarily *underinterpreted.* Reviewers will not usually allow the author of a single investigation to draw sweeping conclusions that go beyond the limitations of sample and procedure. Literature reviewers can however make such broad conclusions and interpretations. For people who are interested in grand ideas and broad questions, literature reviews constitute an excellent and exciting means of addressing them.

NARRATIVE AND META-ANALYTIC REVIEWS

There are two different strategies for reviewing literature, and these are called narrative review and meta-analysis. Narrative review approaches are more traditional, and indeed almost all literature reviews prior to 1980 used them. They consist of providing qualitative descriptions of the results of many previous studies. Meta-analysis, in contrast, is a newer approach that uses a quantitative method of combining the results of previous studies.

Although there is some tension between the users of the two methods, and some experts who favor meta-analysis disdain narrative approaches as obsolete, my opinion is that the two methods serve different goals and therefore both have a valuable place in science.

Meta-analysis is the preferred method for combining the results of many studies that use comparable methods to address the same question. In contrast, narrative reviews are more useful for combining results from studies that may use very different methods and procedures and that address different questions. For example, if you wanted to combine the results of many studies on gender differences in domestic violence you would certainly use meta-analysis. Gender always means the same thing, and domestic violence is measured in a few rather standard ways, and so it is appropriate to combine the results of many studies to determine what the result is. Thus, Archer (2000) did precisely that, and he was able to conclude that women are more likely than men to initiate physical violence toward a spouse or dating partner, as well as showing that the difference across many studies is quite a small one.

In contrast, narrative reviews can be useful for combining quite different kinds of evidence to formulate a broad theoretical formulation. Baumeister and Leary (1995) reviewed very diverse literatures in order to conclude that a "need to belong" is one of the most pervasive and powerful human motivations. To make their case, they sought to show that the need to belong is involved in a wide range of very different patterns of behavior, including thought processes, emotional reactions, forming and breaking off relationships, physical and mental health, and lifelong happiness.

In addition, most empirical articles and dissertations contain some review of relevant previous literature, and these are typically narrative. They are used to set up the hypotheses for the present study by linking the various steps in the theoretical argument to previous findings.

Thus, the first step in writing a literature review is to decide what kind of review to write. If you are looking at many different studies on the same hypothesis, meta-analysis is generally better than narrative. If the goal of your review is to formulate a new theory that will link together diverse strands of work, then you may favor a narrative method instead. Put another way, meta-analysis is the better method when it is viable, but there many things meta-analysis cannot do, and in those cases narrative reviews can be quite valuable.

Searching the Literature

Regardless of what kind of literature review you plan to write, a first step is finding the evidence. The research literature in psychology has been expanding rapidly for several decades, each month hundreds or even thousands of new articles are published, and so the task of finding everything you want can be formidable. If you intend to write a good literature review, you should strive to be as thorough as possible. You will lose credibility if the people who read your literature review can say, "Hey, you forgot to include such-and-such a study."

Recent advances in computer indexing have greatly expanded the literature reviewer's ability to search large databases for every potentially relevant article. These are becoming ever easier to use. With only a few instructions, you can learn to conduct such searches. Typically they will give you a (long) list of abstracts of articles that refer to whatever key words you type into the computer. You can restrict the search not only by topic but also by time (e.g., you might request only the publications from the last ten years), by journal, and by other factors as well. Still, the odds are you will end up skimming a long list of abstracts to identify the articles relevant to your cause.

You should keep notes of how you run the computer searchers, because you should report your search method in the manuscript itself. Indicate what database(s) you searched, what keywords you entered, and how you restricted the search. The purpose is to let the reader know how you got the information that you are summarizing in your paper.

For some topics, computerized searches are not helpful, because the topic has not been specified. For example, Baumeister (2000) reviewed diverse literatures to formulate and test a hypothesis about female erotic plasticity (i.e., the degree to which the sex drive is affected by social, cultural, and situational factors). Because erotic plasticity was a new theory and a new concept, that article relied on reinterpreting studies that were conducted to test quite different ideas. Using "erotic plasticity" as a term to search a database would have yielded nothing, and a broader term such as "sexual desire" would have yielded many irrelevant findings. In such cases, reviewers must fall back on older methods of finding sources. The obligation to be careful and thorough remains strong, however.

One valuable method of searching the literature without computerized aids is to find the most relevant journals and examine every article they published. In some fields there are prominent journals that are devoted to a topic and are likely to contain most of the relevant articles (as well as many irrelevant ones). For example, to do the paper on erotic plasticity I began with the *Journal of Sex Research*, and in an earlier paper on suicide (Baumeister, 1990) I could rely on *Suicide and Life-Threatening Behavior*. Typically I begin with the most recent years, on the assumption that new articles will contain references to important older works. A good strategy is to read every abstract in the journal. (An abstract is a short summary of the article, and nearly all research journals have these for every article, so it is often possible to cover a lot of ground in fairly short time, just by reading these summaries.) If the abstract shows that the work is relevant to what you are doing then you read the article itself. Otherwise you move on.

When reading the article, it is important to pay special attention to sources that it cites, especially ones that lie outside the journal you are studying. Make a list of other sources to look up. Don't be discouraged if your list soon grows long, for many articles will turn out to be not all that relevant, whereas everything you do find (that is relevant) will strengthen your paper.

Meta-Analysis

There are standard procedures for conducting a meta-analysis, and if you plan on using that method you may want to work with someone who is already an expert or consult one of the published sources as a guide. Helpful works include Wolf (1986), Hedges and Olkin (1985), Rosenthal (1983, 1991), Cooper and Hedges (1994), and Cooper (1990).

In general, meta-analysis works by converting the findings of many different studies into a common measure that can be used to combine them. Typically you translate your independent variable into two categories or experimental conditions. For example, you might want to compare men against women. Then you look at the difference between them in each study. The standard way of expressing this difference is in standard deviation units. That is, you take the average for men, subtract the average for women (to produce the difference), and divide the result by the size of the standard deviation. (You may have to compute an average standard deviation, if the paper gives separate standard deviations for men and for women.) This is called d. You will therefore have a d for every study, and indeed in some cases you will have several d's for each study.

Be sure that you always subtract in the same direction and preserve the sign of the difference. Thus, if you subtract the women's mean from the men's mean, then a positive number signifies that men scored higher, whereas a negative number indicates that women scored higher—which is something quite different. In many cases, you can get all the information you need from the tables published in the article. If the article does not publish standard deviations along with the means, you can sometimes estimate them from the other statistics that are reported, but for this you should get a statistical expert (at least a professor) to help you.

From there, it is a short step to get an overall result. You compute an average d across all the different studies, simply by averaging all the d-values you have obtained. (Again, be sure to preserve the positive and negative values, so that these may cancel each other out when you add them together.)

The combined (average) value of d sums up the results of all the studies you have included. You can establish whether it is significantly different from zero and also how large it is. By convention (Cohen, 1977), a d of about .3 is a small effect, .5 is medium, and .8 or more is large.

Meta-analysis can be made more complex and more theoretically interesting if you sort the studies by important factors. To do this, you code each study when you look at it and then see how d varies with your codings. For example, Oliver and Hyde (1993) conducted a meta-analysis of gender differences in sexual behavior, and they coded their findings by the year in which the study was published. In this way, they could look at changes across time. For example, they found that gender differences in many variables (such as support for the double standard of sexual morality) were larger in older articles and smaller in new ones, indicating that men and women had become more similar over time.

Narrative Reviews

Even if you do not use a meta-analysis, it is important to make an effort to be thorough and balanced and to indicate how all the information you present fits together. In contrast to meta-analysis, narrative reviewing has not elicited many books or papers to explain the procedures, although some useful tips have been furnished by Bem (1995) and Baumeister and Leary (1997).

One particular benefit of a narrative review is that it can integrate results from very different methods and procedures. When you try to evaluate all the information you have found, you should give some thought to how many different research methods pointed toward the same conclusion. To illustrate: five studies that led to the same conclusion from different methods are quite convincing, as compared to five studies that found the same result using the same method. To be sure, five studies getting the same result with the same method are somewhat good, and they show that an effect is reliable and can be obtained repeatedly (perhaps by different researchers). It is however possible that that method contains a hidden source of bias or error, and so each study that uses the same method simply repeats the same error, thereby producing a distorted result. In contrast, if five studies with different methods point to the same conclusion, one can have high confidence that the conclusion is not the result of some bias or flaw in any one method. It is also unlikely that the different methods will all lead to the same flawed conclusion because of all different biases. Methodological convergence is therefore a valuable tool for the literature reviewer, and the greater the methodological diversity, the stronger the paper and its conclusions.

For example, Baumeister, Catanese, and Vohs (2001) sought to investigate the question of whether men or women have a stronger sex drive. There is no one optimal way of measuring the strength of sex drive, and any one measure might be questioned. Thus, if men report thinking about sex more often than women, this might reflect merely a greater willingness of men to report their sexual thoughts. Accordingly, we came up with almost a dozen different indices of strength of sex drive and then sought evidence of gender differences on all of them. The convergence was decisive: On every measure (desired frequency of sex, frequency and variety of sexual fantasies, frequency of arousal, desired number of sex partners, willingness to forego sex, initiating versus refusing sex, frequency of sexual thoughts, scope of sacrifices made for sex, and so forth) men exhibited higher sex drives. The point is that only the convergence across multiple methods and measures permitted a strong conclusion. If men had scored higher on some measures and women on others, the conclusion would have been very different.

At present, meta-analysis does not have a procedure for integrating methodological diversity into its calculations, and so the five studies with different methods will not score any better than the five studies with the same method. Recognition of methodological diversity is therefore (for the present, at least) a major advantage of the narrative reviewer.

Hypotheses in Advance?

Most courses in experimental methods insist that researchers should have their hypotheses clearly spelled out before they collect their data. This requirement is made partly to prevent people from "capitalizing on chance." That is, if someone conducts a large study with many different measures and conditions, by random chance alone something is likely to turn out to be statistically significant. Researchers call such approaches "fishing expeditions," because the researcher is like someone who goes fishing and does not know what he is going to catch but will settle for almost anything. Such exploratory studies do have a role in science, but mainly as ways of generating ideas for further research. For a researcher to describe such findings as if they were predicted in advance is therefore misleading, and capitalizing on chance can lead to false conclusions getting published and thereby lowering the value of the knowledge base that all future scientists will use to guide their own work. Some researchers treat the practice of developing hypotheses after the results are known (called "HARKing"—an acronym for Hypothesizing After Results are Known; see Kerr, 1998) as an unethical violation of scientific honesty. By requiring researchers to specify their hypotheses in advance, the field protects itself from these errors.

A literature reviewer does not need to be so scrupulous about having hypotheses in advance, however. First and foremost, the danger of capitalizing on chance is greatly reduced in a literature review as compared to a single study. A single study might by chance produce an odd, misleading result here and there, but a literature review combines the results of many different studies, and it is highly unlikely that a chance result will occur over and over.

Indeed, my view is that literature reviewers should be much more flexible in their thinking than experimentalists. If you have a firm hypothesis and are committed to testing it alone, you may miss valuable and important patterns in the data. Perhaps you initial theory will not be supported, but by working with large numbers of published studies you might find other patterns that make important, valuable contributions to the field. You might realize that your initial hypothesis framed the question wrong.

If anything, strong commitment to an initial hypothesis might create bias in a literature reviewer. A reviewer who is locked into one idea or one way of looking at a phenomenon may end up imposing his or her rigid ideas onto the data and thereby produce a conclusion that is misleading.

In short, I recommend that literature reviewers try to remain open-minded when reading the literature and be willing to revise their theories substantially. There is no consensus among experts on this issue, and so it is possible that some experts would disagree with my recommendation. Still, my own experiences in writing many literature reviews has found that my initial theories and hypotheses were often quite wrong and in other cases seriously oversimplified. It would be a shame to fail to learn and change one's thinking during the process of reading a large amount of research findings.

The Value of Null Findings

Every laboratory experimenter dreads the "null finding," which is essentially the no-difference conclusion. The null hypothesis is that no difference exists between the control condition and the experimental conditions. Typically researchers are trying to support their theories by finding positive evidence that some differences exist, and so the null hypothesis is the opposite of what they want to find. Usually null findings are considered unworthy of publication, because they are inherently ambiguous: For example, sloppy work or poor measures will produce null findings, and in those cases it would be fallacious to conclude that the researcher's theory was wrong. Hence a null result is very discouraging to the experimenter, because it is a kind of failure, and it is not possible to advance one's career by publishing null results.

The literature reviewer is in a quite different situation, however, and null results can be important. For one thing, it is important for researchers (especially meta-analysts) to include null findings in their calculations. For example, suppose ten studies found no difference (and weren't published) whereas two studies did find a difference. A meta-analysis that concentrated only on the two successful studies might conclude that there is positive support for the theory, but a meta-analysis that included the ten null findings would probably draw the opposite conclusion. Yet because null findings are generally not published, there is a real danger that literature reviewers will end up only finding the two successful studies.

One solution to this problem is to include theses and dissertations. In recent years, meta-analyses have come under increasing pressure to include unpublished theses and dissertations, simply because these will give some indication of null results. That is, if a professional researcher comes up with null findings, he or she will probably never write them up (because the journals generally refuse to publish them), but dissertations get written even if the study yields null results. The use of dissertations is at best a partial solution to the problem of unpublished null results, but it is a step in the right direction.

What about if the literature review itself produces null results? A literature reviewer is not as vulnerable as an experimenter to the danger of null results. Indeed, a literature review that concludes there is no difference can be published. For example, DePaulo, Charlton, Cooper, Lindsay, and Muhlenbruck (1997) meta-analyzed the results from many studies on people's ability to detect lying and deception in others. In particular, they focused on whether people's objective accuracy was linked to their subjective confidence. In countless courtroom scenes in movies and television, there is a crucial point at which the lawyer points to the defendant and asks the witness "Are you sure that this was the person you saw?" DePaulo and her colleagues concluded that the statistical relationship between confidence and accuracy across all the studies in their sample averaged out to a paltry .04, which was not significantly different from zero. In plain terms, lawyers should not bother asking witnesses whether they are certain, because their degree of certainty bears no relationship to whether they are right or wrong.

A literature review may also succeed in showing that the totality of existing evidence is inconclusive. Perhaps many of the studies are flawed or confounded, or they point in opposite directions. Such a literature review might conclude that "we simply don't know yet." It still performs a valuable service to the field by highlighting the limitations in current knowledge. It can help advance the field by pointing out that an issue that experts have assumed to be settled is in fact unresolved, and so more (and perhaps better) research is needed.

Types of Possible Conclusions

Four possible conclusions can emerge from a literature review. This is far more than from a standard experimental study, which typically can only draw one positive conclusion or the ambiguous failure to reject the null hypothesis.

The first conclusion is that the theory or hypothesis is correct. After reviewing many different studies and combining the information from them, the reviewer draws a confident conclusion that the idea has been well supported and should be considered true, at least until and unless some strong contradictory evidence emerges from future work.

The second is that the hypothesis is not proven but is currently the best guess. The reviewer says that it would be premature to draw a strong conclusion that the truth has been found, but there is enough quantity and variety of evidence to permit a tentative conclusion. This conclusion says that the burden of proof should be shifted onto anyone who wishes to conclude otherwise, but it is quite conceivable that this will happen. For the time being, the field should proceed as if the theory is correct, even though more research is needed before one can consider the matter settled once and for all. Such conclusions are especially important in matters relevant to psychotherapy or applied psychology, because many practitioners cannot wait around for twenty-five years until somebody decides that an issue is definitely proven. Therapists have to use the best available evidence to deal with problems in the immediate present. It may be helpful to them to know the difference between a definite, proven fact and a best guess, but in most cases they may find it necessary to base their work on these conclusions. In other words, a "best guess" is much more useful and helpful for them than the "wait and see" shrug that purists might favor.

The third conclusion is that the available evidence does not permit a confident conclusion (even a best guess) either way. This may arise because there is not enough evidence available because different studies cancel each other out by coming to opposite conclusions, or because a few pervasive methodological flaws render the evidence unreliable. It is often helpful to the field to be told what it does not know—perhaps especially if people have assumed that some view is strongly supported when it is not. If your literature review draws this conclusion, it is especially important that you spell out the requirements for future researchers who wish to provide more conclusive evidence.

The fourth conclusion is that a hypothesis is false. After reviewing all the available evidence, you find that the theory has consistently failed to gain support. Possibly the evidence points to the opposite theory, or in other cases a meta-analysis may show that there is no difference. In either case, the literature review concludes by saying that a theory should be abandoned and regarded as wrong.

COMMON PROBLEMS AND ERRORS IN LITERATURE REVIEWS

Because few people receive explicit training in how to conduct a literature review, many end up having to learn it by themselves, often by trial and error. This section will summarize some of the common problems among literature reviews.

Uncertain Purpose

It is important to know what the goal of your literature review is. Many people think, "The goal is just to summarize past work on the topic!" However, a simple summary of previous findings does not generally make much of a contribution, and so that kind of review ends up being difficult to publish.

Ideally, a literature review should have a clear goal of advancing the field's theoretical understanding of some issue. It may propose a new theory that links together a diverse array of findings. Alternatively, it may evaluate a theory by testing it against the wealth of published work. In both these cases, the article will offer a new, improved understanding of the phenomena. Simply providing a list and summary of findings on some topic is not enough.

Vague Introduction, Poor Organization

The introduction to your literature review should spell out the goals of your review (see previous section). It should also explain the theory carefully and thoroughly. This may seem obvious, but many writers of literature reviews do not follow this plan. Some are tempted to offer only a short introduction that focuses on the importance and interest value of the question. Then they present all the research findings. Only after all the material is described do they begin to offer their own theoretical ideas of what the important patterns and conclusions are. Many writers may feel that this organization accurately reflects how they produced the paper. Often a person will start reading with only a basic curiosity about some phenomenon or a sense that it is important. Then the person accumulates findings, and after they are all in hand the person starts to think about what they mean.

Unfortunately, this style of organization produces a paper that is very difficult to read. Readers need to know where the paper is going. You cannot expect a reader to keep dozens of research findings straight in memory before finding out how they all fit together.

Hence it is important to put all your theorizing in the introduction, even if you actually did construct your theories after you finished reading the literature. You should not mislead the reader by falsely claiming that you had these theories in advance, but the reader needs to have the broad theoretical ideas in mind when reading through the summaries of research findings. Of course, you do not have to offer only one single theory in the Introduction. It is often useful to set up your literature review as a competition between two or more theories. Explain how each of them is reasonable and plausible, and indicate how you will look for evidence that will show which of them is correct.

Your presentation of research findings should then be organized on the basis of your theory. For example, if your theory has three steps, you would probably organize your presentation of the research by those three steps. Do not make the mistake of feeling that you have to summarize the literature in the way it has usually been understood or presented. Remember, the goal of your literature review is to achieve a new understanding of some phenomenon, so it is quite appropriate to break free from the conventional ways of thinking about the topic. Developing or evaluating the theory is the purpose of your review, and the way you organize your presentation of findings should reflect and serve that purpose.

Once you have presented all the material, you can then provide a General Discussion section that sums up what you have found. Which aspects of the theory are well supported? Which have been disproven? Which require modification? Which require further evidence? Try to imagine how someone who supported the theory would evaluate the weight of evidence, and then imagine how someone who opposed the theory would evaluate the same evidence.

Thus, the plan of the paper is to present the theory first, then the review of findings, and then a discussion of what has been learned. This organization is not all that different from how one writes up an experiment or other empirical report. That is no mere coincidence: Rather, following that organization is an effective way to communicate information with readers.

Not Enough Information

Another common mistake is to fail to provide enough information about the literature you review. Occasionally one makes the opposite mistake, such as by providing excessive detail about some of the studies one covers. But simply because of the constraints of how long a manuscript can be, the more common error is to present too little information.

The most common form of this error is to say what some study concluded without indicating how it reached that conclusion. After all, this is what many researchers do when writing the introductions to their empirical reports. But it is not sufficient for a literature review. An empirical report contributes original data. A literature review relies on its presentation of previous work to justify its conclusions. Hence it is necessary to spell out the nature of that evidence.

In general, a literature review should summarize the specific methods and findings of the studies it cites, rather than just the conclusions. In a narrative review, this is a matter of summarizing how each study was done and what it found. In a meta-analysis, one indicates precisely what kinds of procedures and measures were used. Sometimes this can be done in a large table. One way or another, however, the reader must be told what the substance of the previous investigations was.

In many cases, a sentence or two may be sufficient for summarizing each study. It is not necessary to spend multiple paragraphs on every previous article. But readers should be given sufficient information so that they can make up their own mind as to whether the evidence supports the conclusion.

Failing to Connect to Take-Home Message

When Robert Sternberg (1991) took over as editor of Psychological Bulletin, he directed authors to make sure that their manuscript had a "take-home message." In a sense, his directive conforms to my earlier comments about making sure that your paper has a purpose of developing or evaluating a theory, rather than just summarizing the current state of knowledge on some topic or other. The take-home message should be stated explicitly in your General Discussion and in your abstract. You can recognize it easily: It is what you would answer when someone asks you what the point of your paper is. If your answer to such a question is along the lines of "There's a lot of research on attitudes," or "There are plenty of sex differences," you should hear an alarm go off, because that is hardly important enough to be worth publishing.

The take-home message may not have been in your mind when you started the project. Indeed, if you remained open-minded as I recommended, you may not have known what the take-home message would be until you completed reading the literature and spent some time re-reading your notes and thinking about how they fit together. Still, the take-home message is the capsule value of your paper, and *everything in the paper should refer to it.*

The obligation to make the connections to your take-home theme may seem obvious with the Introduction and General Discussion, but it is also important in your coverage of the research findings. Do not fall into the trap of describing study after study on its own terms, such as by presenting methods and results but without stating the implications for your theory. Readers need to be told explicitly how the various findings fit into the theoretical scheme of your paper and how they contribute to the take-home message. You may do this for individual studies or for groups of studies, but it is not adequate to leave this until the end of the paper.

Be Critical!

Another common mistake is to forget to criticize the research you cover. In psychology and the other social sciences, hardly any methods are perfect. You should indicate their limitations. Again, this is something you can do study by study or in groups of studies, but it needs to be done. One format I have found useful is to organize the presentation of research findings into subsections, each of which has a single theoretical point to make, and provide a summary critique at the end of each subsection (e.g., Baumeister, 1990). This summary critique can evaluate the group of studies as a whole. Thus, if one study has a problem or shortcoming but another study has reached a similar conclusion but avoided that problem, you do not need to waste space criticizing the problem in the first study—you can point out that the conclusion is not tainted by that problem, insofar as studies have reached the same conclusion without that problem. A summary critique can also evaluate the amount and methodological diversity (ie, converging evidence) of the evidence.

Forgetting to criticize is especially common among authors who have a favorite theory and are presenting evidence to support it. They might even feel they are undermining their take-home message by criticizing the evidence that supports it. They are wrong, however. The contribution of your paper is that much stronger if you can indicate the weaknesses (as well as the strengths) of the evidence. If the critique means that you have to downgrade your conclusion from a proven fact to a best guess, so be it: All that means is that researchers should continue to study the problem rather than considering the matter settled. Remember, flaws or gaps in the published literature are not your fault—but neglecting to point out flaws or gaps in the literature is your fault. Your role is not that of a lawyer who tries to make the best case for one side of the argument. Rather, your role is to be a judge and jury, skeptically evaluating the evidence for both sides and rendering the fairest judgment possible.

Assuming you want to publish your literature review, it is helpful to consider the perspective of the editor who will decide whether to accept it. Editors do like to have novel theories and interesting ideas presented in their journals. They do not, however, want their journal to have articles that overstate the case for these ideas. Imagine that you are an editor who publishes many articles that are later proven to be wrong because of overzealous statement of unjustified conclusions: You would probably feel ashamed. When you write a literature review, make your case, but be frank about the limitations in the evidence you review.

A related error is the failure to adjust your conclusions based on your critique. I have seen this in particular when an author submitted a paper without any critique of the evidence and then was told by reviewers to add such a critique. Some authors will dutifully furnish the critique, but they then leave the same strong, optimistic conclusions they had in the first place. Before you state that the evidence for or against some theory is "strong" or "clear" or "convincing," you should evaluate the weight and diversity of that evidence as well as your critique of its flaws, shortcomings, and ambiguities. In other words, look at both the strengths and weaknesses of the literature you have reviewed, and only then decide how strong a conclusion is warranted.

Exceptions and Counterexamples

The normal, everyday thought processes of ordinary people involve selective coverage or selective critique of evidence (e.g., Kunda, 1990; Lord, Ross, & Lepper, 1979). For example, people may recognize evidence contrary to their position but apply stricter critical standards when evaluating it. Writers of literature reviews are subject to similar tendencies, which can bias their results and conclusions. Such biases are especially likely when a conclusion accords with prevailing wisdom or seems politically correct. Hence it is important to guard against these tendencies as much as possible.

One device is the deliberate search for exceptions and counterexamples. Most of your work in putting together a literature review is probably devoted to seeking positive examples that support the pattern or theory you are describing (your take-home message). The approach of looking for confirming examples is however what produces the infamous "confirmation bias," in which people selectively attend to evidence that supports their conclusion and overlook contrary evidence (e.g., Darley & Gross, 1982). To overcome this bias, you should spend some time late in the project searching for any sort of contrary evidence. That is, once you have your general conclusions in mind and have formulated your take-home message, stop and ask "Is there any evidence that anyone might interpret as contradicting that conclusion?" You may even be moved to look in some new places for relevant evidence.

Devoting a small section toward the end of your paper to a deliberate search for contrary evidence has several advantages. First, it will help you find such evidence, which might require you to temper or qualify your conclusions. Second, it will make your overall presentation more accurate. Third, it will make it more convincing to readers, because if they see you have exerted yourself to examine both sides of an issue, they will be less likely to assume that your approach was biased or selective.

Fourth, this section may even help you develop a more sophisticated, complex, and interesting (and probably more accurate!) theory. For example, in my literature review on erotic plasticity (Baumeister, 2000), I had reached the general conclusion that female sexuality is more responsive than male sexuality to a variety of social, situational, and cultural factors.

A deliberate search for possible exceptions led me to find a handful of findings that pointed in the opposite direction. When I lumped them together, I noticed that they all involved early childhood experiences. Hence I revised my general theory to say that male sexuality seems to go through a period of plasticity during childhood, when environmental influences and experiences can have a significant effect, but starting at adolescence male sexuality remains fairly constant whereas female sexuality continues to respond and develop. Thus, focusing on exceptions helped develop a better and more balanced theory.

Tell Them Where to Go

A good literature review should nearly always contain some statements about what are the priorities for future research. Normally these will occupy a subsection in the General Discussion. By this point you will have presented and criticized the available evidence and then summarized the main conclusions. You have told the reader what segments of the evidence are strong and which ones are weak or ambiguous. It is therefore not difficult to extend your discussion by saying what you think researchers should focus on during the next decade or so.

Thus, you may conclude that some issues have been resolved, and no further research is needed. This is helpful to prospective researchers so that they will not waste their time continuing to prove things that are already well established. On other matters, however, you may conclude that the evidence suffers from serious flaws, and so further work may be directed to try to remedy those problems. You might even suggest what methodological improvements or controls are needed in further work. On yet other aspects of the issue, evidence may be sparse, and so you would call for more studies of the topic.

In my experience, editors nearly always expect a literature review to include some recommendations for empirical research. After all, a literature review is re-publishing information that has already been published, and so it needs to serve some additional function beyond reporting what has already been done. Helping to guide empirical researchers as to what they should do next is one such valuable service. Indeed, it may help your paper get cited. Researchers may justify their investigation by saying that your review highlighted the need for precisely the kind of study they are doing.

When you have completed a literature review, you are in an unusual position of having a broad grasp of a great deal of information. You may have a perspective that gives you an overview of an entire field of work. No one else has that same perspective unless he or she is willing to do all the reading you have done. Hence it is valuable for you to use that perspective to say what you think should be emphasized in further research. Even though it may seem obvious to you that one question is definitively settled whereas another issue needs plenty of more and better research, it is worth saying so explicitly.

Matters of Style

Your literature review can be more effective if it follows several guidelines for style and presentation. One of these is to be careful and scrupulous about what you mean when you make a statement followed by a name and date in parentheses. In particular, it is vitally important to maintain a distinction between what someone may have said versus what someone showed or proved on the basis of strong data. In your literature review, you probably want to cover both what people may have said by way of theorizing and what researchers have shown with empirical findings. Unfortunately, the format for citing someone is the same in both cases. As a literature reviewer, the responsibility falls on you to make the difference clear.

To some extent, this problem of confusing assertion with proof can be minimized if you follow my earlier advice to describe the methods and results of studies (instead of merely their conclusions). I recommend going a step farther, however. When you wish to cite someone's assertion that was in the form of a theory, speculation, casual observation, clinical impression, or the like, say so! Thus, instead of saying "Women are nicer than men (X, 1982)" you should say something along the lines of "X (1982) speculated that women are nicer than men" or "Based on her personal experiences, X (1982) concluded that women are nicer than men." The crucial point is to prevent readers from confusing such a statement with an empirical finding such as "In a carefully controlled study with young adult college students, X (1982) showed that women were nicer than men insofar as the women were more friendly and tolerant toward a newcomer who did not know how to behave."

My suggestion to indicate precisely what a given previous author had done seemingly runs counter to Bem's (1995) injunction that names of researchers should always be in parentheses rather than serving as the grammatical subject of a sentence. Bem recommended that authors should focus on the research findings themselves rather than the researchers. Although I agree with the general attitude behind Bem's comments, I do think there are many circumstances in which it is helpful, even necessary, to take the name outside the parentheses. Indicating that someone said rather than proved something is just one important instance.

Generally, though, you should avoid letting the names play too prominent a role in your writing. One rule of thumb is never to start a paragraph with a name. When you start with a name, you have effectively neglected any transition, and the reader does not know how the new paragraph fits into your evolving argument. Graduate students who write their first literature reviews are particularly prone to starting paragraphs with names, because they tend to cover the published works one at a time and devote a paragraph to each one. That style of writing is very hard to read, however, because the reader has to figure out what the continuity across paragraphs is and where the line of evidence is supposed to lead. Use the first or last sentence of each paragraph to connect with your take-home message.

CONCLUSION

The psychology journals contain the diligent efforts, indeed in many cases the life's work, of thousands upon thousands of researchers. This is an immensely valuable stock of information, but it exists in a state of near anarchy and chaos, with articles on the same topic scattered across different journals and different years, while the same issue of one journal will contain pieces that have nothing in common.

To help the field cope with such a mass of unorganized information, literature reviews serve valuable purposes. They bring together the information that is otherwise dispersed in many places. They summarize and integrate many individual findings, permitting much stronger and more confident assertions about which ideas are correct and which are false. They can address broad, integrative questions that single empirical papers cannot. They can propose broad theories and evaluate them against a diverse assortment of work. Literature reviews seem destined to play an ever-increasing role in psychological science, as experts want to have reliable answers to broad questions and as it becomes ever more difficult to cope with the burgeoning mass of information.

Although this chapter has focused on the difficulties, dangers, and pitfalls of writing literature reviews, let me close by saying a few words about its pleasures. Writing literature reviews can be fun as well as deeply satisfying. They are certainly not for everyone, but for some they are ideal. It is, after all, nice to be able to work with other people's published data rather than always having to struggle with your own! More important, literature reviews permit you to tackle broad questions that have a resonance and intellectual stimulation that goes beyond what can be addressed in a single empirical paper.

From my own perspective, a special appeal of literature reviews is that they allow you to study different questions, and so they increase the breadth and diversity of your thinking. To collect data on a new problem typically requires a new set of skills, and so it is difficult to collect data on very many new topics. (That is why most laboratory-oriented researchers devote their entire careers to a small set of issues and questions.) But to write a literature review on a new topic involves the same set of skills, namely reading and thinking and discerning patterns, or possibly meta-analysis. Once you have mastered how to write a literature review, you can move from one interesting question to another fairly easily, and you are on your way to a very interesting career and life.

As I have said, writing literature reviews is not for everyone. It is activity best suited to people who are good at spotting patterns in large masses of information, who like to write and think (perhaps more than they like to collect and analyze data), who enjoy thinking about broad questions, and who have many different interests.

REFERENCES

Archer, J. (2000). Sex differences in aggression between heterosexual partners: A meta-analytic review. *Psychological Bulletin, 126*, 651–680.

Baumeister, R. F. (1990). Suicide as escape from self. *Psychological Review, 97*, 90–113.

Baumeister, R. F. (2000). Gender differences in erotic plasticity: The female sex drive as socially flexible and responsive. *Psychological Bulletin, 126*, 347–374.

Baumeister, R. F., Catanese, K. R., & Vohs, K. D. (2001). Is there a gender difference in strength of sex drive? Theoretical views, conceptual distinctions, and a review of relevant evidence. *Personality and Social Psychology Review*. (in press, to appear shortly.)

Baumeister, R. F., & Leary, M. R. (1995). The need to belong: Desire for interpersonal attachments as a fundamental human motivation. *Psychological Bulletin, 117*, 497–529.

Baumeister, R. F., & Leary, M. R. (1997). Writing narrative literature reviews. *Review of General Psychology, 1*, 311–320.

Bem, D. J. (1995). Writing a review article for Psychological Bulletin. *Psychological Bulletin, 118*, 172–177.

Cohen, J. (1977). Statistical power analysis for the behavioral sciences. New York: Academic Press.

Cooper, H. (1990). Meta-analysis and the integrative research review. In C. Hendrick, & M. Clark (Eds.), *Research methods in personality and social psychology* (p. 142–163). Thousand Oaks, CA: Sage.

Cooper, H., & Hedges, L.V. (1994). *The handbook of research synthesis*. New York: Russell Sage Foundation.

Darley, J. M., & Gross, P. (1983). A hypothesis-confirming bias in labeling effects. *Journal of Personality and Social Psychology, 44*, 20–33.

DePaulo, B. M., Charlton, K., Cooper, H., Lindsay, J. J., & Muhlenbruck, L. (1997). The accuracy-confidence correlation in the detection of deception. *Personality and Social Psychology Review, 1*, 346–357.

Hedges, L. V., & Olkin, I. (1985). *Statistical methods for meta-analysis*. Orlando, FL: Academic Press.

Kerr, N. L. (1998). HARKing: Hypothesizing after the results are known. *Personality and Social Psychology Review, 2*, 196–217.

Kunda, Z. (1990). The case for motivated reasoning. *Psychological Bulletin, 108*, 480–498.

Lord, C. G., Ross, L., & Lepper, M. R. (1979). Biased assimilation and attitude polarization: The effects of prior theories on subsequently considered evidence. *Journal of Personality and Social Psychology, 37*, 2098–2109.

Oliver, M. B., & Hyde, J. S. (1993). Gender differences in sexuality: A meta-analysis. *Psychological Bulletin, 114*, 29–51.

Rosenthal, R. (1983) Assessing the statistical and social importance of the effects of psychotherapy. *Journal of Consulting and Clinical Psychology, 51*, 4–13.

Rosenthal, R. (1991). *Meta-analytic procedures for social research.* Thousand Oaks, CA: Sage.

Sternberg, R. J. (1991). Editorial. *Psychological Bulletin, 109*, 3–4.

Wolf, F. M. (1986). Meta-analysis: Quantitative methods for research synthesis. Beverly Hills, CA: Sage.

CHAPTER 6

Presenting Your Research

LINDSEY L. COHEN AND LAURIE A. GRECO

REASONS FOR PRESENTING RESEARCH

When you consider submitting your research for conference presentation, is it is wise to weigh the costs and benefits of the endeavor. The costs might include the time commitment of writing and constructing the presentation, the potential for rejection from the reviewers, and the anxiety inherent in formal presentations. The benefits include disseminating information to appreciative audiences, such as professors, students, clinicians, teachers, and other professionals interested in new ideas to assist them in their own work. As a personal gain, feedback can be invaluable to you in the development of your research program. Presenting research at conferences also allows for the opportunity to meet potential future advisors, employers, collaborators or colleagues. Conferences are ideal settings for networking and, in fact, many conferences have forums organized for this exact purpose (e.g., job openings listed on a bulletin board). Although the benefits of presenting at conferences appear to outweigh the costs, you should consider the specific pros and cons for you, your research, and your particular situation before embarking on this experience.

PRESENTATION VENUES

There are many different outlets for presenting research findings ranging from departmental presentations to international conferences. The decision of submitting a proposal to one conference over another should be guided by both practical and professional reasons. In selecting a conference, you might answer the following questions: Can I afford to travel to this location? Will my presentation be ready in time for the conference? Am I interested in visiting the city that is hosting the conference? Do the dates of the conference interfere with personal or professional obligations? Will my friends and colleagues also be attending this conference? Are the philosophies of the association consistent with my perspectives and training needs? Is this the audience to whom I wish to disseminate my findings? Are there other professionals that I would like to meet attending this conference? Are the other presentations of interest to

LINDSEY L. COHEN • Department of Psychology, West Virginia University, Morgantown, WV, 26506-6040
LAURIE A. GRECO • Cincinnati Children's Hospital Medical Center, Division of Psychology, Cincinnati, Ohio 45229-3039

me? Is continuing education credit offered? By answering these questions you should be able to pinpoint the conference that is best suited for you and your research.

TYPES OF PRESENTATIONS

After selecting a conference, you must decide on the *type* of presentation. In general, presentation categories are similar across venues and include poster and oral presentations (e.g., papers, symposia, panel discussions) and workshops. In general, poster presentations are optimal for disseminating preliminary or pilot findings, whereas well-established findings, cutting-edge research, and conceptual/theoretical issues often are reserved for oral presentations and workshops. If you are unsure about whether your research is best suited for a poster or oral presentation or workshop, consult with more experienced colleagues. Keynote and invited addresses are other types of conference proceedings typically delivered by esteemed professionals or experts in the field.

The most common types of conference presentations, poster presentations, symposia, panel discussions, and workshops, deserve further discussion. Typically, these scientific presentations follow a consistent format, which is similar to the layout of a research manuscript. For example, first you might introduce your topic and highlight related prior work, and outline the purpose and hypotheses of the study. Second, you could review your methodology, and, lastly, present and discuss salient results (see Drotar, 2000).

Poster Presentations

Poster presentations are the most common medium through which researchers disseminate findings. In this format, researchers summarize their primary aims, results, and conclusions in an easily digestible manner on a poster board. Poster sessions vary in duration, often ranging from between 1–2 hours. Authors typically are present with their posters for the duration of the session to discuss their work with interested colleagues. Poster presentations are relatively less formal and more personal than other presentation formats with the discussion of projects often assuming a conversational quality. Typically, many posters within a particular theme (e.g., health psychology) are displayed in a large room so that audiences might walk around the room and talk one-to-one with the authors. In addition, conference reviewers accept many more posters for presentations than symposia, panel discussion, and workshops, and thus, the acceptance criteria are more lenient. Related, researchers might choose posters to present findings from small projects or findings of relatively less importance (e.g., preliminary or pilot results). Symposia, panel discussions, and workshops allow for the formal presentation of significant findings or of multiple studies.

Research Symposia

Symposia involve the aggregation of several individuals who present on a common topic. Depending on time constraints, 4–6 papers typically are featured, each lasting roughly 20 minutes, and often representing different viewpoints or facets of a broader topic. For example, a symposium on the etiology of anxiety disorders might be comprised of four separate papers representing the role of familial influences, biological risk factors, peer relationships, and emotional conditioning on the development of maladaptive anxiety. As a presenter, you might discuss one project or the findings from a few studies. Like a master of ceremonies, the symposia Chair typically organizes the entire symposia by selecting presenters, guiding the topics and style of presentation, and introducing the topic and presenters at the beginning of the symposium. In addition to these duties, the Chair often will present a body of work or a few studies at the beginning of the symposium. In addition to the Chair and presenters, a Discussant is part of a symposium. The Discussant concludes the symposium by summarizing key findings from each paper, integrating the studies, and making more broad-based conclusions and directions for future research. Although a Discussant is privy to the presenters' papers prior to the symposium in order to prepare the summary comments, he or she will often take notes during the presenters' talks to augment any prepared commentary. The formal presentation is often followed by a period for audience inquiry and discussion. Although presenters are often researchers of varying levels of experience, Chairs and Discussants are usually senior investigators.

Panel Discussions

Panel discussions are similar to research symposia in that several professionals come together to discuss a common topic. Panel discussions, however, generally tend to be less formal and structured and more interactive and animated than symposia. For example, discussants can address each other and interject comments throughout the discussion. Similar to symposia, these presentations involve the discussion of one or more important topics in the field by informed discussants. As with symposia presentations, the Chair typically organizes these semi-formal discussions by contacting potential speakers and communicating the discussion topic and their respective roles.

Workshops

Conference workshops typically are longer (e.g., lasting at least three hours) and provide more in-depth, specialized training than symposia and panel discussions. It is not uncommon for workshop presenters to adopt a format similar to a structured seminar, in which mini-curricula are followed. Due to the length and specialized training involved, most workshop presenters enhance their presentations by incorporating interactive (e.g., role-plays) and multi-media (e.g., video clips) components. Workshops often are organized such that the information is geared for beginner, intermediate, or advanced professionals.

THE APPLICATION PROCESS

After selecting a venue and deciding on a presentation type, the next step is to submit an application to the conference you wish to attend. The application process typically involves submitting a brief abstract (e.g., 200–300 words) describing the primary aims, methods, results, and conclusions of your study. For symposia and other oral presentations, the selection committee might request an outline of your talk, curriculum vitae from all presenters, and a time schedule or presentation agenda. Some conferences also request information regarding the educational objectives and goals of your presentation. One essential rule is to closely adhere to the directions for submissions to the conference. For example, if there is a word limit for a poster abstract submission, make sure that you do not exceed the number of words even by one. Whereas some reviewers might not notice or mind, others might view it is as unprofessional and possibly disrespectful.

Although the application process itself is straightforward, there are differences in opinion regarding whether and when it is advisable to submit your research. A commonly asked question is whether a poster or paper can be presented twice. Many would agree that it is acceptable to present the same data twice if the conferences draw different audiences (e.g., regional versus national conferences). Another issue to consider is when, or at what stage, a project should be submitted for presentation. Submitting research prior to analyzing your data can be risky. It would be unfortunate, for example, to submit prematurely, such as during the data collection phase, only to find that your results are not significant or contrary to study hypotheses. Although some might be willing to take this risk, remember that it is worse to present low quality work than not to present at all.

PREPARING AND CONDUCTING PRESENTATIONS

Choosing an Appropriate Outfit

Dress codes for conference proceedings typically are not formally instated; however, data suggest that perceptions of graduate student professionalism and competence are influenced by dress (e.g., Gorham, Cohen, & Morris, 1999). Although the appropriateness of certain attire is likely to vary, a good rule of thumb is to err on the side of professionalism. You also might consider the dress of your audience, and dress in an equivalent or more formal fashion. Females, for example, might consider a dress, skirt, or pants suit. For males, either a suit or slacks with a dress shirt and tie is recommended. Although there will be people at conferences wearing other styles of dress, students and professionals still early in their careers are best advised to dress professionally. In addition to selecting your outfit, there are several preparatory steps you can take to help ensure a successful presentation.

Preparing for Poster Presentations

THE BASICS. The first step in preparing a poster is to be cognizant of the specific requirements put forth by the selected venue. For example, very specific guidelines often are provided, detailing the amount of board space available for each presenter (typically a 4-foot by 8-foot standing board is available). To ensure the poster will fit within the allotted space, it may be helpful to physically lay it out prior to the conference. This also may help to reduce future distress, given that back-to-back poster sessions are the norm; knowing how to arrange the poster in advance obviates the need to do so hurriedly in the few minutes between sessions.

TIPS FOR POSTER CONSTRUCTION. The overriding goal for poster presentations is to summarize your study using an easily digestible, reader-friendly format. As you will discover from viewing other posters, there are many different styles to do this. If you have the resources, professional printers can create large glossy posters that are well received. However, cutting large construction paper to use as a mat for laser printed posters pages can also appear quite professional. Regardless of the framing, it is advisable to use consistent formatting (e.g., same style and font size throughout the poster) and large font sizes (e.g., at least 20-point font) that can be read from a distance of approximately six feet. Another suggestion for enhancing readability and visual appeal is to use bullets, figures, and tables to illustrate important findings. Generally speaking, brief phrases (as opposed to wordy paragraphs) should be used to summarize pertinent points. In short, it is important to keep your presentation succinct and avoid overcrowding on pages. Although there are a variety of fonts available and poster boards come in all colors imaginable, it is best to keep the poster professional. In other words, Courier, Arial, or Times New Roman are the probably the best fonts to use because they are easy to read and they will not distract or detract from the central message of the poster (i.e., your research). In addition, dark font (e.g., blue, black) on a light background (e.g., yellow, white) is easier to read in brightly lit room, which is the norm for poster sessions.

WHAT TO BRING. When preparing for a poster presentation, consider which materials might be either necessary or potentially useful to bring. For instance, it is wise to bring tacks with which to mount the poster, as well as other types of adhesives (e.g., glue and double-sided tape). It also is advisable to create handouts summarizing the primary aims and findings and to distribute these to interested colleagues. The number of copies one provides often depends on the size of the conference and the number of individuals attending a particular poster session. We have found that for larger conferences, 50 handouts are a good minimum. In general, handouts are in high demand and supplies are quickly depleted. In which case, you should be equipped with a notepad to obtain the names and addresses of individuals interested in receiving the handout via mail or e-mail.

CRITICALLY EVALUATE OTHER POSTERS. We also recommend critically evaluating other posters at conferences. You will notice great variability in poster style and formatting, with some researchers using glossy posters with colored photographs and others using plain white paper and black text. Make mental notes regarding the effective and ineffective presentation of information. What attracted you to certain posters? Which colors stood out and were the most readable? Such informal evaluations likely will be invaluable when making decisions on aspects such as poster formatting, colors, font, and style.

Conducting Poster Presentations

In general, presenting a poster is straightforward—tack the poster to the board at the beginning of the session, stand next to the poster and discuss the details of the project with interested viewers, and remove the poster at the end of the session. However, we have found that a surprisingly high number of presenters do not adequately fulfill these tasks. Arriving to the poster session at least ten minutes early will allow you to find your allocated space, unpack your poster, and decide where to mount it on the board. When posters consist of multiple frames, it might be easiest to lie out the boards on the floor prior to beginning to tack it up on the board.

During the poster session, remember this fundamental rule—be present. It is permissible to browse other posters in the same session; however, always arrange for a co-author or another colleague knowledgeable about the study to man the poster. Another guideline is to be available

TABLE 1. Poster Presentations

• Constructing Your Poster	• Follow conference guidelines • Summarize study using a professional and reader-friendly format (e.g., short phrases, large font size, plain font) • Use consistent formatting throughout poster (e.g., same style and font type) • Use bullets, graphs, tables, and other visual aides • Keep succinct and avoid overcrowding on pages
• Deciding What to Bring	• Tacks to mount poster • Adhesives (e.g., glue or double-sided tape) • Handouts summarizing primary aims and findings • Notepad and pen for addresses
• Evaluating other Presentations	• Observe variability in poster formats • Note effective and ineffective presentation styles • Incorporate effective aspects into your next presentation
• Presenting Your Poster	• Arrive at least five minutes early to set up • Be present or arrange for co-author(s) to man the poster • Be available to answer questions • Avoid engaging in interfering activities (e.g., reading, talking to friends)

to answer questions and discuss the project with interested parties. In other words, refrain from reading, chatting with friends, or engaging in other activities that interfere with being available to discuss the study. In terms of answering difficult questions, see suggestions in Table 4. At the conclusion of the poster session, it is important to quickly remove your poster so subsequent presenters have ample time to set up their posters. Suggestions for preparing and presenting posters are summarized in Table 1.

Preparing for Oral Presentations

THE BASICS. Similar to poster sessions, it is important to be familiar with and adhere to program requirements when preparing for oral presentations. For symposia, this might include sending an outline of your talk to the Chair and Discussant several weeks in advance and staying within a specified time limit when giving your talk. Although the Chair often will ensure that the talks adhere to the theme and do not excessively overlap, the presenter also can do this via active communication with the Chair, Discussant, and other presenters.

WHAT TO BRING. As with poster presentations, it is useful to anticipate and remember to bring necessary and potentially useful materials. For instance, individuals using Power Point should bring their slides and back-up overheads in case of equipment failure. Equipment, such as microphones, VCRs, and overhead machines, often are available upon request; it is the presenter's responsibility, however, to reserve equipment in advance.

CRITICALLY EVALUATE OTHER PRESENTERS. By carefully observing other presenters, you might learn valuable skills of how to enhance your presentations. Examine the format of the presentation, the level of detail provided, and the types and quality of audiovisual stimuli. Also try to note the vocal quality (e.g., intonation, pitch, pace, use of filler terms such as 'um'), facial characteristics (e.g., smiling, eye contact with audience members), body movements (e.g., pacing, hand gestures), and other subtle aspects that can help or hinder presentations.

PRACTICE, PRACTICE, PRACTICE. In terms of presentation *delivery*, repeated practice is key to effective preparation (see Williams, 1995). For many people, students and seasoned professionals alike, public speaking can elicit significant levels of distress. Given extensive data supporting the beneficial effects of exposure to feared stimuli (see Wolpe, 1977), repeated rehearsal is bound to produce positive outcomes, including increased comfort, increased familiarity with content, and decreased levels of anxiety. Additionally, practicing will help presenters hone their presentation skills and develop a more effective presentational style. We recommend practicing in front of an "audience" and soliciting feedback regarding both content and presentational style. Solicit feedback on every aspect of your presentation from the way you stand to the content of your talk. It might be helpful to rehearse in front of informed individuals (e.g., mentors, graduate students, research groups) who ask relevant and challenging questions and subsequently provide constructive feedback. Based on this feedback, determine which suggestions should be incorporated and modify your presentation accordingly. As a general rule, practice and hone your presentation to the point that you are prepared to present without any crutches (e.g., notes, overheads, slides).

BE FAMILIAR AND ANTICIPATE. As much as possible, try to familiarize yourself with the audience both before and during the actual presentation. By having background information, you can better tailor your talk to meet the professional levels and needs of those in attendance. It may be particularly helpful to have some knowledge regarding the educational background and general attitudes and interests of the audience (e.g., is the audience comprised of laymen and/or professionals in the field? What are the listeners' general attitudes toward the topic and towards you as the speaker? Is the audience more interested with practical applications or with design and scientific rigor?). By conducting an informal "audience analysis," you will be more equipped to adapt your talk to meet the particular needs and interests of the audience.

Similarly, it might be helpful to have some knowledge about key logistical issues, such as room size and availability of equipment. For example, will the presentation take place in a large, auditorium-like room or in a more intimate setting with the chairs arranged in a semicircle? If the former, will a microphone be available? Is there a podium at the front of the room that might influence where you will stand? Given the dimensions of the room, where should the slide projector be positioned? Although it may be impossible to answers all such questions, it is a good idea to have a general sense of where the presentation will take place and who will be attending. Suggestions for preparing and conducting oral presentations are summarized in Table 2.

Conducting Oral Presentations

USING AUDIO-VISUAL ENHANCEMENTS. One strategy for enhancing oral presentations is to use audio/visual stimuli, such as slides, overheads, video clips, or flip charts (e.g., Hoff, 1988; Wilder, 1994; See Table 3). When using visual enhancements, keep it simple, and clearly highlight important points using readable and consistent typeface. Information should be easily assimilated and reader-friendly, which generally means limiting text to a few phrases rather than complete sentences or paragraphs and using sufficiently large font sizes (i.e., 36–48 point font for titles and 24–36 point font for text). In addition, it is a good idea to keep titles to one line and bullet to no more than 2 lines of information. Additionally, color schemes should be relatively subdued and "professional" in appearance. For overheads, a light background and dark text are recommended, whereas the reverse is true for slide presentations (i.e., dark

Table 2. Oral Presentations

• Preparing for Your Oral Presentation	• Adhere to program requirements (e.g., stay within time limit) • Check on equipment availability • Reserve necessary equipment (e.g., VCRs, laptop for Power Point presentation, overhead machine) • Bring necessary materials (e.g., Power Point slides, overheads, video clips) • Be prepared to present without any materials in case of equipment failure
• Familiarizing Yourself with the Environment	• Conduct informal "audience analysis"—Familiarize yourself with audience before and during presentation • Tailor your talk to meet the professional levels and needs of the audience • Anticipate room size (e.g., will talk be held in a large auditorium or in a more intimate setting?)
• Giving Your Talk	• Dress professionally • Maintain good posture; avoid standing in one place • Avoid distracting mannerisms (e.g., pacing and filler words such as "um") • Avoid standing in one place or behind a podium • Maintain eye contact with your audience • Be vocally energetic and enthusiastic
• Enhancing Your Presentation	• Practice, practice, practice! • Solicit feedback from colleagues and make appropriate modifications • Observe other presenters; imitate effective presentational styles and incorporate effective modes of delivery • Use enhancements and audio/visual aides such as video clips, Power Point slides, cartoons or comics • Use humor and illustrative examples (e.g., metaphors, real-life stories, cartoons, comic strips, jokes) • Avoid information overload; Instead, clearly deliver 2–4 "take-home messages"

background and light text). See Figure 1 for an example of a poor and good slide for an oral presentation.

Using audio-visual aids, such as video clips, also can contribute substantially to the overall quality and liveliness of a presentation. When incorporating video clips, pre-set volume levels and cue up videotapes in advance. We also recommend announcing the length of the video, dimming lights before playing the tape, and giving a concluding statement following the video.

Multimedia equipment and audio-visual aids have the potential to liven up even the most uninspiring presentations; however, caution against becoming overly dependent on *any* medium. Rather, be fully prepared to deliver a high-quality presentation without the use of enhancements. It also might be wise to prepare a solid "back-up plan" in case your original mode of presentation must be abandoned due to equipment failure or some other unforeseen circumstance. Back-up overheads, for example, might rescue a presenter who learns of a broken slide projector five minutes before presenting.

When using slides and overheads, it is important to avoid "going overboard" with information. Many of us will present research with which we are intimately familiar and invested. With projects that are particularly near and dear (e.g., theses and dissertations), it may be tempting to tell the audience as much as possible. It is not necessary, for example to describe the intricacies of the data collection procedure and present *every* pre-planned and post hoc analysis, along with a multitude of significant and non-significant *F*-values and coefficients. Such information overload might bore audience members who are unlikely to care about or remember so many fine-grained details. Instead of committing this common presentation blunder, present

TABLE 3. Audio-Visual Enhancements

• Examples of Audio-Visual Aides	• Slides • Overheads • Video clips • Flip charts • Cartoons and comic strips
• Tips for Using Overheads and Slides	• Test equipment in advance • Keep it simple; use to clarify and enhance • Avoid going overboard (too much might detract from presentation) • Use reader-friendly format (e.g., short phrases, avoid overcrowding) • Use bullets rather than sentences • Remember *One* × *Six* × *Six*: Only **ONE** idea per visual; Less than **SIX** bullets per visual; Less than **SIX** words per bullet • Highlight important points using readable, consistent typeface • Use professional color schemes (e.g., light background, dark text for overheads and dark background, light text for slides) • Speak to audience, not to visual aides • Stand to the side of your screen to avoid blocking audience's view • Pause as you change slides/transparencies; practice for smooth transitions • Be prepared to present without your overheads/slides
• Tips for Using Videos	• Test equipment in advance • Pre-set volume levels and cue tape in advance • Introduce video clip and announce its length • Dim the lights before playing • Give a concluding statement following the video • Use video clips to illustrate and enhance presentations

key findings in a bulleted, easy-to-read format rather than sentences. To avoid overcrowding of slides and overheads, you might remember the *One* × *Six* × *Six* rule of thumb: Only *ONE* idea per visual, less than *SIX* bullets per visual, and less than *SIX* words per bullet (see Figure 1). Also, as a general guideline, the goal of your presentation should be to clearly disseminate a few (e.g., 2–4) "take-home messages" that the audience truly *will* take home!

In short, remember and hold fast to this basic dictum: Audio/visual aides should be used to *clarify* and *enhance* (Cohen, 1990; Wilder, 1994). Aides that detract, confuse, or bore one's audience should not be used (soliciting feedback from colleagues and peers will assist in this selection process). Overly colorful and ornate visuals, for example, might detract and distract from the content of the presentation. Likewise, visual aids containing superfluous text might encourage audience members to read your slides rather than attend to your presentation. Keeping visuals simple also might prevent another presentation faux pas: reading verbatim from slides.

USING HUMOR AND EXAMPLES. The effective use of humor might help "break the ice," putting you and your audience at ease. There are many ways in which humor can be incorporated into presentations, such as through the use of stories, rich examples, jokes, and cartoons or comic strips. As with other aides, humor should be used in moderation and primarily to enhance a presentation. When using humor, it is important to be natural and brief and to use non-offensive humor related to the subject matter.

Another strategy for spicing up presentations is through the use of stories and examples to illustrate relevant and important points. This can be accomplished in many ways, such as

Example Slides

Distraction for Pediatric Distress

- Background
  - Children exhibit high medical procedure distress
  - Coaches and distraction are helpful
  - Dissemination has been poor
- Purpose
  - Develop a practical intervention to decrease children's medical procedure distress

Good slide

NURSE COACHING AND MOVIES FOR PRESCHOOLERS IMMUNIZATIONS

Preschooler exhibit high medical escape/avoidant behaviors during painful medical procedures. Although research has shown that coaches can help children cope with procedural distress, dissemination of these findings into actual practice is quite poor.

Bad slide

- In dimly lit rooms, it is better to use slides with a dark background and light text.
- Keep titles to one line and avoid using all capital letters.
- Bullets are preferable to sentences.
- Use underlining, italics, or bold font to help organize the information.
- Use a consistent font style throughout the presentation.
- Attempt to use parallel construction of text.
- Present related information together and avoid including other points.
- Keep the information succinct.
- Avoid acronyms, unless they were clearly defined on a prior slide.
- Including relevant clip art can enhance a slide, however, avoid distracting from your talk by having too many images in the presentation or more than one image per slide.

FIGURE 1. Examples of good and bad oral presentation slides

by providing practical and real-life examples or by painting a mental picture for the audience using colorful language (e.g., metaphors, analogies). Metaphorical language, for instance, might facilitate learning (Skinner, 1953) and help audience members to remember pertinent information. Similarly, amusing stories and anecdotes can be used to engage the audience and decrease the "impersonal feel" of more formal presentations. Regardless of whether or how humor is used, remember to do what "works" and feels right. Trying *too hard* to be amusing likely will come across as contrived and stilted, thus producing the opposite of the intended effect.

ATTENDING TO OTHER SPEAKERS. When presenting research in a group forum (e.g., symposia), it may be beneficial to attend to other speakers, particularly those presenting before you. Being familiar with the content of preceding talks will help to reduce the amount of overlap and repetition between presentations (although, some overlap and repetition might be desirable). You might, for example, describe the similarities and differences across research projects and explain how the current topic and findings relate to earlier presentations. The audience probably will appreciate such integration efforts and have a better understanding of the general topic area.

ANSWERING QUESTIONS. Question and answer sessions are commonplace at conferences and provide excellent opportunities for clarifying ambiguous points and interacting with the

TABLE 4. Handling Difficult Questions

Type of question	Suggestions
• Questions without readily available answers	• Admit your unfamiliarity with the question • Ask the questioner if he/she has thoughts as to answer • Hazard a guess, but back it up with literature and acknowledge that it is a guess • Pose an answer to a related question • Simply state that the questioner raised an important point and move on to other questions
• Irrelevant questions (e.g., "Where were you born?")	• Avoid digressing from the topic • Offer to meet with the questioner following the presentation
• "Dumb" questions (e.g., "What does 'hypothesis' mean?")	• Offer a brief explanation and move on • Do not insult the questioner
• Politically sensitive questions (e.g., being asked to comment on opposing theoretical viewpoint)	• Stick to empirical data and avoid personal attacks
• Multiple questions asked simultaneously	• Choose either the most pertinent question or the question you would like to answer first (e.g., "I'll start with your last question.") • Ask the questioner to repeat the questions
• Offensively worded questions (e.g.,	• Avoid becoming defensive • Avoid repeating offensive language
• Vague questions	• Ask for clarification from the questioner • Re-state the question in more specific terms

audience. When addressing inquiries, it is crucial to maintain a professional, non-defensive demeanor. Treat every question as legitimate and well intentioned, even if it comes across as an objection or insult. As a general rule, in large auditoriums it is good to repeat the question so that everyone in the room hears it. If a question is unclear or extremely complicated, it may be wise to pause and organize your thoughts before answering. If necessary, request clarification or ask the questioner to repeat or rephrase the question. It also may be helpful to anticipate and prepare for high-probability questions. Wilder (1994), for example, recommends anticipating questions likely to be asked and preparing responses in advance.

There are several types of difficult questions that can be anticipated, and it is important to know how to handle these situations (Table 4). Also, we recommend preparing for a non-responsive audience. If audience members do not initiate questions, some tactics for preventing long, uncomfortable silences are to pose commonly asked questions, reference earlier comments, or take an informal survey (e.g., "Please raise your hand if you work clinically with this population."). Even if many questions are generated and lead to stimulating discussions, it is important to adhere to predetermined time limits. End on time and with a strong concluding statement.

Above all, avoid becoming defensive and critical, particularly when answering challenging questions. Irrespective of question quality or questioner intent, avoid making patronizing remarks or answering in a way that makes the questioner feel foolish or incompetent. Try to avoid falling into an exclusive dialogue with one person, which might cause other members of the audience to feel excluded or bored. If possible, offer to meet with questioner and address his or her questions and concerns at the end of the talk. Another suggestion is to avoid engaging in mini-lectures by showcasing accumulated knowledge and expertise in a particular area.

Instead, only provide information that is directly relevant to the specific question posed by the audience (Wilder, 1994).

CONCLUSION

There are great benefits to presenting research, both to the presenter and the audience. Before presenting, however, you should consider carefully a number of preliminary issues. For instance, you must decide whether your study is worthy of presentation, where to present it, and what type of presentation to conduct. Once these decisions are made, prepare by practicing your presentation, examining and learning from other presentations, and consulting with colleagues. Sufficient preparation should enhance the quality of your presentation and help decrease performance anxiety. We are confident that you will find that a well-executed presentation will prove to be a rewarding and valuable experience for you and your audience.

REFERENCES

Cohen, J. (1990). Things I have learned (so far). *American Psychologist, 45*, 1304–1312.

Drotar, D. (2000). Presenting scientific data. In D. Drotar (Ed.), *Handbook of research in pediatric and clinical child psychology*, (pp. 329–345). New York: Plenum.

Gorham, J., Cohen, S. H., & Morris, T. L. (1999). Fashion in the classroom III: Effects of instructor attire and immediacy in natural classroom interactions. *Communication Quarterly, 47*, 281–299.

Hoff, R. (1988). *I can see you naked: A fearless guide to making great presentations*. New York: Universal Press.

Skinner, B. F. (1953). Science and human behavior, (pp. 242–256). New York: Macmillan Company.

Wilder, C. (1994). *The presentations kit: Ten steps for selling your ideas*. New York: Wiley & Sons.

Williams, J. B. W. (1995). How to deliver a sensational scientific talk. In W. Pequegnat, & E. Stover (Eds.), *How to write a successful research grant application: A guide for social and behavioral scientists*, (pp. 171–176). New York: Plenum.

Wolpe, J. (1977). The acquisition, augmentation and extinction of neurotic habits. *Behaviour Research and Therapy, 15*, 303–304.

CHAPTER 7

Publishing Your Research

ALAN E. KAZDIN

Publication of research is an essential part of science. Indeed, one often hears of the accumulation of knowledge in science. This accumulation depends not only on the completion of research but also on preparation of reports that disseminate the results. Publication can serve other goals as well. Preparing a manuscript for publication helps the investigator to consider the current study in a broader context and the focus of the next studies. There are of course many professional and career goals served by publishing one's research. Publication of one's research signals a level of competence and mastery that includes development of an idea, designing, executing and completing the study, analyzing the results, preparing a written report, submitting it for publication, and traversing the peer-review process. Knowledge, talent, and persistence are required to complete the sequence and these characteristics are recognized to be evident among those who publish. This chapter focuses on publishing one's research. The topics include preparing a manuscript, selecting a publication outlet, submitting the manuscript for review, and revising the manuscript as needed for publication.

There are many outlets to communicate the results of one's research. Prominent among these are presentations at professional meetings, chapters in edited books, full-length books, and professional journals. Journal publication, the focus of this chapter, holds special status because it is the primary outlet for original research. In terms of one's career, journal publication also plays a special role primarily because articles accepted for publication usually have undergone peer review. Acceptance and publication attest to the views of one's peers that there is merit in what was completed. For any given article, only a few peers (1 editor, 2–3 reviewers) may actually see the manuscript. Multiple publications add to this and after a few publications one can assume there is a building consensus about one's work, i.e., others view the contributions as important and worthy of publication.

ALAN E. KAZDIN • Child Study Center, Yale University School of Medicine, New Haven, CT 06520

PREPARING A MANUSCRIPT FOR PUBLICATION

Writing the Article

A central goal of scientific writing is to convey what was actually done so that the methods and procedures can be replicated. Concrete, specific, operational, objective, and precise are some of the characteristics that describe the writing style. The effort to describe research in concrete and specific ways is critically important. However, the task of the author goes well beyond description.

Preparation of the report for publication involves three interrelated tasks that I refer to as description, explanation, and contextualization. Failure to appreciate or to accomplish these tasks serves as a main source of frustration for authors, as their papers traverse the process of manuscript review toward journal publication. *Description* is the most straightforward task and includes providing details of the study. Even though this is an obvious requirement of the report, basic details often are omitted in published articles (e.g., sex, socioeconomic status, and race of the participants; means and standard deviations) (Case & Smith, 2000; Weiss & Weisz, 1990). *Explanation* is slightly more complex insofar as this refers to presenting the rationale of several facets of the study. The justification, decision-making process, and the connections between the decisions and the goals of the study move well beyond description. There are numerous decision points pertaining to such matters as selection of measures and control and comparison groups. The author is obliged to explain why the specific options elected are well suited to the hypotheses or the goals of the study.

Finally, *contextualization* moves one step further away from description and addresses how the study fits in the context of other studies and in the knowledge base more generally. This latter facet of the article preparation reflects such lofty notions as scholarship and perspective, because the author places the descriptive and explanatory material into a broader context. Essentially, the author is making the case for the study based on the knowledge base. Relatively vacuous claims (e.g., this is the first study of this or the first study to include this or that control condition or measure) are rarely a strong basis for the study. Without context, any "first" is not very important by itself. Indeed, it is easy to be first for a topic that is not very important and has been purposely neglected.

Description, explanation, and contextualization are essential. Of course, good writing helps, especially if the author can tantalize or entice the reader to convey there is an important element missing of a critical story. That story is about the problem of interest and prior research leaves open a critical element that this new study will redress. The extent to which description, explanation, and contextualization are accomplished increases the likelihood that the report will be viewed as a publishable article and facilitates integration of the report into the knowledge base. Guidelines are provided later in the chapter that emphasize these tasks in the preparation and evaluation of research reports. The guidelines focus on the logic of the study, the interrelations of the different sections, the rationale for specific procedures and analyses, the strengths and limitations, and where the study fits in the knowledge base. Consider main sections of the manuscript that are prepared for journal publication and how these components can be addressed.[1]

[1] Preparing a manuscript for publication entails several format requirements, such as print style and size, citations of sources, use of abbreviations, structure of tables and figures, and order in which sections of the article appears. These are detailed in the *Publication Manual of the American Psychological Association* (APA, 2001) and are not covered in this chapter.

Sections of an Article

TITLE. The title of an article includes the key variables, focus, and population with an economy of words. The special features of the study are included to convey the focus immediately to potential readers. It is critical here to be direct, clear, and concise (e.g., "Memory loss and gains associated with aging" or "Predictors of drug use and abuse among adolescents"). These examples are especially concise. Ordinarily an author is encouraged to fit the title within 10–12 words.

Occasionally, comments about the method are included in the title or more commonly in the subtitle. Terms like "a pilot study" or "preliminary report" may have many different meanings, such as the fact that this is an initial or interim report of a larger research program. These words could also be gently preparing readers for some methodological surprises and even tell us not to expect too much from the design. (For example, my dissertation coined the subtitle: "A pre-preliminary, tentative, exploratory pilot study©.") In some cases, terms are added to the study such as, "A Controlled Investigation," which moves our expectation in the other direction, namely, that the present study is somehow well conducted and controlled, and perhaps by implication stands in contrast to other studies in the field (or in the author's repertoire). Usually words noting that the investigation is controlled are not needed unless this is truly a novel feature of research on the topic.

ABSTRACT. The Abstract is likely to be read by many more people than is the full article. The Abstract probably will be entered into various databases and be accessible through Internet and on-line library searches. Many journals list the tables of contents for their issues and provide free access on the Web to abstracts of the articles. Consequently, the Abstract is the only information that most readers will have about the study. For reviewers of the manuscript and readers of the journal article, the Abstract is the first impression of what the author studied and found. Ambiguity, illogic, and fuzziness here are ominous. Thus, the Abstract is sometimes the only impression or first impression one may have about the study.

Obviously, the purpose of the Abstract is to provide a relatively brief statement of goals, methods, findings, and conclusions of the study. Critical methodological descriptors pertain to the participants and their characteristics, experimental and control groups or conditions, design, and major findings. Often space is quite limited; indeed a word limit (e.g., 100 or 120 word maximum) may be placed on the Abstract. It is useful to deploy the words to make substantive statements about the characteristics of the study and the findings, rather than to provide general and minimally informative comments. For example, vacuous statements ("Implications of the results were discussed" or "Future directions for research were suggested.") ought to be replaced with more specific comments of what one or two implications and research directions are (e.g., "The findings suggest that the family and peers might be mobilized to prevent drug abuse among adolescents and but that cultural influences need to be considered as well.")

INTRODUCTION. The Introduction is designed to convey the overall rationale and objectives. The task of the author is to convey in a crisp and concise fashion why this particular study is needed and the current questions or deficiencies the study is designed to address. The section should not review the literature in a study-by-study fashion, but rather convey issues and evaluative comments that set the stage for the study. Placing the study in the context of what is and is not known (contextualization) and the essential next step in research in the field requires mastery of the pertinent literatures, apart from reasonable communication skills.

Saying that the study is important (without systematically establishing the context) or noting that no one else has studied this phenomenon (measure or sample) usually are feeble attempts to short-circuit the contextualization of the study.

It may be relevant to consider limitations of previous work and how those limitations can be overcome. These statements build the critical transition from an existing literature to the present study and the rationale for design improvements or additions in relation to those studies. It is important to emphasize that "fixing limitations" of prior work is not necessarily a strong basis for publishing a study. The author must convey that the limitations of prior work are central to a key building block in theory or the knowledge base. Alternatively, the study may build along new dimensions to extend the theory and constructs to a broader range of domains of performance, samples, and settings. The rationale for the specific study must be very clearly established.

In general, the Introduction will move from the very general to the specific. The very general refers to the opening of the Introduction that conveys the area, general topic, and significance of a problem. For example, in studies of diagnosis, assessment, treatment, or prevention of clinical dysfunction, the Introduction invariably includes a paragraph to orient the reader about the seriousness, prevalence or incidence, and economic and social costs of the disorder. Reviewers of the manuscript are likely to be specialists in the area of the study and hence know the context very well. Yet, many potential readers would profit from a statement that conveys the significance, interest, and value of the main focus of the study.

After the initial material, the Introduction moves to the issues that underlie this particular study. Here the context that frames the specific hypotheses of the study are provided and reflect theory and research that are the impetus for the investigation. Essentially, the author is making a case for conducting the study. Extended paragraphs that are background without close connections to the hypotheses of the study serve as a common weakness of manuscripts rejected for publication.

The Introduction does not usually permit us to convey all of the information we wish to present. In fact, the limit is usually 2–5 manuscript pages. A reasonable use of this space is in brief paragraphs or implicit sections that describe the nature of the problem, the current status of the literature, the extension to theory and research this study is designed to provide, and how the methods to be used are warranted. The penultimate or final paragraph of the Introduction usually includes a statement of the purpose of the study and the specific hypotheses and predictions. By the time the reader reaches this paragraph or set of paragraphs, it should be very clear that these hypotheses make sense, are important, and address a critical issue or need in the knowledge base. In short, the Introduction must establish that the study addresses a central issue. To the extent that the author conveys a grasp of the issues in the area and can identify the lacunae that the study is designed to fill greatly improves the quality of the report and the chances of acceptance for journal publication.

METHOD. This section of the paper encompasses several points related to who was studied, why, and how. The section not only describes critical procedures, but also provides the rationale for methodological decisions. Initially, the subjects or clients are described. Why was this sample included and how is this appropriate to the substantive area and question of interest? In some cases, the sample is obviously relevant because they have the characteristic of interest (e.g., parents accused of child abuse) or is in a setting of interest (e.g., nursing home residents). In other cases, samples are included merely because they are available. Such samples of *samples of convenience* may include college students or a clinic population recruited for some other purpose than this study. The rationale for the sample should be provided to convey why *this* sample provides a good test of the hypotheses and whether any special features may be relevant to the conclusions. Subject selection, recruitment, screening, and other features warrant comment. The issue is whether features of the subject-selection process could restrict the conclusions in some unique fashion, or worse, in some way represent a poor test given the purpose of the study.

The design is likely to include two or more groups that are treated in a particular fashion. The precise purpose of each group and the procedures to which they are exposed should be clarified. Control groups should not merely be labeled as such with the idea that the name is informative. The author should convey precisely what the group(s) is designed to control. The author is advised to identify the critical methodological concerns and to convey how these are controlled in the design. Plausible threats to experimental validity that are uncontrolled deserve explicit comment to arrest the reasonable concerns of the reviewers.

Several measures are usually included in the study. Why the *constructs* were selected for study should have been clarified in the Introduction. The specific *measures* and why they were selected to operationalize the constructs should be presented in the Method section. Information about the psychometric characteristics of the measures is often highlighted. This information relates directly to the credibility of the results. Apart from individual assessment devices, the rationale for including or omitting areas that might be regarded as crucial (e.g., multiple measures, informants, settings) deserves comment.

Occasionally, ambiguous statements may enter into descriptions of measures. For example, measures may be referred to as "reliable" or "valid" in previous research, as part of the rationale for their use. There are, of course, many different types of reliability and validity. It is important to identify those characteristics of the measure found in prior research that are relevant to the present research. For example, high internal consistency (reliability) in a prior study may not be a strong argument for use of the measure in a longitudinal design where the author hopes for test-retest reliability. Even previous data on test-retest reliability (e.g., over 2 weeks) may not provide a sound basis for repeated testing over annual intervals. The author ought to present information to convey the suitability of the measures for the study.

RESULTS. It is important to convey why specific statistical tests were selected and how these serve the goals of the study. A useful exercise is for the investigator to read that paragraph about hypotheses and predictions from the Introduction and then immediately start reading the Results section. The results ought to speak directly to and flow from that narrative statement in the Introduction.

Analyses often are reported in a rote fashion in which, for example, the main effects are presented and then interactions for each measure. The author presents the analyses in very much the same way as the computer output. Similarly, if several dependent measures are available, a particular set of analyses is automatically run (e.g., omnibus tests of multivariate analyses of variance followed by univariate analyses of variance for individual measures). The tests may not relate to the hypotheses, predictions, or expectations outlined at the beginning of the paper (Wampold, Davis, & Good, 1990). Knowledge of statistics is critical for selecting the analysis to address the hypotheses and conditions met by the data.

It is often useful to begin the Results by presenting basic descriptors of the data (e.g., means, standard deviations for each group or condition), so the reader has access to the numbers themselves. The main body of the Results is to test the hypotheses or to evaluate the predictions. Organization of the Results (subheadings) or brief statements of hypotheses before the analyses are often helpful to prompt the author to clarify how the statistical test relates to the substantive questions and to draw connections for the reader.

Several additional or ancillary analyses may be presented to elaborate the primary hypotheses. For example, one might be able to reduce the plausibility that certain biases may have accounted for group differences based on supplementary or ancillary data analyses. Ancillary analyses may be more exploratory and diffuse than tests of primary hypotheses. Manifold variables can be selected for these analyses (e.g., sex, race, height differences) that are not necessarily conceptually interesting in relation to the goals of the study. The author may wish to present data, data analyses, and findings that were unexpected, were not of initial interest, and were not the focus of the study. The rationale for these excursions and the limitations of interpretation are worth noting. From the standpoint of the reviewer and reader, the results should make clear what the main hypotheses were, how the analyses provide appropriate and pointed tests, and what conclusions can be reached as a result.

DISCUSSION. The study began with a statement of the need for this study and issues or lacunae the study was designed to address, i.e., the Introduction. The Discussion continues the story line by noting what we know now and how this addresses or fulfills the points noted previously. With the present findings, what puzzle piece has been added to the knowledge base, what new questions or ambiguities were raised, what other substantive areas might be relevant for this line of research, and what new studies are needed? From the standpoint of contextualization, the new studies referred to here are not merely those that overcome methodological limitations of the present study, but rather focus on the substantive next steps for research.

More concretely, the Discussion usually includes paragraphs to provide an overview of the major findings, integration or relation of these findings to theory and prior research, limitations and ambiguities and their implications for interpretation, and future directions. These are implicit rather than formally delineated sections and the author ought to consider the balance of attention to each topic. Usually, the Discussion is completed within 3–5 manuscript pages.

Description and interpretation of the findings can raise a tension between what the author wishes to say about the findings and their meaning versus what can be said in light of how the study was designed and evaluated. It is in the Discussion that one can see the interplay of the Introduction, Methods, and Results sections. For example, the author might draw conclusions that are not quite appropriate given the method and findings. The Discussion may convey flaws, problems or questionable methodological decisions within the design that were not previously evident. That is, the reader of the paper can now state that if these are the statements the author wishes to make, the present study (design, measures, sample) is not well suited. The slight mismatch of interpretative statements in the Discussion and Methods is a common, albeit tacit basis for not considering a study as well conceived and executed. A slightly different study may be required to support the specific statements the author makes in the Discussion; alternatively, the Discussion might be more circumscribed in the statements that are made. (To avoid the potential problems noted here, I omitted the Discussion section from my dissertation, a decision not uniformly appreciated by my committee.)

It is usually to the author's credit to examine potential limitations or sources of ambiguity of the study. A candid, nondefensive, appraisal of the study is very helpful. Here too, contextualization may be helpful because limitations of a study are also related to the body of prior research, what other studies have and have not accomplished, and whether a finding is robust across different methods of investigation. Although it is to the author's credit to acknowledge limitations of the study, there are limits on the extent to which reviewers grant a pardon for true confessions. At some point, the flaw is sufficient to preclude publication, whether or not the author acknowledges it. For example, the authors of the study might note, "A significant limitation of the present study is the absence of a suitable control group. We are aware that this might limit the strength of the conclusions." Although awareness may have its own intrinsic value, in this case reviewers may view the limitations as sufficiently damaging as to preclude drawing valid inferences.

At other points, acknowledging potential limitations conveys critical understanding of the issues and guides future work. For example, in explaining the findings, the author may note that although the dependent measures are valid, there are many specific facets of the construct of interest that are not included. Thus, the results may not extend to different facets of the construct as measured in different ways. This latter use of acknowledgment augments the contribution of the study and suggests concrete lines of research.

Questions to Guide Manuscript Preparation

The section-by-section discussion of the content of an article is designed to convey the flow or logic of the study and the interplay of description, explanation, and contextualization. The study ought to have a thematic line throughout and all sections ought to reflect that in a logical way. The thematic line consists of the substantive issues guiding the hypotheses and decisions of the investigator (e.g., with regard to procedures and analyses) that are used to elaborate these hypotheses.

A more concrete and hence perhaps more helpful way of aiding preparation of the manuscript is to consider our task as authors as that of answering many questions. There are questions for the authors to ask themselves or, on the other hand, questions reviewers and consumers of the research are likely to ask as they read the manuscript. These questions ought to be addressed suitably within the manuscript. Table 1 presents questions according to the different sections of a manuscript. The questions emphasize the descriptive information, as well as the rationale for procedures, decisions, and practices in the design and execution. The set of questions is useful as a way of checking to see that many important facets of the study have not been overlooked. As a cautionary note, the questions alert one to the parts rather than the whole; the manuscript in its entirety or as a whole is evaluated to see how the substantive question and methodology interrelate and how decisions regarding subject selection, control conditions, measures, and data analyses relate in a coherent fashion to the guiding question.

SELECTING A JOURNAL

Preparation of the manuscript is logically before selecting a journal and submitting the journal for publication. However, investigators occasionally have the journal or a couple of journals in mind before the manuscript is prepared. Journals have different emphases and research with particular sorts of foci (e.g., theory, application), samples (e.g., animals, college students, community samples), settings (laboratory, field), and research designs (cross-sectional, longitudinal; experimental, observational). Consequently, it is not odd for the investigator to plan/hope that a study when completed will be appropriate for a journal he or she targeted well before preparing the manuscript for publication. I mention selecting a journal here on the assumption that this logically follows in the sequence of completing a study, preparing the write up, and submitting the article for publication. Selecting a journal is part of the submitting the article.

TABLE 1. Major Questions to Guide Journal Article Preparation

ABSTRACT

What are the main purposes of the study?
Who was studied (sample, sample size, special characteristics)?
How were participants selected?
To what conditions, if any, were participants exposed?
What type of design was used?
What are the main findings and conclusions?

INTRODUCTION

What is the background and context for the study?
What in current theory or research makes this study useful, important, or of interest?
What is different or special about the study in focus, methods, or design to address a need in the area?
Is the rationale clear regarding the constructs (independent and dependent variables) to be assessed?
What specifically are the purposes, predictions, or hypotheses?
Are there ancillary or exploratory goals that can be distinguished as well?

METHOD

Participants
Who are the participants and how many of them are there in this study?
Why was this sample selected in light of the research goals?
How was this sample obtained, recruited, and selected?
What are the subject and demographic characteristics of the sample (e.g., sex, age, ethnicity, race, socioeconomic status)?
What, if any, inclusion and exclusion criteria were invoked, i.e., selection rules to obtain participants?
How many of those subjects eligible or recruited actually were selected and participated in the study?
Was informed consent solicited? How and from whom (e.g., child and parent), if special populations were used?

Design
What is the design (e.g., group, true-experiment) and how does the design relate to the goals?
How were participants assigned to groups or conditions?
How many groups were included in the design?
How are the groups similar and different?
Why are these groups critical to address the questions of interest

Procedures
Where was the study conducted (setting)?
What measures, materials, equipment, or apparatus were used?
What is the chronological sequence of events to which participants were exposed?
What intervals elapsed between different aspects of the study (e.g., assessment, exposure to the manipulation, follow-up)?
If assessments involved novel measures created for this study, what data can be brought to bear regarding pertinent types of reliability and validity?
What checks were made to ensure that the conditions were carried out as intended?
What other information does one need to know to understand how participants were treated and what conditions were provided?

RESULTS

What are the primary measures and data upon which the hypotheses or predictions depend?
What analyses are to be used and how specifically do these address the original hypotheses and purposes?
Are the assumptions of the data analyses met?
If multiple tests are used, what means are provided to control error rates (increased likelihood of finding significant differences in light of using many tests)?
If more than one group is delineated (e.g., through experimental manipulation or subject selection), are they similar on variables that might otherwise explain the results (e.g., diagnosis, age)?

TABLE 1. (*Continued*)

Are data missing due to incomplete measures (not filled out completely by the participants) or due to loss of subjects? If so, how are these handled in the data analyses?
Are there ancillary analyses that might further inform the primary analyses or exploratory analyses that might stimulate further work?

DISCUSSION

What are the major findings of the study?
Specifically, how do these findings add to research and support, refute, or inform current theory?
What alternative interpretations, theoretical or methodological, can be placed on the data?
What limitations or qualifiers are necessary, given methodology and design issues?
What research follows from the study to move the field forward?
Specifically, what ought to be done next (e.g., next study, career change of the author)?

Note: These questions are adapted from Kazdin (2003).

Several hundred journals are available in the behavioral and social sciences. The American Psychological Association (APA, 1997, www.apa.org/journals) has enumerated journals in psychology within the English language. Also, on the Internet there are excellent sites that search for journals in given area (e.g., clinical psychology) and provide (at this writing) over access to over 1800 journals (www.psycline.org/journals/psycline.html, www.isinet.com/isi/journals/index.html). These sources provide information about the editorial policy, content area or domain, type of article (e.g., investigations, literature reviews, case studies), guidelines for manuscript preparation, and tables of contents of current and past issues.

Many criteria are invoked to select a journal to which one will submit a manuscript, including the relevance of the journal in relation to the topic, the prestige value of the journal in an implicit hierarchy of journals in the field, the likelihood of acceptance, the breadth and number of readers or subscribers, and the discipline and audience one wishes to address (e.g., psychology, psychiatry, medicine, social work, health, education). As for the prestige value, clearly some journals are regarded as more selective than others. For example, some of the APA journals are premier journal outlets in their respective areas (e.g., *Journal of Personality and Social Psychology*, *Journal of Consulting and Clinical Psychology*). Yet, journals from other organizations, journals not sponsored by an organization, and journals from other professions or disciplines can be as or more highly regarded. Indeed, in some areas (e.g., behavioral neuroscience), some of the most discriminating and selective publication outlets are not psychology journals (*Science*, *Nature Neuroscience*). One can identify the best outlets by familiarity with the literature (e.g., where do the best studies seem to be published) and by chatting with colleagues. There is research on the impact that a given journal has on the field. For example, the Institute of Scientific Information (www.isinet.com/isi/products/citation/jcr/index.html) lists many journals and has information to assess the impact of a particular journal on a scientific field (e.g., social sciences). The impact factor usually refers to the extent to which articles from that journal are cited.

Some journals are not very selective and, indeed, have to hustle (e.g., invite, accept many) articles so they can fill their pages. The more obscure and low impact journals may actually be in a little trouble in accepting enough papers. A few journals in psychology charge authors for publishing their papers. So when one's paper is accepted, the author is charged on the basis of how many journal pages the article will require. These outlets do not necessarily take all submissions (e.g., like my dissertation) but they often take most. These journals tend not to be as carefully peer reviewed and hence publications in such journals are commensurately much less well regarded. Within psychology, career advice is to focus on peer-reviewed and well-regarded journals, leaving aside other issues (e.g., who publishes the journal, whether there are charges). Knowledge of the area of research, journal citation impact, and contact with ones colleagues can readily identify the ideal outlets for one's research.

The audience one wishes to reach may be a critical and indeed primary consideration in selecting a journal. Who might be interested in this study (beyond blood relatives)? One way to answer this is to consider the reference section of one's article. Are one or two journals emphasized in the Reference section of the manuscript? If so, one of these journals might be the most appropriate outlet. Citation of the journal on multiple occasions indicates that the journal publishes work on the topic and readers likely to be interested in the topic are also likely to see the article. Also relevant, journals vary markedly in their readership and subscription base. Some journals have relatively few subscribers (e.g., 200–600 up to several thousand) and are in relatively few libraries. The visibility of one's study and the chance that others will see it are influenced by these considerations. Fortunately, most professional journals have their abstracts included on databases that can be accessed from the Web. This makes even the most obscure study (e.g., my dissertation) accessible.

Most journals are in print (hard copy form) but many are only Web based and are sometimes referred to as electronic journals. This is not the place to discuss that topic except to note often publication on the Web is much faster (less delay in review of the manuscript and acceptance of the manuscript) than is publication in a printed journal. The central issue for one's career is the extent to which the publication outlet is well regarded by one's peers and the care with which manuscripts are reviewed before they are accepted and published. Electronic versus printed journal format is not as critical as the quality of the publication. If publication in the journal requires little or no peer review, if most manuscripts are accepted, and if manuscripts are accepted largely as they are (without revision), quality of the research and the value of the publication to one's career may be commensurately reduced. (If the reader knows of such outlets, please write me and let me know right away. I have a "friend" is trying to publish his doctoral dissertation.)

MANUSCRIPT SUBMISSION AND REVIEW

Overview of the Journal Review Process

Alas, through careful deliberation and 30 minutes with your coauthor at a Oija board, you select a journal and are ready submit it for publication. Before you do, consult the Instructions to Authors written in the journal to make sure you submit the correct number of copies and that your letter notes that you wish to have the manuscript considered for publication. In some cases, you may be required include sentences or paragraphs that say this study is not being considered elsewhere in another journal, has not been published before, and that you will give the copyright to the publisher if the manuscript is accepted. Processing of the manuscript could be delayed if your letter does not meet the guidelines provided in the journal. It is a little sloppy not to read the Instructions to Authors in advance of submitting the article.

Once the manuscript is submitted, the journal editor usually sends the paper to two or more reviewers who are selected because of their knowledge and special expertise in the area of the study or because of familiarity with selected features of the study (e.g., novel methods of data analyses). Some reviewers are consulting editors who review often for the journal and presumably have a perspective of the type and quality of papers the journal typically publishes; other reviewers are ad hoc reviewers and are selected less regularly than consulting editors. Reviewers are asked to evaluate the manuscript critically and to examine whether or the extent to which:

- The question(s) is important for the field,
- The design and methodology are appropriate to the question,
- The results are suitably analyzed,
- The interpretations follow from the design and findings, and
- The knowledge yield contributes in an incremental way to what is known already.

Once the paper is reviewed, the editor evaluates the manuscript and the comments of the reviewers. In some cases, the editor may provide his or her own independent review of the paper; in other cases he or she may not review the paper at all but defer to the comments and recommendations of the reviewers. The editor writes the author and notes the editorial decision. Usually, one of three decisions is reached: the manuscript is accepted pending a number of revisions that address points of concern in the reviewers' comments; the manuscript is rejected and will not be considered further by the journal; or the manuscript is rejected but the author is invited to resubmit an extensively revised version of the paper for reconsideration.

The *accept* decision usually means that the overall study provides important information and was well done. However, reviewers and the editor may have identified several points for further clarification and analysis. The author is asked to revise the paper to address these points. The revised paper would be accepted for publication. The *reject* decision means that the reviewers and/or editor considered the paper to include flaws in conception, design, or execution or that the research problem, focus, and question did not address a very important issue. For the journals with high rejection rates, papers are usually not rejected because they are flagrantly flawed in design. Rather, the importance of the study, the suitability of the methods for the questions, and specific methodological and design decisions conspire to serve as the basis for the decision. The *reject-resubmit decision* may be used if several issues emerged that raise questions about the research and the design. In a sense, the study may be viewed as basically sound and important but many significant questions preclude definitive evaluation. The author may be invited to prepare an extensively revised version that includes further procedural details, additional data analyses, and clarification of many decision points pivotal to the findings and conclusions. The revised manuscript may be re-entered into the review process and be evaluated again.

Of the three letters, clearly a rejection letter is the most commonly received. Authors and perhaps new authors in particular are not sufficiently prepared for this feature of the journal publication business.[2] Journals often publish their rejection rates, i.e., proportion of submitted manuscripts that are rejected and this figure can be quite high (e.g., 70–90 percent). Often the prestige value of the journal is in part based on the high rejection rate. (If this same criterion were invoked in judging careers, the rejection rate for my manuscripts—now approaching 99.99 percent—would place me in a rather elite group.)

Although beyond our purpose, the review process deserves passing comment. The entire process of manuscript submission, review, and publication has been heavily lamented, debated,

[2] Excellent readings are available to prepare the author for the journal review process (*The Trial* by Kafka, *The Myth of Sisyphus* by Camus, and *Inferno* by Dante). Some experiences (e.g., root canal without an anesthetic, income tax audit) also are touted to be helpful because they evoke reactions that mimic those experienced when reading reviews of one manuscript.

and criticized. The imperfections and biases of peer review, the lack of agreement between reviewers of a given paper, the influence of variables (e.g., prestige value of the author's institution, number of citations of one's prior work within the manuscript) on decisions of reviewers, and the control that reviewers and editors exert over authors have been vigorously discussed (e.g., Bailar & Patterson, 1985; Cicchetti, 1991; Lindsay, 1988).

Understanding the review process can be aided by underscoring the one salient characteristic that authors, reviewers, and editors share, to wit, they are all human. This means that they (we) vary widely in skills, expertise, sensitivities, motives, and abilities to communicate. Science is an enterprise of people and hence cannot be divorced from subjectivity and judgment. In noting subjectivity in the manuscript review and evaluation process, there is a false implication of arbitrariness and fiat. Quality research often rises to the top and opinions of quality over time are not idiosyncratic.

You Receive the Reviews

Alas, the editorial process is completed (typically within 3 months after manuscript submission) and the reviews are in. You receive the letter from the editor noting whether the paper is accepted for publication and if not whether it might be if suitably revised. It is possible that the letter will say the manuscript is accepted as is (no further changes) and praise you for your brilliance. If this occurs, it is the middle of the night and you are dreaming. Remain in this wonderfully pleasant state as long as you can. When you awake, your spouse or partner hands you the real letter and you read one of the three decisions noted previously.

If the manuscript is accepted, usually some changes are needed. These do not raise problems. More often than not, the manuscript is rejected. There are individual differences in how one reacts to this decision. Typically, one feels at least one of these: miffed, misunderstood, frustrated, or angry at the reviewers whose identity will be contemplated by scrutinizing the language, font style, key words, and possible DNA remnants on the reviewers' comments sheets. Some authors select one of the very effective psychotherapies or medications for depression; others use coping strategies (e.g., anger management training, stress inoculation therapy) or alternative medicines (e.g., acupuncture, mineral baths, enemas).

The task is to publish one's work. Consequently, it is useful and important to take from the reviews all one can to revise the manuscript. Maladaptive cognitions can harm the process. For example, when reading a review, the author might say, the reviewer misunderstood what I did or did not read this or that critical part. These claims may be true, but the onus is always on the author to make the study, its rationale and procedures, patently clear. A misunderstanding by a reviewer is likely to serve as a preview of many other readers of the article. If the author feels a rejected manuscript can be revised to address the key concerns, by all means write to the editor and explain this in detail and without righteous indignation and affect.

Authors often are frustrated at the reactions of reviewers. In reading the reactions of reviewers, the authors usually recognize and acknowledge the value of providing more details (e.g., further information about the participants, or procedures). However, when the requests pertain to explanation and contextualization, authors are more likely to be baffled or defensive. This reaction may be reasonable because much less attention is given to these facets in graduate training. Also, reviewers' comments and editorial decision letters may not be explicit about the need for explanation and contextualization. For example, some of the more general reactions of reviewers are often reflected in comments such as: "Nothing in the manuscript is new," "I fail to see the importance of the study," or "This study has already been done in a much better way by others."[3] In fact, the characterizations may be true. Authors (e.g., me) often feel like they are victims of reviewers who wore sleep masks when they read the manuscript, did not grasp key points, and have had little exposure to, let alone mastery of, the pertinent literature. Occasionally two or more of these are true. As often as not, it is the reviewers who might more appropriately give the victim speech. The author has not made the connections among the extant literature and this study and integrated the substantive, methodological, and data-analytic features in a cohesive and thematic way. Reviewers' comments and less than extravagant praise often reflect the extent to which the author has failed to contextualize the study to mitigate these reactions. The lesson for preparing and evaluating research reports is clear. Describing a study does not establish its contribution to the field, no matter how strongly the author feels that the study is a first.

Let us assume that the manuscript was rejected with an invitation to resubmit. As a rule, I try to incorporate as many of the reviewers' and editor's recommendations as possible. My view is that the reviewer may be idiosyncratic, but more likely represents a constituency that might read the article. If I can address several or all issues, clarify procedures that I thought were already perfectly clear, and elaborate a rationale or two, it is advisable to do so. Free advice from reviewers can and ought to be used to one's advantage.

There are likely to be aspects of the reviews one cannot address. Perhaps reviewers provide conflicting recommendations or a manuscript page limit precludes addressing or elaborating a particular point. Even more importantly, perhaps as an author one strongly disagrees with the point. Mention these in the letter to the editor that accompanies the revised manuscript. Explain what revisions were or were not made and why. If there are large revisions that alter the text (few sentences), methods or data analyses, help the editor by noting where the change can be found in the manuscript and even submit an extra copy of the manuscript in which the changes are highlighted in marker.

The investigator may receive a rejection letter and decide simply to submit the manuscript as is to another journal. I believe this is generally unwise. If there are fairly detailed reviews, it is to the author's advantage to incorporate key points and often not-so-key points, even if the manuscript is to go to another journal. I have often seen the same manuscript (not mine) rejected from two different journals in which there were no changes after the first rejection. The authors could have greatly improved the likelihood of publication in the second journal but were a bit stubborn about making any revisions. Even if the manuscript were to be accepted as is in the second journal, it is still likely the author missed an opportunity to make improvements after the first set of reviews was provided. In general, try to take all of the recommendations and criticisms from the reviews and convert them to facets that can improve the manuscript. Obstacles to this process may stem from our defensive reactions as authors and the often brutish way in which reviewers convey cogent points. (I remember being highly offended the first two or three times reviewers noted such comments, "the author [me] would not recognize a hypothesis if it fell on his lap" and "the design of this study raises very important issues, such as whether it is too late for the author [me] to consider a career change.")

It is worthwhile and highly rewarding to publish one's research. The process takes time and persistence. Also, contact with others through the review process can greatly improve one's work. In my own case, reading the reviews occasionally has stimulated next studies that I carried out. In one case, I befriended a person who was a reviewer of my work earlier in my career. Years later over dinner, I mentioned his review in a distant past, the study it generated,

[3] Thanks to my dissertation committee for letting me quote from their comments.

and the very interesting results and, of course, expressed my gratitude. (His review was not entirely positive, which probably is the main reason I hid in bathroom of the restaurant until he paid the check for dinner.)

The journal review process is not the only way to obtain input on one's manuscript. I occasionally send a penultimate draft of a manuscript to experts in the field whom I do not know. I convey in a letter what I am trying to accomplish and ask if they would provide feedback. I have done this on a few occasions and cannot recall anyone colleague who has refused to provide comments. The comments are usually detailed and quite constructive and have a different tone from those that emanate from the journal review process. The comments in turn can be used to devise the version that is submitted for publication.

CLOSING COMMENTS

Designing and completing a study requires many skills. Publication and communication of results of research represent a separate set of skills and most of these skills are not mentioned or detailed in graduate training. I have mentioned three tasks that are involved in preparing a manuscript for journal publication: description, explanation, and contextualization of the study. The writing we are routinely taught in science focuses on description, but the other portions are central as well and determine whether a study not only appears to be important but also in fact actually is. Recommendations were made in what to address and how to incorporate description, explanation, and contextualization within the different sections of a manuscript (e.g., Introduction, Method). In addition, questions were provided to direct the researcher to the types of issues reviewers are likely to ask about a manuscript. Another concrete way to aid in preparing a manuscript is to identify one or two published articles that are very clearly written. Consider the organization, presentation, story line, and thrust of these articles and try to emulate their structure.

Publication of one's research has many rewards. The external rewards (fame, fortune, promotion) are often mentioned first. Apart from any of these, publication helps one's own thinking that began with conceptualization of the study and understanding the phenomenon. Writing up the results often helps for extends one's own thinking further and hence is a critical step in the next study or in conceptualization of the topic or area. This is a reciprocal process where we too are influenced by the publications of others and hopefully exert influence with our own publications.

ACKNOWLEDGEMENTS: Completion of research was facilitated by support from the Leon Lowenstein Foundation, the William T. Grant Foundation 98-1872-98), and the National Institute of Mental Health (MH59029).

ADDITIONAL RESOURCES

American Psychological Association (1997). *Journals in psychology: A resource listing for authors* (5th ed.). Washington, DC: Author.

American Psychological Association (2001). *Publication manual of the American Psychological Association* (5th ed.). Washington, DC: Author.

Kupfer, D. J., Kraemer, H. C., & Bartko, J. J. (1994). Documenting and reporting the study results of a randomized clinical trial (spicy meatballs, not pabulum). In R. F. Prien, & D. S. Robinson (Eds.), *Clinical evaluation of psychotropic drugs* (pp. 237–260). New York: Raven Press.

Maher, B. A. (1978). A reader's, writer's, and reviewer's guide to assessing research reports in clinical psychology. *Journal of Consulting and Clinical Psychology, 46*, 835–838.

Pryczak, F., & Bruce, R. R. (2000). *Writing empirical research reports: A basic guide for students of the social and behavioral sciences* (3rd ed.). Los Angeles, CA: Pyrczak Publishing.

Wilkinson, L., & the Task Force on Statistical Inference, APA Board of Scientific Affairs (1999). Statistical methods in psychology journals: Guidelines and explanations. *American Psychologist, 54*, 594–604.

REFERENCES

American Psychological Association (1997). *Journals in psychology: A resource listing for authors* (5th ed.). Washington, DC: Author.

Bailar, J. C. III., & Patterson, K. (1985). Journal of peer review: The need for a research agenda. *New England Journal of Medicine, 312*, 654–657.

Case, L., & Smith, T. B. (2000). Ethnic representation in a sample of the literature of applied psychology. *Journal of Consulting and Clinical Psychology, 68*, 1107–1110.

Cicchetti, D. V. (1991) The reliability of the peer review for manuscript and grant submissions: A cross-disciplinary investigation. *Behavioral and Brain Sciences, 14*, 119–186.

Kazdin, A. E. (2003). *Research design in clinical psychology* (4th ed.). Needham Heights, MA: Allyn & Bacon.

Lindsay, D. (1988). Assessing precision in the manuscript review process: A little better than a dice role. *Sociometrics, 14*, 75–82.

Wampold, B. E., Davis, B., & Good, R. H. III (1990). Hypothesis validity of clinical research. *Journal of Consulting and Clinical Psychology, 58*, 360–367.

Weiss, B., & Weisz, J. R. (1990). The impact of methodological factors on child psychotherapy outcome research: A meta-analysis for researchers. *Journal of Abnormal Child Psychology, 18*, 639–670.

CHAPTER 8

Recommendations for Teaching Psychology

WILLIAM C. RANDO AND LEONID ROZENBLIT

Teaching is one of the legs in the academic tripod, along with research and service. As a typical academic psychologist, you will find that teaching will occupy a significant percentage of your time, despite the fact that you may never get any formal training in pedagogy. Today, with increasing numbers of universities offering training in teaching to graduate students, more people are starting their professional careers prepared to teach. This preparation comes in many forms. Some psychology departments receive funding through the Preparing Future Faculty (PFF) program. Funded by the PEW Foundation, PFF provides teaching skills to graduate students and introduces them to academic institutions different from their own. Other psychology graduate students receive teaching preparation from their academic department, while the majority take part in training organized by a campus teaching and learning center. Graduate students who take advantage of this kind of training are fortunate; they entire the job market ready to teach well, and they have a much easier time making the transition from student to academic professional. With such a solid professional start, these well-prepared teachers are likely to become better throughout their careers, able to adapt their style and approach as needed along way. They more likely to be in control of the teaching process in a way that allows them to vary the style they use and the amount of time they spend on teaching, while always maintaining a very high standard for themselves and their students. Faculty members who never master the art of teaching, are more likely to feel burdened by their "teaching load" throughout their career, never giving their full potential to their students, and never achieving the rewards of great teaching that so many senior faculty experience (McKeatchie, 1999).

Teaching well is important throughout your career, but it is particularly important in the early years. The "publish or perish" scenario that once applied only to highly competitive research universities, now apply to almost all academics, even those who chose careers in so called teaching oriented, liberal arts colleges. And publishing is not the only pressure placed on a new faculty member. Increasingly, new psychology Ph.D.'s are seeking adjunct faculty positions for reasons of preference or necessity. These per/course positions are typically free

WILLIAM C. RANDO • McDougal Graduate Teaching Center, Yale University Graduate School, New Haven, CT 06520
LEONID ROZENBLIT • Department of Psychology, Yale University, New Haven, CT 06520

of pressure to publish, once you actually land one. However, in certain markets where good adjunct faculty positions are competitive, the standards for hiring remain focused on scholarly production, even when the position is entirely about teaching. And the fact remains, that while adjunct faculty members may not feel direct pressure to publish, most will feel the pressure of having to cobble together two or three adjunct positions or other types of work to make ends meet. This is no time to struggling as teacher.

Regardless of the position, if you have not received adequate preparation in teaching as a graduate student, you may find you have a lot to learn at a time when you probably have little time to learn it. Faculty members who try to learn to teach under these conditions naturally look for the fastest way to prepare and teach a class. One such way is to teach as you were taught, that is, teach a carbon copy of the Introduction to Psychology course that you had as an undergraduate. There are some predictable problems with this approach. For one, you probably do not have the same skills or style as the professor you are trying to emulate, so attempts to replicate his or her classes will likely fall short of your expectations. Moreover, we rarely have the exact same philosophy as our mentors, which means that if we follow their behaviors, we're likely to end up in practical binds, unable to determine practical solution because we lack a coherent pedagogical rationale for the course of action we've taken. In the end, drawing on our best teachers to build a teaching philosophy and style is an excellent idea. Doing exactly what they did because it worked for them is not. You can borrow some strategies from your mentors, but if you want to be a successful teacher, you have engage in some serious analysis and reflection about what you are doing and how you are doing it.

Simply put, you have to choose what kind of teacher you will be. The profession is full of people unsatisfied with their teaching, though they spend little time on their lectures and even less on their students. They have achieved tenure and/or professional prominence on the merits of their research. That is one kind of career in psychology. If you choose another type of career in psychology, one in which you are rewarded by teaching, you will need to devote time to it. The fact remains that the time you devote to teaching will have to come from some other important endeavor, like research. If that trade off seems terribly high, consider the following:

- Evolving methods of teaching assessment are allowing schools to give greater weight to quality teaching at hiring, promotion and tenure time.
- Teaching, like any skill, becomes easier as you get better. Skilled teachers can achieve great results with less time and effort than unskilled teachers.
- As a new professor, a reputation for good teaching allows you to attract graduate students and talented undergraduates to you and your work. This can create enormous professional benefits at a time when you really need them.
- Teaching well is a joy. Teaching poorly is a burden, or worse, a drain on your time and energy.

It is nearly impossible to learn to teach simply by reading, but chapters such as this one can provide a valuable framework for improving your teaching. A serious attempt to master the art of teaching requires resources, time, practice and feedback. Make inquiries as to whether your institution offers assistance in this area, through mentoring programs, teaching grant initiatives, or through some kind of teaching improvement center.

The remainder of this chapter contains tips and strategies for success in the college classroom. These suggestions point to many different styles of teaching, all of which have proven effective in their own way. However, there is one concept that unifies every idea herein, and that this: That the goal of any class or course is not to cover material or get through the book. The goal of a class to is to reach students in ways that will help them learn. Teachers must decide how they want their students to be different—smarter, wiser, more clever, more skilled, more appreciative—as a result of being in class. Then they must find a way to achieve that goal.

FOUR STEPS TO DESIGNING A COLLEGE COURSE IN PSYCHOLOGY

Use Student Learning to Define the Overall Purpose of the Course

As stated above, there is enormous benefit in framing or defining your class around core learning goals. First, teachers experience renewed motivation in teaching when they move from a content centered approach (i.e., getting through the material) to a learning centered approach (i.e., helping students achieve). This renewed sense of purpose typically generates more creative and innovative approaches to classroom teaching, which, if nothing else, makes the process more interesting. Second, teachers who successfully communicate their purpose to students may find their students have increased motivation and willingness to work and learn. In classes where the purpose seems to be defined around teacher's lectures and interests, students are more likely to feel like and act like spectators. However, when a class and all its activities are defined around student learning, students are more likely to feel and act like interested participants.

The process of defining your goals and objectives begins with taking an inventory of all the skills and abilities you want your students to acquire during the term. The difficulty in accomplishing this stems from the challenge of prioritizing: figuring out which goals are most important, and how some goals are prerequisite to other goals. In addition, teachers typically have objectives of different types. For example, there may be facts we want students to know, or skills we want them to acquire or feelings and appreciations we hope they develop. We may also have goals around how students experience us, our course, and our field, and all of these might reflect our own values and beliefs about undergraduate education. All of these goals should be part of your inventory, but then, as mentioned above, the challenge is making sense of them, giving certain goals priority, and turning them into a plan of action. One way to do this is to define a large, terminal goal—the main objective you want your students to be able to achieve by the end of the course—and then work backward, identifying as many of the subordinate skills students will need as you can. Here is an example:

Terminal Goal or Objective: I want my students to demonstrate the ability to use data and reasoning to address a major issue in public health, education or social policy.

Subordinate Goals or Abilities: In order to complete the Terminal Objective, my students will need to demonstrate the following:

- the ability to distinguish among different sub-areas of psychology.
- the ability to critically evaluate social science findings reported in journals or the popular press.
- the ability to write at least three paragraphs that demonstrate the distinction between observation and inference.
- the ability to articulate the power and complexity of experimental design.
- the ability to identify 10 threats to validity in a well-respected journal article.
- the ability to apply the scientific method to questions about human behavior, and be able to identify misapplications of the method.

Notice that in the example above, the emphasis in on the demonstration of well defined abilities. The common trap of many teachers is their tendency to define their goals in terms of what students will "understand" without defining the depth and breadth of the understanding, nor the way that the understanding will demonstrated. The complexity of the learning process, and the fact that all of our students start out with different skills, and styles of learning make teaching difficult to begin with. However, the more clearly you can define the skills and abilities that students should acquire during semester, as well as how each and every activity and assignment furthers those goals, the more likely your students are to actually learn something. Notice also that the Terminal Goal has real-world application. It is the kind of task that might motivate students. The Subordinate Goals are less real-world, more academic, but if you organize the course around the more engaging applications of the terminal goal students will be more motivated to develop subordinate stills.

Get to Know Something about Your Students

Claiming to know anything about students is tricky. Experienced teachers have the sense that students vary from one another; they vary from class to class, and from institution to institution. The literature on learning styles reminds us that individual students learn in different ways, and that, in any class, we may have learners who are more or less visual, verbal, social, competitive, cooperative, linear, global, independent, creative, and well-organized, etc. (Upcraft, 1996). Most experts in this area agree that in any given class, a mix of methods and modes of delivery and assessment is best. They also suggest that we may want to introduce our students to different modes of studying and preparation, joining a study group, for example, so that students can learn to capitalize on their strengths or to practice underdeveloped skills.

It may be easier and more productive to think about the way that students differ between institutions. Obviously, this means taking stock of the academic culture of the place your teaching and learning from colleagues, and from students themselves, about the habits and expectations that are most common. If you are new to an institution, you may be surprised at the norms students have developed for teaching and learning. Some are part of the formal institutional structure, such as the lecture/section method used at many research institution. Most norms arise informally, and are passed down from student to student, and from teacher to teacher. The purpose of understanding teaching and learning norms is not to copy what has been done before, but to understand what parts of your teaching may be viewed as new or innovative by students and what parts are standard operating procedure. If you are new to a campus, AND you are asking students to learn in a whole new way, you may want to ease them into the change and be prepared for a little resistance. It is not always easy to discern the norms and culture of institution, and you may want to take some assertive steps to get the information you need. We suggest talking to as many colleagues and students as you can. Here are some questions you might ask:

- What kinds of lectures are students used to? PowerPoint? Stand-up comedy?
- Is there precedent for students working together in groups? Do they do group projects?
- What kinds of assignments are typical? Long, formal, end-of-term papers or shorter more idiosyncratic essays and exercises?
- How much of the teaching is experiential? Formal? Innovative?
- Once you have a better sense of your students, you can look back at your goals and determine ways to achieve them.

Get to Know Yourself as a Teacher

Effective teaching is as much self-knowledge as it is anything else. Sure, a charming, funny, and charismatic teacher will likely have an easier time reaching students. And on some campuses, students may flock to the Nobel and Pulitzer Prize winners. But it is also true that every day, in classes all across the country, faculty members with average charm, and with only average prospects of getting a midnight call from Stockholm, find ways to reach students and even to inspire them. The key here is to find your strengths as a teacher and use them in the service of your goal. Here are some strengths you can build on:

- Writing and delivering great lectures. Summarizing huge amounts of material. Explaining complicated concepts. Making dull material fascinating. Telling jokes and stories.
- Facilitating great seminar discussions. Asking provocative questions and summarizing complicated dialogue.
- Orchestrating large classes into small groups or all-group discussions. Dealing with noise and controversy.
- Designing mini-experiments or analytical tasks for in-class group work. Creating challenges on the spot. Debriefing.
- Working with and managing teams over the course of a semester. Creating motivation through team competition. Dealing with interpersonal situations.
- Consulting with students individually. Doing individual diagnosis and planning. Mentoring.

The key here is to take stock of your strengths and use them to develop goals that will keep you and your students motivated throughout the semester.

In the process of taking stock of your strengths, it is beneficial for a faculty member to simultaneously think about weaknesses and areas for improvement. Assessing weaknesses in teaching is difficult because reliable constructive feedback to teachers is scarce. Constructive negative feedback is notoriously difficult to get from students or junior colleagues who may fear reprisal, and few professionals feel comfortable discussing their shortcomings with peers or superiors. However, feedback about shortcoming can be enormously useful for faculty members who want to become better teachers. You can reflect on the questions below:

- Organization and Clarity: Does the structure of your course as described in the syllabus really make sense to students? Is there continuity and flow in lectures from day to day and in the assignments and classroom activities that accompany those lectures?
- Rapport with Students: Do students really understand that you respect them and want them to learn? Do they feel comfortable approaching you with questions and problems? Have you earned their respect? Have you lost your respect for them?
- Fairness in Grading: Related to organization, do tests and graded assignments reflect the work being done in class in a consistent and reasonable way? Are your standards clear, internally consistent and in-line with students' standards in other classes? Are there opportunities to discuss problems and misunderstandings?
- Expressiveness and Enthusiasm: Does your lecture delivery or discussion leading style increase students' interest in material or detract from it? Do you communicate positive feelings—curiosity, importance, critical interest, passion—for the material? Is your body language or verbal style energizing or enervating?

Develop a Course Plan that Pulls Everything Together

Broken down into its most basic parts, the pedagogical plan has five elements—purpose, motivation, content, actions, and assessment. These elements structure the course overall, but they also guide the course on the micro level. In other words, for every unit or every class meeting, you can bring these five elements to bear as design guides. The end-product of a course plan is a course syllabus which reflects the details of your plan and communicates them to your students. The degree to which your pedagogical plan is transparent to students is an issue we will discuss in a later section. For now consider using the questions below to develop your plan for how you will teach each aspect of the course.

- What is the purpose of this section or chapter (develop a skill, practice a technique, master an area of knowledge)?
- How will I motivate students to learn this? Is the material or skill innately interesting or valuable? What does it teach students do? Will I need to create a demonstration or model? Will I use a graded test or assignment to increase motivation?
- What new information will students need (theories, studies, examples, etc.) and how will they get it (lecture, reading, video, observation, etc.)?
- What action will students perform on that new information (write about it, discuss it with peers, experiment on it, reflect on it, etc.?)?
- How will I assess what students are learning? (graded paper, un-graded written assignment, observation)?

SOME PRACTICAL CONSIDERATIONS IN CREATING A COURSE

Once a faculty member establishes goals and rationales for a course, the pragmatic steps and choices become much easier. In the alternative, the structure of the text or the vagaries of semester calendar end up driving the purpose of the class, which is not ideal. In this section, we discuss four choices that every faculty member has to make: textbooks and readings; use of class time; assignments and other out-of-class work; and grading.

Choose a Textbook that Helps You Teach

The trick here is to resist the temptation to let the tail wag the dog by allowing the content and structure of the text to structure the goals of your course. Few faculty members ever find the perfect textbook, until they breakdown and author their own, and even then, there always seems to be something out of place, missing or overemphasized. Some easy ways to find a respectable pool of good textbooks to consider are: ask your colleagues to make recommendations (They will know the level and type of textbook students at your institution are used to, and they may even have direct experience teaching with that book.); the core collection or reserve room of the library will have copies of all the textbooks currently in use; write to publisher for review copies of books you have heard of or seen advertised; consult an on-line resource, e.g., A Compendium of Introductory Psychology Texts at www.lemoyne.edu/OTRP/intotexts.html.

Your first consideration is the content. You cannot teach effectively from a book that you neither respect nor agree with, unless you design the entire course around debunking the text, which many students find confusing. This does not mean that you have to agree with everything the authors present. Allowing students to see you display a little healthy disagreement with authority of the text is probably good for most students, but it should not be a daily ritual. Find a book that provides intelligent and scholarly treatment of most topics, and that does so in language that you and your students can understand and appreciate. If the book organizes material in way that advances your understanding of things, then you have an additional advantage. Quality of content is the most important consideration, but textbooks contain many other qualities that can help you teach more effectively. Some of these qualities include: illustrative examples that explain concepts in various ways; exercises and activities that you can use during class or as out-of-class assignments; side bars and special inserts that discuss related topics like teaching students about the field, real-life or policy applications, personal biographies of researchers or historically important research. Most books these days also include student study aids, such as review questions or self-test. A textbook today my include a CD which can help you develop lectures or add web-based material to the class. Textbooks come with a myriad of bells and whistles, not all of which will be helpful. Remember, the book is just a tool to help you teach better. It is not the entire class, nor is it a bible that you have to follow. On the other hand, students are used to focusing on "the book" and looking to it for answers and guidance, so you are smart to get one that really compliments your approach.

Be Creative in Your Use of Class Time

There are many things you can do with class time other than lecture. Class time is your most valuable teaching commodity, but to make the most of it, we need to design it in the context of what students will do in other settings—outside alone, outside with other, one-on-one with us. With this in mind, class time is probably not the best time for students to encounter new material for the first time. Use this opportunity to let students work together, and for you to observe students at work and give them timely appropriate feedback. If you are a stimulating lecturer who can motivate, stimulate and inspire students to greater heights of academic achievement, then some amount of lecture will likely serve you and your students well. Lectures designed to simply cover material or go over chapters are usually not worth it. If you need to introduce new material, do it quickly—within 15 or 20 minutes. Use the remainder of the time to:

- organize small group tasks that allow students to work on material; or
- All-class discussions about interesting controversial topics. These can be organized as debates, or extended role-play exercises that ask students to take the perspective of a point of view or theoretical orientation;
- Demonstrations with discussion and analysis.

The design of class time is even more important if your class is longer than 50 minutes or only meets once a week. In these cases, it is important to break the class into clear segments with clear goals. Asking students to sit though 50, 90 or 120 minutes of straight lecture is not the best use of your time or theirs.

Design Assignments that Allow Students to Make Better Use of Class Time

Students spend more time completing assignments than any other aspect of school, so it is vital that assignments require students to do significant, targeted, academic work. Students' performance on assignments can be improved by connecting some aspect of the assignment to the work students will do in class the next day. For example, if students are writing reports on research articles, have them use some aspect of those reports to do an in-class analysis. Motivation can be further increased by setting up in-class peer groups that require individuals to come to class prepared. As you begin to develop your first assignments, look back on some of the assignments you were given, and ask colleagues for their ideas. Consider the assignments that are typically used in psychology classes—the research report, the case analysis, compare and contrast, journal article review, lab report—because these are forms that may be familiar to students. Then focus on the specific goals and objectives you have created for that section of that course, and modify the assignment in the following ways:

- Identify the specific skills that students need to master in order to complete the assignment. An assignment that requires students to demonstrate several skills once or twice, is better than assignment that requires students to demonstrate one skill again and again.
- Find a task that clearly requires the skills you've identified, and which produces some kind of identifiable product, or requires finding the answer to a specific question or puzzle. Try to focus on real questions rather than rote exercises. Be creative in how you frame the assignment so that students will have to use new skills and modes of expression. If possible, allow students some choice in what they do or how they approach the task, but do not sacrifice the core purpose of the assignment. Unique assignments are also more difficult to plagiarize.
- Match the length, difficulty and scope of the task to the skills you want students to demonstrate. Shorter, focused assignments typically offer more stimulating educational experiences than longer, more complex works. At some point, it may become necessary for undergraduates to demonstrate their ability to sustain an analysis or project for forty pages. This is not the case for most undergraduate work in psychology.
- Communicate the purpose of the assignment in clear terms of high academic standards. Focus on what students are actually accomplishing for themselves.
- Effective assignments are easy to identify. Students will be drawn into the work and they will exceed your expectations. In addition to demonstrating the required skills of the assignment, you will begin to see evidence of humor, creativity, and critical thinking. Some additional suggestions for creating assignments appear below.
- Effective assignments are clearly defined and have well-established standards. It does no good to wait until you grade a paper to tell students what you were looking for.
- Effective assignments are no larger than the skills they are designed to teach. Don't ask students to produce huge products and long papers to demonstrate small skills over and over again.
- Effective assignments produce real products, with form and structure. Rather than asking students to write a 5 page paper on X, ask them to write up a case analysis or grant proposal, mock legal brief, committee report, letter to the editor or a publishable book review.
- Effective assignments may make use of imagination and perspective, ask students to take on a role and write from that perspective, e.g., take the role of a patient, or speculate on a hypothetical situation.
- Effective assignments combine the demonstration of well-defined skills and abilities with opportunities for creativity, uniqueness and personal expression.

- Effective assignments ask students to demonstrate skills that are directly related to the core goals of a course. That is, students should have to rely on what they learned in class to successfully complete an assignment.
- Effective assignments often include students working in pairs or teams, though students should be individually accountable for their own work and their own grades.
- *Use grading as an opportunity to assess student work and give them necessary feedback*: Grading students' work effectively is a critically important part of teaching. However, evidence suggests that it is often done poorly, and without appropriate attention, which has left students and faculty members alike with a dismissive or cynical view about the entire process. Your colleagues and students may have this view, in which case you will have to make a conscience effort to think and act otherwise. Grades, after all, are not simply a reflection of how our students have done, they are a reflection of how carefully and thoughtfully we have taught. It is somewhat demoralizing to scan a group of your students' end-of-term grades, and not really know how well they reflect what your students have learned. Additionally, we can find ourselves with a host of practical problems when students come back to complain.
- Grading begins with your very first thoughts about the course. Once you identify the skills and abilities you want students to demonstrate, you must assign value to the achievement of those skills and to the partial achievement of those skills, and then translate that value into what every grading scheme your institution requires. Listed below are a set of considerations that you can apply to every assignment or test you grade, as well as to the overall grade.
- Establish and communicate specific standards for everything you grade. Inform students upfront what will be graded and how. Reaffirm those standards in the comments that accompany your grades. Remember, the primary purpose of grades is to give students useful feedback about their progress.
- Begin grading short assignments and in-class work early in the term. This will help students become familiar with your standards and their level of preparation.
- Establish ground rules to achieve fairness in grading. Inconsistency in rules and procedures will communicate favoritism and capriciousness. It is not necessary to establish rigid practices to achieve a sense of fairness, however your rules must apply to all your students, and in the same way.
- Grade a variety of student work. Make sure your grading structure reflects all of the objectives you have identifies for the course. Naturally, you will want to give greater weight to the core objectives. However, you can keep students working and learning at a steady pace throughout the term if your grading scheme gives them continuous feedback about how well they are doing along the way.
- The grading of participation in-class should, like all other grades, include clearly defined standards.

Write a Course Syllabus that Establishes a Contract Between You and Your Students

The final step in designing a course is the presentation of the syllabus. The syllabus accomplishes one essential goal: it supplies students with all the information they need in order to understand and complete the course in a way that helps them set their expectations and guide their behavior. It can be useful to think of the syllabus as an informal contract between you and your students.

There are many styles of syllabii. Some faculty members choose to put everything in writing, including the purpose of the course and the rationale for its design, while others include just bare-bones logistical information about due dates, grade requirements and texts. To help you decide how much detail to include, think about what is important to you and to your students. Also, use the syllabus as a reference or teaching tool, throughout the semester. Tone and style are both personal choices, however, be aware that the tone of the syllabus does communicate something to your students. You've seen hundreds of syllabi in your lifetime, so we don't have to describe one. Still, you might want to consider these suggestions for writing a good one.

- Do not take for granted that you students know more about your institution than you do. Remember, many students in any classroom are just as new as you are. Avoid abbreviations and lingo. Remember, first-year students and part-time students may not be familiar with nicknames and other local jargon. Stick to the facts and include as many as you can.
- Highlight the most important ideas or processes of the course. Don't be afraid to include some big ideas in the syllabus, especially if they provide a context or purpose for the course.
- Edit carefully the calendar information you include. Be aware of holidays and other campus activities. Remember, students will use this syllabus to plan their semester.
- Make the document as useful as possible, so that students will keep it and look to it, often. Whether on paper or on the web, the syllabus should be a useful document that you and your students refer to because it has good, reliable information.

TEACHING PSYCHOLOGY WITH TECHNOLOGY

Extolling the virtues of new technologies in a published text is a risky business. Tools that seem cutting-edge and exciting at the time of writing tend to sound dated by publication. Yet, as teachers, we are hard-pressed to ignore the information technology revolution. After all, our business is, in some sense, information.

First we will consider some reasons you might want to use information technology in your teaching. Second, we will ask when you should use the technology (and, conversely, when you should pass). Finally, we will consider how you should use the technology. By concentrating on general principles, we can compensate for the short projected shelf-life of the technological specifics.

Why Should I Use Information Technology?

- *To sell and market your course.* Both deans and students at times appear unduly impressed with glamorous course web sites, and polished Power Point presentations. Cynical as this sounds, sales and marketing may be the most immediately practical set of reasons to supplement chalk and paper with electrons.

- *To solve logistical problems.* Put your notes on the web, print out your power point presentations as handouts, collect and distribute assignments without wasting valuable class time. Tools developed for easy exchange of information in business can simplify the logistical challenges of teaching.
- *To help your students learn.* Help student apply new concepts, actively engage the course material by discussing it with their peers, develop rich knowledge structures, and find additional resources. It can give teachers and students new abilities earlier generations could only dream about. Some particularly relevant examples might be the use of videos to show clinical interviews, computer animation to illustrate complex causal relationships, computers with projectors to show actual experimental stimuli in real-time, and on-line data collection to conduct sample research in a methods course.

When Should I Use Information Technology?

Any effort to introduce innovation into the classroom is fraught with potential difficulties of unknown magnitude, all in pursuit of uncertain rewards. The last thing you want to do as a teacher is to spend hundreds of hours doing web-design for a site students won't use.

In the previous section, we emphasized the importance of articulating your goals in terms of student achievement. Technology is just another tool for enhancing student achievement, so we propose you think about the use of instructional technology as a four-part process.

1. Define your goals. In student-centered terms: what changes (learning or abilities) do I want to see in my students? What teaching/learning problem am I trying to solve.
2. Consider what tools are available (e.g., email, web, newsgroups, chat, multi-media software). Are there institutional resources you can draw upon? Are there resources available on the Internet? What tool will really help my students learn?
3. Define a strategy for integrating technology into the rest of the class. This is the difficult part, and where most instructional technology fails. It's not enough to put up a website. Why would your students visit it? It's not enough to create a course chat room. Who will chat there and why? The motto for technology merely appended to a course seems to be: "If you (just) build it, they won't come." Your integration strategy—how you fit the innovation with your pedagogical objectives and the rest of your course structure—will determine success.
4. Assess how well your strategy has met your goals. Was the effort worth it? Did using this technology increase student learning or motivation?

When you consider the framework above, the answer to the question "When should I use technology in my teaching?" becomes straightforward: whenever it helps you achieve a clear pedagogical goal in a cost-effective way.

How Do I Get Started Using Instructional Technology in My Teaching?

Psychology researchers are often proud of being Jills-of-all trades. Many of our research projects call on a broad spectrum of skills, and we may often have to switch hats from manager, to programmer, to carpenter in a space of an afternoon. It's tempting to bring some of those skills to bear on developing technological solutions to teaching problems. However, the costs of developing teaching technologies from scratch are often prohibitive (in terms of your time). Activities like web-site design may be fun for some of us, but they compete for scarce time with syllabus design, lesson planning, and student contact. Keeping it simple should be a paramount consideration for implementing any technological innovation. Fortunately, many pre-fabricated components for technological solutions are probably already at your disposal. The most important resource should be your college or university. Many universities, and quite a few small colleges have already developed, or are currently developing, ways to support faculty use of IT for teaching.

- Check with your version of Information Technology Services, or Media Initiatives, or Audio-Visual Services to see what kind of help they have available.
- Check for automated tools for placing courses on the web. Our home institution, for example, provides web-browser based construction and management of course web-sites that includes web-page design, materials upload and download, chat, and newsgroups.
- If your institution doesn't have such services yet, ask them to outsource the services, or go through an outside solutions provider yourself (e.g., http://www.blackboard.net/)

Web-Resources

The Internet has placed a panoply of previously esoteric resources at the fingertips of teachers. Many of the best resources are discipline specific, and there is no shortage of those geared specifically for teaching of psychology. Here are a couple of index sites to get you started:

- APS Resources for Teachers of Psychology http://www.psychologicalscience.org/newsresearch/teach.html
- The Society for the Teaching of Psychology http://teachpsych.lemoyne.edu/teachpsych/div/divindex.html

INTRODUCTORY VS. ADVANCED COURSES

This section explores the fundamental differences between introductory and advanced courses, suggests ways that you might best prepare for each, and highlights some traps you may want to avoid.

In psychology, as in other disciplines, there are predictable differences between the approach to introductory and advanced courses in the field. Introductory course enrollments are typically large and therefore courses are taught in a lecture format. The basic goal of the introductory course is to expose students to a breadth of content. Assessment usually involves some kind of objective test with a combination of multiple choice and short answer items. The explicit goal of most introductory courses is to introduce students to basic information and to test their abilities to comprehend it.

Advanced courses, in contrast, are typically small, sometimes very small. The goal is to explore one area of psychology in detail through reading, lecture and discussion. Students are often asked to write papers or design experiments, in other words, to start doing some of the real activities that psychologists do. The goal here is to test for advanced analytical abilities and to give students a more authentic experience in psychology. In this way, these courses may also be designed to socialize students into values and norms of the field.

As a new faculty member, you will likely be assigned to teach some combination of introductory and advanced courses in your very first year. Here are some hints for developing successful courses at each level, and for avoiding common pitfalls.

Teaching Introductory Courses in Psychology

Breadth can be boring, and bored, unmotivated students do not learn much. Boredom has repercussions beyond your class; at many universities, the intro to psychology course is the gateway into the major. And since bored students tend to find other majors, you are doing yourself, your students and your department a big favor if you can find ways to bring Introduction to Psychology to life. Not that teaching an introductory course is all about entertainment—your content still has to be solid, your lectures well-organized, your visuals clear, your assignments well-designed and your tests lucid and fair—but there are special motivational challenges inherent in reaching students at the introductory level. Here are some suggestions:

- Build the course around some big questions that have relevance for students.
- Learn to use small group or paired work exercises in your large lecture course. Break up the lecture and get students working on interesting questions together. This is especially crucial if your class meets for more than 50 minutes at a shot.
- If you have to use objective tests as your primary mode of assessment, try to create on assignment during the semester that allows students to explore their own interests. Even in the big class, find a way to see or acknowledge every student.
- If you are going to lecture, lecture really well. If you don't know how well you lecture, have a colleague or consultant observe you. Once you've mastered the art of delivery, design lectures around the most interesting feature of any chapter. Tell stories. Find a way to demonstrate a concept or give students a chance to experience it.
- Use end-of-class assessment activities and un-graded writing, e.g., two-minutes paper assignments, to help students realize what they have learned in every class.

Teaching Advanced Courses in Psychology

In most academic departments, teaching advanced courses is considered a privilege, and a reward for higher standing in the department. Often, advanced courses will include graduate students as well as advanced undergraduates, and the number of students is often less than 15. In some cases, junior faculty will be allowed to teach a course that is directly related to their research, which, if you are on the tenure track, is an excellent way get students to join your research team.

As a rule, advanced courses are even less structured than introductory courses. This is true for a number of reasons. First, advanced courses are less likely to be taught from a standard textbook, though texts do exists for many advanced topics. Second, as mentioned above, advanced courses are often a direct reflection of the professor's take on the subject or may be build around the interests of the students in the class. Finally, advanced courses are designed to offer students the opportunity to explore a topic in depth and in their own way, which means that students are likely to approach the core topic of the class from a variety of perspectives.

Advanced courses are taught in all types of formats, but for the purpose of this discussion we'll consider the seminar. In a seminar class, students are given a collection of readings for discussion each week. It is understood that each student is working on his or her own paper throughout the semester, and drawing the on readings and discussion when appropriate. Student are often expected to go beyond the assigned readings in the completion of their paper, which is often a long, research paper of over 20 pages in the appropriate journal style.

The advanced seminar is rarely the topic of attention is discussions of teaching, because it is expected that the advanced nature of the students and the material, combined with the individual focus of the work make the seminar "run itself." Contrary to this expectation, most of have participated in seminars that felt dull and unsatisfying. Remember, advanced seminars are extremely important courses, especially when they represent capstone experiences for psychology majors. The challenge is to balance the opportunity for individual exploration, with the creation of a common learning experience. Here are some suggestions.

- Just as you would for any course, have a plan that describes what will be accomplished in the seminar, and how. Describe how intellectual work will progress throughout the term. Prepare strategies for changing the discussion, raising the level of dialogue, and breaking unproductive patters of interaction. Commit to leading the seminar and being responsible for it's success.
- Allow for some individual exploration, but make sure that the group as a whole is dealing with the same material at the same time. The purpose of a seminar is to bring minds together on common questions or problems. If everyone is doing their own thing, there is no common content and no dialogue.
- Set very high standards, make them explicit, and then have the courage to hold everyone to them. This doesn't mean being a tyrant, but it does mean making sure that students adhere to your expectations in their writing and speaking. This means...
- Designing the seminar so that nearly everyone has some direct responsibility for advancing the dialogue, every single day. If all but a few people are coming to seminar unprepared every day, the seminar is not a success.
- Start each meeting with a one-paragraph, ungraded-but-submitted writing assignment on the key question or issue for the day.
- Use student pairs, triads, or groups in the seminar, with responsibility to respond to material each day. Students are less likely to ignore the reading if they know it will disappoint their peers. When a key question or issue emerges in discussion, require everyone to respond.
- Give constant, critical-but-constructive feedback, teach students to do the same, and encourage them to do so. No one wins and no one learns when 30 minutes of unsubstantiated and unclear comments go unquestioned.

MANAGING TEACHING ASSISTANTS

In many ways, the Teaching Assistant (or Teaching Fellow) is a strange creature—his role is rarely well defined. He walks the shadow world between colleague, student, and servant, as all apprentices must. It's the supervising professor who determines, often implicitly, which role a teaching assistant will play. The TA experience is likely to feel servile when TAs aren't allowed to help set goals of courses they help teach (in contrast with collaborative research projects, where graduate students have some input on what project to pursue and how to pursue it), when their roles are unclear, or their tasks menial. For example, TAs commonly feel least satisfied when they grade exams they've had no part in creating and papers they've had no part in assigning. On the other hand, a great relationship between faculty member and TA can be a graduate student's most rewarding experience. Supervising faculty can, and often do, have a profound impact on the lives and careers of their students by introducing them to teaching and the life of an academic.

Just as you may not have received training in undergraduate teaching, you almost certainly had no training in management or mentorship. Here are some strategies to help you become a better manager and mentor for your TAs:

- Make your TAs more engaged and more accountable by involving them in setting goals at various levels.
- Meet with the TAs prior to the beginning of class. Explain your pedagogical goals and ask for their input. If the TAs are teaching sections, ask them to articulate, preferably in writing, what their section will do for the students.
- Involve your TAs in planning the course, the lessons, and the assignments as much as possible. This will not only help you come up with better material, but will also be an invaluable learning experience for the future faculty members under your wing. The more invested each TA feels in the course the more rewarding the work will be. For example, you can have each TA give a guest lecture, then generate exam questions about the guest lecture, and grade the specific questions they've generated.
- Give your TAs more autonomy to run their section as they see fit. Once you have agreed on what the goals of section are, let the TA experiment with means.
- Clarify expectations at the outset. What will the TAs do? What will they be trying to accomplish? How will they be evaluated?
- Give your TAs the support they need to function effectively. Usually this means meeting early and often, especially in the very beginning of the course. It also means keeping track of your end of the course paperwork, and clearly delegating various assignments to different TAs. For example, who will be responsible for compiling all the section grades at the end of the course? A few other ideas:
  - Offer to observe your TA's section to help them become better teachers.
  - If your institution offers TA training and development, require your TAs to avail themselves of the training before teaching your course. Make it your business to let your TAs know about the resources available to them.
  - Effectively delegate grading authority to your TAs, if your TAs are responsible for assigning grades. One of the most frequent and bitter complaints heard from TAs is that the course instructors summarily overrule the TA's grading decisions without consulting the TA. If you feel you have a question about a grading decision, meet with the TA about it. The TA will often have directly relevant information about the grade and the student in question. Remember, the TAs probably know more about the students in their sections than you do.
  - Demand accountability. The consequence of effectively delegating authority to the TAs, for both grading and goal-setting, is that they will feel accountable for the success or failure of their efforts. Once they have set their own goals, and you have given them the support they need, the responsibility rests squarely with the TA.
  - By investing energy in effective delegation you will save time in the long run, develop better mentoring relationships with your TAs, and have a better class. Although

the rewards are large, successful delegation is difficult. Consider that you must be emotionally prepared to give the members of your team the freedom to fail, as well as succeed.

CONCLUSION

We hope this short introduction to teaching will help you navigate the uncertain waterways towards establishing yourself as a classroom teacher. The first years are important, but don't be discouraged if they don't go well. Keep trying new things and asking for help. We've seen great teachers emerge after years of average performance. As a faculty member, teaching will be a big part of your life, so it's important to figure out how to do it well and also how to enjoy it. We've only scratched the surface in this chapter. Here are some additional resources:

- You Campus Teaching Center. Chances are your campus has a teaching center with consultants who can help you define goals, think of strategies for meeting those goals, and observe your teaching. There, you are also likely to find a library of books on teaching, and access to a network of people on campus who can give you advice.
- The American Psychological Association http://www.apa.org/
  Type "teaching" into the search box for the latest articles on teaching in psychology
- APS Resources for Teachers of Psychology http://www.psychologicalscience.org/newsresearch/teach.html
- The Society for the Teaching of Psychology
  http://teachpsych.lemoyne.edu/teachpsych/div/divindex.html

REFERENCES

McKeachie, W. J. (1999). *Teaching tips: Strategies, research and theory for college and university teachers* (10th ed.) Boston, MA: Houghton Mifflin.

Upcraft, M. L. (1996). Teaching and today's college students. In Robert J. Menges and Maryellen Weimer and Associates, *Teaching on Solid Ground*. San Francisco: Jossey-Bass.

CHAPTER 9

Proposing and Completing Your Dissertation

KATHLEEN MALLEY-MORRISON, MARCUS PATTERSON, AND LIANG YAP

INTRODUCTION

The dissertation is the oldest consistent requirement for becoming a doctor in most academic disciplines in the United States. The dissertation, which has its roots in the 19th Century German educational system, is the central requisite for the highest level of educational attainment, the doctor of philosophy (Rosenberg, 1962). It is distinguished from pedagogical training, which happens at earlier stages in the educational process, and is the formal demonstration that a student has attained the skills necessary to independently produce relevant scientific research and scholarship. In the United States, the dissertation was first adopted as a requirement for the doctorate by Yale University in 1861 (Furniss, 1965) and quickly became the central exposition in the passage from student to doctor for most academic disciplines in most universities. Within psychology, completion of the dissertation has been central to training at the doctoral level since the Ph.D. degree was first granted to G. Stanley Hall in 1878 (Street, 1994). This requirement is common to most doctoral psychology students and, in that sense, might be seen as the unifying or binding activity for doctorial training in our field. In its most recent survey, the US Department of Education (2000) found that 46,010 doctoral degrees were granted in 1998. Almost 10% of those degrees (4,073) were Ph.D.s in psychology.

As it was originally introduced, the dissertation was to be an "original research project" that "clearly extended the boundaries of knowledge in one's discipline" (Olson & Drew, 1998, p. 57). Thus, it is crucial to the development and growth of a discipline and is not simply a rite of passage or means of evaluating the student. This tradition has continued, as is evident in the policy statement on The Role and Nature of the Doctoral Dissertation by the Council of Graduate Schools (1991). According to the Council, the dissertation serves two important functions: 1) "the successful completion of [professional training] demonstrates the candidate's ability to

KATHLEEN MALLEY-MORRISON AND MARCUS PATTERSON • Department of Psychology, Boston University, Boston, MA 02215
LIANG YAP • Department of Neurology, Massachusetts General Hospital, Boston MA 02114

address a major intellectual problem and arrive at a successful conclusion independently and at a high level of professional competence and 2) its results constitute an original contribution to knowledge in the field" (p. 21).

In psychology, the dissertation has typically been an empirical study—for example, with either an experimental or correlational design. In research programs, this empirical requirement has been almost universal, although there has been some variation within programs in clinical psychology. The scientist-practitioner model focused on the integration of research into clinical practice and promoted an empirical model of research (Raimy, 1950). More recently, the Vail Conference suggested that professionals should be educated consumers of the scientific research, but not necessarily scientists themselves, taking the emphasis off empirical research for the dissertation (Sanchez-Hucles & Cash, 1992). A survey of Vail-model programs revealed that 90% required a dissertation, but only 25% required that the dissertation be an empirical study. Interestingly, 66% of students in these programs completed an empirical dissertation, while 34% selected a non-empirical approach (Sanchez-Hucles & Cash, 1992). Non-empirical approaches include survey research, clinical projects, theoretical papers, case studies, literature reviews and phenomenological studies. While empirical studies are the most common and most commonly accepted designs for the dissertations in psychology (Shemberg, Keeley, & Blum, 1989), some students may undertake non-empirical research. The suggestions that follow will focus mainly on empirical designs, but will be useful for those working on all types of dissertations designs.

One of the first critical questions that many students face in the quest for a dissertation topic is who will ultimately be the dissertation advisor. The way this question is answered is of crucial importance because strong supervisory relationships are associated with timely completion of the degree (Muszynski & Akamatsu, 1991). For some, this question is answered prior to or as part of the process of admission to graduate school. For others, selecting a professor to work with may be seen as part of the doctoral educational process itself.

Graduate programs vary in the extent to which they admit students with the understanding or obligation to work with specific faculty members. On one end of the spectrum are programs that take an apprenticeship or mentoring approach. These programs typically accept students specifically to work with a particular professor. The student's financial support may or may not be tied to the professor's grant funding and the student is admitted with the understanding that s/he will be working with a particular professor from the outset of his/her training and often through to the dissertation.

In these programs, students are likely to be talking with their mentor and exploring ways of building on or extending that mentor's research from the beginning of their training. To publish a dissertation growing out of this process in an American Psychological Association journal, the student must have made "a primary contribution to and hold primary responsibility for the data concepts, and interpretation of results"—which is a requirement for authorship on any article submitted to an American Psychological Association Journal (American Psychological Association, 2001, p. 6). This can be a challenge in a competitive academic program with well-developed, mentoring programs.

It will be important for students in these and other programs to be clear about their own role in and contribution to the project (as well as their mentor's role and contribution), so that conflicts about the ownership of the data or authorship issues do not arise later on. It is important to define these boundaries at the outset of the project, because it will be increasingly difficult to do this once the project is underway. Such issues might be resolved when one writes an IRB proposal, as the primary author. One may also want to draw up a contract outlining roles and responsibilities in the project. While this might seem overly formal, it will help to ensure clear roles and responsibilities.

On the other end of the spectrum are less "structured" programs in which it is the student's responsibility to find an advisor. In such departments, students may have the option of choosing among several professors and may make their own connections in selecting a dissertation advisor, often through their coursework or research work. Students in these programs have less guidance in determining whom they can work with and what they can propose, but may have a wider array of options available to them. Taking advantage of this flexibility, which helps both student and faculty member determine with whom they are most compatible and with whom they work best, is often the best approach to finding a mentor (Zachary, 2000). Additionally, it is important for the student to determine which faculty members are willing and able to take on the responsibility for supervising another doctoral dissertation.

In all programs, the groundwork for writing a dissertation begins the first day of graduate school. Students are expected to pass certain milestones prior to undertaking work on the dissertation. These can include completing coursework, passing qualifying or comprehensive examinations, passing a language examination, and participating in professional training activities (including working in clinical practica, presenting at research conferences, and engaging in research). These activities are not only preparation for the dissertation but can also be steps toward writing the dissertation. Alternatively, they can be impediments to this process. In this context, it is important to try to integrate the dissertation into one's training, to make it relevant to one's interests and goals, and to make it part of a "logical" progression toward the completion of the dissertation. Otherwise, requirements can become stumbling blocks—that is, "discontinuities in training" that can delay progress toward completion of the dissertation and, ultimately, graduation (Marshall, 1993).

THE GOAL OF THE DISSERTATION

While it might seem premature, the objective of the dissertation is often closely tied to one's career goals. There are obviously many paths that one can follow and these will be closely tied to the form one's dissertation project takes. The dissertation might be preparation for a career as a practitioner, as a professor in a two-year or four-year college or as an academic, among other possibilities.

Students aiming for a practice career have specific considerations and constraints. If they are not intending ultimately to do independent, empirical research, they may want to select a project that is going to have relevance to their clinical work—that is, a project that has relevance to real-world clinical practice. Such students may also be open to alternatives to the traditional empirical dissertation, such as the non-empirical methodologies mentioned above. [Some have suggested that alternatives to the traditional dissertation might be more useful for students interested in professional practice (Porter & Wolfle, 1975)].

Graduate students whose goal is to teach in an undergraduate institution might have more flexibility in selecting their dissertation topic and their topic may be less tied to their career choice. Being skilled in research topics and methodologies taught to undergraduates may be more important for becoming an attractive candidate for such positions, than the topic of the dissertation itself.

Students aiming for a career in psychological research, either in a university or applied setting, will want to choose a topic which has the potential to make a significant contribution to the field. Dissertations that produce promising results and that are continued after graduation are associated with high levels of scientific output over the span of one's career (Porter & Wolfle, 1975). Thus, a dissertation that is likely to yield promising results and has the potential to lead to a series of studies is best for individuals aiming for a lifetime, research career.

Students aiming for a research career will want to select a topic that will provide a foundation for a job talk. Such a talk should demonstrate: a mastery of the relevant literature, the ability to identify and design a study around an important issue, methodological expertise, knowledge of multivariate statistics, and promising and provocative results. It is also valuable to have a sufficiently rich set of findings for several publications. For all students, the completion of the dissertation should be the top priority, since making this a priority is predictive of time to completion (Muszynski & Akamatsu, 1991).

CONSIDERATIONS IN CHOOSING A DISSERTATION COMMITTEE

If you are expected to find your own dissertation advisor ("First Reader"), as well as the rest of your dissertation committee (typically at least three members), there are a number of useful guidelines to follow:

- Talk to students working with faculty members whose research interests you. Determine which of these faculty members are likely to be both available and helpful. These qualities in a supervisor have been associated with successful completion of the dissertation (Dewey, 2002). Also determine whose students graduate in a timely fashion (and whose do not).
- Consider the match between your personal styles. Finding a compatible supervisor is of critical importance, since a strong advisor/advisee relationship has been related to timely completion of the dissertation (Muszynski & Akamatsu, 1991). One stylistic consideration might be whether your mentor expects you to work closely with him/her or to work independently.
- Consider the standing of faculty within the program. Faculty members who are untenured, or about to move or retire present obvious issues. Newer, untenured faculty may become personally or overly invested in your project.
- Consider the resources that you might need to complete your project and which faculty members can offer these.
- Consider your goals beyond completing your Ph.D. If you wish to continue working on scholarly research, you might want to consider which faculty might make long-term collaborators, individuals with whom you can write grants and develop joint programs of research.

Once you've selected your advisor, you will need to begin assembling the rest of your committee. Advanced graduate students should work closely with their dissertation supervisors in choosing the committee. It is important to have a well-matched and harmonious committee, since this will provide the most supportive and consistent environment for the difficult task ahead. Your advisor is likely to have some insight into how to accomplish this. One should obviously avoid selecting members who have personal conflicts or who are highly critical of one another's work. One should also be cautious about selecting two faculty members of very different orientations, since they may make incompatible demands. In selecting the committee, you may want to keep the following considerations in mind: 1) It is often helpful to have at least one member of the committee be knowledgeable in statistics. 2) If the research is designed to bridge a gap between two somewhat disparate areas, it will be very important to have a committee member who is an expert in each area. 3) Many students have opportunities for clinical or field research experiences outside of their department. As a way of adding someone with a specific background or area of expertise, students may want to invite "external" professionals to be part of the dissertation committee. 4) There are risks associated with having an outside reader on the dissertation committee—especially if s/he is a First Reader.

If you are interested in asking an outside person to serve on your committee, there are a number of useful steps to follow:

- First, determine whether your department allows "outside" professionals to be committee members and, if relevant, to be First Readers.
- Determine whether the potential "outside reader" has ever served as a First Reader or dissertation committee member in your department and whether s/he knows how the dissertation hearing and evaluation process works in your department. This is important because there can be considerable variation in this procedure among departments.
- If it is permissible to have an outside reader, determine whether this professional has ever been a First Reader on a dissertation examination committee. The First Reader's name goes right after the student's name on the dissertation abstract that is submitted to "Dissertation Abstracts International." Consequently, one may want to consider whether this person will be recognized as someone who has done relevant research in the area.
- Determine whether s/he will have the time to provide close, ongoing supervision of doctoral work. This is important because s/he will likely not be paid or will be paid a nominal sum for his/her work with you.

There are other practical issues to consider when selecting a dissertation committee. You should determine whether any of the potential members are due for a sabbatical, tenure-review, or retirement around the time the dissertation will be completed. If so, this could interfere with the kind of supervision or guidance that would be needed from them. It could also hinder the process if there were difficulties communicating with or reaching your committee members.

CHOOSING A TOPIC

Topics often start with a question about some psychological phenomenon—for example, about group differences on some interesting characteristic, or the causes of some kind of behavior, or the outcomes of particular experiences, or the correlates of some aspect of personality. It may be a vague question that piques your curiosity or it may be a specific question that no one seems to have an adequate or definitive answer for. It is often suggested that topics emerge from areas of interest that have already developed. While this may be true in part, an area of interest is often too vague to provide a specific topic.

There are some pitfalls to avoid when choosing a topic for a dissertation. One should resist being too suggestible or so open to different possible topics that one appears overly eager to finish and indiscriminate in the selection of a topic. The danger in a lack of selectivity is that topics that are pursued without being of interest to the graduate student have been associated with delay in completion of the degree (Muszynski & Akamatsu, 1991). The contrasting pitfall is to search for the "perfect" project, one that will revolutionize the field. The danger in this is that one will never settle on a topic and never complete the degree.

In selecting a topic of study, clinical students have the added consideration of whether to chose a laboratory analogue study versus treatment outcome study. Treatment studies have been associated with delays in completion of the degree, so this is something to consider when choosing the type of study (Muszynski & Akamatsu, 1991).

REVIEWING PRIOR RESEARCH

The first step in the development of a doctoral prospectus is an extensive review of the relevant literature. You conduct your review in order to arrive at the relevant hypotheses. It is important to remember that hypotheses for a research project must always be derived from the available conceptual and/or empirical literature. In the course of your literature review, you may discover that the question of interest to you has already been adequately addressed or addressed in the particular way that you envisioned. If so, this discovery can become a spur to developing a better-focused or more sophisticated question that builds upon previous research. Alternatively, the most productive approach may be to abandon the original idea for another topic altogether. Your review may also convince you that the current state of the relevant research is murky in ways that would be difficult to resolve. This may be due to the fact that your topic or question has been poorly constructed (and needs to be revised) or to the fact that there is simply very little or no relevant research on it. One of the pitfalls in selecting a topic is that people often choose obscure topics in an effort to ensure creativity or originality. The danger is that there will be very little literature to build on (and, therefore, the review will be on loose conceptual ground) and obscurity will not ensure creativity.

The fact that your hypotheses must be derived from a critical review of literature does not mean that you cannot study a novel topic; you just need to ensure that your investigation is based on materials worthy of such a review. An adequate dissertation prospectus must show your intellectual competence, your competence in conducting a circumspect and critical review of literature, and your ability to build on previous work.

HOW TO WRITE A PROPOSAL

As noted, the process of developing a dissertation prospectus generally begins with a research question. In some cases, a research project is designed to answer research questions. In other cases, the research is designed to test specific, operationalized hypotheses. In both cases, the final research questions or hypotheses are derived from and based upon a critical review of the literature. This critical review is the first major section of a dissertation prospectus.

The review of literature that is needed for a doctoral prospectus may be the most extensive review you ever undertake. If the dissertation is the first step in the development of a major research program, the critical review is the conceptual and empirical foundation on which a whole series of studies may be built. There are two major dangers to avoid in undertaking this review: 1) surveying the literature too broadly, and 2) focusing too narrowly. Sometimes researchers believe that they must so thoroughly investigate the literature on every variable they find in their reading that is related in any way to their major constructs of interest that they never feel confident that they have developed an adequate basis for their research. In other cases, they focus so narrowly on the few studies that seem to provide the most direct rationale for their own study that they betray a lack of general and contextual knowledge.

To do a successful critical review of the literature, it is essential to be organized and efficient. Here are some tips:

- You do not take notes on every article you find.
- Make duplicate copies of the abstracts you find useful.
- Organize those abstracts into piles thematically. Those piles may end up yielding the organizational structure of your review.

- Make a summary table of the findings of the articles that are most directly related to the issue you are pursuing. Such a table is particularly useful when there are discrepancies among the findings of the studies being reviewed.
- Develop a conceptual model, in diagrammatic form, showing the relationships you expect among variables. If appropriate, map the predictor variables, outcome variables, and mediator and/or moderator variables into an integrated system, identifying the positive and negative associations you expect among the variables and the possible role of any intervening variables between your predictors and your outcomes.

The American Psychological Publication Manual (2001) is helpful in this process. If the review is developed effectively, it will lead readers to anticipate the final set of unresolved questions or knowledge-advancing hypotheses and find them compelling.

For the second major section, the method section, you should conduct a power analysis to determine the sample size necessary for the study. Sources are available online that will calculate power based on the number of variables, and the strength of the correlation or difference that is desired. Other, useful sources include Cohen (1988) and Wilkinson (1999). If you are working with humans or animals, you will need to describe the steps to conform to the ethical guidelines of the APA (see Sales & Folkman, 2000) as well as of the National Institute of Health.

Ensuring the adequacy and appropriateness of the proposed analyses may require consultation, which is why it is important to have someone knowledgeable in statistics on the committee. To test a hypothesis about group differences, be sure to make reference to a group difference statistical test like analysis of variance. To determine the relative contribution of a number of different variables to some outcome, make reference to a procedure such as multiple regression or discriminant function analysis.

PROPOSING THE DISSERTATION

Each Ph.D. program has its own specific procedures and guidelines for the proposal of the doctoral dissertation. As already noted, the dissertation prospectus will most likely have a) an empirical literature review section leading up to research questions and/or hypotheses, b) methods and procedures for conducting the research, and c) proposed statistical methods for data analyses. It is useful to work closely with the dissertation committee members during the prospectus development process to ensure that the Institutional Review Boards at your department or university are likely to approve your research methods and procedures, and that things will go smoothly during the prospectus hearing.

The prospectus itself might be viewed as an agreement one makes with oneself and one's committee as to how the dissertation project shall proceed. It is important to have everyone's agreement that it shall progress in this way. The prospectus is also like a road map that one will follow. It is particularly important that this map be clearly laid out in the beginning. Planning for the prospectus and fidelity to it have both been linked to successful completion of the dissertation (Dewey, 2002).

Some aspects of the preparation for the prospectus hearing are intimidating to student. Often the faculty who attend the hearing are not interested in the details of the review of literature. They will focus on practical issues—for example, what you plan to do, how you plan to do it, why you plan to do it that way, and what you expect to find. They may have questions like "What will you do if you can't recruit enough participants by the methods you've proposed?" Or, "If you plan to see participants more than once, how will you reduce attrition?" Or, "If you are going to perform an experiment, how will you control for static due to....?" "How will you make your deception convincing?" The best way to prepare for this interrogation is to practice it with some fellow graduate students, especially ones who have already been through the process. In addition, if prospectus hearings in your department are open to everyone, it's advisable to attend one or two of them before facing your own.

Do also refer to your graduate department's guidelines for the most up-to-date information with regard to the dissertation style and format, and all the academic and residency requirements for the degree. These guidelines are usually accessible via the department's home pages on the Internet. An example of a useful schedule for the proposal and timely completion of your dissertation requirements can be found under "Creating a Timeline for Completion of the Dissertation."

RESOURCES AVAILABLE TO FUND DISSERTATION, TO GATHER AND ENTER DATA

An important practical question to keep in mind when reviewing the literature and developing the prospectus is whether the research can be done with little or no financial support. Some researchers complete their dissertations without using any funds but their own, but seeking financial support for the research can be desirable for a number of reasons:

- Financial support has been linked to timely and successful completion of the dissertation (Peacock, 1996; Dewey, 2002).
- The very process of applying for funds provides experience in writing grant proposals, which is a marketable skill in the world of academia.
- If the application for funding is successful, it may then be possible to conduct a better and more sophisticated study than could have been done without it.
- If the application is successful, you will gain invaluable experience in grant management.
- Listing grant support on a C.V. is an accomplishment, and improves one's chances for a post-doctoral fellowship and/or academic position.

Funding is available from a variety of sources. Most if not all universities have an office that provides supportive services to members of the university community seeking external funding. Often called a "Grants and Contracts Office" or a "Sponsored Programs Office," this office may be willing to send a representative to the department to explain their functioning to junior faculty and graduate students. Your First Reader or department chair can often provide some advice about contacting helpful people in that office.

Much of the information you will need about sources of funding is available over the Internet. Your sponsored programs office may have its own website where information is posted about fellowships, grants, contracts, and other types of awards. There are also a number of excellent websites that can be accessed by anyone. The Community of Science, Inc. (http://fundingopps2.cos.com) has hundreds of listings for sources of support for research in psychology. Graduate students are eligible for many of these awards. The information provided on this website includes: the name of the awarding agency, amount of award, purpose of award, eligibility information, submission requirements, deadlines, and contact persons.

There are awards to support a variety of activities related to the dissertation, including direct support for dissertation research, support for completed dissertations, travel funds to conferences (to present dissertation research), support for students with disabilities, support based on economic need and support for students of particular ethnic backgrounds. Recent offerings have included the following types and sources of support, with no citizenship requirements:

- International Dissertation Field Research Fellowships from the Social Science Research Council (SSRC)—USA, which will provide support for 9 to 12 months of field research and related expenses. The Council has particular interests in proposals that identify the United States as a case for comparative studies.
- Henry A. Murray Dissertation Awards of up to $2,500, sponsored by the Henry A. Murray Research Center at the Radcliffe Institute for Advanced Study at Harvard University, for dissertations on some aspect of "the study of lives," with a focus on issues in human development or personality for populations within the United States.
- Social Issues Dissertation Awards of $600 and $400, from the Society for the Psychological Study of Social Issues (SPSSI).

Another website with information about sources of funding in psychology is: http://www.lib.msu.edu/harris23/grants/3psych.htm. This website lists lots of links for sources that provide various types of funding for graduate students, including the American Psychological Association and the American Academy of Child and Adolescent Psychiatry. Some of these funding/awards are intended primarily for minority students.

The websites of professional organizations and foundations such as those listed below are also excellent resources for grants and awards for graduate students:

- American Psychological Association
  http://www.apa.org/ed/grants.html
- American Psychological Society
  http://www.psychologicalscience.org/apssc/default.cfm
- National Science Foundation
  http://www.nsf.gov/home/students/start.htm#grad
- Psi Chi: National Honor Society in Psychology
  http://www.psichiorg.content/awards/home.asp

GETTING STARTED

Once you have obtained formal approval from your dissertation prospectus hearing committee to begin your research, you should commence gathering your data in a systematic and efficient manner. While data-gathering methods will vary as a function of the research hypotheses and types of studies (e.g., field experiments, archival research, interviews, surveys, etc . . .) being conducted, you should devise a log. This log should keep track of participants and their demographics, procedures administered, and whether the data have been fully collected and entered into the computer. In cases where monetary (or other) compensation is involved, record whether or not participants have acknowledged receipt of such compensation. To ensure confidentiality regarding participants (where relevant), separate and/or remove all forms of identification (e.g., their informed consent forms) from the data. However, if you are intending to conduct a follow-up study as part of or following your dissertation research, be sure to have a way of tracking participants and matching their later responses with their earlier responses.

TABLE 1. Common Myths (and Realities) about the Ph.D. Dissertation

Myth 1. You must read every article on your subject matter.
Reality. You will probably not be able to do this, but in the course of your reviews, you will encounter most relevant articles. Main point: do not use perfectionism as an excuse to avoid beginning the research!
Myth 2. You should not pursue a topic unless there is the potential for making a revolutionary discovery.
Reality. You cannot know this from the outset. Again, consider whether this pursuit is an avoidance strategy.
Myth 3. You must include every variable found to relate to your major constructs.
Reality—(see above)
Myth 4. The dissertation will determine your entire future in the field.
Reality. This is one of many determinants, but not the only one and sometimes not the most important one.
Myth 5. A dissertation has to be a tome with the heft of a first novel.
Reality. There is always debate about the acceptable page limit to the dissertation. In their survey of 100 dissertations in psychology, Cone and Foster (1993) found that the length of the dissertation ranged between 59 to 679 pages with a median page length of 174.
Myth 6. A dissertation will differ from your previous studies only in length.
Reality. As suggested earlier, the dissertation is meant to be a significant and original contribution to the field and is being overseen by a committee of experts.

The American Psychological Association has two truly excellent books on multivariate statistics—Reading and Understanding Multivariate Statistics (Grimm & Yarnold, 1995) and Reading and Understanding More Multivariate Statistics (Grimm & Yarnold, 2000).

CREATING A TIMELINE FOR COMPLETION OF THE DISSERTATION

Creating a timeline and then remaining faithful to it is important for successful completion of the dissertation. Time-management skills will need to be brought to bear on this project, since the project is likely to be the most important and most time-consuming project that has ever been under your control.

Unpleasant truth #1: Completing a dissertation is likely to be more difficult than you think, even if you are someone who finishes papers easily. This is much more comprehensive and involves many variables, some of which are not in your control. Also, your supervisor, your department chair, your graduate school dean, your university president all consider it important not to award Ph.D.s in the name of your university on the basis of dissertations that are not of top quality. The reputation of your department and your university is at stake with every doctoral dissertation, so the review process is usually rigorous.

Unpleasant truth #2: Completing a dissertation is going to take longer than you think. Steps in the process vary across universities and departmental programs, but typically, you will have to develop a critical review of the scholarly literature first. At many universities, it may be expected that this review will itself be publishable in a professional journal such as the Psychological Bulletin. If this is true at your university, it is a good idea to start by reading a number of Psychological Bulletin articles that were based on reviews of literature for doctoral dissertations. Read the footnotes at the beginning of articles in these journals—they will indicate whether the review was part of a dissertation.

A typical next step will be the development and formal submission of the dissertation prospectus—the proposal for the research you want to do, including the critical review of literature and proposed methods for examining research questions and/or testing hypotheses. During (or even before) the development of your prospectus, you should create a timeline to

TABLE 2. Suggested Timeline for Dissertation Defense

Departmental Requirements	Target Semester/Date for Completion
Required Courses (e.g., statistics)	
Electives	
Qualifying Examination	
Petition for Ph.D. Candidacy	
Prospectus Hearing	
Institutional Review Board Approval	
Data-Collection Timeframe	
Data-Analyses Timeframe	
Dissertation Write-up (1st Draft)	
Dissertation Write-up (2nd Draft)	
Dissertation-Final Draft	
Dissertation Defense-1st Practice	
Dissertation Defense-2nd Practice	
Actual Dissertation Defense	
Submission of Dissertation Approval Forms to Graduate School	
(Clinical Training/Practica)	
Other(s)	

reassure yourself that all your departmental requirements have been met, and for setting target dates ensuring a timely progress towards your dissertation defense. An example of such a schedule is provided in Table 2.

One consideration for clinical students is whether to complete the dissertation before internship. The concerns are that the students will not complete the dissertation after internship and that they will be distracted by it while on internship. While only 20% of all interns start the year with their dissertations complete (Krieshok, et. al. 2000), programs are increasingly making it a requirement that students finish prior to internship. Student who have completed proposals make more progress on the dissertation than students at the pre-proposal stage (Krieshok, et. al. 2000). So it seems that clinical students should consider at least proposing their prospectus prior to embarking on internship.

WRITING THE DISSERTATION

To complete your dissertation in a timely fashion, there are a number of steps that can be helpful.

- Create a data set, with variable labels, at the beginning of the data collection process and enter your data as you go along.
- If you revise your methodology revise the methods section of your proposal (which is now evolving into your dissertation) immediately.
- If your institution restricts the length of the prospectus, begin adding material into your review of literature to provide a broader basis for your study that will then be used in the actual dissertation.
- When all the data are collected, begin the initial data analysis right away.
- When the data are all entered into the computer, calculate your descriptive statistics before taking on the task of testing your hypotheses.

- Once you are familiar with your own data and have debugged the study, you are ready to start addressing your research questions and/or testing your hypotheses.

Typically, most of your readers, except perhaps the statistician, will want to wait until you have debugged the study, and have a completed write-up of your results, approved by your first reader, before they look at it. There will be variations across committees, depending on the personalities and policies, but typically most readers will not be asked to deal with the same rough and incomplete draft at the same time.

Typically, your first reader will indicate when the dissertation draft is ready for perusal by the other committee members. They in turn will make their suggestions. Sometimes there will be differences among committee members about whether you've done all the necessary analyses, written them up adequately, and interpreted them convincingly. If you and your first reader have chosen your committee wisely, these differences should be worked through fairly efficiently. You will know that you are close to scheduling a final doctoral oral when your committee agrees that your draft is ready to be defended.

PREPARING FOR THE DISSERTATION DEFENSE

It is wise to start early to prepare for the dissertation defense. One way to do this is to present and defend your work in a variety of settings to a variety of audiences. You can practice in front of a research group and present aspects of your data (preliminary findings) at colloquia or at professional meetings. By the time you defend your dissertation, you should be comfortable presenting research in your field. But don't let that experience make you overconfident: As the time for your dissertation defense approaches, practice your presentation in front of a group of fellow graduate students. Ask them to question you critically. Brainstorm the issues that seem likely to surface during the actual dissertation defense, and make sure that you know your responses to such inquiries.

Table 3 provides examples of the kinds of questions that could be asked at a dissertation orals.

As the date of your actual dissertation defense draws near, garner social support in preparation for the defense. You should actually utilize social support throughout the dissertation process since this is an important predictor of timely completion of the dissertation (Peacock, 1996), but this will be acutely important as the defense date nears. Self-care strategies may also be particularly important in days and weeks just before the defense to avoid being "burned-out" on the day. Contact your committee members about a week in advance of your hearing to confirm with them the time, date, and venue of your doctoral defense.

TABLE 3. Sample Questions for a Dissertation Oral Examination

1. Why do you think you did not get full support for your hypothesis that.... ?
2. Did you consider broadening your sample to include..... ?
3. Why did you decide to develop your own measure of... ?
4. What do you think would have happened if you had analyzed your data separately by gender?
5. What evidence do you have that your experimental manipulation was successful?
6. If you were going to do the study over again, what would you do differently?
7. Based on your findings, what do you think of X's theory that.... ?
8. If you were at a cocktail party and wanted to tell a lay person about your findings, what would you tell them in a sentence or two about the most important thing you found.

After you have successfully passed your hearing, it is likely that you will still need to do a little work. Dissertation committee will often ask you to make revisions. These are usually minor and somewhat predictable. In less pleasant situations, committee members may ask you to make more extensive changes. This can happen if your advisor did not read closely enough or if a committee member "discovers" something that s/he previously missed. It is a rare event, but less traumatic if one is aware that it can happen. Also, this is another unforeseen event that can arise to delay graduation. Once revisions are complete, you will need to prepare your dissertation for submission to your graduate school and library. (See below.)

PUBLISHING YOUR DISSERTATION

In past, publishing the dissertation was a requirement for receiving the Ph.D. University presses and Microfilm both originated as vehicles to publish dissertations (Olson & Drew, 1998). University presses are no longer readily available as outlets for the new Ph.D. and s/he must seek other means of publishing part or all of the dissertation. Because of the nature of the Ph.D. in psychology, it is most likely that it will be published in a scientific journal and not as a complete book. This constraint has both advantages and drawbacks. Although it may provide an opportunity to derive several publishable articles from the same project, the readers do not get to see the entire study in all its richness and possible complexity.

In publishing the dissertation, one must first consider what the best source will be. In performing literature searches for term papers and for the dissertation, you will become familiar with the range of professional journals that are available in the various sub-fields of psychology. In choosing a suitable journal to submit your dissertation, you can consult the literature that you have cited in your own dissertation for ideas as to where to submit your findings. Consider which journals you cited most often and which journals are publishing studies similar to yours. When you have chosen a professional journal, check and follow its "guidelines for submission" in submitting your prepared manuscript.

AFTER THE DISSERTATION DEFENSE

The period after the successful defense of a doctoral dissertation is typically spent editing and revising the manuscript in accordance with feedback from the dissertation committee and the stylistic/formatting requirements of the University's Graduate School Office. Usually appointments must be made with an Academic Records Officer of the Graduate School before and/or after the dissertation defense for a thorough review of the carefully-prepared manuscript.

To preserve a record of the doctoral candidate's scholarly achievement and to disseminate his or her research findings to the academic community, copies of each approved dissertation are usually submitted to the University's library for archival records and circulation purposes. In addition, it is also common practice on the part of the University libraries to have each dissertation microfilmed for global distribution through University Microfilms International (UMI). Do ensure that the edited dissertation manuscripts that are presented to the University's library have been proof-read for errors, as manuscripts are usually microfilmed by UMI without any further editing (with the exception of copyrighted materials included in the manuscripts). As literature search-engines such as Dissertation Abstracts International locate manuscripts based on key words and phrases used in each manuscript's title and abstract, particular attention should be paid to the wordings of these items so that scholars and researchers are able to determine the main contents and frameworks of each retrieved manuscript.

GETTING THE DISSERTATION BOUND AND OBTAINING COPYRIGHTS

Each University's library or Graduate School Office has its own procedures for assisting with the binding of dissertation manuscripts. UMI usually provides a one-time publication discount offer for candidates at the time when manuscripts are submitted, and candidates may therefore wish to take the opportunity to obtain additional bound copies of their manuscripts for their personal and professional usage.

For a nominal fee, UMI can also assist with the registration of copyrights of manuscripts at the time a candidate submits the dissertation to the University's library or Graduate School Office. If a candidate wishes to secure copyrights for the dissertation manuscript at a future date, he or she can obtain further information from the Register of Copyrights, U.S. Copyright Office, Library of Congress, Washington, DC 20559.

There are a few remaining details that one will need to attend to prior to publication. These may include: meeting deadlines to submit dissertation manuscripts (check with the University's Library and Graduate School Office for this); determining the number of unbound copies of the dissertation manuscript that are needed for submission; ascertaining that the type of quality paper used for the manuscripts is in compliance with the university's guidelines; reviewing format and style of dissertation manuscripts with Academic Record Officer of the Graduate School Office; and obtaining permission from the proper authorities for any copyrighted material.

CONCLUSION

The road from being a Ph.D. graduate student in psychology to a newly-minted Ph.D. psychologist is full of unexpected intellectual discoveries, frustrations, pitfalls, and immeasurable rewards. It is a journey that will test your persistence and patience in the face of uncertainties and ambiguity, but its ultimate reward is one of intellectual fulfillment and pride in attaining the highest academic and professional degree in psychology and as one's first substantive, scientific contribution in an emerging career.

REFERENCES

American Psychological Association (2001). Publication manual of the American Psychological Association (5th ed.). Washington, D.C.: Author.

Cohen, J. (1988). *Statistical power analysis for the behavioral sciences* (2nd ed.) Hillsdale, NJ: Erlbaum.

Cone, J. D., & Foster, S. L. (1993). *Dissertations and theses from start to finish: Psychology and related fields.* Washington, DC: American Psychological Association.

Council of Graduate Schools (1991). *The role and nature of the doctoral dissertation: A policy statement* [Electronic version]. Retrieved July 15, 2002, from http://www.cgsnet.org/PublicationsPolicyRes/role.htm

Dewey, M. (2002). Medical dissertation: differences between successful and aborted research projects. *Deutsch Medikal Wochenschrift, 127*, 1307–1311.

Furniss, E. S. (1965). *The graduate school of Yale: A brief history*. New Haven: Carl Pruington Printing.

Grimm, L. G., & Yarnold, P. R. (Eds.) (1995). *Reading and understanding multivariate statistics*. Washington, D.C.: American Psychological Association.

Grimm, L. G., & Yarnold, P. R. (Eds.) (2000). *Reading and understanding more multivariate statistics*. Washington, D.C.: American Psychological Association.

Krieshok, T. S., Lopez, S. J., Somberg, D. R., & Cantrell, P. J. (2000). Dissertation while on internship: Obstacles and predictors of progress. *Professional Psychology: Research and Practice, 31*, 327–331.

Marshall, W. L. (1993). Anachronistic obstacles to effective training in research: The dissertation, the thesis, and the comprehensive examination. *Canadian Psychology, 34*, 176–183.

Muszynski, S. Y., & Akamatsu, T. J. (1991). Delay in completion of doctoral dissertations in clinical psychology. *Professional Psychology: Research and Practice, 22*, 119–123.

Olson, G. A., & Drew, J. (1998). (Re)Reenvisioning the dissertation in English studies. *College English, 61*, 56–66.

Peacock, S. Y. (1996). The timely completion of the dissertation. *Dissertation Abstracts International Section A: Humanities and Social Sciences, 56*, 3474.

Porter, A. L., & Wolfle, D. (1975). Utility of the doctoral dissertation. *American Psychologist, 30*, 1054–1061.

Raimy, V. C. (Ed.) (1950). *Training in clinical psychology*. New York: Prentice Hall.

Rosenberg, R. P. (1962). Eugene Schuyler's Doctor of Philosophy Degree: A theory concerning the dissertation. *Journal of Higher Education, 33*, 381–386.

Sales, B. D., & Folkman, S. (2000). *Ethics in research with human subjects*. Washington, D.C.: American Psychological Association.

Sanchez-Hucles, J., & Cash, T. R. (1992). The dissertation in professional psychology programs: 1. A survey of clinical directors on requirements and practices. *Professional Psychology: Research and Practice, 23*, 59–62.

Shemberg, K., Keeley, S. M., & Blum, M. (1989). Attitudes toward traditional and nontraditional dissertation research? Survey of directors of clinical training. *Professional Psychology: Research and Practice, 19*, 190–192.

Street, W. R. (1994). *A chronology of noteworthy events in American Psychology*. Washington, DC: American Psychological Association.

US Department of Education (2000). Projection of Educational Statistics to 2011 [Electronic version]. Retrieved July 15, 2002, from http://nces.ed.gov/pubs2000/digest/

Wilkinson, L., & the Task Force for Statistical Inference. (1999). Statistical methods in psychology journals: Guidelines and explanations. *American Psychologist, 54*, 594–604.

Zachary, L. J. (2000). *The mentor's guide: Facilitating effective learning relationships*. New York: Jossey-Bass.

SECTION III

YOUR CAREER AS A PRACTITIONER

CHAPTER 10

Gaining Clinical Experience In and After Graduate School

ALAN D. KATELL, RONALD F. LEVANT, AND ANN S. LOONSTRA

Clinical psychologists in training have an ever-increasing array of career opportunities, and pursuing them requires making many important decisions. These decisions can be challenging ones, as the consequences for career options are far-reaching. Many also need to be made early in the doctoral training sequence. Selecting among these opportunities and making the necessary decisions are thus crucial steps requiring both current information and a decision-making model. This chapter will identify important sources for such information, and provide a framework for integrating them. Key points for consideration include: (1) academic program's training model, (2) specialization training, (3) choosing among intervention models, (4) practicum training and supervision, (5) internship training, and (6) postdoctoral supervision.

ACADEMIC TRAINING MODEL

In considering career objectives, one of the first and most important tasks is determining which training experiences will facilitate your goal attainment. Clinical training experiences are crucial in this regard, whether your career objectives are academic, service oriented, or a blend. Early training experiences are particularly important in determining future direction. Those who do not plan their training curriculum with the future in mind may later find themselves at a competitive disadvantage. A broad range of experiences will increase your potential for match with many desirable internship programs. Because internship training is viewed as the narrowest point in the road from entering doctoral training to achieving career goals, attention to internship preparedness is crucial. A key objective at the graduate training stage, therefore, is to achieve clinical competence in areas that will be most useful to your internship year and beyond.

ALAN D. KATELL, ANN S. LOONSTRA AND RONALD F. LEVANT • School of Psychology, Nova Southeastern University, Fort Lauderdale, FL 33314

Most doctoral curricula include coverage of both general and more concentrated areas of study. Clinical practicum opportunities generally range from general to specific as well. In the latter instance, the terms general and specific refer to populations served, range of problems treated, and types of interventions utilized. If your courses begin with a broad and general perspective, you should consider choosing your practica accordingly. What makes such a generalist model attractive is its extraordinary versatility and robustness in a rapidly changing health care service environment. Such a model will provide a solid foundation from which you can then pursue more focused training. Such preparation will give you the greatest flexibility in adapting your clinical skills to new problems, populations, and/or settings. Importantly, many internships look for such well-rounded training in their applicants. Beyond the internship, you will find your newly acquired skills and knowledge to be applicable in a wide range of clinical settings.

Empirically Supported Treatments

A very positive trend in the evolution of clinical psychology training has been its increasing incorporation of empirically supported treatments (EST's). Paralleling this trend has been an expansion in managed health care systems' efforts to delineate treatment protocols for specific disorders. The implications of these developments for trainees in clinical psychology are several. First, with growth in the profession's capacity to identify and refine therapeutic interventions with scientific rigor, the value of training in unsupported methods becomes increasingly questionable. With the growing impact of managed health care systems on psychological service delivery, you must be prepared to work in a health care system moving toward greater specification of treatment protocols. Second, reliance on treatment methods with documented efficacy will bolster not only the profession's perceived utility, but also your own. Third, as consumerism expands into the health care arena, providers who employ empirically supported treatments will fare best.

The American Psychological Association (APA) has devoted attention to the issue with both practice and treatment guidelines. In addition, APA's Division 12 appointed a task force in 1993 to identify empirically validated treatments (Patrick & Olson, 2000). The Task Force on Promotion and Dissemination of Psychological Procedures (1995) established criteria for the validation of psychotherapies, and provided efficacy data to interested parties, including those funding third party payment for treatment. Chambless et al. (1998) updated the initial report. Their revision delineated criteria and summarized evidence of efficacy for both well established and probably efficacious treatments.

Some examples taken from the updated report of well established treatments in the realm of anxiety and stress are illustrative. Cognitive behavior therapy for the treatment of panic disorder with and without agoraphobia, cognitive behavior therapy for generalized anxiety disorder, exposure treatment for agoraphobia, and exposure and response prevention for obsessive-compulsive disorder have been empirically established as efficacious. Well established and probably efficacious treatments are delineated in numerous other domains, including depression, health problems, trauma, and problems of childhood.

Patrick and Olson (2000) listed important factors bearing on the citation of efficacy evidence. They also provided a concise summary of other literature reviewing empirically supported therapies. Importantly, they outlined current trends in establishing empirical support for interventions, as treatment methods identified as efficacious often differ from one segment of the profession to another.

Your clinical training should include solid grounding in the use of EST's. One way to enhance your opportunities for such training would be to work with faculty who (1) acknowledge the importance of EST's, and (2) will help you prepare to evaluate such treatments on your own. With continued growth in clinical science, treatment methods deemed to have empirical support are likely to change. You would be well advised to keep abreast of such changes. A list of additional resources on the subject of EST's appear at the end of this chapter.

PRACTICUM TRAINING

Developing clinical competence begins with acquiring a solid background of knowledge and generic skills. Therapeutic skills are further developed and refined through the practicum experience. Seek to begin clinical training with a practicum that can provide experience with as diverse a population and as broad a range of pathologies and life circumstances as possible. For example, a well-rounded training experience might include treatment of clients across the age spectrum, members of ethnic and cultural minorities, and clients with long-term mental illnesses and such frequently occurring disorders as anxiety and depression. To facilitate your development of therapeutic relationship enhancement skills, seek opportunities to treat persons differing from you in age, ethnicity, socioeconomic status, religion, and worldview.

Begin to obtain assessment experience as early in the training sequence as possible. Assessment in its many forms is an essential component of clinical psychology training. It is important to obtain supervised experience not only in test administration and scoring, but also in interpretation and integrated report preparation. Clemence and Handler (2001) reported that many graduate programs historically have not required students to complete the type or amount of training in assessment techniques that will make them competitive or even eligible candidates for internship. It is probable that effective preparation for internship requires the inclusion of elective assessment courses and other assessment experiences, including work with projective techniques.

In sum, it is up to you to be aware of and seek what is needed to meet the requirements for internship, postdoctoral training, licensure, and professional practice. You must strive to increase your general knowledge and skills in as many areas of clinical training as possible. It is important to recognize that you have the primary responsibility to ensure the breadth of your clinical training. By the time your first practicum is completed, you will likely have received some exposure to one or more specialized populations, disorders, and/or settings, and some experience in associated assessment. You should have learned to understand how to utilize the research available to you to inform your practice. You should also have begun to consider your options for future specialization. These considerations will shape your choices for a second and possibly third year of practicum. By the time you are eligible for internship, you should have a general idea of what specialization areas, if any, you wish to pursue.

It is also helpful to know how much experience will be required to make you a competitive internship applicant. Some internship programs require as few as 600 practicum hours, but 1200 hours has become more common. Many students attempt to increase their competitive edge by completing 1500 hours or more (Gloria, Castillo, Choi-Pearson, & Rangel, 1997). Available data have shown, however, that the number of practicum hours is not a predictor of internship placement (Boggs & Douce, 2000). The primary issue, therefore, appears to be the extent to which your academic training, practicum experiences, and professional goals match the training objectives of the internship. In short, goodness of fit is the key selection factor.

SUPERVISION

An important component of maximizing your gain from clinical practica is seeking a first one that includes substantial structure and guidance. This structure will help alleviate some of the uneasiness so often a part of early attempts at therapy. You may initially feel as if you are being required to assimilate an overwhelming number of variables during your earliest interactions with clients. You may feel similarly about your first interactions with supervisors. It is generally reassuring, however, to know that your supervisor will offer support while assisting in the planning and implementation of appropriate interventions. Such an arrangement allows you to focus on basic skill and relationship development. After the rudimentary skills are developed and practiced, you may then most benefit from supervision which allows you to be more autonomous while still providing a readily accessible avenue for knowledgeable consultation (Maki & Delworth, 1995).

Models of supervisory development are important in understanding how to approach clinical supervision. Stoltenberg and Delworth (1987) outlined the widely utilized developmental model of training and supervision known as the Integrated Developmental Model (IDM). This model describes the issues trainees encounter through several identifiable stages of professional development. Stoltenberg and Delworth recommend that training and supervision be adapted to each progressive stage. The IDM describes three basic structures that supervisors use to assess counselor functioning at each stage. They are: (1) self-awareness and awareness of others, (2) motivation, and (3) autonomy. As a new professional in clinical psychology, the structured environment provided during the first stage of development will keep your initial level of anxiety manageable. As your confidence grows, you will become less reliant on your supervisors, and this marks your shift to the second stage of development. You should then anticipate the eventual assignment of more difficult clients, as your supervisor expects you have developed the competence to use more complex therapeutic techniques.

According to Stoltenberg and Delworth (1987), it would not be unusual for you to experience some ambivalence during this second stage of development. You may begin to struggle with motivation, behave in an adolescent fashion, and experience more aspects of countertransference and overidentification with the client. Stoltenberg and Delworth advise you to consider psychotherapy for yourself during this stage of development.

Once you have achieved stability at the second stage of development, you will be ready to move to the third, wherein prior skills are consolidated and new ones are added. This is typically the level of development that you might expect to reach during the latter part of your internship and at the postdoctoral level of training. As your skills develop and the scope of your experiences broadens, you will continue to move toward a more autonomous supervisory experience. The increased stability evident during the third stage facilitates rapid development and refinement of skills and therapeutic techniques (Stoltenberg & Delworth, 1987). As you progress through the skill and knowledge development derived from practicum and supervision, a crucial aspect of your learning will be systematically monitoring and examining any developmental issues of your own that arise. Consult with your training director and other faculty members about options for addressing such issues.

Another supervisory consideration is your clinical mentors' professional identification and credentials. The staffs at many practicum sites include mental health professionals other than psychologists (e.g., psychiatrists and clinical social workers), and you may have the opportunity to be supervised by them. Bear in mind, however, that while they have valuable skills and knowledge to impart, APA accreditation of academic programs stipulates that supervisors be appropriately credentialed, as they will facilitate an important part of your learning. They will also serve as role models for your socialization as a psychologist. These considerations lead the great majority of doctoral training programs to require practicum supervisors to be licensed psychologists. Internship applications typically require you to document hours of supervision received from licensed psychologists as well.

The capacity to choose your practica and supervisors will be determined by your program, your faculty, and your training director. However, you should seek to express whatever preferences you can. To this end, some common sense pointers are: (1) seek practicum sites that have supervisors with substantial experience with the populations and problems with which you will be working, and (2) evaluate the extent of your supervisor's current or continuing involvement in a particular area of concentration, whether through research, consultation, or grants. A supervisor's level of continuing involvement will greatly contribute to his or her level of expertise.

CLINICAL EXPERIENCE DURING INTERNSHIP

Internship has been described as the "didactic-experiential bridge between doctoral programs and professional practice" (Boggs & Douce, 2000). It is required by APA-accredited training programs for degree completion. Application is competitive on a national basis, and good preparation is necessary to obtain a placement that will enhance your professional development. Founded in 1968, the Association of Psychology Postdoctoral and Internship Centers (APPIC), has helped standardize the internship application process by adopting a uniform application, promoting fairness and common sense in application deadlines, and developing an equitable method of selection. Their website, provided in Appendix 1, is an excellent source of information regarding policies and training issues.

Clinical training at the internship level typically promotes competence in assessment, intervention, research, program evaluation, outcome measurement, and quality assurance. Your opportunities at this level typically include specialized training in evolving areas of the field, which will allow you not only to sharpen your general clinical skills, but also to begin developing expertise with particular disorders, populations, and/or treatments of interest.

In recent years, the number of internship applicants has exceeded the number of available positions. Internship training is crucial, and so it is incumbent upon you to stay informed of the implications of this shortfall. As there are many APPIC member internships that are not APA-accredited, one such implication has been that you may increase the likelihood of a match by applying to unaccredited as well as accredited programs. Such a strategy remains controversial, however. For instance, it is not clear what the ramifications for postdoctoral fellowship or employment are of completing an unaccredited internship (Delworth & McNeill, 1985). It is not known whether completion of an APA-approved internship may someday be required for licensure in various states. It is important to stay well informed on these issues, and to consult with your academic and/or clinical mentors well in advance of starting the application process. A list of websites providing more information on this subject is included in Appendix 1.

Gaining clinical experience during matriculation may seem like a complicated, extended, and even daunting undertaking. This chapter has attempted to simplify it by providing you with a general sense of how your development should progress, and what you should expect to have accomplished by the time you graduate. Table 1 presents a summary of assessment and treatment experiences or competencies to achieve during each year of graduate training.

TABLE 1. Sample Timeline for Clinical Assessment and Treatment Experiences and Competencies

Year One:
- Attain a solid background of academic knowledge in:
  foundations of clinical psychology
  theories of clinical interventions
  empirically supported therapies

Year Two:
- Attain initial clinical practicum experience in assessment and/or treatment (including supervision and case consultation)
- Begin to attain therapy skills and experience with common disorders
- Begin to attain assessment skills, including but not limited to the following types of assessment:
  personality assessment
  behavioral assessment
  intelligence testing
  projective assessment measures
- Begin to attain experience in the treatment of:
  diverse populations
  varied pathologies and life circumstances
- Begin to attain experience in report-writing and clinical case presentations

Year Three:
- Attain more focused clinical practicum experience in assessment and/or intervention and/or consultation, particularly with more difficult disorders or populations
- Begin or continue to participate in group or peer supervision
- Increase your experience in the administration, scoring, and interpretation of assessment measures.
- Increase your experience in report-writing and clinical case presentation

Year Four:
- Continue to augment your clinical skills by providing assessment and treatment to more specialized populations and disorders
- Begin to provide clinical supervision under close supervision of your own
- Conduct assessment with multiple measures leading to integrated reports
- Pursue options for specialization, whether through clinical or research experiences

Year Five:
- Internship training year (2000+ clinical training hours)
- Continue to refine your clinical skills, including work with couples, families, and/or groups
- Extend focus toward possible area(s) of specialization

POSTDOCTORAL SUPERVISION

Postdoctoral training has become virtually universal, whether one is pursuing a career in an academic or other research setting, an assessment or treatment environment, or the consultation arena. The primary purpose is to finish preparation for professional practice, including the attainment of a range of postdoctoral credentials. For licensure, for instance, virtually all states require supervised postdoctoral hours. The most common number of hours is 2000, but the percentage that must be direct client contact varies widely. In all states that require supervised postdoctoral hours, the supervision must be provided by a licensed psychologist, and typically in a face-to-face manner. Check the APPIC website (www.appic.org) for a link to a summary of state licensing requirements. Also check with the psychology licensing board in the state(s) where you intend to practice.

Postdoctoral settings range from fellowships built around a formal, organized program of training to informal residencies with a psychologist in private practice. Applications to

TABLE 2. Gaining Clinical Experience In and After Graduate School: Principal Points to Consider

Curriculum and related issues
- Be mindful of how the changing marketplace and current supply and demand issues impact your options for clinical experience.
- Familiarize yourself with the predominant schools of thought, their approaches to clinical work, and the differences in their principal methods of treatment.
- Acquire a strong fundamental knowledge of empirically supported therapies.
- Plan your curricular options (e.g., electives) with an eye toward the future. Select training experiences that will meet both long-term and short-term goals. Consider your options for postdoctoral specialization.

Practicum
- Gain initial practicum experience with as diverse a population and as broad a range of pathologies as possible.
- Familiarize yourself with assessment techniques that will be useful for internship, postdoctoral training, licensure, and practice.
- Learn how to utilize research to inform practice.

Supervision
- Seek supervisors who have had experience with the population you are treating.
- For your first practicum, look for a supervisor who will provide structure and guidance.
- Seek supervisory experiences that will allow for increasing levels of autonomy.
- Be aware of your own developmental transitions within the supervisory relationship.
- Consider personal therapy to address issues that may arise during your clinical training.

Internship and postdoctoral considerations
- Preferences for internship, postdoctoral, and specialty training will significantly impact your career options, so gather information about them early.
- Licensure is determined in large part by having appropriate academic credentials, the required number and type of supervised hours, and a broad knowledge of the field.
- Achievement of Fellow and Diplomate status is largely determined by the level of commitment and the significance of contributions made to the profession.
- Acquire as much information as possible about expectations for your supervised postdoctoral experience before applying. Be sure to obtain a written contract before accepting.

postdoctoral training opportunities are generally sought in consultation with, but not under the aegis of your academic program. Most application deadlines are in the late fall or early spring of the internship year. In fellowships, client contact occurs in the sponsoring facility, often a medical center, hospital, or other large treatment facility. Additional information about fellowships is provided elsewhere in this handbook. Informal residencies, on the other hand, can be quite variable in how clients are provided, settings utilized, and form and nature of supervision. Applicable state law generally dictates the parameters of the supervision. Because of the variability of supervision provided in informal residencies, you would be well advised to enter such relationships only after obtaining complete information about the supervisor, the nature, frequency, and cost of the supervision, and how any disputes will be resolved. A written contract should be obtained before entering such informal arrangements. In general, postdoctoral training without a specified stipend should be approached with great caution.

CONCLUSION

While there are many ways to obtain clinical experience in and after graduate school, having a framework for doing so is invaluable. There are several key issues to keep in mind, some set by your academic program, but many determined by your career goals, licensure laws, and various credentialing bodies. This chapter has outlined the principal points you must consider.

ADDITIONAL RESOURCES

Web Resources

American Board of Professional Psychology (ABPP): www.ABPP.org
American Psychological Association (APA): www.apa.org
APA Div. 12, Clinical Psychology: www.apa.org/about/division/div12.html
APA Div. 16, School Psychology: www.apa.org/about/division/div16.html
APA Div. 17, Counseling Psychology: www.apa.org/about/division/div17.html
APA Graduate Students (APAGS): www.apa.org/apags/
Association of Counseling Center Training Agencies: accta.ucsc.edu
Association of Psychology Postdoctoral & Internship Centers (APPIC): www.appic.org
Association of State and Provincial Psychology Boards (ASPPB): www.asppb.org
Canadian Psychological Association (CPA): www.cpa.ca
Council of Counseling Psychology Training Programs (CCPTP): www.lehigh.edu/ccptp/
Credentialing Opportunities for Professional Psychologists: www.nationalregister.org/grad.html
Examination for Professional Practice in Psychology (EPPP): www.asppb.org/eppp.htm
National Register of Health Service Providers in Psychology: www.nationalregister.org

Print Resources

Barnett, D. W., Daly, E. J. III, Hampshire, E. M., Hines, N. R., Maples, K. A., Ostrom, J. K., & Van Buren, A. E. (1999). Meeting performance-based training demands: Accountability in an intervention-based practicum. *School Psychology Quarterly, 14*(4), 357–379.

Boylan, J. C., Malley, P. B., & Reilly, E. P. (2001). Practicum and Internship: Textbook and resource guide for counseling and psychotherapy.

Kendall, P. C. (1998). Empirically supported psychological therapies. *Journal of Counseling and Clinical Psychology, 66*(1), 3–6.

Levant, R. (2000). Pre-doctoral pre-specialization training. Paper presented in a symposium, "Bridging the scientist-practitioner divide: Implications for training" at the 108th Annual Convention of the American Psychological Association in Washington, DC, Sunday, August 6, 2000.

Levant, R. F., Reed, G. M., Ragusea, S. A., DiCowden, M., Murphy, M. J., Sullivan, F., Craig, P. L., & Stout, C. E. (2001). Envisioning and accessing new roles for professional psychology. *Professional Psychology: Research and Practice, 32*(1), 79–87.

Luborsky, L. (2001). The meaning of *empirically supported treatment* research for psychoanalytic and other long-term therapies. *Psychoanalytic Dialogues, 11*(4), 583–604.

O'Donohue, W., Buchanan, J. A., & Fisher, J. E. (2000). Characteristics of empirically supported treatments. *The Journal of Psychotherapy Practice and Research, 9*(2), 69.

Snyder C. R., & Ingram, R. E., Eds., (2000). *Handbook of Psychological Change.* New York: John Wiley & Sons, Inc.

REFERENCES

Boggs, K. R., & Douce, L. A. (2000). Current status and anticipated changes in psychology internships: Effects on counseling psychology training. *Counseling Psychologist, 28*(5), 672–686.

Chambless, D. L., Baker, M. J., Baucom, D. H., Beutler, L. E., Calhoun K. S., Crits-Christoph, P., Daiuto, A., DeRubeis, R., Detwiler, J., Haaga, D. A. F., Johnson, S. B., McCurry, S., Mueser, K. T., Pope, K. S., Sanderson, W. C., Shoham, B., Stickle, T., Williams, D. A., & Woody, S. R. (1998). Update on empirically validated therapies II. *The Clinical Psychologist, 51*(1), 3–16.

Clemence, A. J., & Handler, L. (2001). Psychological assessment on internship: A survey of training directors and their expectations for students.

Delworth, U., & McNeill, B. (1985). College counseling center internships: Clarifying the issues. *Professional Psychology: Research and Practice, 16*(4), 468–469.

Gloria, A. M., Castillo, L. G., Choi-Pearson, C. P., & Rangel, D. K. (1997). Competitive internship candidates: A national survey of internship training directors. *Counseling Psychologist, 25*(3), 453–472.
Maki, D. R., & Delworth, U. (1995). Clinical Supervision: A definition and model for the rehabilitation profession. *Rehabilitation Counseling Bulletin, 38*(4), 282–293.
Patrick, C. L., & Olson, K. (2000). Empirically supported therapies. *Journal of Psychological Practice, 6*(1), 19–34.
Stoltenberg, C. D., & Delworth, U. (1987). *Supervising counselors and therapists: A developmental approach.* San Francisco: Jossey-Bass Inc.
Task Force on Promotion and Dissemination of Psychological Procedures (1995). Training in and dissemination of empirically validated psychological treatments. *The Clinical Psychologist, 48*(1), 3–23.

CHAPTER 11

Training to Begin a Private Practice

JEFFREY E. BARNETT AND ELIZABETH HENSHAW

Preparation for entering and succeeding in private practice is one vital area that graduate programs typically cannot give adequate attention to due to the long list of "academic" courses that must be offered. And it seems that there is never enough time to learn all we need to know to be fully prepared for our professional roles after graduation day. But the preparation specific to having a career as a private practitioner is an important aspect of career growth and planning. This chapter will provide guidance on how to prepare for a career in private practice.

Years ago, psychologists would receive their degree, become licensed, have business cards printed, take out a yellow pages ad, rent an office, and begin treating patients. Unfortunately, the practice landscape has become much more crowded, competitive, and complicated over the years. There are numerous mental health professionals with various amounts and types of training who are all competing for many of the same patients. While clinical proficiency is mandatory, it is not nearly enough to ensure success in private practice. Running a private practice is a business enterprise that requires advanced planning, market analysis, a business plan, targeted marketing, and solid business practices.

PREPARATION FOR PRIVATE PRACTICE

But rather than just learning as you go along, it is best if you prepare to enter private practice well in advance. You can begin by using the resources that surround you to explore options that will allow you to become more marketable and better prepared to be a successful private practitioner. Use your graduate school professors, professionals in your community, and Internet websites to explore your options as early as possible. Refer to the checklist below to familiarize yourself with some of the issues you will want to consider both before and after receiving your degree:

JEFFREY E. BARNETT • Independent Practice and Department of Psychology, Loyola College, Baltimore, Maryland 21210
ELIZABETH HENSHAW • Department of Psychology, Loyola College, Baltimore, Maryland 21210

While You Are Still in Graduate School

- Take elective courses in specialty areas that interest you. Possibilities include group or family psychotherapy, clinical hypnosis, stress management, and neuropsychological assessment.
- Explore specific internship opportunities that will prepare you for the type of private practice you would like to have.
- Talk to those professors who also work in private practice and ask questions such as:
- How did your training help you to prepare for a career in private practice?
- What challenges and obstacles did you face while entering private practice and how did you overcome them?
- What successes and failures have you experienced in beginning and running a private practice?
- What are the lessons you've learned that you wish you knew when you first entered private practice?
- How did you learn about the business aspects of running a private practice?
- What are the most important things you've learned about running a successful private practice?
- What impact has your theoretical orientation played on the nature of your private practice and on your level of success?
- What can I do now to begin preparing so that I can be successful in private practice after graduation?

After Obtaining Your Degree

- Explore post-doctoral opportunities that will enhance your skills as a private practitioner. See Chapter 23 of this volume for further information on the potential importance and role of post-doctoral fellowships.
- Research geographical areas that interest you and determine their needs. Ask yourself the following questions when deciding to practice in a certain area:
- Is the area saturated with practitioners with a certain specialty?
- Are there any groups of potential patients whose needs are not being adequately met?
- Is the region I've selected for my private practice saturated with managed care or do most private practitioners in that area have fee-for-service practices?
- Will I be able to join managed care panels and if so, how long does this process take and when can I begin this process?
- Should I open my private practice immediately or will I need to start with other work and build my private practice into a full-time enterprise over time?
- Do I have a business plan for establishing and running my private practice? Do I need to consult with any experts to assist me with this endeavor?

IS PRIVATE PRACTICE FOR YOU?

A career as a private practitioner is not for everyone. However, for those who are well-prepared and who have realistic expectations, it is an enriching and rewarding career choice. Personal characteristics such as strong internal motivation and an entrepreneurial spirit will

TABLE 1. Pros and Cons for a Career in Private Practice

Pros	Cons
• Being your own boss. • Ability to decide practice location, hours, areas of specialization. • Unlimited earnings potential. • Flexibility. • Control over business decisions. • Full responsibility for success of practice.	• Financial uncertainty and risk with possible periods of low earnings. • Responsibility for all expenses and overhead. • Possible professional isolation for solo practitioners. • Responsibility for billing, collections, insurance, employee and staff decisions.

certainly play a role in your success in private practice. But these factors alone are not enough. Consider the pros and cons in Table 1 to establishing and maintaining a private practice.

After making the decision to enter private practice and considering the personal characteristics and professional issues above, it is important to start thinking about some of the more practical issues you will face as a private practitioner. For instance, how will you start your practice? Just jumping right into full-time private practice is not necessarily a viable option for all recent graduates. Consider the most realistic and beneficial options particular to your situation. Specifically, take the time to understand the amount of time it takes to build a full-time private practice, the financial demands of opening a practice in your area, making ends meet while building your clientele, the need for health insurance and other benefits, and the need for professional support, especially early on. Some recent graduates prefer to start out in another setting and transition to private practice slowly.

One way to do this is to work full-time in a salaried position and start your private practice in the evenings and weekends. This will provide you with a full-time salary, benefits, collegial interaction, and supervision if needed. This is a good time to develop competence in specialty areas of practice that you can begin marketing in the local community. You will also have the opportunity to network with other professionals in the local area and to build your reputation while not experiencing the financial instability of slowly building your practice. Or, if you have the financial flexibility, you might want to work part-time in a salaried position with benefits and build your practice in the remaining time. This arrangement gives you the security and benefits of a salaried position along with the needed time to devote to building your private practice without working the numerous hours required if you work full-time plus have a private practice. The drawback is that the amount of income is less during the time that the private practice is being developed.

An additional option is to dedicate yourself full time to the development of your private practice. This choice provides the fastest route to a full-time private practice, but carries the greatest challenges financially. With each of the first two choices you can decide, based on your success and/or preference, just how much of your time you want to spend in the private practice setting. Some practitioners cut back on the number of hours worked in a salaried position as their private practice grows. Others will find that working part-time in two positions provides them with the best possible combination of financial stability, benefits, varied work activities, and collegial interactions to meet their needs.

Another important decision to make also concerns your practice setting. You may choose to open your own 'solo' private practice, you may form a group practice with one or more colleagues, or you may join an already existing group practice. If you choose to participate in a group practice, an additional point to consider is the composition of the group. It may be

Table 2. Considerations for a Solo Practice or Group Practice

Solo practice	Group practice
Pro: Practitioner independence. Set your own hours, salary, benefits; decide how to run your practice.	Pro: When you have a psychiatrist on staff you will have easy access and ongoing communication about your patients who need treatment with psychotropic medications in addition to their psychotherapy.
Con: You must find mentorship and supervision on your own as you need it. This might come at a cost.	Pro: Inter-professional collaboration and within-group referrals.
Con: No administrative support, you will have to allow time for paperwork and correspondence.	Pro: Access to clerical and administrative support
Con: Higher costs of operation unless operating from your home, which has drawbacks of its own.	Pro: Lower overhead/sharing of costs.
Pro: Absolute authority over all decisions	Con: Sharing of decisions and of profits.
Con: Unlimited personal liability.	Con: Each member of the group must accept some liability for the actions of all group members.

Note: A sole proprietorship is not taxed as a business entity. (Depending on your total income, this can be either an advantage or a disadvantage.)

comprised entirely of psychologists or it may be a 'multidisciplinary group'. Table 2 provides an overview of the benefits and drawbacks of each arrangement.

Again, it is helpful to speak with private practitioners in a variety of practice settings to hear about their various experiences. This will help you decide on the best plan of action for you. Keep in mind, however, that many practitioners look for positions, get interviewed, accept an offer, and *then* see how it works. There is only so much we can know in advance; some of it must be learned through experience. But, if you consider all these issues and get a clear sense that one practice arrangement best suits your needs, personality, and comfort level, then that is what you should try.

Questions to Ask When Considering Joining a Group Practice

- Who owns the group and who makes business decisions?
- How are referrals shared and what assistance will be provided to help me get started?
- What administrative support do I receive from the group?
- What percent of the income I generate goes to the practice and what percent to me?
- What if I decide to leave the practice; can I take my patients with me?
- What benefits am I provided; malpractice insurance, continuing education, etc.?
- Am I allowed to decide which patients I will treat?
- What supervision and on-call coverage opportunities and obligations are there?
- What are the criteria for evaluation and how does one become an owner or partner?

As you begin to attempt to set yourself apart from the many 'psychotherapists' competing with you for a limited number of potential patients it is important to be able to be more than just another generic mental health professional. It is important that you have a set of skills that meet particular patient needs and that set you apart from others. This is not to suggest that providing psychotherapy and assessment services with excellence is not a worthy endeavor, but these skills should be viewed as the foundation for your private practice. Beyond that, consider developing an area of expertise that can be marketed to targeted audiences (and that also are typically fee-for-service endeavors where you will earn more and not have to hassle with managed care).

Psychologists in Independent Practice, Division 42 of the American Psychological Association, has an excellent series of niche practice guides that provide an excellent introduction to developing a specialty. Each guide provides a detailed description of the specialty area, information on how to enter it, what training is needed, and where to obtain it and training resources available, ethics issues to consider, marketing considerations, and a list of resources to access for additional information. Thirty six niche practice guides are presently available for such diverse areas of practice as health psychology, infertility, psycho-oncology, eating disorders treatment, marital therapy, working with stepfamilies, smoking cessation, ADHD assessment and treatment, geriatrics, sport psychology, treatment of personality disorders, neuropsychology, women's issues, psychologist-dentist collaboration, child custody evaluations, men's issues, and many others. These very useful guides may be ordered through the Division 42 website at www.division42.org. Developing specialty areas is an important step for setting yourself apart from other practitioners in your community. Select areas that interest you, obtain the needed training, and then begin marketing the services you have to offer.

Also, in addition to providing clinical services, you should consider how you might apply the knowledge and skills you already possess to other areas that would augment your clinical practice. Suggestions include business consultation and team building, personal and executive coaching, divorce mediation, school consultations, and forensic evaluations. While one should only enter these specialty areas with supervision from an experienced colleague, you may be surprised how little additional training and experience you'll need to be competent in these areas of practice as well as with some of the niches described above.

THE BUSINESS OF PRACTICE

Even the most competent clinician can end up sitting alone in the office waiting for the phone to ring. After assessing your local area's needs, developing a specialty area or practice niche, deciding on group or solo practice/multidisciplinary or all psychologists, purchasing business cards and even taking out a yellow pages ad possibly, you must now tackle the business of practice; and it is a business. Ask yourself the following questions regarding the business of running a private practice:

First, will I work as an Independent Contractor or an Employee? An employee is hired by, and works for, an employer, is directed by the employer which patients to treat, when, and how, and the employer takes out withholding for taxes and pays a portion of the individual's social security tax. IRS Tax Topic Bulletin 762 (Independent Contractor vs. Employee) states: an independent contractor is defined an individual who is not an employee, but who works with another individual under a contractual agreement. Independent contractors treat whichever patients they like, and when and how they might like. They purchase their own supplies and set their own hours. They pay quarterly estimated taxes and no taxes are withheld by the other person. For additional information see the Internal Revenue Service's website at www.irs.ustreas.gov/forms_pubs/.

If you should choose to work as an employee, ask yourself how you will establish your fee structure for services rendered *and* within the practice. The typical arrangement is to pay the practice owner a certain fee or certain percentage of fees collected for each patient seen. Typically, employees pay the practice owner 40% of all fees collected and keep 60% for themselves. If you are offered a lower percentage of fees collected, such as 50%, be sure your contract stipulates criteria for it increasing over time. A typical arrangement would be to start with paying 50% to the practice and then having this percentage decrease as you begin generating your own referrals. Should you begin providing referrals to others in the group due to your success the percentage paid to the practice would decrease even further. All of this should be clearly laid out in the contract agreement signed upon joining the group. Being aware of these long-term issues when starting out is very important to your success in private practice.

Next, what are you receiving for the percentage of collections you pay to the practice? The practice owner is providing the office space, furnishings, office staff and supplies, and perhaps most importantly, referrals of patients for you to evaluate and treat. Typically, practice owners who are very busy and have more incoming referrals than they can personally treat will take on independent contractors. For the new psychologist just entering private practice this can be an excellent way of starting out. There is a ready stream of referrals, a furnished office with trained staff and infrastructure already in place, and the possibility of supervision, if needed. Other contractual arrangements are possible, such as leasing space in another practitioner's or group's office, so consider the options available to you to find the arrangement that is in your best interest based on your particular circumstances.

Finally, be sure to educate yourself on certain business principles such as non-competition clauses, a major area of concern for independent contractors. The non-competition clause will be laid out and agreed upon between you and the practice owner when signing your initial contract. This clause specifies that if you leave the practice you may not practice psychology for a specified period of time within a certain distance of the practice you are leaving. This will protect the practice owner from direct competition from you should you decide to leave. Unless you have a specialty area not otherwise available in the local area, such contractual clauses are generally deemed enforceable. The practice owner is providing you with referrals and assisting you to develop your reputation in the local area. Without such a clause in the contract you could fill your schedule, build your reputation, and then leave and open your own practice across the street or across town.

RULES OF BUSINESS SUCCESS

Consult the Experts

The first thing you need to know, even if you open a solo practice, is that you can never enter or run a private practice on your own. You will need the services of experts in two key areas of expertise; legal issues and accounting. Unless you have graduated from law school we strongly suggest that you *never* enter a business arrangement or sign any contract before first consulting with your attorney. Too many practitioners have learned the hard way just how costly a mistake being your own attorney or accountant can be. While their fees may seem expensive, these professionals will save you a great deal of money, anguish, and legal difficulties in the long run. Speak to experienced practitioners to find out who they use, if they are happy with the fees charged and services provided, and use this input to guide you. You may also obtain referrals for attorneys through your local or state psychological association as well as through the local bar association. But be sure to check their references and reputation. Don't rely on fancy advertisements for guiding you in such an important decision. Just to clarify the point made above... never sign any contract without first having it reviewed by your attorney who will ensure it is in your best interest and suggest any needed modifications *before* you sign it.

Market Your Practice at Every Opportunity

Even if you are an independent contractor in a group practice, but especially if you decide to open your own practice, marketing yourself to the local community and to a variety of possible referral sources is of great importance. Potential referral sources may include physicians in your community, schools, attorneys, other mental health professionals, and a variety of others. Possible strategies to secure referrals include:

- Send an announcement of your practice opening.
- Follow up with a brief letter describing your training, background, and expertise. Be sure to tailor the letters to the perceived needs of each referral source and the specific population they serve. (See Appendix One for an example.)
- Telephone potential referral sources and request a brief meeting to meet and describe the services you offer (and how you can help them and their patients).
- Offer free presentations to the patients of your referral sources. For example, you could offer a seminar on behavior management strategies to the parents of a pediatrician's patients, a presentation on stress management skills to an internal medicine physician's or cardiologist's patients, or a seminar on strategies for working with certain types of learning disabilities for teachers at a school you hope will refer patients to you.
- If you give presentations or seminars, be sure to bring business cards, brochures, and fliers describing you, your practice, and the services you offer. You can utilize marketing professionals and create your own brochure or you can purchase brochures from the APA's Division 42 and then attach your business card to them.
- Available brochures include "Psychotherapy with children and adolescents" and "Choosing a psychologist."
- Keep likely referral sources updated on additional training you receive and new types of patients you can treat.
- Some private practitioners write a monthly or bi-monthly newsletter that they send to members of the community. Others write columns in local newspapers or do radio talk shows on mental health topics, and some give presentations to local groups such as C.H.A.D.D., the PTA, support groups, or at sites such at the YMCA, senior centers, and schools. These indirect forms of marketing may also be very effective in establishing your reputation as a local expert and can increase your referrals over time.
- Use technology to market yourself as well. Create a web page for your practice and link in to a variety of mental health sites. Be sure to keep it up-to-date and include useful information for visitors similar to a brochure or newsletter (visit these practitioners' websites for ideas to use in creating your own website:
  www.teammasters.com
  www.kolt.com
  www.mindspring.com/~docld/
  www.drelainerodino.com
- You should also market yourself to your colleagues. Utilize your contacts in the State Psychological Association and let them know of your practice and the services you offer.

- Explore the successful practices in your local area and offer to take the practitioner(s) out to lunch to introduce yourself and meet with them. Many practitioners with busy practices are frequently looking for colleagues to whom they may refer patients they can't see. They also need competent practitioners to refer patients whose needs fall outside their areas of expertise. They can only refer these patients to you if they know of you and the services you provide.

Keep in mind that only half the work is done when you have received a referral. By nurturing the contact, you will be sure to keep the referrals flowing in. For instance, when a referral is received, always send a letter of acknowledgment of the referral. In the case of specific services, be sure to keep the referral source in the loop at pertinent stages. For instance when doing an evaluation, forward a copy of your report to the referral source, and for treatment, provide periodic written updates on the patient's treatment progress. Always be sure to first obtain the patient's written consent before doing so. Also bear in mind that your job is to solve or reduce the referral source's problems. Initially, they may send you their most difficult and demanding patients. A successful, happy patient and a successful treatment outcome are your most powerful marketing strategies (see Appendix Two for a sample letter).

In summary, you must provide high quality services, give referral sources timely and useful feedback, and market your services both directly to referral sources and indirectly to the community. Actively follow-up all these marketing efforts on a regular basis.

SETTING UP YOUR PRACTICE

If you work as an employee or an independent contractor this will be taken care of for you. But, if you open and run your own private practice you must consider and address these important issues (see Table 3).

First consider the physical office. The actual office must be set up so that patient privacy is protected. The use of sound proofing, white noise machines, and even insulated ceilings, walls, and doors all help to keep confidential communications private. Secretarial staff should have an area apart from the patient waiting room where telephone calls can be made. A locked

Table 3. Checklist for Beginning Your Private Practice

- Analyze the local community's needs.
- Select a location.
- Develop areas of expertise.
- Develop a comprehensive business plan.
- Hire an attorney and accountant.
- Rent or lease office space; ensure soundproofing and handicap accessibility.
- Obtain needed insurance.
- Furnish the office, hire needed staff, begin phone service, utilities, etc.
- Establish office policies and train staff on ethics standards such as confidentiality.
- Set fees using prevailing community standards as a guide.
- Develop a multifaceted marketing plan and implement it.
- Become involved in your community and professional associations.
- Obtain needed supervision and additional training.
- Periodically reassess your strategies and practices. Modify as needed.
- Continue providing high quality services and never stop marketing your practice.

room with lockable file cabinets for treatment record storage is mandatory. Faxes should be received in an area to which unauthorized individuals do not have access.

Next, consider insurance coverage. At a minimum you will need malpractice insurance. It is typically recommended that your coverage be for $1,000,000 per claim and $3,000,000 per year. If you obtain hospital privileges or work on any managed care panels this is typically the amount of coverage they require you obtain and keep in force. You may also wish to obtain disability insurance to provide you with coverage should you be unable to work for a period of time and you should consult your attorney about additional types of insurance for your office and staff. You may purchase two types of malpractice coverage; occurrence and claims made. Occurrence insurance provides coverage for claims made against you any time during your career, even if you discontinue your coverage. Claims made insurance only provides coverage while the policy remains in effect. While occurrence insurance is more costly, many choose it due to the coverage provided. The largest malpractice carrier for psychologists is the American Psychological Association Insurance Trust (www.apait.org). Others include the American Professional Agency (www.americanprofessional.com) and Psychotherapist Professional Liability Insurance Program (www.applip.com).

Next, unless you plan to do all jobs (answering the phone, greeting patients, collecting fees, billing, doing insurance paperwork, filing, and the like) you will likely hire a staff. Consult with your attorney and accountant and learn about applicable laws concerning interviewing and hiring practices, employment law, taxes, and related issues. Then be sure all persons hired understand both their job duties and all applicable ethical standards. Train your staff about confidentiality and related issues. Have written office policies that you instruct them in and have them agree to in writing. Be sure to supervise them adequately to be sure they do not exceed the agreed upon limits of their roles.

Another important area is fee setting. While you certainly should be paid what you are worth, it is advisable conduct an informal survey of private practitioners in your local area to see what fees they charge. You may either ask them directly or telephone their offices as a potential patient requesting information about their practice. Not only will you learn their fees, but you will also learn about their office policies from the information they share. You may also consult with the newsletter *Psychotherapy Finances*. This is a useful newsletter that posts the results of their annual salary survey of mental health professionals. It may be accessed online at www.psyfin.com.

You will then need to establish procedures for, and forms or documents for, informed consent, release of information, payment policies, billing and the use of insurance, the use of collections agencies, intake forms and questionnaires, follow-up letters to referral sources, follow-up letters for patients who drop out of treatment and for those who successfully complete treatment. You may also choose to do some patient satisfaction surveys, treatment outcome measures, and other measures. Rather than try to develop all these policies and forms yourself, you should request copies of those forms used by colleagues when you meet with them. You may also find several resources very helpful in this endeavor.

First, the annual edited book *Innovations in Clinical Practice: A Source Book*, edited by VandeCreek and Jackson and published by Professional Resource Press of Sarasota, FL (www.prpress.com), regularly includes a wide variety of useful office forms. Typical forms include those for informed consent; a practice information form to distribute to patients that includes explanations of such issues as appointments and fees, billing, cancellation policy, emergencies and after hours contact, the process of therapy, confidentiality, and related issues; a patient intake form; an informed consent to submit insurance form; and an employee agreement to maintain confidentiality form.

You may also obtain a model informed consent to treatment form on the website of the American Psychological Association's Insurance Trust at www.apait.org. You may download this and modify it for your use.

An additional valuable resource is the *Documentation Survival Handbook* by Soreff and McDuffee, published by Hogrefe & Huber Publishers. This volume provides many useful forms such as for the evaluation of the violent patient, for the evaluation of suicide or suicide risk assessment, for an initial patient evaluation, for psychological testing, treatment summaries and discharge summaries, psychotherapy session progress notes, and for the documentation of telephone conversations and consultations. Additionally, several companies market software for tasks such as documentation and patient billing. Many psychologists find the use of such software a great benefit in terms of efficiency and consistency. Examples include TheraScribe (www.therascribe.wiley.com) and QuicDoc (info@quicdoc.com). Finally, practice management software such as Office Therapy™(www.mbcsystems.com) provide software that assists in automated client management, scheduling, billing, insurance filing, and related services.

Finally, supervision is especially important as you begin your career. In addition to individual supervision you may form or join a peer supervision and support group to connect you with other new private practitioners as well as more experienced colleagues. This may be of great help clinically, to generate referrals, and to help you better cope with the many demands of opening and running a private practice. You should also consult with the information provided in Chapter Four of this volume for much more detailed suggestions for addressing this important area of our professional development.

In conclusion, the private practice of psychology is an exciting and rewarding endeavor. With adequate advanced thought, preparation, and the use of the resources and strategies described in this chapter you should have a good head start. While a single chapter can not be an exhaustive reference on all aspects of preparing for and being successful in private practice the information presented above and the checklist below should be of assistance.

APPENDIX ONE
SAMPLE TARGETED FOLLOW-UP LETTER

Jenny Jones, M.D.
Jones Cardiology Group
Jonesville, MD 21108

Dear Dr. Jones:

I am writing to follow-up the practice opening announcement you recently received. I am a licensed psychologist in your community who specializes in treating stress-related disorders. The enclosed brochures describe my practice and more information is available on my website at www.stressrelief.com

I understand that many of your patients suffer from stress-related disorders and many of them may benefit from several of the services I provide. I recently presented a stress management workshop at the Healthy Hearts Program at Community Hospital. I would be please to offer such a workshop to your patients free of charge. I will telephone you shortly to discuss this possibility.

My practice provides a full range of mental health assessment and treatment services. I focus on health and wellness, working to provide patients with the strategies and skills to overcome their difficulties. I know many cardiology patients need assistance with stress management, combating anxiety and depression, as well as with making difficult but crucial lifestyle changes. I use a full range of effective techniques and will work collaboratively with you to ensure that your patients receive the best possible care.

I look forward to meeting with you to discuss further how I may be of assistance to you and your patients. I will contact your office in the next week to schedule a time to speak.

Sincerely,

Jeffrey E. Barnett, Psy.D.
Licensed Psychologist

APPENDIX TWO
SAMPLE LETTER TO FOLLOW-UP A REFERRAL

Jane Smith, MD.
Smith Primary Care
Smithville, MD 99999

Dear Dr. Smith:

Thank you for your recent referral of Ms. Jen Jones for evaluation and treatment. I met with Ms. Jones initially today and we had the opportunity to discuss her reported difficulties with depression. I began my assessment of these difficulties and will continue this over the next two to three sessions. Once my initial assessment is completed I will be back in touch with you to provide you with my findings, recommendations, and our agreed upon treatment plan. I anticipate having this to you within the next two to three weeks.

(Insert patient's relevant history and mental status examination here)

While no crisis or emergency exists at present Ms. Jones' depression is a serious concern. She understands that if her symptoms worsen she should contact me immediately. Despite the serious nature of Ms. Jones' depression I am hopeful of being of assistance to her. I utilize a comprehensive treatment approach that will focus on reducing Ms. Jones' distress and provide her with the skills and techniques to help her move forward quickly. I will work closely with you to ensure that Ms. Jones receives the best possible care and will keep you informed of her progress and all significant changes in her functioning as they occur.

I have enclosed several of my business cards for your use along with several pamphlets that may be of use to your patients. I am also separately sending you copies of a stress management tip sheet that I hope will be of value to your patients.

Once again, thank you for this very timely and appropriate referral. I appreciate the opportunity to be of service to Ms. Jones. Please feel free to contact me at any time if you have any questions or concerns about her treatment.

Sincerely,

Jeffrey E. Barnett, Psy.D.
Licensed Psychologist

CHAPTER 12

Navigating the Internship Application Process

MITCHELL J. PRINSTEIN, SHANE J. LOPEZ, AND HEATHER N. RASMUSSEN

THE INTERNSHIP APPLICATION PROCESS: A RITE OF PASSAGE

For many, anxiety regarding the internship application process begins shortly after the excitement of graduate school acceptance subsides. The predoctoral internship is a curriculum requirement in all accredited doctoral programs in psychology, typically occurring during the penultimate or final year of doctoral training. It is not uncommon for students just beginning their graduate education to already feel inundated with information regarding internship opportunities, strategies for improving one's potential for securing a desired placement, and even tales of distress regarding the application procedure itself. Indeed, although an arduous, time-consuming, and occasionally stressful process, the internship application procedure offers many an opportunity to contemplate and organize their career goals, establish a professional identity beyond the walls of their doctoral program, and develop important networking relationships that will last years after internship training has ended. This chapter will review some important facts, strategies, and suggestions to minimize anxiety and maximize success throughout the application process (see also Williams & Prinstein, 2004[1]).

Debunking Myths and Reducing Anxiety

Unfortunately, a great deal of misinformation is readily available regarding predoctoral internship placement; several of these fallacies serve to heighten anxiety among those involved

MITCHELL J. PRINSTEIN • Department of Psychology, Yale University, New Haven, CT 06520
SHANE J. LOPEZ AND HEATHER N. RASMUSSEN • Psychology and Research In Education, University of Kansas, Lawrence, Kansas 66045

[1] All royalties from this book are used to help support the American Psychological Association of Graduate Students (APAGS).

in the application procedure. Some calming facts using data from the past four years (see the APPIC website; Keilin, Thorn, Rodolfa, Constantine, & Kaslow, 2000):

- Approximately 2900–3100 doctoral students apply for predoctoral internships each year
- Between 82–85% of these applicants are successfully matched
- Of these, approximately 46–50% match at their first choice site; 78–83% match at one of their top 3 placements
- The number of available slots has increased in the past several years
- Of students who are unplaced on Match Day, 65–70% are able to secure a slot within the same application year.

THE APPLICATION PROCESS: HOW AND WHEN TO BEGIN

Recording Information

As part of the internship application process, students are asked to report their clinical experience, including the number of hours of direct contact with clients, hours spent preparing, reviewing, and organizing case material, and supervision hours. Students also are asked to record their experience administering, scoring, and interpreting assessments throughout their graduate training. A common, but important suggestion is for students to begin recording this information as they complete each practicum assignment throughout graduate training. While this may take only an hour or so at the end of each semester, the task of tabulating this information while preparing application materials years later is taxing to one's time, memory, and patience.

A simple, confidential Client Log can be constructed to record all of the information above. In addition to the number of hours spent with each client (including direct contact, case preparation, and supervision) and a list of any assessments conducted before or during the course of treatment, be sure to record the clients' age, presenting complaint, diagnosis, the treatment modality/orientation used, and the setting in which clinical treatment took place (see Williams & Prinstein, 2004). Completion of the AAPI (APPIC Application for Psychology Internship; see www.appic.org for the most current version) will ultimately require you to sum the number of hours and/or cases during training in a variety of ways. A Client Log kept up-to-date makes this task relatively simple, and is useful ritual to mark the end of each practicum experience as you progress through training.

Setting Goals

Arguably the most important process of the internship application process occurs before you review the materials for a single internship site, complete any applications, or schedule interviews. The suggestion to 'set goals' is easily disregarded as the kind of trite motivational rhetoric that is used to sell mail-order products on late night television. However, a carefully considered set of goals will help guide your selections, and ultimately will inform the decisions of the admissions committee more than may initially seem evident. In addition to the opportunity to review your career trajectory, goals serve practical purposes in selecting internship sites to which you will apply, writing your application essays, responding to questions during interviews, and ultimately constructing your rank ordered match list.

What kind of internship experience would you like? What rotations, clinical populations, treatment modalities, or orientations are of most interest to you? What types of careers are you considering for your future? Although most doctoral students spend a considerable proportion of their time dedicated to graduate study in psychology, it is not at all uncommon for students to reach the last phase of their formal training without clear answers to these questions. Excellent graduate training offers structured exposure to numerous clinical and research experiences, and as many possibilities for future career paths. This is educational in its comprehensive nature, but also can be disorienting and overwhelming to students planning a career, particularly when focused on more immediate concerns, such as the completion of a dissertation, etc. The internship application process offers an opportunity to create an individualized career path that builds upon graduate experiences and forges forward in a direction that is specifically suited to you.

Setting goals is a collaborative activity. Meet with your mentors. Ask them to review your clinical strengths and weaknesses. Also, inquire about the strengths and weakness of clinical training at your graduate training program, and elicit specific suggestions on the types of internship experiences that would best complement your practica training. For instance, if you are from a doctoral program that offers mostly outpatient treatment experience, you may want exposure to more severe presentations of psychopathology, such as that on an inpatient or day treatment unit. Or, if your training has predominantly focused on one theoretical orientation, you may wish to gain exposure to alternate approaches.

Review career options with your mentors. Applicants interested in pursuing careers at a research institution may want to seek internship experiences that will cultivate their development as a clinical scientist. Applicants who wish to develop a clinical specialty may seek training with a specific population, diagnosis, or treatment approach during internship. While meeting with your mentors, be sure to ask for a list of sites to which applicants from your program have successfully applied—and apply to these if they fit your goals. A summary of questions you may consider when forming your goals is listed in Table 1.

THE APPLICATION PROCESS: SOLICITING MATERIALS AND CHOOSING SITES

Obtaining information on possible sites to consider is relatively easy using the searchable directory on the APPIC website. Web links will quickly take you to the sites of those programs that match initial search criteria, or provide addresses to request hard copies of application materials. A simple postcard will do when requesting hard copies; this is not part of the application procedure.

Once you have received these materials, use your goals to help select the sites that appear to match your interests. Try ranking each site on a 1–10 scale for each of your goals, leaving an extra category for your overall impressions of the training environment. Keep in mind that most application materials typically offer only a brief description of each rotation and a briefer glimpse of the requirements, environment, and setting at each site. However, this information can be used to rule out sites that simply do not match your needs. Beware of the temptation to apply to a site that meets most your needs, yet imposes a stringent requirement (e.g., a half-year assessment rotation) that is of no interest to you. The money spent on an interview to this site

TABLE 1. Decisions and Goals

Training Needs

What do you need to address gaps in your training experiences?

- Do you want/need more clinical experience with:
  - a specific population (i.e., age group or presenting problem)
  - a treatment modality/approach/orientation (e.g., more group treatment, experience with exposure/response prevention, more didactics on empirically-supported treatments)
  - clients from a specific treatment setting (e.g., a counseling center, inpatient unit, VA)

What experiences would help you build skills you would like to develop?

- Do you want to develop your assessment skills? (test administration, interpretation, report writing)
- Do you want develop your ability to work within a multidisciplinary team?
- Do you want to develop your ability to supervise others?
- Do you want to learn how to conduct clinical trials?
- Do you want to specialize, or get generalist experience?

Career Needs

What experiences will make you most marketable for the careers you are interested in?

- Clinical research experiences (e.g., data analysis, grant writing, publishing)
- Opportunities for postdoc placement
- Ability to build a client base, community connections
- Opportunities to develop a practice niche in the marketplace

Personal Needs

What do you need to balance your personal and professional lives?

- A specific geographic area you need to live in
- A placement that with nearby job opportunities for your partner
- Working less than 80 hours a week
- A flexible schedule

Sample Goals

1. I'd like to gain exposure to clients with severe psychopathology, preferably on an inpatient unit
2. I would like to continue to develop my expertise in empirically-supported treatments
3. I would like to work with autistic children
4. I would like to live in Idaho

will ultimately reveal what you already know (i.e., you will have to spend a half-year doing something you are not interested in), and this may prove frustrating by the end of the process. However, also keep in mind that few sites will offer a perfect match to your goals, and some flexibility and open-mindedness is warranted.

How many programs should you apply to? Keilin and Williams (in Williams & Prinstein, 2004) report that the mean number of applications submitted by each applicant over the past three years has ranged between 13–15. Interestingly, results from past application rounds statistically demonstrate that applicants' chances of successfully matching do not increase by applying to more than 15 sites. Thus, for almost every applicant, it should be entirely possible to limit your selections to no more than 15; completing this many applications is an enormous task, and visiting this many sites if extended invitations to all is virtually impossible in the limited time available to schedule interviews. Remember, be sure to include some sites to which others in your program have successfully applied. Also include sites that range in competitiveness, but do not choose a site you would not seriously select simply as a "safety." It is far better to wait a year than to accept an undesired placement. For the current application timeline, a final list of your sites should be compiled by September in your application year (see Table 2).

TABLE 2. A Suggested Schedule for the Internship Application Process

Before your Application Year: March to June

- Compute all practica hours, including anticipated hours. Include the number of supervised client contact hours you have had, types of tests administered, diversity of case load, etc.
- Begin evaluating programs. Use the APPIC *Directory* to find sites that match your interests. Review each site's Web-based materials or request their materials via email or regular mail. Discuss sites with your training director and past/current interns, as they may be able to offer comments about how the site fits your needs.
- Create a budget. Filling out applications and traveling to interviews can take many thousands of hours and thousands of dollars.

The Application Year: July to September

- Decide on the sites you to want to apply. Think about your internship, professional, and personal goals to ensure a good "fit" with a site. Once you decide, order packets from highest to lowest interest. Review your site preferences with your mentor or a trusted faculty member for their input.
- Review the information for important dates and information about the application and selection process (e.g., when applications are due, whether or not they require an on-site interview, etc.). Take note of the appropriate way to contact staff to discuss the program.
- Register for the MATCH (www.appic.org).
- Prepare your curriculum vitae. Have a faculty member or another student critique and edit your vitae.
- Identify four people whom you would like to ask for letters of recommendation. Most sites require three, however it is good to have one extra as a backup. Provide references with a copy of your vitae, your goals for internship, and other important information that will help them draft a strong letter. Ask references if they prefer you to provide them with stamped envelopes.
- Draft application essays.
- Complete the APPI and write individualized cover letters.

October to January

- Submit applications.
- Wait patiently.
- Begin to schedule interviews.
- Practice a sample case presentation and practice for possible interview questions.
- Review materials from each site and decide whether to complete a literature search on some of the people you might interview with. In other words, know each site well.
- Compose questions for internship sites.
- Send thank you notes or follow-up letters.

February

- Submit rank order for MATCH before the deadline

THE APPLICATION PROCESS: PREPARING THE APPLICATION

Once you have selected your sites, identify the earliest deadline and use this date to complete all of your applications. This is a time-intensive process; it is best to start early and anticipate that it will take as many hours as would a graduate course.

Letters of Recommendation

Although very little work on your part, a good place to start with the preparation of your application is to solicit letters of recommendation from referees. You should ask your major professor/mentor for a letter, and anyone else who can offer a positive evaluation of your clinical skills. Although letters are generally from psychologists, a single letter from another mental health professional is fine, if necessary. Letters from an extremely well known psychologist are a good idea only if they can offer informed comments about your ability; otherwise this is not a good idea at all. Letters from a referee who is or was somehow affiliated with the internship site (e.g., a former intern) are also a good idea if an informed critique of your ability is included.

Virtually all letters of recommendation are glowing. Most all state that the applicant is extremely skilled, motivated, and perhaps "one of the best." Letter writers are consistenly enthusiastic and recommend applicants very, very strongly. Given this restricted range, only two letters tend to stand out: 1) those that offer lukewarm praise, and 2) those that truly stand apart with exceptional, unique, and heart-stopping praise. Be sure you do not get the former, but do what is reasonably possible to get the latter.

It is a professional courtesy to give your referees a 1) list of your sites/addresses, 2) the recommendation forms with their contact information already completed, 3) a set of typed envelopes, 4) a list of deadlines, and 5) a copy of your AAPI and/or CV.

Curriculum Vitae

Your CV should document your training experiences and accomplishments in an efficient, clear, and organized manner. In addition to the information provided on the CV, it is a measure of your professionalism, organizational and communication abilities. It is not a measure of your computer skills (no special fonts, no abundance of formatting tricks necessary) or your Kinko's budget (no scented, high bond, hologram paper necessary), nor is your CV evaluated by its weight or bulk. Simple, clear, professional, concise. Remember, the admissions committee will read dozens and dozens of CVs in a sitting—you want to be noticed for your experience, not because you submitted a garish or incomprehensible CV.

The AAPI

As noted above, the APPI is a lengthy document with questions regarding your training experiences. It was created by asking several hundred APPIC internship sites to submit questions for inclusion, and not all questions will be relevant to the sites you are applying to, nor will all questions be relevant to your own experience. The APPIC website (also see Williams & Prinstein, 2004) offers detailed instructions on completing the application. Invariably, applicants encounter vagaries and ambiguities that make the APPI somewhat challenging to complete. Given the hundreds of training sites and graduate programs, it is inevitable that some attempts to accurately describe your experiences using the application question blanks will be like fitting square pegs into round holes. Simply do you best to convey your experiences as accurately as possible given for each question on the APPI. An honest error in calculation, or point of confusion, will not lead to an ethics charge against you or your extradition from the field. If you must, a brief note or supplemental sheet may be attached to the application to explain any special circumstance or unique calculation quagmire.

Remember that some parts of the application will be for applicants who have very different graduate experiences and are applying to very different internship programs than you—you are not expected to have experience in each area of competence included on the APPI.

In fact, you are not necessarily expected to be competent—but rather, trainable. The internship year is a training experience, and the best applicants are those who present as confident, with skill, potential, and some humility. More (hours, assessments, etc.) are not necessarily better. Completing 5 WAIS-IIIs means that you generally know how to administer and interpret the measure. Completing 50 WAIS-IIIs does not necessarily make you a better applicant. A total of 1200 clinical hours indicate that you have had a sufficient number of opportunities for clinical training. A total of 4200 clinical hours suggests that you may come from an atypical graduate program and/or may have had insufficient supervision, coursework, or research experience. Keep in mind that your pedigree (i.e., your training program, advisors) may convey a fair amount of information about your potential to succeed as an intern. Admissions committees may merely glance at your application to ensure that you are generally similar to the many other excellent candidates they have reviewed from your graduate program over the years.

The Essays

Other than insuring that your application is completed professionally and accurately, there are few things you can do to enhance your attractiveness as an applicant by the time you are completing your applications. Your referees will likely already have formed their impressions of you and the experiences documented on your CV and APPI will already have been accrued before you start this process.

At this point in the process, the essay section may be your one opportunity to substantially contribute to the strength of your application. Rather than simply documenting your experience, the essays provide you with an opportunity to convey your goals for internship and for your career. Most importantly, the essays allow you to express your belief that the internship site offers a unique match to these goals. This belief should be expressed clearly, convincingly, and repeatedly throughout the essay section.

The APPI includes five 500-word essays, but this could be reinterpreted as an opportunity to tell the site about your interests and goals in 2500 words or less. In other words, although each essay asks for a statement on a specific topic, use each question as a springboard for stating your interests, and the match with specific opportunities offered at that internship site. Each essay is briefly discussed below.

The autobiographical statement (Essay #1) is often the most perplexing assignment, tempting some to reminisce personal childhood memories, and others to restate the educational and training experiences already listed on their CV. Neither is an optimal approach. More appropriately, the autobiographical statement often begins with a brief discussion of the factors, interests, or experiences that led to the pursuit of graduate training in psychology, and/or a preview of ultimate career goals, with specific, educated guesses on the responsibilities, setting, or focus of one's ideal job as a psychologist. Efforts to use a humorous anecdote or creative opening to the autobiographical statement are certainly permissible if this is the best way to convey the applicant's character, but unlike a college admission essay, this assignment should probably be geared towards a more professionally written statement—especially for internship sites that have adopted a clinical scientist perspective.

Although a restating of your CV is not a good idea for the remaining paragraphs in your autobiographical statement, it is wise to help the reader "walk through" the most relevant points in your training background and fill in the picture beyond what could be understood from reading the names of your previous practica placements. A helpful way to do this is to organize your statement around central themes or interests. For instance, if you have accrued assessment experience during several points in your training, and this is something you wish to highlight to the readers of your application (i.e., perhaps because you wish to continue to develop these skills as a specialty area, or because it matches with an internship rotation of particular interest), then you might review your assessment experiences in a brief paragraph. Most importantly, it is not recommended that you merely list the numerous experiences you have had conducting assessments, but rather you should aim to offer an educated observation or critical evaluation of your skills and experiences (e.g., You might note that these experiences helped you to develop an interest in inter-rater correspondence in the assessment of childhood externalizing problems. Or, you might describe how these experiences led you to become interested in working on a multi-disciplinary assessment team during internship, or later in your career). Thus, you can briefly recount the experiences that were most important to you in graduate training, but the emphasis is on how these experiences led you to develop specific notions about your role as a psychologist, or goals for your training. Recall the goals you developed at the beginning of this application process (i.e., including how you initially selected these goals), and you will have the information you need for this essay.

At the end of this essay, as with all others, it is essential that you explicitly state how your goals and interests match the training objectives and experiences of this particular site. Note that if you have selected your sites according to your goals, this paragraph may be quite similar from application to application, and this is fine. It is very important to be aware that although you will have spent many hours reviewing application materials and discovering that your interests match the site, the admissions committee will be reviewing your application in only a few minutes in the context of dozens or hundreds of other applications. Help the committee see the match as clearly as you do—be very specific (e.g., "I am interested in XX. The rotation on XX at your site would be an ideal match for this goal").

The second essay asks for your thoughts regarding case conceptualization. This should not be regarded as a quiz, but rather a second opportunity to state your ideas and experiences, and how this has led to training goals that are ultimately matched by the internship site's training opportunities. Of course, it will be important to demonstrate that you have achieved a basic level of competence in case conceptualization, and that you are using a theoretically-, and perhaps empirically-informed approach to the selection of treatment techniques. You might find a brief case presentation helpful to illustrate your points, or perhaps a description of your systematic, stepwise approach to thinking about cases. You will likely have a variety of strengths and weaknesses (e.g., little exposure to specific theoretical orientations, little exposure to more complex presentations of psychopathology) in your case conceptualization skills at this point in your training. It is acceptable to state these in your essay, and again use this as an opportunity to state how your particular educational experiences have led to your goals for internship training. Again, the last paragraph should tie these goals to specific training opportunities offered at the internship site.

The third essay on the APPI allows you to discuss your experiences and thoughts regarding diversity, as it pertains to clinical and research training. Although the question is worded in such a way as to imply that you should discuss your prior experiences working with clients from diverse backgrounds, not all trainees will have had enough of these opportunities to describe in approximately 500 words. However, your training experience is not all that is being evaluated here; and in fact, your CV and APPI already has made clear what experiences you have or have not yet had in this domain. Use this essay to discuss your thoughts and ideas regarding the importance of diversity issues in psychology, and how you would/could/should be considering diversity issues in your research and clinical work (see Chapter 2 in this volume). Remember that diversity can be defined in many ways, and recall that as a psychotherapist, you have been viewed as demographically-different from many of your clients. Your own background experiences have been different from virtually every client you have seen, and thus, you have already had several opportunities to consider diversity issues, if only in subtle ways. Again, a brief case example may be appropriate in this essay, but personal disclosures that are not directly relevant to your training as a psychologist may not be.

For those who may wish to pursue an research oriented career and/or accrue additional experiences during the internship year as an investigator, the fourth essay (i.e., statement of research interests) offers a particularly important opportunity to describe a program of research and future goals. This is an excellent opportunity to practice writing the statement that will ultimately be expanded and used when applying for research-oriented postdocs and faculty appointments. In addition to a description of the responsibilities you have had on specific research projects, and perhaps a brief reminder of your independent contributions to presentations or manuscripts, be sure to discuss your *program* of research in its preliminary stages. Not all of your experiences will necessarily fit into a cogent package, but your attempts to identify common themes in at least some of your work (particularly culminating in the dissertation for now), would be to your benefit.

Not all applicants are interested in pursuing a research career; indeed, some may anticipate that their dissertation will represent their final work as an investigator. This essay should be taken seriously nonetheless, and can be used to describe past interests and the applications of these experiences to clinical practice. Your ability to speak intelligently about your understanding of the research process and your own prior experiences as an investigator offers some measure of your general knowledge of psychology, your critical thinking skills, your enthusiasm and passion for psychology, and your dedication to a clinical science training model. Be sure to state the status of your dissertation and its expected completion date. Your statements regarding research and/or their applicability to clinical practice should again be used to illustrate your goals for training and your perceptions of a match.

Lastly, the fifth essay explicitly allows you to discuss the match between your training goals and the experiences offered at the specific internship site to which you are applying. This should be a reiteration of points that you have made throughout essays #1–4. A helpful way to organize this essay is by simply stating the three or four goals you developed at the beginning of the application process, followed by a paragraph to discuss each in more detail. Each of these paragraphs should state the names of specific rotations, faculty, or didactic seminars at the internship site that best match your goals. Most importantly, the tone of this statement should reflect a high level of enthusiasm for the training site, as well as your strongly stated belief that this training is absolutely essential for you to achieve those well-conceived, requisite goals you need to advance your career. Admissions committees are very interested in having someone who will most benefit from what their site has to offer, and those applicants who will be very excited to have the opportunity to complete their internship training at their site.

The Cover Letter

A brief cover letter is a helpful addition to your application, but certainly not a necessary component. The cover letter usually includes a brief statement regarding the submission of your application materials and a list of your contact information. The cover letter also offers an excellent chance to introduce your goals and strong enthusiasm for internship training. This helps to prime the reader for all that will follow in the application materials. Lastly, the cover letter is an appropriate place to mention personal factors that may influence your decision. For instance, it is completely acceptable to offer a brief statement regarding your strong desire to move to a specific geographical region, making the admissions committee aware that you are seriously interested in relocating.

THE INTERVIEW PROCESS

After you have submitted your application materials and endured the agonizing latency period while interview decisions are made, you will most likely begin to receive a series of letters, phone calls, and emails inviting you to interview at specific training programs. Some of these interviews will be scheduled (by you or the site) as phone-interviews. Although this does not allow you to visit the site in-person, phone-interviews are much easier to schedule and will not ultimately decrease your chances of selection. Most interviews are conducted in-person, however, and the amount of time required to organize the many transportation, hotel, and car rental reservations should not be underestimated. It is quite common to spend the second half of December and the entire month of January scheduling and traveling to interviews; do not expect to get much work done (e.g., on your dissertation) during this time period. When scheduling your interviews, try to keep at least one day of rest between each interview day regardless of how much stamina you may believe you have before the process begins. Also, once you have started to hear from a few programs, feel free to contact others to check the status of your application and possible dates for interviews. Many of the administrative assistants or training directors handling these calls have been involved in the process before and will be understanding; however, your respect and consideration for their time will also be appreciated. Similarly, it is common for applicants to find that they need to reschedule interview dates to help coordinate travel itineraries; this is allowed by many sites, although again keep in mind the complexity required for the site's coordination of visits.

Although initially anxiety producing, you will quickly master the interview experience. You may be the only person to visit a particular site on your interview day, or you may have an opportunity to visit along with every other applicant who has been invited for an interview (typically 5–10 interviewees for each available slot). If the latter, you will probably meet several of these applicants at another site later in the process, and you should most certainly take advantage of this mobile support group to compare notes on the process and to develop networking relationships and friendships.

Many sites will offer a tour of the facility or an opening information session to begin the interview day, followed by a series of individual interviews with faculty and interns (who may formally sit on, or informally advise the admissions committee) to ask and answer questions. Yet, there is great variability between sites on some of these dimensions. Group interviews (involving several faculty or several other applicants) are possible. Some interviewers will ask many challenging questions; others will ask none, but allow you to solicit information about the training site. Some interviews will consist of colloquial, friendly chit-chat; others will be exclusively focused on topics related to psychology training. Pay special attention to the response you have to each training environment and each interviewer—this is a fair measure of what your experience may be like as an intern located at that site, or under that faculty member's supervision for an entire year.

By the time you have been invited for an interview, the admissions committee has typically determined that you are most likely qualified for an internship position, and the selection criteria has changed. You are being evaluated on at least three qualities, and this should guide your presentation and self-evaluation for each interview. These are: Social Skills, Enthusiasm, and Match.

Social Skills

Surprisingly, some doctoral candidates in psychology who have successfully navigated the curriculum requirements for a degree and skillfully obtained an invitation to interview for internship are fairly bereft of social skills. If you suspect that you may be one of these people, you should schedule a frank discussion with your mentor or peers and solicit constructive feedback on how to best present yourself in a professional, appropriate manner.

Others may strongly believe that they possess appropriate social skills, but are, in fact, grossly mistaken. A quick review of consistent successes or failures in past interpersonal relationships may help to reveal whether you belong in this category.

Still others with acceptable social skills may find that when confronted with an anxiety producing stimulus, they quickly devolve into an unfortunately inept buffoon. A variety of anxiety management strategies are available for those who fit within this category. The value of practice in mock interviews (with mentors, friends, family members, pets) cannot be overstated.

Luckily, the vast majority of applicants will find that they do not belong in any of these categories above, but rather feel reasonably confident that, like in clinical situations, they should be able to manage the interview experience relatively effectively. Most important, given the restricted range of this variable, it will be important to convey the manner in which you stand apart from other applicants (due to your enthusiasm or match, see below). However, note that attempts to select interview clothing that will help you to be noticed, such as a 'power tie' (for men), or a bright red dress (a particularly bad idea for men), are usually misguided.

Enthusiasm

Imagine that you are an internship supervisor on the admissions committee. Would you like an apathetic or enthusiastic co-worker/trainee to arrive to work everyday? Would you like supervision meetings to be dull, perfunctory, and mundane, or enlightening, rewarding, and stimulating? An enthusiastic intern is energetic, grateful, and motivated, eliciting the same in his/her supervisors. With all other qualities being equal, the enthusiastic intern applicant is always the desired choice.

Expression of enthusiasm during your interview can be accomplished in subtle ways (Note: the use of pom-poms to spell out the name of the internship site during the interview is generally unnecessary). When asked to discuss your interests or to describe your past experiences, a smile and brief, prefatory remark (e.g., "OK, here's an experience that was particularly rewarding." "That opportunity is something that is especially exciting for me" "That is just the kind of activity that I am really looking forward to.") is very effective. It is of course important that this is sincere, and if you are sitting in the office of a faculty member who will supervise you on the rotation that perfectly matches those training goals that you have developed to guide you towards the ideal career of your choice, then it should be fairly easy to muster the appropriate level of enthusiasm. If you believe that you are a relatively "low-key" person who doesn't frequently express giddy happiness, however, you may want to practice a little in mock interviews before visiting sites.

Match

Rather than an evaluation period, the interview process could be accurately described as a sorting process between applicants and sites. Because most applicants will be placed, the interview period offers a time for all to determine 'fit' more than anything else. Like on the essays, your job on the interview is to reveal the match—explicitly, clearly, repeatedly. Note that many interviewers will have reviewed your application materials long ago, or not at all; thus, it is crucial that you state the names of rotations, faculty, and other experiences that you think makes the site match your needs.

You will be asked for your internship goals numerous times during the interview process. Your work during the initial phase of this process once again will pay off. State your goals followed by your assessment of how the site will meet them.

Virtually every question asked on an interview can be used to launch a discussion about the match (while showing enthusiasm). If asked about your theoretical orientation, reply, and then immediately ask about the related opportunities available at the site—if you are excited by the response, say so—clearly (see Williams & Prinstein, 2004 for a list of common interview questions). If asked to discuss career goals, reply, and ask about the types of careers typically pursued by interns from this site. Again, if you like what you hear—say so. If you don't like what you hear, but you are intrigued and feel you can be open-minded, then indicate this. By the end of the interview, it should be readily apparent to you and the interviewer that you are (or are not) well suited for a position at this site. Remember, the goal of this process is not merely to get a slot, but to get a true match.

Thank You Notes

Be a courteous, respectful visitor to each site. A brief note following your visit is a nice way to express gratitude, and a great final opportunity to once again state how the site matched your goals. If you are especially interested in the site, be sure to state this in the note. However, remember that thank you notes are not at all necessary, nor is the form of the note (i.e., email, handwritten on personal stationary, singing telegram) at all important.

MAKING YOUR DECISIONS

Be sure to keep careful notes of your impressions as you finish each interview day. Your initial (and most accurate) impressions are very susceptible to interference during this process, and you will want to make sure that you select a site that you will be comfortable with upon placement. When you finish all of your interviews, use these notes to review each site and the initial goals you had constructed for internship training. Based on your experiences interviewing at each site, it is common to discover some new priorities, and you may wish to add or delete a goal from your list. A rating of each site on each of these goals can give you some concrete information on how each program fits your needs. However, an un-quantifiable "gut" feeling may ultimately prevail in making your decisions.

Remember to solicit the feedback of your mentors when making your final decisions. Also take into consideration any additional information you have encountered subsequent to the interview day. It is quite common for training sites to call you or your mentor with an opportunity to ask additional questions, or with a subtle statement indicating their level of interest in your application. Although this should not ultimately affect your rank order list (see Chapter 13 in this volume), this could prove informative nonetheless.

CONCLUSION

The internship application process is the first step towards establishing an independent identity in the field. Although admittedly difficult to appreciate while experiencing the process, most who have survived report that the applications and interviews allowed for critical self-evaluation of professional goals, and establishment of professional connections that last throughout an entire career. You will emerge from this process not only with an internship placement at the site of your choice, but also a more clear direction regarding your professional future than before.

ADDITIONAL RESOURCES

Williams, C., & Prinstein, M. J. (2004). *Internships in psychology: The APAGS workbook for writing successful Applications and finding the right match.* Washington, DC: American Psychological Association.

Instructions for joining the APPIC INTERN-NETWORK listserve for questions and discussion can be found at www.appic.org

REFERENCES

Keilin, W. G., Thorn, B. E., Rodolfa, E. R., Constantine, M. G., & Kaslow, N. J. (2000). Examining the balance of internship supply and demand: 1999 Association of Psychology Postdoctoral and Internship Centers' match implications. *Professional Psychology: Research and Practice, 31*, 288–294.

Williams, C., & Prinstein, M. J. (2004). *Internships in psychology: The APAGS workbook for writing successful Applications and finding the right match.* Washington, DC: American Psychological Association.

CHAPTER 13

Predoctoral Internship

The APPIC Computer Match

W. GREGORY KEILIN

In 1999, the Association of Psychology Postdoctoral and Internship Centers (APPIC) began using a computer-based matching program to place students in available internship positions. This new system (called the "APPIC Match") was implemented because of the significant difficulties experienced by participants in the previous selection process (Keilin, 1998; Stedman, 1997). In fact, the APPIC Match was found to be a significant improvement, with applicants reporting far fewer policy violations by internship sites and less "game-playing" overall, while feedback from academic training directors suggested that students experienced greater satisfaction with their internship placement and reduced levels of stress during the process (Keilin, 2000).

This chapter will provide you with an overview of both the APPIC Matching Program and the APPIC Clearinghouse (the mechanism through which unmatched applicants can learn about available internship positions after the Match is completed). While the information in this chapter is accurate as of this writing, changes and enhancements are generally made each year. Thus, you should always consult the current Match instructions for the most up-to-date information available.

OVERVIEW OF THE APPIC MATCH

The APPIC Match is administered by National Matching Services, Inc. (NMS), a company based in Toronto, Canada. NMS has extensive experience in administering matching programs for various professions. NMS and APPIC work closely throughout the process to ensure that the Match is conducted in a fair and orderly process. Extensive information about the Match may be found at both of these web sites:

APPIC: http://www.appic.org/
National Matching Services: http://www.natmatch.com/psychint/

W. GREGORY KEILIN • Counseling and Mental Health Center, The University of Texas at Austin, Austin, TX 78712

Here is a brief overview of the internship selection process:

1. Each applicant registers for the APPIC Match, which involves completing a registration form (available at the NMS web site) and submitting the appropriate non-refundable Match fee.
2. From approximately November through January, applicants submit applications directly to internship sites and participate in interviews.
3. Prior to a specified deadline date, applicants and programs submit "Rank Order Lists" (ROLs) to National Matching Services. An applicant's ROL is a list of all internship programs to which he or she would like to be matched, in order of preference. The Matching Program uses this information to place the applicant in his or her highest-ranked program that has not filled its positions with applicants ranked higher on its ROL. Applicants' and sites' rankings are given equal weight in the process. Specific information about how the matching algorithm works is available on the NMS web site.
4. On a pre-determined date, results of the Match are released to applicants and programs. The results of the Match are binding on all parties, in that applicants are required to attend the internship site to which they have been matched, and programs are required to accept the applicants to whom they have been matched.

INTERNSHIP SUPPLY AND DEMAND

In recent years, much has been written about the apparent shortage of internship slots in comparison to the number of applicants (e.g., Dixon & Thorn, 2000; Oehlert & Lopez, 1998). Many students are concerned about how this "Supply and Demand" imbalance will impact their chances of securing an internship position.

Fortunately, this situation appears to be improving. Since the APPIC Match was instituted in 1999, the number of available internship positions has increased while the number of applicants has stayed about the same. At this writing, the most recent selection process was in 2000–2001, and APPIC estimated that approximately 95% of all internship applicants were placed that year in a position. This reflects an improvement from the 1998–99 selection process, in which 91% of applicants were successfully placed (Keilin et al., 2000).

There are several things that you can do to increase the likelihood of finding a position:

1. Apply to a reasonable number of internship sites. A recent study (Keilin, 2000) recommended applying to between 11 and 15 sites, as applying to more does not appear to significantly increase one's chances of being matched. Applicants who are geographically limited in their internship search (and thus apply to fewer sites) generally have a more difficult time getting placed (Keilin et al., 2000).
2. Apply to a diversity of internship sites. Applicants who apply to mostly very popular or competitive sites may run a greater risk of not being matched. You may wish to consult the APPIC Online Directory for information about the number of applications that sites receive.
3. Seek out a full-time, rather than a part-time, internship placement. Unfortunately, the number of part-time internship positions that are available nationally is extremely limited, and those who are seeking such positions (due to family or other obligations) can have a difficult time finding a placement. Some applicants have successfully negotiated the creation of a half-time position; thus, you may wish to contact Training Directors to see if they have some flexibility in this regard.

4. If you are not successfully placed via the APPIC Match, don't give up. Many positions are still available after the Match, and the majority of unplaced applicants are still able to find a position.

NAVIGATING THE APPIC MATCH

One of the best ways to stay informed about the Match is to subscribe to the APPIC e-mail list MATCH-NEWS. This is a low-volume list (i.e., you will usually receive no more than five e-mail messages per month) that provides news, information, and tips about the Match and the selection process. Specific instructions for subscribing to this list are available at the APPIC web site. Some students subscribe to this list well before they intend to apply for internship as a way of preparing themselves for the process.

Match Registration

All applicants who intend to participate in the APPIC Match are required to register with NMS. Registration forms may be downloaded to your computer directly from the NMS web site. Simply print out a copy of the registration materials, fill them out, and submit them via regular mail to NMS along with the appropriate Match fee. If you are enrolled in a doctoral program that is an "APPIC Subscriber" (i.e., pays an annual fee to APPIC for a subscription to the Directory), you will receive a discounted Match fee.

Approximately 2–3 weeks after submitting your registration materials, you will receive a confirmation from NMS that includes your unique Applicant Code Number and a password. This Code Number should be communicated to internship sites at some point during the process, as it will be used to uniquely identify you when they submit their rankings. The password should be kept confidential, and you will use it later in the process to login to the NMS web site to submit your rankings and to obtain your Match result.

You should register prior to the announced applicant registration deadline; in fact, you may wish to register earlier so that you will have your Applicant Code Number in time to enter it on your internship applications. However, if you are unsure whether or not you will be ready to apply to internship in the current year, you may wish to wait to register until you are more certain (but not later than the registration deadline) as the Match fee is non-refundable.

Once you have completed the Match registration process, you can focus on the application and interview portions of the process. There is little to do as far as the Match is concerned until your interviews are completed.

Match Policies

It is extremely important that you take the time to carefully read the APPIC Match Policies. These Policies dictate the operation of the Match, and outline the responsibilities that are expected of both applicants and programs throughout the selection process.

As of this writing, the Match Policies specifically prohibit applicants and programs from soliciting or communicating any ranking-related information. This means that you are not permitted to communicate to a site where you intend to rank them, nor are you allowed to ask a site where they intend to rank you. Similarly, sites are not permitted to share their rankings of you or inquire as to how you rank them. However, even with this prohibition, it is still permissible to express normal and genuine interest in a site, as long as such expressions do not communicate ranking information.

Here are some examples of statements that might be considered either acceptable or unacceptable under the current Match Policies:

ACCEPTABLE:	"I've really enjoyed this interview."
	"I believe this rotation will really meet my training needs."
	"I'm not very interested in the neuropsychology training that you offer."
UNACCEPTABLE:	"Your site is my top choice."
	"Your site will be very high in my rankings."
	"Where do you intend to rank me?"

APPIC provides two separate mechanisms for students who run into difficulties during the process or experience a violation of the Match Policies:

1. "Informal Problem Resolution" process: this allows you to confidentially consult with an APPIC representative regarding your situation. The representative will help you examine the various options available to you and, when appropriate, may intervene on your behalf (with your permission). You may also get assistance in determining whether the filing of a formal complaint is appropriate. Applicants are often more comfortable contacting APPIC on an informal basis, and many problems are quickly and efficiently resolved using this approach.
2. APPIC Standards and Review Committee (ASARC): This committee was established by APPIC to review and adjudicate formal complaints filed by Match participants. If you experience a violation of a Match Policy, you may file a formal complaint with ASARC. In addition, if you violate any of the Match Policies, an internship program could file a complaint against you. ASARC reviews these complaints and makes recommendations to the APPIC Board, which may then choose to impose sanctions on participants.

Constructing Your Rank Order List

As you go through the interview process, you will develop both positive and negative impressions of the various internship programs that you are considering. Many applicants like to take notes after each interview or use some other method of organizing these impressions. Such organization will be very helpful to you in deciding how to rank the internship programs to which you have applied.

You will be required to submit to NMS a confidential "Rank Order List" (ROL), which is simply your list of internship programs ranked in the order in which you prefer them. Thus, the internship program that you most want to attend should be listed as your #1 choice; your second most-preferred program should be listed second; and so on. Because your ROL will remain confidential, you are free to rank programs in any order that you wish without being concerned that sites will ever know how you have ranked them.

It is *extremely important* that you rank your programs in the order in which you prefer them, and that you do *not* take into consideration such things as: how you believe these programs are ranking you, how competitive the programs are, whether others from your program are applying to these programs, how many applicants have applied to these programs, etc. In other words, the program that you most want to attend should be listed first on your ROL *regardless* of how you perceive your chances of being matched to that program. The matching program has been designed such that the *only* correct approach is to rank your sites in the order that you prefer them; any other strategy will very likely result in a match that you are less happy with.

For example, if your top choice is program "A," but you believe that your chances of getting matched to "A" are very small, you should still list "A" as your top choice. Doing so will *not* decrease your chances of being matched to sites lower on your list if the computer is unable to match you to program "A." Similarly, if program "Z" is the site that you least prefer, but you believe that your chances of getting matched to "Z" are very high, you should still list "Z" are your last choice. Doing so will allow the computer to attempt to match you to the more-preferred choices on your list without reducing your chances of being matched to "Z."

To further illustrate the importance of ranking programs based on your true preferences: let's say that you consider program "A" to be your top choice and program "B" to be your second choice, and your submitted ROL reflects these preferences. Furthermore, assume that program "A" ranks you tenth, while program "B" ranks you as its top choice. The computer will first make every attempt to match you to your top choice, program "A," before attempting to match you to any program lower on your list. If the computer is able to match you to program "A," it is finished (and you are very happy!). However, if the computer is unable to match you to program "A," it then moves to the next program on your list—in this scenario, program "B." Since program "B" ranked you as its top choice, you would definitely be matched to program "B." As you can see from this example, ranking programs based on your true preferences allows you to try for your top-ranked programs without hurting your chances at lower-ranked programs if your higher-ranked choices don't work out.

When constructing your ROL, you will need to use the unique Program Code Number assigned to each of the internship programs that you are ranking. These numbers are available directly from each internship program and may also be found on the NMS web site. Some internship sites have more than one "program" (i.e., rotation or training experience) in the Match, and would thus be assigned more than one Program Code Number. For example, a site could have three separate programs in the match: a neuropsychology program, a geropsychology program, and a "general psychology" program, each with its own Program Code Number. Another site could have two programs, one for paid positions and one for unpaid positions. In the latter example, if you were very interested in a paid position at that site but not very interested in an unpaid position, you would rank the program number for paid positions relatively high on your ROL while ranking the unpaid position relatively low (or you could leave it off of your list altogether).

There is no limit to the number of programs that you can list on your ROL. You should rank all programs at which you are still under consideration and which you still find acceptable. If you decide that any internship program is not acceptable to you, simply leave it off of your ROL and you will not be matched to that program under any circumstances.

If you applied to any internship programs that are not participating in the Match, you may have a difficult decision to make: whether to withdraw from the Match in order to accept a position at a non-participating site, or to participate in the Match by submitting a Rank Order List.

Submitting Your Rank Order List

Once you have determined your rankings, you must submit them to NMS via the internet no later than the Rank Order List submission deadline (currently in early February but subject to change). Internship programs are also required to submit their ROLs by this deadline. Remember that submitting your ROL means that you are committing yourself to attend the internship program to which you are matched by the computer.

To submit your rankings, you must first login to the NMS web site using your Applicant Code Number and password. Then, simply follow the instructions to enter your ROL. You must use the appropriate Program Code Numbers to identify the programs that you are ranking. If you later change your mind about your rankings, you are permitted to make changes to your ROL as long as it is prior to the deadline.

Once you have entered your ROL, the final step is to certify your rankings. Certification means that you are designating that your ROL is complete and may be used in the Match processing. You may still make changes to a certified ROL, but doing so decertifies it and you must re-certify it once you have finished making changes.

After electronically submitting your ROL, there is nothing more to do other than to relax and wait for your results. These is generally about a two-and-one-half week wait between the ROL submission deadline and the release of the Match results. This waiting period can be somewhat difficult and anxiety-provoking, but it is necessary because NMS uses this time to perform extensive verification of all applicants' and programs' ROLs. This verification process catches some of the errors made by applicants and programs, and ensures that no one is accidentally left out of the process.

Receiving Your Match Results

Currently, the results of the Match are released in a two-step process. The first step (currently on a Friday) involves all applicants being told whether or not they were matched but *not* the name of the site to which they were matched. On the following Monday (known as "APPIC Match Day"), applicants are told the names of the internship programs to whom they are matched, and programs are told the names of the applicants to which they are matched. The reason for this two-step process is to provide a three-day advance notice to applicants who were not matched to any program so they have time to prepare for the opening of the Clearinghouse on Match Day.

Generally, about half of all applicants are matched to their top-ranked internship program, while four out of five are matched to one of their first three choices.

The results that you receive from the Match are binding—in other words, you are required to attend the internship program to which you are matched, and that internship program is required to accept you as an intern. On Match Day, matched applicants and their new Training Directors generally contact each other to acknowledge and celebrate the Match result. Shortly after Match Day, your new Training Director will mail you a written contract that confirms the terms of your appointment.

REMAINING UNMATCHED: THE APPIC CLEARINGHOUSE

Each year, many qualified applicants are disappointed to learn that they have not been matched to an internship program. Similarly, some excellent internship programs do not fill all of their positions. For the unmatched applicant, this can be a very difficult and frustrating experience, particularly after the many months of effort and considerable expense involved in the application and interview process.

If you discover yourself in this position, it is important to remember that there are many opportunities to secure an internship position after the Match. In fact, recent research has shown that nearly two-thirds of unmatched applicants are able to find an internship position after Match Day (Keilin et al., 2000). Thus, while not being matched can be a very discouraging and disheartening experience, it is important to stay focused and continue moving forward, as your chances of finding a position are still quite good.

Currently, applicants are told several days prior to APPIC Match Day about whether or not they have been matched to an internship program. Thus, if you learn that you have not been matched, you have several days to prepare for the next step. As an unmatched applicant, your primary source of information about available positions will be the APPIC Clearinghouse. The Clearinghouse opens on Match Day and operates essentially as an electronic bulletin board of available internship positions. The Clearinghouse consists of two different parts:

- *Listing of Unfilled Positions*: A list of programs that have unfilled positions from the Match. This list is initially posted on the NMS web site on APPIC Match Day, is not updated once it has been posted, and is removed from the web site after ten days. While some Training Directors may choose to be excluded from this list, you will find that the list contains the vast majority of unfilled positions from the Match.
- *Clearinghouse E-mail List*: This is an e-mail distribution list to which internship Training Directors can post announcements about their available positions. Subscribing to this list means that you will receive these postings directly into your e-mailbox. Instructions for subscribing to the Clearinghouse e-mail list are provided on the APPIC web site.

Both the Listing of Unfilled Positions and the Clearinghouse e-mail list are important sources of information, and you should expect to use both extensively throughout the process.

Upon learning that you are unmatched, there are several important steps to take in preparing for the opening of the Clearinghouse:

1. Consult with your Director of Clinical Training, other faculty members, family, and friends about your options, as these individuals can provide you with valuable information and support throughout the process. It can be very helpful to discuss some of the following issues in advance:
   - Whether you are willing to consider a broader range of internship options (e.g., different training experiences or settings, other geographical locations, unfunded positions)
   - Whether you are willing to accept placement at a non-APA accredited or non-APPIC member internship site (you should discuss the implications of doing so, particularly with regard to licensure and future employment, with your faculty)
   - Clarify what types of sites or training experiences you are <u>not</u> willing to consider
2. Prepare multiple copies of your application materials, including your vita, APPIC Application, cover letter, and transcripts. Talk with the individuals who wrote your letters of recommendation to see how you can best work with them to get these materials sent out quickly to internship sites.

3. Since the Clearinghouse moves quickly, it is very important that you clear your schedule for at least the first several days beginning on Match Day. You should ensure that you have essentially unlimited access to a fax machine, a computer with internet and e-mail access, and a telephone. It can also be helpful to have some envelopes and labels available in case you need to send materials via an overnight delivery service.
4. Recruit family members and friends who can provide you with emotional and logistical support during this period.
5. Carefully review the materials on the operation of the Clearinghouse that are located on the APPIC web site.

Applying for Positions

Once the Clearinghouse opens, you will have access to the Listing of Unfilled Positions, and (if you are subscribed to the Clearinghouse e-mail list) you will begin receiving e-mail messages containing vacancy announcements. The information contained in the Listing of Unfilled Positions is very limited, and many Training Directors will use the Clearinghouse e-mail list to provide far more detailed information about their positions, application procedures, qualifications they are looking for in applicants, etc. The Listing of Unfilled Positions and the Clearinghouse e-mail list can differ significantly, in that you could find a position listed in one but not the other. Thus, it may be helpful to have a system in place that allows you to organize and prioritize this rapid influx of information.

It is vitally important to understand that the Clearinghouse moves very rapidly, with positions being filled in a matter of a few days or, in some case, a few hours. A recent study (Keilin et al., 2000) found that 40% of all unfilled positions were filled within the first week after Match Day. This means that you should move very quickly to apply to those positions that are of interest to you.

You will also find that the structured nature of the application, interview, and results notification process that occurred up until Match Day is now completely different. When filling positions after the conclusion of the Match, sites are free to set their own application, interviewing, and hiring procedures. For example, you may find that a site may discontinue accepting applications before you have had a chance to apply. Or, a site could tender you an offer and expect a response within a very short period of time.

APPIC is not the only organization that provides a Clearinghouse of unfilled positions. Currently, at least one other organization (ACCTA, the Association of Counseling Center Training Agencies) operates a Clearinghouse for the benefit of students and programs. More information on other organizations' Clearinghouses can be found at the APPIC web site.

CONCLUSION

While the internship application and interview process can be challenging to navigate, many students find it to be a rewarding and validating experience. The APPIC Match was designed to reduce the pressure and anxiety that has been traditionally associated with this process. You should feel free to contact APPIC or NMS at any time if you have any questions.

Best of luck with your internship search!

REFERENCES

Dixon, K. E., & Thorn, B. E. (2000). Does the internship shortage portend market saturation? 1998 placement data across the four major national training councils. *Professional Psychology: Research and Practice, 31*, 276–280.

Keilin, W. G. (1998). Internship selection 30 years later: An overview of the APPIC matching program. *Professional Psychology: Research and Practice, 29*, 599–603.

Keilin, W. G. (2000). Internship selection in 1999: Was the Association of Psychology Postdoctoral and Internship Centers' Match a success? *Professional Psychology: Research and Practice, 31*, 281–287.

Keilin, W. G., Thorn, B. E., Rodolfa, E. R., Constantine, M. G., & Kaslow, N. J. (2000). Examining the balance of internship supply and demand: 1999 Association of Psychology Postdoctoral and Internship Centers' Match Implications. *Professional Psychology: Research and Practice, 31*, 288–294.

Oehlert, M. E., & Lopez, S. J. (1998). APA-accredited internships: An examination of the supply and demand issue. *Professional Psychology: Research and Practice, 29*, 189–194.

Stedman, J. M. (1997). What we know about predoctoral internship training: A review. *Professional Psychology: Research and Practice, 28*, 475–485.

CHAPTER 14

Obtaining a License to Practice Psychology

COREY J. HABBEN

In a profession that is rich with complexity and virtually boundless in applications, the simplest of facts remains: if you want to practice as a psychologist, you must be licensed to do so. This is true in every state, province, and territory of the United States and Canada. In several states, you may not legally use the title of "psychologist" without a license to practice psychology. Perhaps the most damaging reality is that a license is required by nearly every third-party payer for reimbursement of services. Without the ability to independently receive reimbursement for services, there is very little you can do without a license to practice and earn a sustainable income. Although the primary rationale for the license to practice is protection of the public, it can sometimes feel like yet another hurdle to a new psychologist.

Many graduates of doctoral-level psychology programs go on to have full and rewarding careers without ever obtaining a license. University professors and research scientists have no practical need for it (although some will obtain a license to supervise clinical students, conduct treatment outcome studies, or to satisfy accreditation requirements). Nevertheless, if your plan is to rely on practicing psychology, then the psychology license represents the first essential requirement for independent practice. You do not become a practicing psychologist when you receive your doctorate; you become one when you obtain your license.

You may have various reasons for wanting a license. You may be training to start a career as a full-time practicing psychologist. Or, you may plan to work in an academic setting with the hopes of doing some clinical work on a part-time basis. Perhaps you want to train and supervise students to become psychologists themselves. Regardless of your reason for seeking licensure, there are many things that you need to know in order to make the licensure process occur smoothly and expeditiously. This chapter is intended to provide you with the main information you need to plan and execute the process of obtaining your license. As you will discover, there is some variability among states, provinces, and territories which may play a role in your future as you plan your career. Table 1 lists a number of suggestions for beginning the licensure application process.

COREY J. HABBEN • Behavioral Health Clinic, Walter Reed Army Medical Center, Washington, DC 20307-5001

TABLE 1. Essential Tips For Getting Licensed

Applying/Preparing (during your pre-doctoral internship year)

- buy the ASPPB Handbook of Licensing and Certification Requirements for Psychologists
- contact your licensing board and request an application packet
- know the requirements of your jurisdiction and make sure your training meets eligibility
- contact supervisors and provide them with necessary documentation
- complete typed application, documentation, and submit transcripts
- submit your application when you are eligible (usually after post-doctoral year is complete), respecting any deadlines
- prepare yourself for numerous fees

Studying (during your post-doctoral year)

- purchase an EPPP study program kit; if it is too expensive, share the expense with another applicant or borrow a recently-used (i.e., within last two years) kit
- take your first practice exam no earlier than 12 months, and no later than 6 months, *within* your anticipated EPPP exam date to identify your baseline "pre-study" score
- begin studying lightly six months prior to your exam
- continue self-administering timed practice exams once or twice per month, reviewing your errors, analyzing weaker content areas, and charting scores and dates
- focus your study time on the content areas with which you are having the most difficulty
- increase study time accordingly based on performance on practice exams
- become familiar and comfortable with the unique style of EPPP questions and multiple-choice answers
- do not cram

BEFORE YOU EVEN GET STARTED: LOOKING AHEAD

Psychology licensure laws are quite different from driver's license laws, in more ways than one. Every state, province, and territory in the United States and Canada has its own unique licensure law. Although the laws are all generally similar, there is enough variability to make some license requirements uniquely different from others (e.g., exam cutoff scores, supervised training hour requirements, etc.). To complicate things further, the license for each state, province, or territory applies *only* for that state, province, or territory. If you have a license to practice in California, you cannot practice in New York unless you have a New York license; your license only applies in California. If you were to move to New York and you wanted to continue practicing, you would then need to also get licensed in New York.

Because of these differences, it is important to know the state(s) in which you plan to be licensed as you begin preparing for the licensure application process. Unfortunately, this requires an assumption that you know in which state(s) you will be living or working within a year or two; an assumption that may not always be realistic. What if you live in New Jersey and you will be looking at jobs in both New Jersey and New York? What if you are considering several different states yet have no idea what jobs will be available? What if your spouse or partner will need to relocate to an as yet undetermined area in the future? What if you decide to relocate to another state many years into your career?

There can be a number of reasons why you may not be certain where you will be practicing, yet you will likely only be able to apply for one state license. Because of this, it is a good idea to become familiar with the requirements for the states you are considering; particularly, your top three preferences. Knowing what these states require will be very important as you complete your internship and post-doctoral training. You want to ensure that your training, whether pre-doctoral or post-doctoral, is meeting the minimum eligibility requirements for all of the states you are seriously considering. Most pre-doctoral internships and post-doctoral fellowships will design their training so that your training hours exceed the eligibility requirements for most states.

GENERAL ELIGIBILITY REQUIREMENTS FOR LICENSURE: WHAT YOU WILL NEED

Although there is some variability, requirements for licensure involve three main areas: education, training/supervised experience, and examinations. As noted, each state, province, and territory has its own specific licensure requirements and the wording can often vary. Eligibility requirements will be described in more general terms.

Education

All licensure laws for independent practice require a doctoral degree in psychology, usually from a regionally accredited institution. Criteria are usually provided for required coursework. Because each jurisdiction is different, you will want to ensure that your transcript includes the required courses specified. Some states prefer the program be APA-accredited. If you do happen to graduate from a non-APA-accredited program, you will need to provide documentation that your program provided all of the required coursework specified.

Training/Supervised Experience

Currently, it is standard that at least two years of approved full-time supervised experience be required. Of these two years, one year is usually pre-doctoral (internship) and the other year is post-doctoral (postdoc). The hours for both pre-doctoral and post-doctoral experience range from 1500 to 2000 per year, although one state (Michigan) and the District of Columbia require two years of post-doctoral experience and another state (Alabama) requires no post-doctoral experience. Criteria for supervision time are usually specified.

Examinations

A passing score on the Examination for Professional Practice in Psychology (EPPP) is required by all states, provinces, and territories. The EPPP will be discussed in more detail later in the chapter. Only applicants for licensure are eligible to take the EPPP; it is not an exam you can take during graduate school or internship. The EPPP is most commonly taken upon completion of the post-doctoral year. Some states also require oral and/or written exams, usually the jurisprudence exam.

Assuming these requirements, it is a good idea to begin contacting any state, provincial, or territorial licensing board for licensure application information before you begin your post-doctoral year. In addition to the application, this should include a copy of the licensure law as well as the rules and regulations of the board. It will be important to determine when you will be eligible to take the EPPP exam, as well as any other required examinations, and to complete any required paperwork prior to the appropriate deadlines. You may find that materials need to be submitted by a deadline that falls during the middle of your post-doctoral year. A list of state, provincial, and territorial psychology licensing board phone numbers and addresses is available at the website for the Association of State and Provincial Psychology Licensing Boards (ASPPB) at www.asppb.org.

Considerations of Differences Among State, Provincial, and Territorial Requirements

As mentioned, each state, provincial, and territorial license law is different. As a result of this, there are roughly 62 slightly different sets of requirements. Although they are similar in many ways, you will want to be aware of the way in which they are specifically different. As you review the licensure requirements for the state, province, or territory you are considering, there are a number of questions you will need to address:

- Does my degree meet the required criteria?
- Do I have the minimum number of required hours for both pre-doctoral internship and post-doctoral training? Do both training experiences meet the criteria?
- Do I have enough documented supervision time? Is that requirement specified?
- What is the cutoff score for the EPPP? When will I be eligible to take the EPPP?
- Am I required to take any other examinations?
- What are the deadlines for submitting my application and documentation?
- What are the various fees I will be expected to pay?

These questions should all be answered in the materials you receive from the licensing board. *The Handbook of Licensing and Certification Requirements for Psychologists in North America* is revised each year and lists the basic requirements for licensure in all 62 states, provinces, and territories. This handbook ($26) is an essential resource and is published by ASPPB. Purchase information is available at www.asppb.org.

As you review the requirements for your state, province, or territory, it is recommended that you consider the requirements for the other 61 licensing boards. It is ideal to exceed the requirements for all 62 licensing boards should you ever wish to obtain licensure in another state later in your career. For example, a 1600-hour pre-doctoral internship is sufficient for licensure in Colorado, yet it falls short for dozens of other states. If you were considering practice in the Washington, DC area, you would want to know that the requirements for face-to-face supervision for post-doctoral training differs from 52 hours per year in the Maryland, 100 hours per year in Virginia, and 150 hours per year in the District of Columbia. It would also be important to know that the most common EPPP cutoff score is 70%, although a few boards have a different cutoff score for each test administration. A review of the requirements for all 62 licensing boards on the three main areas (education, supervised experience, and examinations) will help inform you.

THE EXAMINATION FOR PROFESSIONAL PRACTICE IN PSYCHOLOGY (EPPP)

The Examination for Professional Practice in Psychology (EPPP) was developed by the Association of State and Provincial Psychology Boards (ASPPB) to serve as a standardized examination to evaluate applicants for licensure. Its stated intent is to evaluate the broad-based knowledge expected to be gained, following the appropriate doctoral education and supervised training in psychology. All 62 licensing boards require the EPPP for licensure in psychology.

At the time of writing this edition, the administration of the EPPP was in the process of transitioning from a paper-and-pencil exam to a computer-administered exam. During 2001, computer administration of the EPPP was voluntary; however, as of 2002 the EPPP will be administered entirely as a computerized exam. The paper-and-pencil EPPP was made up of 200 multiple-choice items. Although the basic content and structure of the test remains the same, the computerized administration is made up of 225 items, although only 200 items are scored. The additional 25 items are used as experimental items to be determined whether or not to use in future administrations. The computerized administration of the EPPP has a time limit of four hours and fifteen minutes, which allows for fifteen additional minutes over the original four-hour limit of the shorter pencil-and-paper exam.

The content of the EPPP consists of items representing eight weighted content areas. These content areas are based on a 1995 analysis examining what licensed psychologists do and what knowledge is required of them. Detailed explanations for each of the content areas are available from ASPPB, and are summarized below with their content percentage:

- *Treatment/Intervention* (16%)—Knowledge of (a) individual, group, or organizational interventions for specific concerns/disorders, (b) treatment theories, and (c) consultation models and processes
- *Ethical/Legal/Professional Issues* (15%)—Knowledge of (a) the ethical code, (b) professional standards for practice, (c) legal mandates, (d) guidelines for ethical decision-making, and (e) consultation models and processes
- *Assessment and Diagnosis* (14%)—Knowledge of (a) psychometrics, (b) assessment models, (c) methods for assessment of individuals and organizations/systems, and (d) diagnostic classification systems and issues
- *Cognitive-Affective Bases of Behavior* (13%)—Knowledge of (a) cognitive science, (b) theories of learning, memory, motivation, and emotion, and (c) factors that influence and individual's cognitive performance and/or emotional experience
- *Growth and Lifespan Development* (13%)—Knowledge of (a) age-appropriate child, adolescent, and adult development, (b) atypical patterns of development, and (c) the protective and risk factors that influence developmental outcomes for individuals
- *Social and Multicultural Bases of Behavior* (12%)—Knowledge of (a) social cognition, social interaction processes, and organizational dynamics, (b) theories of personality, and (c) issues in diversity (multiethnic, multicultural, gender, ageism, sexual orientation, and disability)
- *Biological Bases of Behavior* (11%)—Knowledge of (a) neuroscience, (b) the physiological bases of behavior and illness, and (c) psychopharmacology
- *Research Methods* (6%)—Knowledge of (a) research design, methodology, and program evaluation, (b) statistical procedures, and (c) criteria for accurate interpretation of research findings

Although "Research Methods" is the content area with the smallest weighting, it had previously been one of the largest. As a result, individuals who had taken the EPPP prior to the revisions in the later 1990's may note that the EPPP emphasizes research methodology and statistics. This is no longer true, as the content has been modified to emphasize more clinical issues.

One striking advantage of the computerized administration over the pencil-and-paper version is the flexibility of administration dates. The pencil-and-paper EPPP was only administered on two dates per year, once in April and again in October. This led to practical problems such as being delayed several months due to missing an application deadline by a few weeks, or delaying retakes of failed exams. The computerized EPPP can be taken six days a week throughout the year. Should you need to retake the examination, up to four exams are allowed per year; you would only need to wait at least sixty days from your previous administration. The EPPP is administered at an authorized Prometric Testing Centers, of which there are roughly three hundred in the country, and you need not take the exam in the jurisdiction for which you are applying. Prometric Testing Centers in your vicinity can be located at www.prometric.com.

Another significant difference resulting from the shift to computerized testing is the use of scaled scores. The pencil-and-paper EPPP utilized a raw score and was reported as a percentage. For example, an applicant receiving 150 correct answers out of 200 would receive a raw score of 150, or 75%. With the computerized exams, the raw scores are converted to National Scaled Scores ranging from 200 to 800. This is done in an attempt to allow comparisons of different exams with varying difficulties. A National Scaled Score of 500 is considered the equivalent of a raw score of 140, or 70%. A National Scaled Score of 450 is considered the equivalent of a raw score of 130, or 65%. As of 2002, all scores will only be reported as scaled scores.

No computer proficiency is needed to take the computerized EPPP. The program is designed to allow you to skip a question, if necessary, and return to it later on. Upon finishing your exam, results should be received within two to three weeks. This is a marked improvement from the pencil-and-paper examination, which resulted in six to eight week waits for crucial EPPP exam score results.

STUDYING AND PREPARING FOR THE EPPP

Regardless of how you performed in graduate school, the EPPP is an examination that requires preparation, review, and practice. Many senior psychologists will candidly remark that, despite their experience and proficient knowledge of psychology, they would have a difficult time passing the EPPP were they to take it today. Yet, the majority of doctoral-level examinees do receive a passing score on the exam. Success on the EPPP will result from many of the same factors relied on in graduate school: a combination of preparation, knowledge, and anxiety management.

If you speak with others who have taken the EPPP, you will hear a variety of strategies to help prepare you for the EPPP. Perhaps the most focused and helpful of strategies are the EPPP study kits/programs often advertised on psychology publications such as the APA Monitor. The two most common and popular programs are available from the Association For Advanced Training In The Behavioral Sciences (www.aatbs.com) and Academic Review (www.areview.com). Both programs offer comprehensive multi-volume home study programs with analysis of content areas, full-length practice exams modeled after EPPP exams, multi-volume audio cassette programs, computer review programs, live workshops, and other study aids designed to prepare you for the EPPP. Prices are relatively expensive, although different price levels are available and many will argue that the benefits of the program are priceless. Both programs are comparable in effectiveness and reputation.

Perhaps the most integral components of these programs are also the most inexpensive to obtain; that is, the books, tapes, and practice exams. The designers of the program do an impressive job of condensing several years of psychology graduate school into books designed purely for study and review. Some academics may bristle at the notion of creating Cliff Notes versions of graduate school in psychology, however, the comparison fits and fits well. Your old text books were not designed to be reviewed as efficiently as these books were. The audio cassettes offer another mode of ingesting large amounts of information, particularly in times in which you would otherwise be doing very little such as commuting or exercising.

The practice exams, probably beyond anything else, are the most integral tool you can use to prepare you for the EPPP. Both AATBS and Academic Review offer over half a dozen full-length practice exams modeled after the EPPP and provided with detailed explanations for each answer. Sample items from former EPPP exams are also available through ASPPB and are quite helpful. There are a few benefits of the practice exams. First, you become more familiar with the often vague or cumbersome manner in which some EPPP items are presented. Second, you can continually monitor which content areas you understand with proficiency, and in which content areas you are underperforming. Continued administration of the practice exams provides you with opportunities to learn from items answered incorrectly. Finally, practice exams demystify the EPPP and condition you to the timing and fatigue variables and facilitate development of better test-taking strategies.

If you have completed a doctoral program in psychology, then you likely know what study strategies work best for you. Some people prefer to study individually, others prefer to study in groups. Your colleague may prefer to use flash-cards, while you never have. Nevertheless, it is best to avoid comparing your progress to that of others preparing for the EPPP; every person is different and you need to focus on the strategy that works for you. Regardless of what that strategy is, you should set aside several months of progressively intensive study to be adequately prepared for the EPPP. Some have suggested 300–400 hours of study time, although that would depend on your study habits. A sample study schedule is provided in Table 2.

Perhaps your best measure of your level of readiness will be reflected in your performance on the practice exams. Because of this, it is a good idea to take an initial practice exam *at least* six months in advance of your planned EPPP administration date. Both AATBS and Academic Review study programs should provide corresponding content areas for each question, which allows you to calculate percentage scores for each of the eight content areas. For example, you may find you scored 40% of the Treatment/Intervention questions, 51% of the Assessment and

TABLE 2. Studying for the EPPP

Sample study schedule for a six-month study plan

- Month 1—1–3 hours per week; 1 practice exam
- Month 2—2–5 hours per week; 1–2 practice exams
- Month 3—4–8 hours per week; 2–4 practice exams
- Month 4—7–12 hours per week; 2–4 practice exams
- Month 5—10–20 hours per week; 2–4 practice exams
- Month 6—10–20 hours per week; 2–4 practice exams

Additional Suggestions

- make adjustments based on your own study preferences, knowledge of content material, and performance on practice exams
- do not compare your study schedule to someone else's and panic; everyone is different
- plan on finding the EPPP challenging
- expect to get one out of every four questions incorrect (this would still give you an exceptional score)
- pace yourself
- anticipate a few questions that will seem impossible to answer correctly
- guess if you are uncertain; there is no penalty for guessing incorrectly so do not leave any items unanswered

Diagnosis questions, and so on. Do not be alarmed if your performance on the first practice exam is poorer than you expected. Keeping track of your performance on the eight content areas serves to inform you of the areas on which you need to focus your studies. It also provides you with a barometer of your progress over time. It is a good idea to take at least one, if not two, practice exams per month. It is *ideal* to be scoring above the 75% range overall by the time you are preparing to take the EPPP. As you review your scores, take note that the practice tests in both study kits are often more difficult than the EPPP itself. Although it is unlikely you will ever feel completely comfortable and confident, you should feel relatively prepared by the time you are ready to take the EPPP.

AFTER LICENSURE: BANKING YOUR CREDENTIALS

Assuming you have successfully completed all of the requirements for licensure and have obtained your professional license to practice psychology, you should consider banking your credentials (see Table 3). This usually involves the process of submitting and verifying documentation to a centralized credentials "bank" for your education/coursework, practica, internship, doctoral degree, post-doctoral training, EPPP scores, license, and other credentials. This can be very helpful and time-saving in the future as you apply for insurance or managed care panels, jobs, or other credentials. ASPPB offers a Credentials Bank program, which allows you to electronically store your transcripts, exam scores, and documentation of training experience so that it can be sent as needed to future licensing boards. As mentioned, you may find yourself changing jobs and location sometime in the future, whether in the next few years or decades from now. Organizing and submitting documentation can be difficult enough; it can become increasingly difficult years later after supervisors retire, programs modify or close, and addresses change. The Credentials Bank provides a readily accessible archive for necessary licensure documentation. There is an initial fee to set up the record, and then a maintenance fee every two years to keep the record available.

In an effort to streamline the mobility of licensure from state to state, ASPPB also developed the Certificate of Professional Qualification in Psychology (CPQ). The CPQ is a credential given to applicants who meet certain eligibility requirements (similar to most licensure requirements), practiced for a minimum of five years, and have no record of disciplinary action. ASPPB recommends to licensing boards that the CPQ be accepted as a sign of eligibility for licensure. At the time of this writing, 21 states and the District of Columbia accept the CPQ as evidence of eligibility for licensure.

The National Register of Health Service Providers in Psychology also provides the opportunity for credential banking. There are similar eligibility requirements, although once listed in the National Register there are additional benefits such as verifying credentials for applications

TABLE 3. To-do List After Obtaining a License

Upon Licensure

- bank your credentials with ASPPB or the National Register
- display your license in your main office as required by most jurisdictions
- remain current with license fees and continuing education requirements, if required
- retain copies of your licensure application information, which will be needed for various applications such as insurance panels or the American Board of Professional Psychology

to insurance panels and the American Board of Professional Psychology (ABPP). The National Register is available at www.nationalregister.org.

Some states, provinces, and territories will allow an applicant to be "license eligible" if they hold the CPQ, National Register, or ABPP. You would usually only need to take and pass the written or oral local examination, if required, to be licensed in that jurisdiction. Some jurisdictions will also require a certain number of continuing education hours per number of years to maintain licensure.

Throughout the process, obtaining a license can be a difficult, challenging, and even frustrating task. Yet, for the practicing psychologist, it is the most important credential you will ever acquire.

ADDITIONAL RESOURCES

Web Sites

- www.asppb.org—Association of State and Provincial Psychology Boards
- www.prometric.com—Prometric Testing Centers
- www.aatbs.com—Association for Advanced Training in the Behavioral Sciences
- www.areview.com—Academic Review
- www.nationalregister.com—National Register of Health Service Providers in Psychology

CHAPTER 15

Specialty Certification in Professional Psychology

TED PACKARD AND CARLA J. REYES

Since the mid 20th century an increasing number of psychologists have provided a variety of psychological services to the public and have identified themselves as "professional psychologists." This rapid development has resulted in psychology being recognized as a profession by our society in a fashion somewhat similar to the traditional professions of medicine, law, and the clergy. In achieving this recognition, professional psychology has had to measure up to five key criteria that define areas of professional and skilled practice in ours and many other societies.

HALLMARKS OF A PROFESSION

First, the services that practitioners of a profession provide must be perceived by the public as *valuable and necessary.* In a free enterprise society like our own, the market place often is the arbiter of what is perceived as valuable and necessary. With over 100,000 psychology licenses granted to date by U. S. jurisdictions (ASPPB, 2001a) and representation in almost all sectors of our health and mental health systems, psychology is now widely accepted as an important contributor to the common good.

Second, the professional services offered must be based on a *"corpus" or body of knowledge* that has developed over time and that represents foundation concepts, principles, and theories upon which practice is based. In addition, the body of knowledge must be sufficiently developed that it has been subjected to ongoing scientific evaluation and to public scrutiny.

Third, theory in and of itself is not sufficient for practice, and various applications of the corpus of knowledge must be developed. Thus, *methods, techniques, and procedures* employed by practitioners are derived from and connected to the underlying conceptual foundation. The widespread adoption in the educational and training system of the scientist-practitioner model, with its emphasis on the interactive relationship between science and practice, underscores this important point (Belar & Perry, 1992).

TED PACKARD AND CARLA J. REYES • Department of Educational Psychology, University of Utah, Salt Lake City, UT 84112

Fourth, a valued service based on a body of knowledge with related methods of practice is not sufficient, however, for broad recognition as a profession. Many societies, including our own, require statutory recognition by governmental authority. In the United States and Canada this occurs by action of state or provincial legislators rather than on a national level as occurs in a number of countries in other parts of the world (Bass, DeMers, Ogloff, Peterson, Pettifor, Reaves, Retfalvi, Simon, Sinclair, & Tipton, 1996). Thus, societal recognition as a profession requires legislative action and passage of *licensing or certification statues* that define the services offered and the qualifications required for practice at the independent level. Protection of the public from the ill-prepared and from charlatans is a primary rationale that undergirds licensing statutes. However, in almost all instances the laws are "generic" (i.e., general and non-specific) and give broad discretion to the profession in defining further how professionals will practice.

And this brings us to the fifth and, for this chapter, most important hallmark of a profession. Because the licensing statutes are generic, and many important details are left unstated, society in essence entrusts recognized professions to develop voluntarily a variety of *self-regulatory mechanisms* whose fundamental purpose, once again, is to protect the public from harm. Accreditation is one notable mechanism through which psychology attempts to implement this public trust. Programs that meet defined standards are identified as "accredited" by the Committee on Accreditation of the American Psychological Association (APA, 2000a), and the public is assured that graduates of such programs meet basic educational standards agreed upon by professional consensus. Ethics codes are a second important mechanism by which professions demonstrate their commitment to providing high quality and ethically acceptable services and to protecting the public from harm (APA, 1992). Such codes typically define key principles to which all practitioners should aspire (e.g., integrity), prescribe necessary standards of individual practice (e.g., confidentiality), and identify forbidden actions and situations that must be avoided (e.g., dual sexual relationships). The voluntary credentialing, or "certification," of individual practitioners who possess specialized skills is a third self-regulatory mechanism employed by the profession of psychology (Bent, Packard, & Goldberg, 1999). The fundamental purpose of certification is to protect the public by identifying practitioners who meet accepted standards of competence in a particular area of specialty practice. Knowledge of board certification status allows consumers to discriminate between self-proclaimed or ill prepared practitioners and bona fide specialists who have demonstrated competence by successfully passing rigorous peer review and examination procedures.

PROFESSIONAL CERTIFICATION

To certify something as true, accurate, or genuine connotes that a standard has been met and that evidence exists supporting this conclusion. A certificate of deposit from a bank, for example, attests that the identified individual or entity has indeed deposited the indicated sum. Receipt of a certified letter requires the documented signature of the specified recipient. The certification of a particular professional skill presumes that a standard previously agreed upon by a credible professional group has been met in a defined (and often limited) area of practice. The phrase "board certified" has been used for several decades by medical practitioners to describe physicians with documented skills in specific areas of specialization (ABMS, 2000), and it is a term increasingly applied to psychology specialists as our profession continues to grow and mature.

It is important to note at this point that the terms "certified" or "certification" have had more than one meaning in professional psychology. Many early licensing statutes were in fact certification laws, or title acts as they are sometimes called, and only protected use of terms like "psychologist" and "psychological" and did not include definitions of what psychology practice entailed. Licensure laws, or practice acts as they also are known, in addition to protecting use of titles also include "scope of practice" provisions that define the types of services provided by psychologists. Contemporary licensing statutes in almost all U. S. and several Canadian jurisdictions are licensure laws that define practice and protect use of titles. Only a handful of remaining jurisdictions, mainly in Canada, still have certification or title acts in force (ASPPB, 2001a). Use of the term certification in this statutory context is not the primary focus of this chapter, as our emphasis is on voluntary certification administered by recognized professional organizations that documents specialty skills of individual psychologists who already possess a statutory license to practice their profession.

By now it should be apparent that in this voluntary professional self-regulatory context there is a direct connection between the concept of psychology specialty and the certification of individual practitioners of a given specialty. Through its accreditation system, psychology has long recognized the specialty areas of clinical, counseling, and school psychology (APA, 2000a). More recently new areas of specialty practice, sometimes involving postdoctoral training, have emerged such as clinical neuropsychology and forensic psychology (Bent et al., 1999). As will be elaborated later in the chapter, individual post-licensing certification of specialty competence is available to psychologists in a number of traditional and more recently identified areas of practice.

EXAMPLES OF BOARD CERTIFICATION IN RELATED PROFESSIONS

Medicine can be viewed as a mature profession in that it has been recognized for centuries and, in our society, has developed a comprehensive system for recognizing bona fide medical specialties and certifying qualified practitioners in these areas (ABMS, 2000). The history of board certification in medicine goes back to the early 20th century with the concept of a specialty examining board being proposed initially in 1908 followed in 1916 by the creation of the American Board for Ophthalmic Examinations (now titled the American Board of Ophthalmology). Three additional specialty boards were developed over the next two decades leading to the establishment in 1933 of the Advisory Board for Medical Specialties. The rationale, then as now, for the establishment of medical specialty boards is well summed up in the following statement, and the relevance to a maturing professional psychology is apparent immediately:

> The growth of specialty medicine is directly linked to the advancements of medical science and the resulting vast improvements made in medical care delivery since the turn of the century. During this period of growth, there was no system to assure the public that a physician claiming to be a specialist was indeed so qualified. Until the development of the special board movement, each physician had been the sole assessor of his/her own qualifications to practice a given specialty. Specialty societies and medical education institutions encouraged the development of boards to define specialty qualifications and to issue credentials that would assure the public of the specialist's qualifications. (ABMS, 2000, p. 53)

The American Board of Medical Specialties currently lists 24 affiliated specialty examining boards ranging from Allergy & Immunology to Urology that collectively offer 38 general certificates and an additional 87 subspecialty certificates (ABMS, 2000). All physician candidates for any of these medical specialty certificates must pass peer review evaluations and perform at a satisfactory level on oral examinations in their area of intended specialty practice. Notably, the ABMS (n.d.) also reports that 89% of licensed physicians were certified in one or more medical specialty areas as of 1999. In contrast, as of 2002 it is estimated that less than 5% of psychologists are certified in a recognized specialty area by the American Board of Professional Psychology (ABPP, n.d.).

Both professional counseling and social work, two additional mental health professions, recently have developed peer review and examination based systems for identifying specialty practitioners at both masters and doctoral levels. Beginning in 1983, the National Board for Certified Counselors (NBBC, n.d.), an affiliate of the American Counseling Association, began credentialing National Certified Counselors using traditional peer review and examination procedures. Since that time certificate examination and peer review procedures have been developed in the counseling specialties of mental health counseling, school counseling, and addictions counseling. The NBBC reports that over 31,000 mental health professionals currently hold the National Certified Counselor credential, an examination which also is used by many state regulatory agencies as part of the process for licensing professional counselors.

Social Work is a more recent entrant into the voluntary specialty certification arena, with the establishment in 1998 of several social work specialty examinations through the Office of Quality Assurance within the National Association of Social Workers (NASW, n.d.). Certificates of competency are available currently to graduates of accredited social work programs in the specialties of case management; alcohol, tobacco, and other drugs; school social work; and an advanced diplomate in clinical social work for experienced practitioners.

SPECIALTY CERTIFICATION IN PSYCHOLOGY—ABPP AS THE PROTOTYPE

Specialty certification in professional psychology has a long history starting with the establishment of the American Board of Examiners in Professional Psychology (ABEPP) in 1947 (Bent et al., 1999). The ABEPP, as it was then known, was stimulated by a burgeoning demand from the public for mental health services following the conclusion of World War II and a relative lack of organized structures to support the newly emerging profession of psychology. Although the impetus for the establishment of ABEPP came from a committee of the American Psychology Association, the new Board was incorporated independently and, unlike the professions noted in the above paragraphs, set out on a course that has reinforced an unfortunate separation from main stream psychology in general and APA in particular up to the present time. The years immediately after World War II and through the 1950s saw the establishment of additional important professional support structures including a system for accrediting doctoral programs in professional psychology (that stayed within the APA), a movement to establish licensing boards throughout the continent, and the development of APA's first code of professional ethics.

Three "fields of certification" were identified initially, and oral and written examinations developed soon thereafter to test competence in Clinical Psychology, Personnel—Industrial Psychology, and Personnel—Educational Psychology, with the latter two labels eventually evolving into Industrial/Organizational Psychology and Counseling Psychology. After an initial and time-limited "grandparenting" period, examinations were offered, and by the mid 1950s over 2,500 "diplomas" had been earned by psychologists representing one of the three recognized specialties. (Note that the words "diploma" and "diplomate" have been replaced in recent years by the more universally recognized terms "certificate" and "board certified".)

Two significant changes occurred in 1968 when the name of the organization was shortened to the American Board of Professional Psychology (ABPP), and School Psychology was recognized as a fourth specialty with the concurrent development of an examination for board certification in school psychology. Then in 1984 and 1985 the previously independently organized American Boards of Clinical Neuropsychology and Forensic Psychology were accepted under an enlarging ABPP umbrella. The 1990s that followed were a time of rapid expansion of ABPP as new specialties were recognized and credentialing procedures developed for psychologists seeking board certification in Family Psychology, Health Psychology, Behavioral Psychology, Psychoanalytic Psychology, Rehabilitation Psychology, and Group Psychology. Now in the early years of the 21st century, ABPP exists through its Board of Trustees as an umbrella organization coordinating the efforts of the following 12 affiliated but separately incorporated examining boards:

American Board of Behavioral Psychology
American Board of Clinical Psychology
American Board of Clinical Health Psychology
American Board of Clinical Neuropsychology
American Board of Counseling Psychology
American Board of Family Psychology
American Board of Forensic Psychology
American Board of Group Psychology
American Board of Organizational and Business Consulting Psychology
American Board of Psychoanalysis in Psychology
American Board of Rehabilitation Psychology
American Board of School Psychology

Becoming a board certified psychologist in any of these recognized specialty areas involves three essential steps: (1) review of educational credentials, (2) evaluation of a representative professional work sample, and (3) satisfactory performance on a competency examination in one of the psychology specialty areas noted above. *Reviewing a candidate's educational credentials* establishes eligibility for specialty certification, and this occurs at two levels. First, ABPP Central Office personnel check to insure that the candidate has earned a doctorate in professional psychology and also is licensed at the independent practice level as a psychologist in the state, province, or territory in which the psychologist practices. The doctoral degree must be from a program which, at the time the degree was granted, was accredited by the American Psychological Association or the Canadian Psychological Association or was listed in the publication "Doctoral Psychology Programs Meeting Designation Criteria (NR, n.d.). Applicants listed at the time of their application in the "National Register of Health Service Providers in Psychology" or who possess a "Certificate of Professional Qualification" from the Association of State and Provincial Psychology Boards automatically meet these doctoral education requirements. A second level of credential review is then carried out by board certified psychology peers who check to see that the applicant meets the specialty, as opposed to general, eligibility requirements which in most instances include some combination of doctoral foundational study in the specialty, a formal post doctoral residency in the specialty, or a designated number of years (usually two) of supervised experience providing the specialty services.

The second step in the board certification process involves *submission of a professional work sample* that is representative of the candidate's specialty practice. The work sample goes through a process of peer review by board certified psychologists who represent the specialty board to which the candidate has applied. Once the professional practice sample has been evaluated and approved the candidate is eligible to participate in the specialty examination.

The final step in the process entails *satisfactory performance on an examination administered by the specialty board.* The various specialty examinations are designed to be a collegial and respectful and to facilitate candidate demonstration of the defining professional and ethical competencies required to practice the specialty effectively and in a fashion that protects the interests of clients and the public. The scoring of examinations across all ABPP specialty boards is based on criterion-referenced as opposed to norm-referenced procedures, the purpose being to affirm that candidates have met criteria for safe and effective practice. The format of examinations varies somewhat across specialty areas, but in general involves additional discussion of candidate practice samples, exploration of knowledge and skills fundamental to practice of the specialty, response to situations and vignettes representative of specialty practice, and exploration of professional issues and potential ethical problems associated with practice of the specialty. Examinations are held on a periodic basis at convenient locations across the country, often in concert with national meetings of relevant professional organizations, and length of examination varies from 3 to 5 hours across the various specialty boards. Additionally, the clinical neuropsychology board requires satisfactory performance on an objective written examination preparatory to the oral examination. Specialty board examiners observe policies of confidentiality in their reviews of credentials and professional work samples and in the conduct of examinations. ABPP is a non-profit professional organization that relies heavily on the work of volunteer board certified psychologists, and the organization reports ongoing attempts to keep application and examination fee levels as low as possible.

As of 2002 the ABPP charges a $100 fee to cover the cost of credential reviews which is reduced to $50 if the applicant is credentialed as a Health Service Provider in Psychology by the National Register, holds a Certificate of Professional Qualification (CPQ) from the Association of State and Provincial Psychology Boards, or has membership in an APA Division related appropriately to the specialty. An additional $200 fee is required with the submission of the professional work sample, and a $400 fee is charged to cover partially the costs associated with conducting the oral examination. The total application and examination cost of $650 or $700 partially subsidizes actual expenses involved in reviewing credentials, evaluating professional work samples, and conducting examinations. The peer review processes necessary for credible certification are carried out by board certified psychologists who are compensated only for their out-of-pocket expenses and not for the time or energy expended in carrying out their evaluative functions. The payoff to individual psychologists for this investment of time and money can be considerable and, most significantly, includes certification by one's experienced and credentialed peers that a basic standard of competence has been met for safe and effective practice of a psychology specialty.

Graduate students, post doctoral trainees, and licensed psychologists may obtain additional information about the American Board of Professional Psychology, its affiliated twelve specialty boards, and related application materials and processes by going to the organization's web site at www.abpp.org, or by phoning the ABPP Central Office at 800-255-7792, or by writing to American Board of Professional Psychology, 514 East Capitol Avenue, Jefferson City, Missouri 65101.

WHY IS CERTIFICATION NECESSARY AND ESSENTIAL FOR PSYCHOLOGY?

Is certification *really* necessary and essential for professional psychology? A considered and thoughtful answer is very likely to be yes, but the historical answer to the question is no. After an initial surge in the late 1940s and early 1950s, in the following four decades the vast majority of psychologists did not seek board certification (Bent et al., 1999). And, with some exceptions, most contemporary psychologists are not following through in pursuing board certification. Of interest here is the fact that the ABPP Central Office typically receives each year in excess of 2,000 requests for application packets for the various specialty examinations. Approximately 10% of this number ultimately apply. Thus, once again, the answer to the question is, no, the actions of most contemporary psychologists do not support the essentiality or necessity of board certification. But what of the future? Dattilio (2002) concludes that: If we are to take a serious stance on protecting our future profession and our position in the field of mental health delivery, board certification may well become not only necessary but imperative as a way to define advanced qualifications and standards of excellence as the field of psychology continues to expand. (p. 56)

There is compelling evidence that, just as in the more mature profession of medicine, the expansion of board certification and the continued maturation of professional psychology are combined inextricably. Consider the following rationale, much of which is adapted from a brief article written by one of the chapter authors (Packard, 2001).

Exponential Growth of Psychological Knowledge Leaves No Alternative But to Specialize

The scientific foundation that undergirds psychology practice grew at a rapidly accelerating rate during the 20th century and will continue its swift expansion in the first decades of the 21st century. There are large numbers of older practitioners educated in the 1960s and 1970s at respectable institutions who would be amazed in comparing the curriculums they experienced with what is required currently of our psychology trainees. The differences are vast, both in terms of quantity and specificity. Students are overwhelmed with the shear amount of conceptual material and related professional skills to be learned. And by the 3rd or 4th years of their doctoral programs inevitably they begin "to specialize"despite the fact that doctoral curriculums (and the explicit premise of APA's Accreditation system) are built around the premise of "broad and general " doctoral education and training (APA, 2000a). The mass of available conceptual material, related empirical research, and potential practice applications leaves no alternative. "Everything" cannot be learned or mastered, and doctoral students inevitably must make choices about what to emphasize and where to focus their academic efforts.

Our Work Environments Impel Us to Specialize

Academic faculty have known this for years. Earning tenure and respect in a research oriented university requires new faculty to establish quickly a focused and specific program of research. Practitioners have been confronted with this reality in harsh and heavy handed fashion over the past two decades. We are all too familiar with the capture by corporate America of the U.S. health care economy and the related control of health services and practitioners by profit-oriented managed care organizations (Shore, 1998). While the current system is unstable, and continues to evolve, one thing seems certain—we will not return to the nostalgic fee-for-service days of the 1970s when large numbers of psychologists established respectable practices as "generalist" service providers. In recent years, "expensive" psychologists have been squeezed out of the traditional health care system by the cost containment practices of large managed care organizations (MCOs). And their ranks have been filled on MCO provider panels by Masters degree level mental health providers (LPCs, LCSWs, MFTs) and even Bachelors degree level mental health technicians. In order to survive economically, creative psychologists have had to adapt and to develop new patterns of practice. Formerly unknown "niches" have been identified, and new practice patterns have emerged, and in the process "specialization" has become a necessity for many rather than an option for a few.

Our Professional Context Reinforces the Need for Specialization

As detailed in the first section of this chapter, psychology is recognized by our society as a profession because it (1) provides valued services, (2) is based on a "corpus" of knowledge, (3) uses methods, techniques, and procedures derived from the body of knowledge, (4) has developed internal self-regulatory mechanisms (e.g., ethics codes, practice standards, specialty certification, etc.), and (5) is regulated legally through licensing statutes and related laws. The history of most professions recognized currently by our society is in many ways a story of the development of specialties and specialty practice. The clear example of Medicine was outlined in a previous section. Most physicians seek board certification as a necessary credential for practice. Inevitably, psychologists in large numbers will follow suit. Because of the complexity and scope of its scientific and professional knowledge base, the structures and demand characteristics of the environments within which psychologists work, and the models for specialization presented by all health service professions, psychology also must maintain a credible and widely recognized system for specialty recognition and certification in order to insure the continued growth and development of the profession.

Generic Nature of Psychology Licensing in North American Presumes Additional Professional Self-Regulation of Specialty Practice (Dattilio, 2002)

As with medicine and most other regulated professions, the psychology licensing statues are "generic" in almost all U. S. and Canadian jurisdictions (ASPPB, 2001a). Of the 62 licensing jurisdictions represented in the 2001 directory of the Association of State and Provincial Psychology Boards, only two—Virginia and the Territory of Guam—use the title "clinical psychology" in referring to licensed practitioners. Four other jurisdictions make mention in one form or another of the additional designation of "health service provider in psychology" (hardly a focused specialty area) as a broad subclass of licensed psychologists. Thus, being licensed as a psychologist in North America opens up the possibility of providing any of a very large array of psychological services defined in the collective scope of practice sections of the various licensing statutes.

So what is to prevent the generically licensed practitioner from providing whatever psychological services she or he wishes? Without exception, all licensing statutes contain some combination of specific definitions of unprofessional conduct and general references to the APA "Ethical Principles of Psychologists and Code of Conduct" (APA, 1992) and/or the ASPPB "Code of Conduct" (ASPPB, 2001b). Without exception, the codes and the statutes contain explicit references that, for example, admonish psychologists to "provide services, teach, and conduct research only within the boundaries of their competence..." (APA, 1992, p. 1600) and to "...limit practice and supervision to the areas of competence in which proficiency has been gained through education, training, and experience" (ASPPB, 2001b, p. 6). It is abundantly clear that the licensing statutes presume a broad measure of professional self-discipline for both practitioner and organized psychology. And credible board certification in recognized psychology specialty areas is an important component of this voluntary self-regulatory system.

Enlightened Self-Interest Mandates that Individual Psychologists Develop Specialty Skills that Subsequently Are Documented Through Attainment of Specialty Certification

As noted above, "generalist" practice is an option for a rapidly diminishing proportion of psychologists. Some will thrive because of an unusual practice "niche" (e.g., working with the hearing-impaired) or because they have strong multicultural competence or because they possess bilingual or multilingual communication skills. However, an increasing number of psychologists are moving into widely recognized areas of specialty practice. "Primary care" psychologists (e.g., some clinical and counseling psychologists) will be front line specialists consulted by clients with myriad presenting issues. They will work directly with some clients and refer others to specialists. At more focused levels of practice, psychological services will be directed to special groups with special needs and in special ways (e.g., family, health, behavioral, school, and psychoanalytic psychologists). Sharply delineated specialists will provide services, sometimes via referrals from other professionals or agencies, to clients with clearly defined concerns (e.g., forensic, neuropsychological, rehabilitation, and group psychologists).

Psychologists who have documented their specialty skills through certification by a recognized psychology specialty board will have distinct advantages over self-identified or "vanity board" (e.g., no examination) credentialed specialists. As described in the previous section, the American Board of Professional Psychology is in its 55th year of existence and is recognized broadly across the profession and by society in general as psychology's primary specialty certification organization. Certification by an ABPP affiliated specialty board is recognized broadly and increasingly by:

- Hospital, health, and medical organizations
- State and federal courts and related legal institutions
- Psychology licensing jurisdictions
- Military, Veterans Administration, and various government agencies
- Universities and educational systems
- Professional organizations involved directly or indirectly with psychology

Positive consequences to individual practitioners include increased access to job possibilities and work situations; enhanced opportunities in various health facilities, legal institutions, and governmental programs; increased respect and recognition from potential referral sources and fellow health and human services colleagues; earned credibility and enhanced possibilities of effective influence for positive outcomes; and maximization of one's economic potentialities. Enlightened self-interest complements altruism and service motivation, and both can be facilitated by the documentation of skill inherent in recognized specialty certification.

Protecting the Public from Charlatans and the Ill-Prepared Requires Personal and Professional Self-Regulation

Protection of the public is a final strong rationale for the necessity and essentiality of credible board certification in recognized areas of specialty practice. As described above, governmental licensing jurisdictions in North America, whose sole purpose is protection of the public, continue to implement generic psychology licensing statutes. The widely used Examination for Professional Practice in Psychology (EPPP) is constructed and standardized to test for knowledge and skills basic to *all* areas of psychology practice. The peer review processes and examinations constructed and offered by legitimate psychology specialty boards are designed to identify practitioners who possess the knowledge and skills basic to *specialty* areas of psychology practice. Thus, the public protection function of specialty certification supports and complements the primary regulatory function mandated in state and provincial licensing statutes. Professionally sanctioned specialty certification plays a vital role in enhancing public protection by making information available to consumers about board certified psychologists who have demonstrated competence in providing specialty services.

In summary, self-identified specialization is *not* a characteristic of a mature health and human services profession nor in the long run does it serve the public interest. The six rationales presented in this section support the necessity and essentiality of legitimate and credible board certification of specialty competence as psychology grows into a mature and increasingly differentiated profession.

HOW PSYCHOLOGY CURRENTLY RECOGNIZES SPECIALTY PRACTICE AREAS

Board certification presumes that a given profession has developed widely accepted mechanisms that facilitate and document the recognition of newly emerged areas of specialty practice. Psychology's history in this arena has been checkered and fitful from the emergence of professional psychology in mid-20th century until recently. And it is only in the past decade or so that organized psychology has begun to "get its act together" and move towards a broadly integrated and widely accepted system for recognizing emerging areas of psychology specialty practice (Drum & Blom, 2001).

As discussed in an earlier section, The American Board of Examiners in Professional Psychology (later retitled the American Board of Professional Psychology or ABPP) was organized as an independent entity in 1947 including recognition of three psychology specialties that eventually were labeled clinical psychology, counseling psychology, and industrial/organizational (I/O) psychology. Twenty years later in 1967 school psychology was added as the fourth specialty recognized by ABPP. Drum and Blom (2001) have identified these original four areas as "General Practice Specialties" with each playing a formative role in the development of professional psychology in North America. While the I/O specialty moved away from main stream psychology and toward interdisciplinary business consultation activities, clinical, counseling, and school psychology specialties became bulwarks in the professional psychology doctoral training system that developed rapidly after World War II, and the three specialties were recognized quickly as doctoral level specialties by APA's Office of Accreditation. And then for almost three decades the formal system for identifying and recognizing specialty areas in professional psychology remained essentially static until the decade of the 1980s.

In 1980 the APA's Board of Professional Affairs appointed a Subcommittee on Specialization (SOS) charged with developing criteria to be used in recognizing new specialty areas (Drum & Blom, 2001). Although the report of the SOS (APA, 1984) sparked much debate and controversy, it was never adopted as policy by the APA. In an interesting twist of fate, the SOS document was influential in the subsequent development by ABPP (which had struggled on the fringes of professional psychology through the 1960s and 1970s) of an expanded and more comprehensive set of criteria (ABPP, 1993) that were then used to recognize additional new specialty areas. From the mid-1980s until the present ABPP has recognized eight new specialty areas (to be summarized in a later paragraph) in addition to the original four noted above. These newer areas of practice are defined by Drum and Blom (2001) as "Delimited Specialties" and are characterized by post-doctoral training, a narrower focus, and advanced levels of competence within the circumscribed areas. In contrast, the "General Practice Specialties" noted previously emphasize broad and general training in the discipline and profession of psychology and often serve as prerequisites to entry into the more delimited areas of focused specialty practice.

As a response to these varying developments, in 1995 the APA organized its Council for Recognition of Specialties and Proficiencies in Professional Psychology (CRSPPP) and began to assume primary responsibility for the identification and recognition of new areas of specialty practice[1] (APA, n.d.). Since then, CRSPPP has recognized a number of psychology specialties as described below. During this same period of time, the Council of Specialties (CoS) was organized as an independent group representing a broad array of organizations and APA Divisions involved in speciality training, credentialing and practice (CoS, n.d.). Several Specialty Councils collectively make up the CoS, each of which represents relevant APA Divisions (e.g., Division 40, Clinical Neuropsychology), independent specialty organizations (e.g., International Neuropsychological Society), and ABPP-affiliated specialty certification boards (e.g., American Board of Clinical Neuropsychology). The CoS includes in its mission statement increasing public and professional awareness of psychology specialties and facilitating the systematic development of specialty education, training, credentialing, and practice. Despite an uncoordinated developmental history and the current confusing alphabet soup of psychology specialty organizations, there is surprising consensus about current areas of specialty practice in professional psychology. Table 1 summarizes psychology specialties as recognized in 2002 by ABPP, CRSPPP/APA, and the CoS.

Only two specialties, group and rehabilitation psychology, are not recognized currently by CRSPPP, and both have indicated an intention to make application in the near future

[1] Note that CRSPPP recognizes "proficiencies" in psychology as well as "specialties," the main difference being that the former is a more narrowly defined practice skill requiring special training but in a more defined and focused fashion. Psychology proficiencies recognized currently by CRSPPP include biofeedback, clinical geropsychology, psychopharmacology, and treatment of alcohol and substance abuse disorders.

Table 1. Recognized Specialties in American Psychology, 2002

	CRSPPP/APA	ABPP	CoS
Behavioral Psychology	Yes	Yes	Yes
Clinical Psychology	Yes	Yes	Yes
Clinical Neuropsychology	Yes	Yes	Yes
Clinical Child Psychology	Yes	*In process*	Yes
Clinical Health Psychology	Yes	Yes	Yes
Counseling Psychology	Yes	Yes	Yes
Family Psychology	Yes	Yes	Yes
Forensic Psychology	Yes	Yes	Yes
Group Psychology	*No*	Yes	Yes
Industrial/Organizational	Yes	Yes	*No*
Psychoanalytic Psychology	Yes	Yes	Yes
Rehabilitation Psychology	*No*	Yes	Yes
School Psychology	Yes	Yes	Yes

(J. Kobos, personal communication, March, 2002; B. S. Brucker, personal communication, March, 2002). First recognized by CRSPPP in 1998, only Clinical Child Psychology is not recognized currently by ABPP but is in the process of developing its own speciality certification board and applying for this affiliation. And I/O psychology is the only recognized specialty not involved currently with the Council of Specialties. Thus, the palette of recognized specialty practice areas in professional psychology is more stable and known at this point in time than has been the case in the past, and graduate students in professional psychology can begin thinking about or preparing for specialty practice in their future careers with an increased sense of assurance and comfort.

On a final note, another recently organized group titled the Council of Credentialing Organizations in Professional Psychology (CCOPP) has been meeting semi-annually for the past four years for the purpose of developing an overarching conceptual model and taxonomy of specialty areas and specialty practice in psychology (Drum & Blom, 2001). CCOPP is comprised of representatives of the major psychology credentialing organizations in North America[2] and holds promise for not only stabilizing the current landscape of specialization in psychology but developing widely accepted policies and procedures to guide the emergence of new and exciting specialty practice opportunities.

VANITY BOARDS AND QUASI-CERTIFICATION

How to separate the specialty wheat from the chaff is a problematic question faced by all professions. And it is a question of practical concern to psychologists interested in board certification but confused by the advertisements and blandishments of a plethora of competing boards. Although an often ignored problem for decades, several articles and presentations

[2] American Psychological Association, Canadian Psychological Association, American Board of Professional Psychology, Association of Psychology Postdoctoral and Internship Centers, Association of State and Provincial Psychology Boards, National Register of Health Service Providers in Psychology, and Canadian Register of Health Service Providers in Psychology.

have appeared in recent years that address the propriety and ethics of so-called vanity boards or, as some have called them, purveyors of "checkbook credentials." In a 1999 APA annual meeting presentation on issues of qualifications and training of forensic experts (and subtitled "Sheepskins for sale: Shortcut to Slaughter?"), Golding compared specialty certification criteria employed by the American Board of Forensic Psychology (ABFP), an affiliate of ABPP, and the American Board of Forensic Psychological Specialties, part of the American College of Forensic Examiners (ACFE). Some of the notable comparisons included the ABFP's longtime connection with major psychology organizations vs. the ACFE's establishment in 1992 by an individual entrepreneur who lacked credentials typically associated with mental health professionals. Golding also highlighted major differences between the ABFP and the ACFE in forensic training eligibility requirements, peer review mechanisms, work sample procedures, and examination rigor.

The following year an article by Hansen (2000) appeared in the American Bar Association Journal titled "Expertise to Go" that described in detail the creation in 1992 and the subsequent development of the American College of Forensic Examiners (ACFE), the umbrella organization critiqued by Golding in the APA annual meeting presentation described above. The ACFE is reputed to be the largest extant credentialing body in forensic science, with 13,000 members who have received 17,000 board certified diplomas, and includes 11 different specific certifying boards (e.g., Psychological Specialties, Medicine, Dentistry, Accounting, Nursing, Law Enforcement, Engineering, Social Workers, Counselors, etc.). And the ACFE is only one of many such boards that have developed in the field of forensics in the past quarter century. Critics of the ACFE, as quoted in Hansen's article, are surprisingly blunt in their remarks. A New Jersey document examiner, Robert Phillips, states "He's [the founder and current executive director] just in it for the money." (p. 44). James Starrs, a professor of law and forensic sciences at George Washington University, criticizes the organization for a lack of objectivity in its certification process and notes that "It's driven by the felt needs of the people in charge. If they want you in you're in, even if they have to break all of the rules to do it" (p. 45). Andre Moenssens, another law professor and an expert on scientific evidence at the University of Missouri-Kansas City, says that "For the right amount of money, he will certify just about anybody as an expert in anything" (p. 45). However, the ACFE has its defenders, several of whom are cited in the article. Carl Edwards, a Boston lawyer and psychologist who has been an ACFE board-certified life fellow since 1996, indicates that he "has seen nothing suggesting its members are unqualified or are being represented as anything they're not" (p. 49). Mike Baer, a New York state psychologist and president of an ACFE off-shoot organization, states that the founder of the organization is "just trying to build a good organization from the ground up" and says he does not believe that the ACFE is a certification mill, "otherwise, I wouldn't be a part of it" (p. 50). And a Philadelphia-area psychologist, John Brick, who chairs the ACFE's continuing education committee, speaks positively of the organization and notes that the exam he elected to take (he apparently qualified without taking the exam but chose to complete the procedure anyway) "was more difficult that I thought it would be; it was definitely not a Mickey Mouse-type of thing" (p. 50).

So how does one decide whether or not to pursue specialty board certification with a specific organization? And most importantly, in making such decisions, how does one "aspire to the highest possible standards of conduct" and "maintain high standards of competence in their work" and "in describing or reporting their qualifications . . . not make statements that are false, misleading, or deceptive"? (These brief quotations are from the Preamble and Principle A, Competence and Principle B, Integrity of the current ethics code (APA, 1992)).

We suggest that the following nine criteria be used in evaluating the claims of voluntary credentialing bodies and in identifying bona fide specialty certification boards that meet standards accepted widely across the profession. Note that these standards are derived in part from position statements of the American Board of Professional Psychology (ABPP, 2001), and they also reflect recent articles by Dattilio (2002) and Otto and Heilbrun (2002). In our judgment, legitimate and bona fide specialty certification boards meet the following criteria:

1. The specialty must be represented by an *independently incorporated non-profit examining board* which has a stable history, is national in scope, and which reflects the current development of the specialty. And the board makes available to the public descriptions of the specialty area and related patterns of required competencies, and clearly defines the requisite educational, training, and experience standards that applicants must meet.
2. The specialty examining board is *affiliated with a multi-board credentialing organization* that is national in scope, representative of the broader profession, and the board was *not* founded initially by a specific individual or small group representing a special interest or as a for-profit enterprise.
3. The examining board has a history of *association and interaction with recognized general and specialty-specific professional and/or learned psychological organizations* relevant to the practice of the particular specialty.
4. *Multiple members with defined terms* serve on the examining board. They are licensed and board-certified psychologists in the specialty, and their credentials are open to inspection by interested psychologists and the general public.
5. *Professional peer review* permeates all aspects of the board's procedures for evaluating the qualifications of applicants including reviews of applicant credentials, evaluation of professional work samples, and the conduct of competency examinations.
6. *Prerequisite education, training, and experience standards* necessary for admission to candidacy status are defined clearly and implemented consistently as part of the initial peer review process.
7. Candidates are required to submit *samples of professional practice in the specialty* and/or work products associated with the specialty that are evaluated by professional peers with documented expertise in the specialty.
8. All candidates complete *written and/or oral examinations of substance and credibility* that are conducted by board certified professional peers that provide opportunities to demonstrate competence in the practice of the designated specialty.
9. Bona fide specialty examination boards *do not employ "grandparenting" procedures* that allow candidates to waive required examinations or work sample evaluations, nor do they have histories of repeated extensions of grandparenting waivers.

Thus, bona fide specialty certification boards are characterized by clearly stated policies and procedures; non-profit rather than pecuniary motives; connections with recognized national professional organizations; board members whose credentials include specialty certification; peer review procedures; defined educational, training and experience requirements; evaluation of professional work samples; written and/or oral substantive examinations; and an absence of perennial grandparenting waivers. Psychologists who are certified as competent specialists by such boards have assurance that they are aspiring to the "highest possible standards of conduct" and are maintaining "high standards of competence" in their work as specialty practitioners.

THE CREDENTIALING CONTINUUM AND THE MATURATION OF PROFESSIONAL PSYCHOLOGY

Figure 1 immediately below illustrates the "credentialing continuum" associated with a maturing professional psychology committed to providing high quality services to consumers and to protecting the public interest. A fully credentialed psychologist, whose goal included providing behavioral health services, would progress through the various stages of education and training, beginning with graduate school and moving on through licensing and, ultimately, board certification in a recognized area of specialty practice.

A "fast track" psychologist might move through the continuum in 8 years, although taking a decade or more would seem likely for many. Completing a doctoral program and the related internship in 5 years is possible, though many students take longer. Most licensing jurisdictions in the United States and Canada require 1 post doctoral year of supervised experience in addition to the pre doctoral internship. Earning a license thus becomes possible soon after completion of the first year of post degree supervised practice. A few licensing boards have "health service provider" designations built into their licensing statutes; however, most do not. From its founding in 1974, the National Register's primary purpose has been to identify qualified health service providers in psychology (National Register, n.d.). Eligibility for listing in the National Register includes a doctorate in psychology, two years of supervised experience providing psychological health services (i.e., "typical" internship and post doctoral trainee experiences of graduates of professional programs), and a current license to practice psychology at the independent level. Therefore, typical graduates of professional psychology doctoral programs would be eligible to apply for listing in the National Register of Health Service Providers in Psychology immediately after qualifying for their psychology license.

This leaves board certification for advanced practice in a psychology specialty area as the remaining professional challenge on the credentialing continuum. Board certification basic eligibility requirements of the American Board of Professional Psychology are (1) a doctoral degree from a recognized program in professional psychology (APA or CPA accredited in most instances), (2) appropriate supervised experience including an internship, (3) a valid license to practice psychology at the independent level, and (4) completion of an organized post doctoral residency in the specialty area (may be 1 or 2 years) *or* two years of supervised practice in the specialty. Individual boards affiliated with ABPP may have additional specialty-specific requirements, and the interested reader is directed to the listing of specialty board internet sites that follows.

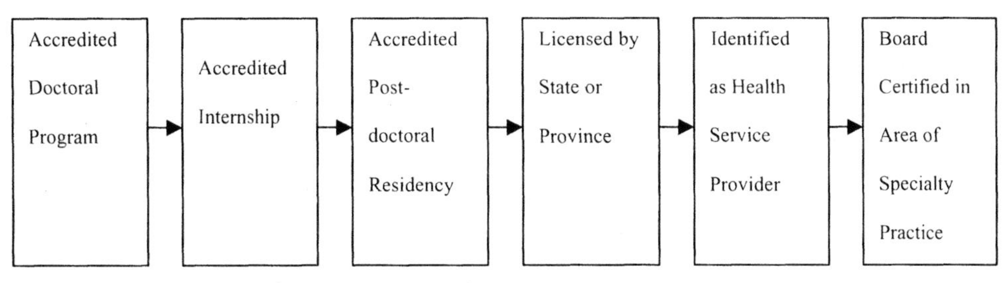

FIGURE 1. The Credentialing Continuum

Some elements of the Credentialing Continuum are reasonably well developed and mature and others are straining to move from childhood into the adolescent stage. Accreditation of doctoral educational and internship training programs through the Committee on Accreditation of the American Psychological Association is now a widely accepted and ubiquitous feature of contemporary professional psychology. As of 2000, for example, approximately 800 doctoral and internship training programs were accredited in the United States and Canada (APA, 2000b). Thus, at the beginning of the 21st century this component of the credentialing continuum is robust and mature. Post doctoral residency training, however, is in a much less developed state. In 1997 the APA Committee on Accreditation adopted guidelines authorizing accreditation of post doctoral programs which led in 2000 to accreditation of the first such program (in clinical health psychology). By 2002 the Committee was receiving significant numbers of applications from post doctoral residency programs (S. F. Zlotlow, Director, Office of Program Consultation and Accreditation, personal communication, March 20, 2002), and prospects seem bright for substantial development of this important component over the next decade.

Beginning with Connecticut in 1945, it took 30 years for licensing statutes to be enacted in all states across the U. S. In 2002 the psychology licensing system across North American is reasonably integrated, functional, and mature and reflects acceptance by our society of the profession of psychology (Bass et al., 1996). The National Register of Health Service Providers in Psychology also has made substantial contributions to the growth of professional psychology and has effectively championed since 1974 the now widely accepted concept of psychologists as integral members of the nation's health service system[3].

But what of specialty certification, the final stage in the credentialing continuum? Despite its lengthy history, until recently the American Board of Professional Psychology and its affiliated specialty examining boards have sometimes seemed like the step-children of professional psychology. Isolated in the backwaters of organized psychology for almost 40 years, ABPP reemerged in the 1990s as a significant and necessary component of our profession. While only a small minority of licensed psychologists currently are board certified, it is abundantly clear that mature professions rest on a large and continually expanding foundation of knowledge and related practice procedures and that specialization is desirable, necessary, and inevitable. ABPP is now involved centrally with key organizations that finally have come together to direct and shape the landscape of specialty practice in North American professional psychology. What will follow inevitably are increasing numbers of practitioners and recent doctoral graduates who seek board certification as a natural and automatic step in completing a credentialing continuum that represents the mature and dynamic profession of psychology.

Taking a decade of one's life to move through the credentialing continuum may seem like an eternity to hard working graduate students beset with course requirements and research obligations, while facing ever increasing educational and living costs. Think back, however, to the first section of the chapter where we discussed characteristics of professions and the expectations of our society for those accorded the privilege of providing services as "professionals." Physicians, architects, bridge builders, and nuclear engineers spend years honing their skills and developing their capabilities to provide services to society, to be helpful to individuals, and to do so with minimal risk and maximum effectiveness. Psychologists bear no less responsibility for becoming mature, skilled, and certifiable providers of human services to a trusting and expectant public.

[3] Interested readers may also want to learn more about the National Register's National Psychologist Trainee Register, a credentials banking service available to graduate students at the completion of their internship and at each additional point on the credential continuum. See the table that follows for the National Register's web site address.

TABLE 2. Some Major Credentialing and Certifying Organizations in Professional Psychology

Organization	Internet Address
American Board of Professional Psychology	http://www.abpp.org/
ABPP Affiliated Boards:	
American Board of Behavioral Psychology	http://www.americanacademyofbehavioralpsychology.org
American Board of Clinical Psychology	http://www.aclinp.org/
American Board of Clinical Health Psychology	http://www.health-psych.org/
American Board of Clinical Neuropsychology	http://www.med.umich.edu/abcn/aacn.html/
American Board of Counseling Psychology	http://www.academyofabpps.org/
American Board of Family Psychology	http://www.apa.org/divisions/div43/
American Board of Forensic Psychology	http://www.abfp.com/
American Board of Group Psychology	http://www.apa.org/about/divisions/div49/
American Board of Psychoanalysis in Psychology	http://www.divpsa.org/
American Board of Rehabilitation Psychology	http://www.apa.org/divisions/div22/
American Board of School Psychology	http://www.apa.org/divisions/div16/
Association of State & Provincial Psychology Boards	http://www.asppb.org/
APA Commission for the Recognition of Specialties and Proficiencies in Professional Psychology (type in "CRSPPP")	http://www.apa.org/
APA Committee on Accreditation (type in "accreditation")	http://www.apa.org/
Council of Specialties	http://www.cospp.org/
National Register of Health Service Providers	http://www.nationalregister.org/

To help with the sometimes confusing task of gathering accurate information, Table 2 provides internet addresses, as of March 2002, of a number of bona fide, major credentialing and certifying organizations in professional psychology.

REFERENCES

American Board of Medical Specialties (2000). *Annual Report & Reference Handbook.* Evanston, IL: Author.

American Board of Medical Specialties (n.d.). Retrieved March 2, 2002, from http//www.abms.org/statistics.asp/

American Board of Professional Psychology (1993). *Application manual for specialty recognition and affiliation with the American Board of Professional Psychology.* Columbia, MO: Author.

American Board of Professional Psychology (2001). *Operations Manual.* Jefferson City, MO.

American Board of Professional Psychology (n.d.). Retrieved March 2, 2002, from http//www.abpp.org/

American Psychological Association (1984). *Specialization in psychology: Principles.* Washington, DC: Author.

American Psychological Association (1992). Ethical principles of psychologists and code of conduct. *American Psychologist, 47,* 1597–1611.

American Psychological Association (2000a). *Book 1: Guidelines and principles for accreditation of programs in professional psychology; Book 2: Accreditation operating procedures of the committee on accreditation.* Washington, DC: Author.

American Psychological Association (2000b). *Committee on Accreditation Annual Report.* Washington, DC: Author.

American Psychological Association (n.d.). Retrieved March 23, 2002 from, http://www.apa.org/crsppp/homepage.html/

Association of State and Provincial Psychology Boards (2001a). *Handbook of licensing and certification requirements for psychologists in the U. S. and Canada.* Montgomery, AL: Author.

Association of State and Provincial Psychology Boards (2001b). *Code of conduct.* Montgomery, AL: Author.

Bass, L. J., DeMers, S. T., Ogloff, J. R. P., Peterson, C., Pettifor, J. L., Reaves, R. P., Retfalvi, T., Simon, N. P., Sinclair, C., & Tipton, R. M. (1996). *Professional conduct and discipline in psychology.* Washington, DC: American Psychological Association, and Montgomery, AL: Association of State and Provincial Psychology Boards.

Belar, C. D., & Perry, N. W. (1992). The national conference on scientist practitioner education and training for the professional practice of psychology. *American Psychologist, 47,* 71–75.

Bent, R. J., Packard, R. E., & Goldberg, R. W. (1999). The American Board of Professional Psychology, 1947 to 1997: A historical perspective. *Professional Psychology: Researach and Practice, 30,* 65–73.

Council of Specialties (n.d.). Retrieved March 23, 2002 from, http://www.cospp.org/

Dattilio, F. M. (2002). Board certification in psychology: Is it really necessary? *Professional Psychology: Research and Practice, 33,* 54–57.

Drum, D. J., & Blom, B. E. (2001). The dynamics of specialization in professional psychology. *Professional Psychology: Research and Practice, 32,* 513–521.

Golding, S. (1999, August). *The voir dire of forensic experts: Issues of qualification and training.* Paper presented at the 1999 annual convention of the American Psychological Association, Boston, MA.

Hansen, M. (2000, February). Expertise to go. *American Bar Association Journal, 86,* 44–52.

National Association of Social Workers (n.d.). Retrieved March 3, 2002, from http//www.socialworkers.org/credentials/default.htm/

National Board for Certified Counselors (n.d.). Retrieved March 3, 2002, from http://www.nbcc.org/

National Register of Health Service Providers in Psychology (n.d.). Retrieved March 25, 2002, from http://www.nationalregister.org/

Packard, T. (2001, Summer). Why ABPP is necessary and essential. *The Diplomate, 20,* 1, 10.

Otto, R. K., & Heilbrun, K. (2002). The practice of forensic psychology: A look toward the future in light of the past. *American Psychologist, 57,* 5–18.

Shore, K. (1998). Managed care and managed competition: A question of morality. In R. F. Small & L. R. Barnhill (Eds.), *Practicing in the new mental health marketplace: Ethical, legal, and moral issues* (pp. 67–102). Washington, DC: American Psychological Association.

CHAPTER 16

Becoming a Clinical Supervisor

SUSAN ALLSTETTER NEUFELDT

Supervision is a critical function in the training of counselors and psychotherapists[1]. As a supervisor, you will be responsible for a significant part of training the next generation of therapists.

Most of you make this choice voluntarily. You probably enjoy the process of counseling or therapy and enjoy the prospect of mentoring others. You are likely to find that supervising someone else adds to your own knowledge and understanding of psychotherapy as well. It is an opportunity to assist therapists, junior to you in experience, to grow and develop their case conceptualization and clinical skills within a multicultural, professional, and ethical environment.

DIFFERENTIATING SUPERVISION FROM PSYCHOTHERAPY

Supervision is a distinctly different process from psychotherapy, although you will use some of your therapy knowledge and skills. It is a challenge to shift from the counseling role to the supervisor role. Frequently novice supervisors refer to their supervisees as "clients" until they really understand the distinctions between psychotherapy and supervision. Sometimes they also have trouble differentiating psychotherapy responses from appropriate supervision responses. When confronted with a person who cries and says that his girlfriend just broke up with him, a therapist would say something like, "It sounds as if this is very distressing to you . . . [and other empathic remarks] . . . Tell me what this means to you." On the other hand, in the context of supervision, a supervisor might say, "I can see how upset you are." [Pause while the supervisee collects himself.] How do you think it is affecting your work with your client who is breaking up with her boyfriend?" The focus shifts from exploring the meaning of the breakup to the way in which this event might affect his work with the client.

A supervisor is more likely to give instruction or advice than a therapist. And while therapists teach and advise in specific situations, they rarely evaluate, except when contracted

SUSAN ALLSTETTER NEUFELDT • Gevirtz Graduate School of Education, University of California at Santa Barbara, Santa Barbara, CA 93106

[1] In this chapter, the words counseling, therapy, and psychotherapy, will be used interchangeably, along with the words counselor, therapist, and psychotherapist.

to do so in cases with a legal component. As a rule, a therapist is nonjudgmental. A therapist turned supervisor, on the other hand, serves as gatekeeper for the profession and must ensure quality of care not only for the client at hand but for future clients. This is a very difficult shift for most therapists to make.

The primary supervisory challenge for the experienced therapist-turned-supervisor, however, is to focus on the therapist and assist the therapist in understanding, conceptualizing, and intervening with the client. In order to do this, the supervisor encourages the therapist to consider the client and the client's problems, characteristics, strengths, and challenges. Graduate student supervisors and interns are close to their own experiences as novices. Unlike supervisors with 15 or 20 years of clinical work behind them, they can remember the sense of being overwhelmed by information provided by the client. They recall their inclinations to focus only on the content of clients' words.

Yet in psychotherapy, words may only tell part of the story. While young children attend acutely to a person's appearance and behavior, often to their parents' embarrassment; "Look, Mommy, at the fat lady eating the big ice cream cone," their parents and teachers train them not to verbalize those observations aloud. The good students who most often frequent graduate schools have been especially well-trained; what the professor says, not what the professor does, determines their academic focus. A competent therapist, however, pays at least as much attention to the nonverbal and paraverbal performance of clients as to the verbal content, and sometimes particularly to the incongruence between them. Learning to reintegrate all that one has been trained to ignore is difficult. The supervisor's task is to assist the therapist to do this. In other words, the supervisor must now attend to the therapist's learning. It is too easy for experienced therapists to focus entirely on the client, to say implicitly to the therapist, in Rogers' words (Goodyear, 1982) "Move over; let me do it!" This is not your chance to do therapy through your supervisee.

While keeping the client's welfare constantly in mind, your task is to focus on training the therapist to provide the finest treatment possible. You begin by instructing in what Bernard (1979) calls the teaching role; how do you teach each supervisee in a manner that fits his or her level of development? With novices (defined by level of development as a professional helper rather than level of training), you may initially explain the importance of the working alliance or the therapeutic relationship to successful therapeutic outcome, and to that end, teach basic rapport building or listening strategies. You might instruct experienced therapists, on the other hand, in the theoretical foundations and requisite skills to implement a new approach to treatment. There are a number of models for doing this.

PRACTICAL MODELS OF SUPERVISION

As a supervisor, you need to establish how you are going to conduct supervision. Often the training program determines a mode, and you carry it out. You may, however, be able to modify it.

Models

Before the days of technology, supervisors did not really know what the client and therapist were doing in therapy. They had to rely on what their supervisees told them to determine what happened during a session. To get the best possible picture, supervisors often asked for process notes; many psychodynamic supervisors still do. Process notes, unlike progress notes, report the therapist's recollection of the dialogue and events in the session and his or her thoughts about it.

With the creation and installation of one-way mirrors in training clinics, supervisors can observe sessions. Using mirrors for in-the-moment observation, family therapists added the delivery of supervision during the session. In live supervision, supervisors also ask therapists-in-training to come out at least once during the session to consult with the supervisor and sometimes a team of their own peers. After the consultation, the supervisee implements the ideas developed with a supervisor or colleagues. Even more directive, "bug-in-the-ear" supervisors ask supervisees to wear a receiver in their ear during the session. From time to time, the supervisor issues directives which the therapist then carries out with clients.

In what is probably the most common form of supervision used in today's training programs, therapists, with their clients' knowledge and consent, record every session on audiotape, or more frequently, videotape. When supervisees meet with their supervisors, they play parts of the session to individual supervisors and, sometimes in group supervision, also to their peers. Upon viewing the therapist and client in action, the supervisor, peer colleagues, and supervisee can explore the supervisee's experience during the session, make new assessments of the client, determine the effect of one intervention, consider another strategy, and assist the supervisee to be more effective.

Advantages and Disadvantages

Each of these strategies is practiced today, and each has advantages and disadvantages, as shown in Table 1.

TABLE 1. Advantages and Disadvantages for Methods of Supervision

Method	Advantages	Disadvantages
Process notes	More precise than an oral report Supervisee necessarily reflects on the session while preparing for supervision Allows understanding of supervisee thinking	No opportunity to observe session directly and experience client or therapist's nonverbal or paraverbal behaviors Supervisee spends more time writing process notes than in actual session
Live or bug-in-the-ear	Supervision occurs in the moment and can be immediately utilized Supervisor can see and interpret nonverbal and paraverbal behavior	Can be experienced by client and supervisee as intrusive Can throw the therapist off course No time for supervisee to reflect
Audiotape and videotape	Allows supervisee direct access to events of session, unmodified by supervisee's interpretation With video, the supervisor also can assess nonverbal and paraverbal behaviors Allows supervisors to stop the tape and ask supervisees to reflect on what they did in the session and the results of their intervention	Can still be experienced by client and supervisee as intrusive Supervision cannot affect what is happening in the current session Supervisees can sometimes select only the parts which show them at their most competent and so avoid the assistance they really need

THEORETICAL MODELS OF SUPERVISION

Whatever mode of supervision you are using, you need more than a "shoot-from-the-hip" approach to your work with therapists in training. There are a variety of theoretical models that can organize the framework within which you supervise. Some of the following models are compatible with one another; some are not. All incorporate the context in which therapy and supervision take place, that is, the physical environment; the racial, ethnic, religious, ability, and socioeconomic class of the client, therapist, and supervisor, and the ways they might interact; the time and circumstances that may shape the counseling experience. On the basis of meta-analysis, Wampold (2001) argued that one therapy approach had not been shown to be much more effective than any other across clients, but that the therapist's commitment to a theoretical orientation affected outcome more. I would argue that the same may be true of supervision.

Supervision According to Theoretical Orientation

This approach is still widely used by many supervisors who exclusively supervise one approach to psychotherapy. In this model, the supervisors conceptualize and respond to their supervisees in a way that is similar to the way they conceptualize and respond to clients. Psychoanalytic supervisors analyze their supervisees' transference, for instance, in order to facilitate their work with clients. Client-centered supervisors treat the therapist with positive regard, empathy, genuineness, and respect as they reflect supervisees' feelings. Behavioral and cognitive-behavioral supervisors encourage analysis of the behaviors and cognitions of the therapist in order to teach the therapist to do the same with clients. Interpersonal therapists work through the relationship with the supervisee to assist the supervisee to facilitate change through their relationship with the client. In other words, supervisors are modeling the therapeutic approach they want their supervisees to enact with their clients.

Developmental Models

In this approach, scholars have examined the development of the supervisee and then applied strategies designed to match supervisees' level of development in order to facilitate current counseling as well as to provoke their progression to the next stage of development. In general, developmental modes assume that therapists go through developmental stages of cognition in a sequenced and unvarying fashion from their initial training to whatever final level of development has been postulated. In many models, development appears to end when the therapist graduates and is licensed, i.e., when one becomes a "master therapist."

On the basis of their experience, others have argued that more than half of therapist development occurs after training is complete. Skovholt and Rønnestad (1992) reported in their qualitative study of 100 counselors and therapists, from paraprofessionals to those with 40 years of experience, that development can continue throughout a therapist's professional career. In fact, they showed that at least half of therapist development occurs after formal training ends. In a recent analysis of data from 5000 therapists who responded to the Development of Therapists Common Core Questionnaire, Rønnestad and Orlinsky (2002, June) found similar patterns of development in therapists from a variety of cultures across the world.

Skovholt and Rønnestad (1992) not only uncovered stages, described in terms of the central task, predominant affect, predominant sources of influence, role and working style, conceptual ideas, learning process, and measures of effectiveness and satisfaction of the therapist; they also examined the processes that facilitated or impeded development. Leading to stagnation and burnout was premature closure, an early choice to use only one therapeutic modality in order to avoid complexity, and pseudodevelopment, an external and rigid style dependent on others' ideas and formal theoretical orientations. When these therapists encountered clients who did not fit their models, they became frustrated at being unsuccessful and either left the field altogether or chose a career, such as research in a psychotherapy lab, where they were not required to conduct psychotherapy themselves.

On the other hand, development occurred, they reported, when therapists continually reflected on their professional work. Elaborated by Neufeldt, Karno, and Nelson (1996) in a series of qualitative interviews with experts on reflectivity in teaching and supervision, reflectivity occurs most often when the therapist is stuck. Like most people, therapists develop when they reflect on their failures. In a spirit of open inquiry, they take risks, allow themselves to be vulnerable, and eschew defensive self-protection, in order to learn from their experiences. They consider their actions, emotions, and thoughts, to understand the session and the interaction between themselves and their clients. Out of this process comes change in their in-session behavior, and in the long term, change in the meaning they make of session events, their work as therapists, and even their lives.

Professional reflection supports development by facilitating both cognitive and personal development in a therapist or counselor. If reflection, indeed, is so important to therapist development, then the supervisor's task is to advance the use of the reflective process as much as to advance specific therapy skills. As a supervisor, you facilitate reflection by asking thoughtful questions about supervisees' feelings, intentions, and results. You support this professional inquiry until it becomes a habit. Questions you might ask include some of the following: "What was it like for you to be with the client in that moment?" "What did you think would happen if you intervened in that way?" "Did it happen?" "Did you learn anything new about the client when the intervention failed?" "How might you use what you learned to modify your approach?"

However, novices do not present their concerns in the same way that advanced therapists do, and they each need supervisory responses tailored to their developmental levels. Novice counselor trainees, after learning the basic listening skills in their first year of training, are looking for support and specific strategies. "What should I do to solve this problem?" they ask, and are surprised and somewhat frustrated when you say, "You need to get more information from the client before you decide. Ask something about where they got this idea that they needed to be so perfect and then see what they tell you. Other questions will follow as you find you need to know more concrete details and examples, until you really have the picture. Then we can talk about what to do next."

Advanced trainees, on the other hand, have more complex questions. "The client is pretty stuck and keeps asking me what to do next. How do you think I should move her forward?" they ask. "You sound as stuck as the client," you say. "It sounds as if you feel stuck when the client gets stuck, and you are asking me what to do next too. Usually you don't get so bamboozled by a client's questions; what do you think is happening here?" Advanced therapists want to understand how their interactions with the client affect their delivery of service. They often welcome interpretations of something like parallel process, while novices frequently find such interpretations of their work intrusive and upsetting rather than helpful.

TABLE 2. Bernard's 3 × 3 Discrimination Model

	Supervisor roles		
Focus of supervision	Teacher	Counselor	Consultant
Intervention			
Conceptualization			
Personalization			

Social Role Models

Social role models can be compatible with developmental models. Social role models describe the supervisor's roles and foci during supervision of a particular case with a particular supervisee, again where roles may be shaped by culture. Their use usually requires an audiotape or better, a videotape, of a counseling session so that the supervisor can observe what actually happened in the session. Social role models allow you, as a supervisor, to understand and analyze the roles and sometimes the tasks you need to carry out with your supervisee. If supervisors use this model, they can discern their own roles and foci. Likewise, supervisors of supervision can use the model with supervisees-in-training. In what role or focus does the supervisor spend most of the time with a supervisee? What is the basis for that? Is this predominant role or focus conditional on a particular supervisee's difficulties or is it a function of a limited flexibility in assuming a variety of roles focused on a variety of tasks? Are supervisors adequately skilled across roles and foci? Many experts have described the roles that supervisors take and where they focus their attention. Currently the most widely used models describe matrices of roles and foci (Bernard, 1979) or functions and tasks (Holloway, 1995). Bernard's 3 × 3 Discrimination Model, is listed in Table 2.

Holloway's SAS model includes a 5 × 5 matrix (see Table 3), which incorporates in particular the supervisor's monitoring/evaluating and modeling functions, stated in verb form, and the counselor's self-evaluation and professional role tasks. It does not name a "counseling" function, simply to confine the limits of the supervisor's supporting/sharing work to appropriate interventions associated with performance in the counseling area.

It is sometimes helpful to ask, "What task or role am I enacting right now? What is my function or where is my focus? "Is this where I want to be?" And in watching yourself supervise, you may find that you spend much more time instructing and evaluating, with a focus on skills, than you do supporting and sharing ideas about case conceptualization. Perhaps you spend almost no time in the counselor role, exploring therapists' emotions that might be interfering

TABLE 3. Holloway's SAS Model

	Supervision tasks				
Supervision functions	Counseling skill	Case conceptualization	Professional role	Emotional awareness	Self-evaluation
Monitoring/Evaluating					
Advising/Instructing					
Modeling					
Consulting					
Supporting/Sharing					

with or effectively informing their performance. While this might be exactly what you should be doing with a novice supervisee with a client who is a college student with a developmental problem, is it appropriate to use the same role and focus with an advanced, emotionally aware, reflective supervisee, who is working with a borderline client? Examining your roles and foci or functions and tasks with each supervisee helps you consider variations matched to the needs of the supervisee at this point in training and with this particular client.

THE SUPERVISION RELATIONSHIP, ETHICAL PRACTICES, AND RISK MANAGEMENT

Holloway's model emphasizes the centrality of the supervisory relationship and its interlocking status with the counseling relationship. The working alliance is critical in both relationships and dependent on a clear understanding of the predominant cultural, i.e., racial, ethnic, religious, gender, sexual orientation, and ability values, as well as levels of ethnic identity development of each participant. As in psychotherapy, without a good relationship, it is difficult to carry out supervision. Defining what will happen in supervision, setting boundaries, explaining the limits to confidentiality, and clarifying both expectations and evaluation procedures, are all essential to that relationship.

While both cross-cultural competence and ethical issues are addressed in other chapters in this book, it is important to note studies from these areas that have direct bearing on the supervisory working alliance. Ladany and his colleagues conducted several studies that related to both cross-cultural issues and to ethics. In one, Ladany, Brittan-Powell, and Pannu (1997) discovered that that supervisees in their study who rated their own and their supervisors' racial identity statuses as parallel reported the highest working alliance ratings, more so if they perceived that both parties had a highly developed racial identity. Parallel high racial or ethnic identities also facilitated the supervisees' development of multicultural competence, and this was most often true when the supervisors were persons of color. Since most supervisors are presently not persons of color, although the percentage is increasing, it is incumbent on white supervisors to learn as much as they can about multiculturalism and develop their racial identities to facilitate the working alliance with all of their supervisees most effectively.

At the same time you, as a supervisor, must attend to ethics and demonstrate your ethical behaviors to your supervisees. In another study, Ladany, Lehrman-Waterman, Molingaro, and Wolgast (1999) found that 51% of supervisees reported at least one ethical violation by their supervisors. As a consequence, their supervision working alliances were weakened.

As a supervisor, you should particularly watch the most frequently violated guidelines noted by supervisees: adequate performance evaluation, confidentiality of supervision sessions, and ability to work with and at least respect alternative perspectives. You cannot count on your supervisees' letting you know about their dissatisfactions. If you can create a safe environment where your supervisees can comfortably reveal their feelings and ideas, and especially their negative feelings about you as the supervisor, you will likely have a successful supervisory relationship.

A particular challenge for advanced doctoral students, however, arises when they supervise beginning student therapists in the same university program. Providing safety requires maintaining a professional distance from the junior students they supervise. Accustomed to the informal relationships among graduate students, which are extended to students as they enter the program, student supervisors sometimes find this difficult. In a small program, students may supervise others who are in classes with them or serve as junior members of the same research teams. Trust is created when supervisors clarify their roles and effectively differentiate between their social, research team, and student roles, and their evaluative supervisory roles. In particular, they explain that they cannot supervise a student who is a roommate, best friend, or romantic partner. This helps supervisees know where they stand in the various relationships. Likewise, defining supervisory confidentiality and explaining its limits can facilitate trust.

In a similar vein, student supervisors who meet together must keep everyone's supervision work confidential. In our supervision seminar, we make a contract that defines all work shown or discussed in the seminar for supervision of supervision as confidential. Student supervisors agree not to discuss the performance of other supervisors or their supervisees outside of the practicum seminar, even among themselves. Of course, when two supervisors work as a team in group supervision, they are expected to talk together about their work with their own supervisees, but we clarify that there should be no "gossip" about supervisors or supervisees. This is harder than one might think in a small program where everyone knows everyone else.

Ethics and disclosure raise an issue not always discussed when therapists consider becoming a supervisor: risk management. More and more frequently, clients are suing supervisors for malpractice carried out by the therapists under their supervision. Likewise, supervisees who felt they were inadequately supervised now sue their supervisors. Potential risks and precautions for avoiding lawsuits and damage awards, include the following. You need to keep records of every supervision session, supervisees' progress, each client's progress, interventions you have recommended or prohibited, and supervisee evaluations. As with clients, your best legal protection is to document everything.

SUPERVISION TRAINING AND SKILLS

In the United States, more and more graduate programs now offer opportunities for supervisor training. Ideally, such training involves a course in supervision theories and practices, followed by at least a semester of a supervision practicum, where supervisors-in-training have the opportunity to supervise trainees junior to themselves. In addition, many internship programs provide training in supervision, even when interns have not had supervision training beforehand. If you are interested in becoming a supervisor or believe it will be a requirement in subsequent employment, you should seek these training opportunities.

However, many psychologists and other mental health professionals discover their desire or need to supervise well after graduation and licensure. In those instances, licensed professionals can get supervision training, often as part of required continuing education. Your training will be considerably more effective if you also receive supervision from experienced supervisors and supervisor trainers for the supervision you provide. In many other countries, licensed psychotherapists must be supervised the entire time they practice.

Supervisor training should provide you with the following:

- Basic theories, models, and research on supervision
- Characteristics and skills unique to supervision and ways in which counseling and supervision differ in scope and responsibilities
- The importance of, building, and facilitating the supervision relationship, with particular attention to cultural factors

- Therapist development and methods for facilitating it
- Supervisory ethics
- Administrative tasks and risk management
- Skills in individual and group supervision
- Appropriate evaluation practices
- Methods for monitoring and ensuring client care

RESOURCES FOR SUPERVISION

No single resource can substitute for supervision training and subsequent supervision of your supervision activities. There is a kind of individualized attention to your skills, style, and supervisees that cannot be duplicated. Observing a good supervisory session with another supervisee can illuminate your understanding and practice. Good training and supervision experiences are enhanced by the use of widely available books and videotapes. A table of good resources is listed below.

As the culmination of my years in study, practice, and teaching, the practice of supervision and the training and supervision of supervisors have been uniquely satisfying. Each year I learn new things and see counselors and supervisors perform in creative and appropriate ways, often ways I never envisioned.

ACKNOWLEDGEMENTS: Acknowledgements are offered with gratitude to all of the students and clients from whom I have learned nearly everything I know about supervision.

ADDITIONAL RESOURCES

Bernard, J. M., & Goodyear, R. L. (1998). *Fundamentals of clinical supervision* (2nd. ed.). Boston: Allyn & Bacon.

Borders, L. D., Bensohoff, J., Armeniox, L., & Coker, K. (1999). *Learning to think like a supervisor*. Alexandria, VA: American Counseling Association.

Brown, M. T., & Landrum-Brown, J. (1995). Counselor supervision: Cross-cultural perspectives. In J. G. Ponterotto, J. M. Casas, L. A. Suzuki, & C. M. Alexander (Eds.), *Handbook of multicultural counseling* (pp. 263–286). Thousand Oaks, CA: Sage.

Chen, E. C. (2001). Multicultural counseling supervision: An interactional approach. In J. G. Ponterotto, J. M. Casas, L. A. Suzuki, & C. M. Alexander (Eds.), *Handbook of multicultural counseling* (2nd ed., pp. 801–824). Thousand Oaks, CA: Sage.

Falvey, J. E., & with Bray, T. E. (2002). *Managing clinical supervision: Ethical practice and legal risk management*. Pacific Grove, CA: Brooks/Cole.

Fong, M. L., & Lease, S. H. (1997). Cross-cultural supervision: Issues for the White supervisor. In D. B. Pope-Davis, & H. L. K. Coleman (Eds.), *Multicultural counseling competencies* (Vol. 7, pp. 387–405). Thousand Oaks, CA: Sage.

Holloway, E. L. (1995). *Clinical supervision: A systems approach*. Thousand Oaks, CA: Sage.

Lefley, H. P., & Pedersen, P. B. (Eds.) (1986). Cross-cultural training for mental health professionals. Springfield, IL: Charles C. Thomas.

Neufeldt, S. A. (1999a). *Supervision strategies for the first practicum* (2nd ed.). Alexandria, VA: American Counseling Association.

Neufeldt, S. A. (1999b). Training in reflective processes in supervision. In M. Carroll & E. L. Holloway (Eds.), *Training counselling supervisors: Strategies, methods and techniques* (pp. 92–105). London: Sage.

Skovholt, T. M., & Rønnestad, M. H. (1992). *The evolving professional self: Stages and themes in therapist and counselor development*. Chichester, England: Wiley.

Stoltenberg, C. D., McNeill, B., & Delworth, U. (1998). *IDM Supervision: An integrated model for supervising therapists*. San Francisco: Jossey-Bass.

Todd, T. C., & Storm, C. L. (Eds.). (1997). *The complete systemic supervisor: Context, philosophy, and pragmatics*. Boston: Allyn and Bacon.

Watkins, C. E., Jr. (Ed.). (1997). *Handbook of psychotherapy supervision*. New York: Wiley.

REFERENCES

Bernard, J. M. (1979). Supervisor training: A discrimination model. *Counselor Education and Supervision, 19*, 60–68.

Goodyear, R. L. (1982). *Psychotherapy supervision by major theorists*. Manhattan, KS: Kansas State University Media Center.

Holloway, E. L. (1995). *Clinical supervision: A systems approach*. Thousand Oaks, CA: Sage.

Ladany, N., Brittan-Powell, C. S., & Pannu, R. K. (1997). The influence of supervisory racial identity interaction and racial matching on the Supervisory Working Alliance and supervisee multicultural competence. *Counselor Education and Supervision, 36*, 284–304.

Ladany, N., Lehrman-Waterman, D., Molingaro, M., & Wolgast, B. (1999). Psychotherapy supervisor ethical practices: Adherence to guidelines, the Supervisor Working Alliance, and supervisee satisfaction. *The Counseling Psychologist, 27*, 443–475.

Neufeldt, S. A., Karno, M. P., & Nelson, M. L. (1996). A qualitative study of experts' conceptualization of supervisee reflectivity. *Journal of Counseling Psychology, 43*(1), 3–9.

Rønnestad, M. H., & Orlinsky, D. E. (2002, June). *The progression, struggle, and decline of psychotherapists: Trajectories of therapist change and stability.* Paper presented at the Symposium conducted at the meeting of the Society for Psychotherapy Research, Santa Barbara, CA.

Skovholt, T. M., & Rønnestad, M. H. (1992). *The evolving professional self: Stages and themes in therapist and counselor development*. Chichester, England: Wiley.

Wampold, B. E. (2001). *The great psychotherapy debate: Models, methods, and findings*. Mahwah, NJ: Erlbaum.

SECTION IV

YOUR PROFESSIONAL SERVICE CAREER

CHAPTER 17

Getting Involved in Professional Organizations

A Gateway to Career Advancement

DANIEL DODGEN, RAYMOND D. FOWLER, AND CAROL WILLIAMS-NICKELSON

Graduate students and new professionals in psychology have many options for career development. One of the most useful decisions a new or emerging psychologist can make is to join a professional association. Psychological organizations provide opportunities for personal and professional development, and offer opportunities to serve the discipline and society at large. Since the late 1800's, psychologists around the world have been organizing themselves into psychological associations to promote clinical, research, or personal interests. The great variety of psychological associations that exist today offer unique opportunities to network, share research, exchange ideas, and learn about critical developments within the field. This chapter will briefly describe relevant aspects of psychological organizations, emphasizing specific opportunities they offer to graduate students and to early-career psychologists.

PROFESSIONAL ORGANIZATIONS IN PSYCHOLOGY

Professional associations seek to advance the body of knowledge in their fields, keep their members informed of professional developments, and provide a variety of services to their members and to the public at large (Fowler, 1999). Joining an association is a critical aspect of career development for new professionals. As far back as 1835, Alexis de Tocqueville noted the tendency of Americans to join together to form voluntary associations. "Americans of all ages, all conditions, and all dispositions constantly form associations," he noted, "They have

DANIEL DODGEN • Public Policy Office, American Psychological Association, Washington, DC 20002
RAYMOND D. FOWLER • 4020 Linnean Avenue, NW, Washington, DC 20008
CAROL WILLIAMS-NICKELSON • American Psychological Association, Washington, DC 20002

not only commercial and manufacturing companies, in which all take part, but associations of a thousand other kinds" (1835). De Tocqueville's assessment continues to be true. With over 23,000 national organizations and 141,000 regional, state, and local organizations and chapters to choose from, 70% of American adults belong to at least one association and 25% belong to four or more (Ernstthal & Jones, 1996). Psychology contributes its fair share to this proliferation of organizations. Because the authors are most familiar with the American Psychological Association (APA), many examples will be drawn from that organization, but APA is only one piece of the discussion.

National and International Psychological Organizations

As early as 1889, psychologists had begun meeting with colleagues from other universities and cities at international congresses (Pickren & Fowler, in press). By 1892, the first national psychological organization, the American Psychological Association (APA), was founded. Since then, psychological associations have been founded in every continent but Antarctica, and national organizations for psychologists exist in over 80 countries (Pickren & Fowler, in press). This expansion created both broadly-focused national psychological organizations and more narrowly-focused societies specializing in specific professional concerns (see Table 1). The latter organizations are comprised of psychologists with similar research interests (e.g., Society of Experimental Social Psychology), applied interests (e.g., Association of Practicing Psychologists), administrative responsibilities (e.g., Society of Psychologists in Management), and employment settings (e.g., National Organization of VA Psychologists) (VandenBos, 1989). Other organizations are based not just on the members' professional responsibilities, but also on their demographic characteristics and how they identify themselves. These include organizations for students (e.g., the American Psychological Association of Graduate Students-APAGS), ethnic minorities (e.g., Society of Indian Psychologists), and geographic locations (e.g., California Psychological Association, Middle Eastern Psychological Network). Finally, many psychologists participate in organizations whose membership includes other disciplines, such as the American Association for the Advancement of Science (AAAS) or the English Association for Child Psychology and Psychiatry (ACPP).

The Function of Professional Organizations within Psychology

All organizations have a mission statement governing their activities. APA's mission statement, for example, outlines three principles: promoting psychology as a science, promoting psychology as a profession, and using psychology as a means of promoting health and human welfare (see Table 2). Most psychological associations, from the European Federation of Sports Psychology to Psychologists for Social Responsibility adhere to one or more of these goals. However, the implications of such a mission are quite far reaching.

One of the primary means of advancing the profession is through the advancement of knowledge. To that end, most organizations sponsor regular conferences that serve as opportunities to exchange information about recent advances in practice and research. The International Union of Psychological Sciences (IUPsyS), for example, holds meetings every four years, while the European Federation of Professional Psychology Associations (EFPA) meets every other year (Fowler, 2000). Other organizations, such as APA, hold yearly conventions.

Journals also advance the knowledge of the field through their role in exchanging information. Nearly every national organization publishes a journal tailored to the interests of its

TABLE 1. Illustrative List of Psychological Associations

Canadian Psychological Associations
- Psychological Association of Alberta
- British Columbia Psychological Association
- Psychological Association of Manitoba
- Manitoba Psychological Society, Inc.
- College of Psychologists of New Brunswick
- Association of Psychologists of Nova Scotia
- Association of Psychologists of the NW Territories
- Ontario Psychological Association
- Corp. Prof. Des Psychologues du Quebec
- Saskatchewan Psychological Association
- Psychological Society of Saskatchewan
- Association of New Foundland Psychologists
- Psychological Association of Prince Edwards Island

U.S. Regional Psychological Associations
- Eastern Psychological Association
- Midwestern Psychological Association
- New England Psychological Association
- Southeastern Psychological Association
- Southwestern Psychological Association
- Western Psychological Association

Affiliated State Psychological Associations

Alabama	Kentucky	Ohio
Alaska	Louisiana	Oklahoma
Arizona	Maine	Oregon
Arkansas	Maryland	Pennsylvania
California	Massachusetts	Puerto Rico
Colorado	Michigan	Rhode Island
Connecticut	Minnesota	South Carolina
Delaware	Mississippi	South Dakota
District of	Missouri	Tennessee
Columbia	Montana	Texas
Florida	Nebraska	Utah
Georgia	Nevada	Vermont
Hawaii	New Hampshire	Virginia
Idaho	New Jersey	Washington
Illinois	New Mexico	West Virginia
Indiana	New York	Wisconsin
Iowa	North Carolina	Wyoming
Kansas	North Dakota	

International Psychological Associations
- International Union of Psychological Science (IUPsyS)
- International Association of Applied Psychology (IAPP)
- European Federation of Professional Psychologists Association (EFPPA)
- Interamerican Society of Psychology (ISP)
- International Council of Psychologists (ICP)

Interdisciplinary Groups with Strong Psychological Interface
- American Association for the Advancement of Science (AAAS)
- American Education Research Association (AERA)
- Society for Research in Child Development (SRCD)
- Gerontological Society of America (GSA)
- Cognitive Science Society
- Society for Neuroscience

(*cont.*)

TABLE 1. (*Continued*)

Human Factors Society
National Mental Health Association (NMHA)
World Federation for Mental Health (WFMH)
Society for Psychotherapy Research
Acoustical Society of America
American Pain Society
Behavior Genetics Association
International Society of Hypnosis
American Correctional Association
Association for Behavior Analysis
International Brain Research Organization
American Psychopathological Association
American Orthopsychiatric Association
American Evaluation Association
Academy of Management
Society for Clinical and Experimental Hypnosis
American Association for Marriage and Family Therapy
Association for the Psychophysiological Study of Sleep
Society for the Advancement of Field Therapy
American Society of Group Psychotherapy & Psychodrama
Association of Business Simulation & Experimental Learning
Association of Mental Health Administrators
Biofeedback Society of America
Comm. On Rehabilitation Counselor Certification
International Society of Research on Aggression
International Society for Psychological Research
International Society for Research on Emotion
Society for Clinical & Experimental Hypnosis
Society for Exploration of Psychotherapy Intervention
Society for Reproductive & Infant Psychology
Society for the Scientific Study of Sex
International Society for Mental Imagery Techniques in Psychotherapy & Psychology
Society for Professionals in Dispute Resolution
Association for Gifted-Creative Children

Student Organizations
American Psychological Association of Graduate Students (APAGS)
Psi Chi
Psi Beta

Education and Training Groups
Council of Graduate Departments of Psychology (COGDOP)
National Council of Schools of Professional Psychology (NCSPP)
Association of Psychology Internship Centers (APIC)
Council of Training Directors (CTD)
Council of Undergraduate Psychology Programs (CUPP)
Association of Medical School Professors of Psychology (AMSPP)
Council of Teachers of Undergraduate Psychology (CTUP)
Joint Council on Professional Education in Psychology (JCPEP)

Credentialing and Licensing Organizations
American Association of State Psychological Boards (AASPB)
American Board of Professional Psychology (ABPP)
National Register of Health Service Providers in Psychology

Ethnic Minority Psychological Associations
Asian American Psychological Association
Association of Black Psychologists

TABLE 1. (*Continued*)

National Hispanic Psychological Association
Society of Indian Psychologists

Other Psychological Association
Psychonomic Society, Inc.
Society of Experimental Psychologists
Society for Multivariate Experimental psychology
Society for Computers in Psychology
Society for Mathematical Psychology
American Psychological Society (APS)
Psychometric Society
National Academy of Practice in Psychology
National Association for School Psychologists (NASP)
American Association for Correctional Psychologists
Association of Practicing Psychologists
Society of Psychologists in Addictive Behaviors
American Academy of Forensic Psychology
National organization of VA Psychologists (NOVA Psi)
Society of Psychologists in Substance Abuse
Psychologists in Long-Term Care
Society of Air Force Clinical Psychologists
Association for Jungian Psychology
North American Society of Adlerian Psychology
Society of Psychologists in Management
Association of Applied Social Psychologists
Association for the Advancement of Applied Sports Psychology
Psychologists for Social responsibility
Association of Women in Psychology
Association of Lesbian and Gay psychologists
Society of Experimental Social Psychology

From VandenBos (1989)

members. Examples include the American Psychological Society's *Psychological Science*, the Society for Research in Child Development's (SRCD) *Child Development*, AAAS's *Science*, and the Australian Psychological Society's *Australian Journal of Psychology.* Like conferences, these journals provide an opportunity for members to share their own expertise and to benefit from the expertise of others as well as to contribute to the literature of the discipline.

TABLE 2. Mission Statement of the American Psychological Association

The objects of the American Psychological Association shall be to advance psychology as a science and profession and as a means of promoting health, education, and human welfare by

- the encouragement of psychology in all its branches in the broadest and most liberal manner
- the promotion of research in psychology and the improvement of research methods and conditions
- the improvement of the qualifications and usefulness of psychologists through high standards of ethics, conduct, education, and achievement
- the establishment and maintenance of the highest standards of professional ethics and conduct of the members of the association
- the increase and diffusion of psychological knowledge through meetings, professional contacts, reports, papers, discussions, and publications
- thereby to advance scientific interests and inquiry, and the application of research findings to the promotion of health, education, and the public welfare.

In addition to their journals, many organizations offer newsletters containing information in a more succinct and readable format. Whether they take the form of magazines, like the *APA Monitor on Psychology*, or a more traditional newsletter format, like the Society for Community Research and Action's (SCRA) *Community Psychologist*, these newsletters serve a vital information-sharing function. Without newsletters, journals, and conferences, no psychologist, regardless of his or her training, would remain competent in the field for more than a few years after completing graduate school.

Beyond information sharing, psychological organizations serve several other critical functions. As Pickren and Fowler (in press) point out, these organizations serve several "gatekeeping" functions. They may determine who can call themselves psychologists or identify themselves as experts in a subspecialty of the field. Through accreditation of continuing education classes, they can influence what people study after completing their degrees, and what they can get credit for studying. Their journals and conferences also determine what information is communicated to the field and how credible it will be when it is disseminated. Fortunately, most organizations exercise this power wisely, since they are themselves governed by the psychologists who make up their membership. In addition, most societies have a complex system of checks and balances that help the system function fairly and democratically (Fowler, 1999).

BENEFITS OF PSYCHOLOGICAL ORGANIZATIONS FOR INDIVIDUALS

A Professional Home

Professional associations, quite simply, provide psychologists with a way to remain current in the field and to develop their professional identity. Without them, psychologists would function in a vacuum. Beyond those global benefits, however, professional associations provide many less obvious ones. In the first place, they provide a place where like-minded psychologists can come together to focus on the issues of most importance to them. Many associations are organized around the unique characteristics and interests of their members. Examples include the Association of Black Psychologists, the Asian-American Psychological Association, the Association of Lesbian and Gay Psychologists, and the Association of Women in Psychology. The 59 state, provincial, and territorial associations affiliated with APA represent a vital home for many psychologists. Other associations organize themselves around topics of interest, such as the Society of Psychologists in Addictive Behaviors or the Association for Jungian Psychology. APA's 53 divisions also reflect a wide array of interests from experimental psychology to psychological hypnosis to the study of lesbian, gay and bisexual issues. For a complete list and description of APA divisions, see http://www.apa.org/about/division.html. In all cases, people choose to affiliate with these specialized groups in order to find a professional home. Professional associations and their divisions and affiliates serve that function.

Interaction with Leaders and Potential Mentors

Interaction with colleagues is a vital component of professional development. Professional organizations offer an excellent opportunity for emerging psychologists to associate with other psychologists and to develop their own professional identity. Through that interaction, graduate students and early-career psychologists gain access to content experts and potential mentors while developing a sense of belonging within their discipline. Only at national conferences are young professionals likely to interact with renowned researchers and have the opportunity to hear them speak. The leaders in the field, regardless of the specific domain or sub-discipline, typically belong to national organizations. After all, it is primarily through the mechanisms organizations provide, such as journals and conferences, that leaders in the field emerge.

These meetings provide one additional benefit to young psychologists and graduate students. At most of the conferences sponsored by professional societies, students can be part of panels or can present their research at poster sessions. In this way, they contribute to the meetings as well as benefiting from them.

Resources

Many organizations offer a wealth of resources to their members. In addition to the primary journals that are usually a benefit of membership, many organizations offer additional journals for more specialized interests. In addition to the *American Psychologist*, which goes to every APA member, APA publishes over 30 journals. Other informational resources include newsletters, books, electronic information databases such as PsychINFO, and Web-based resources.

The resources offered by these national organizations extend far beyond what may typically come to mind. The Ethics Office at APA, for example, provides guidance through written materials, Web sites, and staff members on ethical questions that arise in research and practice settings, as well as other dilemmas that may occur during graduate school (i.e. harassment or dual-role questions). Several organizations also provide guidance on issues regarding human subjects and animal research. Another resource at APA is the Office of Testing and Assessment, which has a large database of information regarding psychological assessment instruments. In yet another example, the APA Research Office conducts ongoing studies that provide timely statistics on students entering and graduating from psychology doctoral programs, psychologists' salaries, employment settings, marketplace trends and more (see http://research.apa.org/). Other resources available through psychological organizations range from employment assistance to financial assistance for students.

Fellowships, Awards, Scholarships, and Grants

Many national organizations provide unique opportunities for their members to receive various fellowships, scholarships, grants and awards. For example, each year APA's graduate student group The American Psychological Association of Graduate Students (APAGS), grants competitive scholarships to graduate students in psychology and awards of excellence to graduate students, mentors, and psychology departments (see http://www.apa.org/apags/members/funding.html). Many other student scholarships, grants, and awards of recognition are sponsored by various national, state, and local psychological associations, as well as divisions of larger organizations (for other examples within APA, see http://www.apa.org/students/student4.html). In addition, SRCD, AAAS, APA and the Society for the Psychological Study of Social Issues (SPSSI) all sponsor fellowships for doctoral-level professionals to come to Washington, DC, for a year and participate in the policymaking process through work at federal agencies, congressional offices, or a national organization's policy office (see http://www.apa.org/ppo/). These Fellowships are open, but not limited, to early career psychologists who often compete successfully for these positions.

BENEFITS OF PSYCHOLOGICAL ORGANIZATIONS TO SOCIETY

National Initiatives

Individual psychologists have much to contribute to our social welfare, but often lack a mechanism for disseminating their knowledge. National organizations are well positioned to develop initiatives that can impact society at a broader level. Two APA projects focused on youth violence serve as examples of the kind of initiatives only a large organization can undertake. *ACT—Adults and Children Together—Against Violence* is a project developed by APA in collaboration with the National Association for the Education of Young Children (NAEYC) to prevent violence by reaching out to adults who raise, care for, or teach children under 8. Based on psychological research, the project includes community trainings and a national multimedia campaign utilizing public service announcements. The television spots for this campaign, developed in conjunction with the Advertising Council, were shown about 30,000 times in media markets across the country between January 2001 and January 2002. The *Warning Signs* project, the result of a partnership between APA and Music Television (MTV), was launched on April 22, 1999 (just 2 days after the Columbine High School shootings) with a 30-minute MTV special co-produced by APA and MTV. Since then, over 4 million young people have seen the program and over 1.25 million copies of the *Warning Signs* brochure have been distributed to offer guidance to young people. APA members have also assisted nearly 175,000 youth and parents by facilitating over 1400 violence-prevention forums using the *Warning Signs* video.

As most readers know, assessment is a vital aspect of psychological research and clinical practice. It is also becoming increasingly important in the educational environment from elementary school forward. For this reason, there is a tremendous need for organizations with expertise and credibility on the national scene to come together to provide principles to guide testing and assessment. The American Educational Research Association, the National Council on Measurement in Education, and APA came together more than 20 years ago to produce the *Standards for Educational and Psychological Testing.* Updated most recently in 1999, the *Standards* are the most widely accepted professional standards in the development, evaluation, and use of tests, and have been cited by the United States Congress and others as a model guide for testing and assessment. Only national organizations could have undertaken this endeavor with such success.

Advocacy for Psychological Research and Practice

Legislation and regulation have a significant impact on all areas of psychology. Many national organizations have Washington-based policy offices that advocate on behalf of psychological research and practice. Given the constant battle for recognition of the value of behavioral and social science research, these efforts are critical to the field of psychology. Psychologists and psychology graduate students who have received funding for their research from the National Institutes of Health (NIH), the Centers for Disease Control and Prevention (CDC), the National Science Foundation (NSF), or other federal agencies probably have the policy staff of a professional organization to thank for their money. National organizations with practitioner members also focus a great deal of effort on issues of interest to clinicians, such as parity in insurance coverage between mental health and physical health. These efforts may also include special attention to the needs of graduate students. In this regard, APA lobbies actively for funding for the Minority Fellowship Program, which supports graduate students of color, and for other loan reimbursement and scholarship programs for psychology graduate students. The voice of national psychological organizations is critical in these efforts, as most of these programs focused exclusively on medical professions, and excluded psychology until recently.

Although much of this advocacy provides direct benefit to psychologists and psychology graduate students, that is not always the aim. Some organizations, such as APA or SRCD, also advocate for programs and services benefiting the populations psychologists serve and research. As an example, APA and SRCD were both highly involved in the recent reauthorizations of the federal Head Start and Elementary and Secondary Education programs. Although these programs do not necessarily benefit psychology directly, the work of psychologists is critical to the understanding of both social and cognitive development. For that reason, these organizations were willing to allocate resources to inform policymakers about relevant research so that federal policy might reflect current knowledge from the field.

It is not only paid advocacy staff who effect policy change. National organizations provide opportunities for their members to become involved in the process as well. Following the Columbine shootings, for example, nearly a dozen psychologists were invited to testify before the Senate Commerce and Health, Education, Labor and Pensions Committees, the House Judiciary Committee, the Congressional Children's Caucus, and at a special closed briefing for members of Congress and their staff convened by Senator Edward Kennedy (D-MA) and Representative Bobby Scott (D-VA) through the auspices of the APA. Psychologists representing various national organizations have testified before Congress on issues ranging from child maltreatment to women's health to terrorism response. These testimonies can have great influence on the congressional committees developing federal initiatives.

While testifying before Congress is an exciting activity, it is also a rare one. Many other opportunities exist, however, for psychology graduate students and psychologists to become involved in policymaking. Most national organizations have electronic Listservs, newsletters, and other vehicles for keeping their members informed about current policy issues affecting their work and providing them with information about how to get involved on a particular issue. Many State Psychological Associations also have advocacy initiatives they are promoting at the state and local level. These include parity initiatives, questions about independent licensure, and other issues of local interest. Typically, any member of a society can get involved in these efforts by signing up for an electronic of fax list.

GETTING INVOLVED

Most of the discussion above focuses on what organizations do for their members or do on behalf of their members. It is important to remember that there is also a great deal that members can do for their organizations. For example, most organizations have multiple opportunities for members to get involved in and influence the leadership of the organizations. The decisions of members, whether expressed directly or through elected representatives, set the policies and direction of their associations. Because organizations need the participation and guidance of their members to function, most organizations have multiple boards, committees, and councils to govern their activities. These groups are made up of members of the association who are elected by the general membership, elected by a subset of the membership, or selected by other members of the association because of the unique contribution they can make. To illustrate further the variety of opportunities and mechanisms for involvement, it may be helpful to examine one organization in more detail. Because of their familiarity with the organization, the authors have chosen to use APA for that purpose.

APA: A Case Study

Many psychologists obviously find professional organizations to be a vital part of their careers. With over 155,000 members and affiliates, APA is the largest association in the world representing organized psychology. APA members are primarily doctoral-level psychologists, about a third of whom are employed in educational settings, a third in private clinical practice, and a third in other settings such as hospitals, clinics, business, industry, and government (Fowler, 2002). Affiliates include graduate students (about one third of the total APA membership), high school teachers of psychology, master's level mental health professionals, psychologists in other countries, and others.

After beginning as an academic-focused organization, APA reorganized in 1945 to incorporate several smaller psychological organizations, evolving into a new organization with a mission that included both professional and scientific issues, as well as the application of psychology to the public interest (see Sidebar 2). Over time, a multifaceted structure that included divisions and state psychological associations developed, reflecting the diversity of the field and APA's members. Today, APA has nearly 600 employees, publishes a number of highly-respected journals, has a respected book publishing arm, holds an annual convention attended by 12,000–17,000 people, provides a monthly magazine to members, and houses multiple offices to address a variety issues with the goal of advancing psychology as a science and profession in the legislative, public, academic and research realms (Fowler, 2000).

Professional Networking

Beyond the activities mentioned above, APA offers many other benefits to its members. In particular, many networking opportunities exist in APA for students and early career psychologists. For example, students may participate in a variety of meetings and conferences, including the annual APA convention, or join any of APA's 53 divisions, enabling them to associate with psychologists and student colleagues who share similar professional interests. Divisions range in size from 300 to 7500 members, with each focusing on a clinical or research interest, or some personal or other factor. Often the personal and research interests overlap, as with the Division 45, the Society for the Psychological Study of Ethnic Minority Issues, so these categories are clearly not exclusive. All the divisions have officers and executive committees (sometimes referred to as boards). These committees provide excellent opportunities to learn about association leadership and to influence the direction of the division. Furthermore, about half of the Divisions now include a graduate student representative on the executive committee, with the number increasing yearly. All Divisions also have newsletters that frequently welcome articles from the membership, providing opportunities for students and early-career professionals to contribute to scientific, although not necessarily peer-reviewed, publications. Some divisions also have divisional journals or other publications that provide information on the domain of interest to the members and provide additional publishing opportunities. Detailed information about APA's divisions are linked through http://www.apa.org/divisions.

Much of the work of the Association is completed by member volunteers who serve on APA's various Boards and Committees. These groups report to the Council of Representatives,

TABLE 3. APA Boards and Committees

1. Board for the Advancement of Psychology in the Public Interest
2. Board of Convention Affairs
3. Board of Educational Affairs
4. Board of Professional Affairs
5. Board of Educational Affairs
6. Board of Professional Affairs
7. Board of Scientific Affairs
8. Policy and Planning Board
9. Publications and Communications Board
10. Elections Committee
11. Ethics Committee
12. Finance Committee
13. Membership Committee
14. Committee on Structure and Function of Council
15. Agenda Planning Group
16. College of Professional Psychology
17. Commission for the Recognition of Specialties and Proficiencies in Professional Psychology
18. Committee on Division/APA Relations
19. Committee on International Relations in Psychology
20. Investment Committee
21. Committee for the Advancement of Professional Practice
22. Committee for the American Psychological Association of Graduate Students
23. Council of Editors
24. Committee on Accreditation
25. Committee on Education and Training Awards
26. Continuing Professional Education Committee
27. Teachers of Psychology in Secondary Schools
28. Committee on Professional Practice and Standards
29. Committee on Animal Research and Ethics
30. Committee on Psychological Tests and Assessment
31. Committee on Scientific Awards
32. Committee on Aging
33. Committee on Ethnic Minority Affairs
34. Committee on Urban Initiatives
35. Committee on Women in Psychology
36. Committee on Lesbian, Gay and Bisexual Concerns
37. Committee on Disability Issues in Psychology
38. Committee on Children, Youth and Families
39. Committee on Psychology in the Public Interest Awards
40. Committee on Rural Health

APA's most powerful governance group. Boards and Committees carry out a wide range of tasks as evidenced by their names (see Table 3), and may frequently have student members or liaisons. Association activities and interests are not limited to the topics of the various continuing Boards and Committees. APA Task Forces and Ad Hoc Committees are formed to address time-limited or newly identified issues that are important to APA members and to psychology in general. Some examples of recent Task Forces and Ad Hoc Committees include: the Ad Hoc Committee on Early Career Psychologists, the Task Force on Psychology in Early Education and Care, the Advisory Committee on Colleague Assistance, the Work Group on Professional Practice Issues in Telehealth, the Working Group on Children's Mental Health, the Electronic Resources Advisory Committee, the Task Force on Serious Mental

TABLE 4. The Mission Statement of the American Psychological Association of Graduate Students (APAGS)

The APAGS Committee shall
• Promote the highest standards in the research, teaching and practice of psychology to further the education and development of all psychology students;
• Represent all graduate study specialties of psychology, facilitating information exchange between these groups;
• Promote leadership development to communicate and advocate for students' concerns; and
• Establish and maintain channels of communication between APAGS and schools, universities, training centers, institutions and other members of the psychological community.

Illness/Severe Emotional Disturbance, the Joint Committee on Testing Practices, and the Task Force on Statistical Inference, just to name a few. Members of these groups can usually be self-nominated or nominated by peers, and graduate students should not be reluctant to nominate themselves for graduate student slots on these committees. Early career professionals should also consider volunteering to serve on these groups as well.

APAGS—THE AMERICAN PSYCHOLOGICAL ASSOCIATION OF GRADUATE STUDENTS

The discussion above only scratches the surface of opportunities for involvement that exist at APA. For graduate students, of course, there is a very specific avenue for greater involvement. APAGS was organized in 1988 and has become the single largest constituency group in the Association (see Table 4 for the APAGS mission statement).

APAGS initial membership of 18,000 has grown to approximately 60,000 members in its 14 years of existence, representing one-third of the current APA membership. Over the years, the list of APAGS activities has lengthened tremendously and its level of integration into the Association has substantially increased. Through participation in governance initiatives and policies, APAGS provides direct student contact and support, develops resources to meet the information and advocacy needs of students, provides leadership opportunities, and offers special convention programming and other distinct training for students.

Involvement in APAGS

There are numerous opportunities for students to become actively involved in APAGS and develop their leadership talents. Students can run for an elected position on the APAGS Committee, or on of one of APAGS five specialized subcommittees: the Committee on Ethnic Minority Affairs; the Committee on Students with Disability Issues; the Convention Committee; the Committee on Lesbian, Gay, Bisexual and Transgender Concerns; and the Advocacy Coordinating Team (ACT) which focuses on national and state legislation that impacts psychology.

APAGS & Career Development

APAGS offers programs and information on topics such as: the business aspects of psychology; internship; post-doctoral training; completing your dissertation; finding a mentor;

balancing work and career; negotiating job offers; presenting and publishing research; and various career paths in psychology. In addition, APAGS features a special Web site and a plethora of resources to help students and early career psychologists prepare for licensure, understand basic business strategies to build an independent practice, get on insurance panels, obtain grants, and pursue the tenure track (see http://www.apa.org/earlycareer/ and http://www.apa.org/apags).

CONCLUSIONS

It should be evident to the reader that the authors believe participation in a psychological organization is a vital part of developing and maintaining a career in psychology. These organizations offer psychologists professional benefits through their journals, conferences, employment assistance, and guidance on ethical standards. They offer personal benefits though opportunities for networking, finding mentors, and receiving scholarships, fellowships, and other awards. Furthermore, these organizations offer an avenue for psychologists at any stage of their careers to make a contribution to the field. They contribute in a global sense by supporting an organization that is furthering critical national initiatives and advocacy efforts. More importantly, they provide opportunities to contribute at an individual level by becoming involved in leadership positions, speaking or presenting posters at conferences, contributing to journals and newsletters, or becoming an advocate. Different benefits will be most salient to different people, but all of them together provide ample evidence that membership in a psychological organization is an investment that yields rich dividends.

REFERENCES

de Tocqueville, A. (1835). *Democracy in America*. New York: J, & H.G. Langley.

Ernstthal, H. L., & Jones, B. (1996). *Principles of Association Management* (3rd ed.). Washington, DC: American Society of Association Executives.

Fowler, R. D. (1999). Managing a professional association. In W. O'Donohue, & J. E. Fisher (Eds.), *Management and Administration Skills for the Mental Health Professional*. New York: Academic Press.

Fowler, R. D. (2000). Psychological Organizations. In A. E. Kazdin (Ed.), *Encyclopedia of Psychology* (pp. 149–152). Cary, North Carolina: Oxford University Press.

Fowler, R. D. (2002). APA's directory tells us who we are. *The Monitor on Psychology*. Washington, D.C.: American Psychological Association.

Pickren, W. E., & Fowler, R. D. (In press). A history of psychological organizations. In I. B. Weiner (General Ed.), & D. K. Freedheim (Vol. Ed.), *Comprehensive Handbook of Psychology: Vol. 1. History of Psychology*. New York: Wiley Books.

VandenBos, G. R. (1989). Loosely organized "organized psychology." *American Psychologist, 44* (7), 979–986.

CHAPTER 18

Advocating for Student Advocacy

MARCUS PATTERSON

A societal trend toward cynicism around politics and a reduction in civic involvement has been documented recently (Putnam, 2001) and psychologists, as a group, seem to be particularly politically disengaged. In a recent study comparing the political giving of various health care disciplines, psychologists were last, giving an average of a approximately $1.05 (per person, per annum). Dieticians gave almost 8 times as much. Psychologists were also behind social workers, occupational therapists, nurses, and speech pathologists (Pfeiffer, 2002). This is an interesting contrast to the fact that as a field, psychology and related mental health disciplines, are often challenged and embattled politically. Because of this and many of the reasons that follow, this chapter will argue that becoming and serving in the role of advocate may be the most important and socially beneficial responsibility that psychologists can take on. This chapter will first will define what advocacy means for psychologists, then discuss the crucial role that students can serve in advocacy and the importance of such involvement during graduate school. Next, the importance of advocacy for the future of our discipline and for the health of our society is highlighted and, finally, opportunities for advocacy that are available to psychologists and psychology graduate students are presented.

Advocacy is the active support or defense of a cause, idea or policy. Advocacy can mean arguing or pleading the cause of other's (as one might for one's students or patients) and/or making particular recommendations (as one might to provide adequate treatment for patients). It can also mean speaking in favor of a cause or proposal (such as supporting the Patient's Bill of Rights). Psychologists advocate in a variety of ways on a variety of levels. These can include activities as different as arguing for adequate or additional services for one's client; recommending changes in state or local licensing laws to more accurately reflect current training or to broaden our scope of practice; and pleading for increased funding for a particular area of research. It can also take forms as different as writing a position statement, calling politicians, making political contributions, e-mailing action alerts to colleagues, and lobbying congress for a particular bill. Given these diverse forms of advocacy, it is inevitable that graduate students and psychologists will serve as advocates in some capacity. Many will even become active in political advocacy on behalf of the profession (Sullivan et al., 1995). Before examining the advocacy opportunities available to graduate student and professionals, we will first discuss the importance of advocacy (for graduate students, for professionals, and for society), since this may not be obvious.

Graduate school is a critical time to become involved in advocacy and it is a time when the importance of advocacy often first becomes evident. As with other aspects of training, graduate school is the time that students develop the habits and set the priorities that will guide their professional lives. In speaking on behalf of one's clients or on behalf of the field, advocacy helps to strengthen one's developing professional identity and provides important connection to the public and to other professionals. There are important similarities between the knowledge and skills that one learns in the classroom and practices during training and those that are utilized in the political or legislative arenas (Sullivan et al, 1995). During training, students are developing the skills that make for good advocates, including the ability to listen and understand another's position, discern the needs of others and represent these positions accurately to others. Advocacy is an important opportunity for students to apply and hone these skills.

Unlike many other professions, the work that psychologists do often involves working with people and, therefore, has considerable social implications. Psychology training, particularly for clinical students, often includes working with impaired and/or oppressed individuals. Thus, graduate school is a time when psychology students might first become aware of their societal role and might begin to experience a sense of civic responsibility. It may also be a time when they first encounter real difficulties within a particular social system. Psychologists and graduate students may become dissatisfied with social structures that fail to meet their patients' or students' needs. Graduate students working in research may also come to realize that there is inadequate funding for research in substantive areas with social implications. In all cases, students may wish to remedy these institutional problems and advocacy becomes an important means of accomplishing this. Jennings (1996) found that dissatisfaction with existing social structures is a dominant theme for those who get involved with advocacy. It also becomes a means of empowerment: to respond actively when one might feel otherwise frustrated or helpless.

GRADUATE STUDENTS ARE NEEDED AS ADVOCATES

The profession of psychology needs student advocates. Graduate students are often in the unique position to advocate for psychology. They represent the current state of training in psychology. They often have a sense of areas of recent advances, they may be working on groundbreaking research which might benefit the public. They are also mindful of the future and trajectory of the field. They also may reach different audiences than those traditionally involved in advocacy. Finally, they may speak to the current generation of students and new professionals.

SHARING THE WORKLOAD

Psychologists and most certainly graduate students are often over-committed and under-compensated for their work, so that adding *pro bono* work in form of advocacy may seem an impossible task. Advocacy has been related to reduced income and less time spent with families (Sullivan *et. al.*, 1995). Thus, suggesting that psychologists and psychology graduate students serve in another capacity may seem counter to self-care and their own best interests. The objective of advocacy, however, is actually to reduce our workload. While this may seem paradoxical, in arguing for institutional changes, advocates are seeking a system that functions more efficiently (e.g. one that more adequately meets the needs of clients). Such a system would ultimately diminish the psychologists' role. Also, if everyone within the profession engaged in advocacy, the time and financial commitment of each would be minimal.

It is also important to recognize that whether we chose to participate in advocacy, professional organizations advocate on our behalf all the time. A number of associations advocate on behalf of students and professionals. These include The American Psychological Association (APA), The American Psychological Society (APS), the Association for the Advancement of Psychology (AAP), and State and Provincial Psychological Associations (SPPAs). This is true for all psychologists and psychology graduate students, regardless of professional leanings or area of specialty. These organizations advocate for everything from increased internship slots, to increases in funds for research, education, and treatment and we benefit from these efforts, even when don't participate in them. As professionals, we, therefore, have some responsibility to support or participate in them. By participating in advocacy efforts, we also are able to play a role in the priority setting of our organizations, which further enhances our investment in and identity with them. In contrast, those not participating in advocacy may feel that others are setting priorities for the field and for themselves.

ADVOCACY BENEFITS PSYCHOLOGY AND SOCIETY

Advocacy benefits psychology as well as society. There are direct public benefits from advocacy, such as when we successfully advocate for services for our clients. There are also broad social benefits, such as when we successfully advocate for increases in research funding or for increases in compensation for mental health treatment. There are also indirect benefits. Advocacy serves an educative function. Psychologists educate legislators about the importance of psychological services, the effectiveness of mental health treatment, the importance of particular kinds of research, and the role of psychology in education. This, in turn, helps the public to understand the contribution that psychology makes in their daily lives. This may be particularly important for psychology, since the lay public often holds misconceptions about psychology and the functions that psychologists perform. Advocacy helps us to correct these mistaken beliefs. (Which means that, in our personal lives, we don't have to always explain or defend our discipline to others). As society increasingly values these contributions, the discipline also benefits. The discipline is enhanced through greater civic responsibility, though increased funding and other opportunities, and through greater public recognition.

ADVOCACY UNITES THE DISCIPLINE

Advocacy helps to unite us as a discipline. As diverse as the field is, we share and benefit from all advocacy efforts on behalf of psychology. When the stature of psychology is raised, we benefit as a collective. Funding increases in any particular area redounds to the benefit of all. More research funds influence treatment funding and the availability of new treatments. Increased funding for education has implications for research funding. We all have something to gain when we advocate for the discipline as a whole and this is something that can (will?) unite us.

PSYCHOLOGISTS MAKE GOOD ADVOCATES AND POLITICIANS

Psychologists well positioned for advocacy and political office. While politicians are often accused of tendentiousness and self-interest, psychologists are trained to listen to and to discern the concerns of one's patients, students, and to accurately represent and advocate for them. Thus, we have the skills to truly represent others and we are trained to do this without personal gain. Advocacy is, thus, an opportunity for employment or future employment

Public policy is a growing area of potential employment for psychologists. Psychology students are being employed in public policy related positions. As suggested above, many of the skills required for this work are attained during graduate school. In addition, a small but growing number of psychologists are becoming legislators (Sullivan et. al., 1995). As with advocacy more generally, psychologists, who are also legislators, report that their training helped them to be particularly effective in these roles (Buffmire, 1995). The presence of psychologists in these positions has also made the need for psychologically minded and psychologist friendly legislators more clear (i.e., more psychologists in these roles). "It is critical to have knowledgeable professional psychologists serving within state legislative bodies as well as lobbying those state legislatures from the outside" (Buffmire, 1995).

ADVOCACY GIVES US CONTROL OVER OUR PROFESSIONAL DESTINY, WHILE IT HELPS TO SHAPE THE FIELD

Finally, advocacy gives us control over our professional destiny. As many psychologists found during the 80s, outside forces can govern and wreak havoc on our profession. Advocacy ensures that psychologists are at the table when decisions that impact the profession are made. Advocacy is a means of proactively protecting the field by extending the reach, understanding, and influence of psychology. It is a way of shaping our professional identity on the world stage. On the other side, it allows us to test and modify our profession in response to the public and their concerns. Public interest may conflict with the interests of psychologists and this may be due to limitations or misconceptions within the profession itself (Kennemer, 1995). Advocacy, however, allows for testing within the marketplace of ideas. Advocacy might not always be successful but a lack of success may reflect public need or interest in an alternative and may serve as a touchstone for the field itself. Advocacy is a sort of public dialogue that informs us about ourselves and our interlocutor (and his/her needs). Ultimately, it is crucial to have psychologists participate within the law making process.

WAYS TO GET INVOLVED

As suggested above, advocacy can take place on many different levels including personal, local, state, regional and national. Large-scale advocacy efforts are often organized by professional associations at the state and national levels and it is often the mission statement of such organization to promote a social action agenda-which is accomplished through advocacy. Thus, one avenue is to become a member of a professional association. Most State, Regional and National psychological associations offer student membership, as do the various divisions within APA.

Deciding where and how to get involved will depend on personal preference, but, in what follows, a list and description of opportunities for involvement is provided.

Department Representative

Most psychology departments have student representatives. These are students in the department who attends departmental meetings and represents the voice and needs of students. Programs that do not have a student representative are encouraged to request one and these initiatives are often successful.

Representative to the Graduate Student Organization (GSO)

Many schools also have GSOs. Psychology students can get involved as the department representative to the GSO. GSOs often addresses graduate student issues, such as those related to stipends, teaching assistantships, and health insurance coverage. Duties include representing particular departmental issues within the GSO, (e.g. should there be more teaching assistantships for psychology graduate students), and reporting the GSO activities to the department. The National Association for Graduate and Professional Students (NAGPS) is the national group of all of these associations. If your school does not have a GSO, NAGPS can help you to organize one. Advice at www.nagps.org.

Collectives

Many departments have collectives that represent specific, student interests within the department. There are ethnic minority collectives, groups for lesbian, gay and bisexual issues, and groups for students with disabilities. These groups are important in ensuring that particular student concerns are addressed and met within a graduate program. Again, students in programs that lack such groups are encouraged to organize these and the American Association of Graduate Students (APAGS) has some models for how one might go about this.

Campus Representative

The APAGS has a campus representative (CRs) program through its Advocacy Coordinating Team (ACT). ACT is comprised of a Chair, who is appointed by the APAGS Executive Committee. The ACT Sub-Committee consists of six Regional Advocacy Coordinators (RACs), State Advocacy Coordinators (SACs), and APAGS Campus Representatives. CRs form a network of students from each university through whom APAGS communicates with most graduate students in psychology across the country. APAGS-ACT was designed to educate students about federal and state legislative issues that affect psychology students and the profession of psychology. Through CRs, APAGS-ACT maintains an active grassroots legislative advocacy network that engages in legislative efforts on behalf of the science and practice of psychology, in the interest of students studying, researching, and practicing psychology, and on behalf of individuals who receive psychological services. CRs are responsible for, not only disseminating information relevant to graduate students, but also voicing the collective concerns of graduate students to APAGS about training, educational, clinical, and research activities. CRs often work with local and state psychological associations in order to increase professional development of students. CRs are the advocates for the students of his or her university. If your program does not have a CR, then you may consider applying through APAGS at www.apa.org/apags.

State or Provincial Psychological Associations (SPPA) Student Membership and Student Groups

Most states offer student membership within their association at a reduced fee. These contacts are often important to get a more comprehensive sense of field, outside one's own academic department. Increasingly, SPPAs are developing graduate student organizations. Within these organizations, students can serve as the representative for one's academic department. Connection with SPPAs can be important for student advocacy, since these organizations lobby for internship slots, ensure that licensing laws reflect current state of training, and ensure that students can receive training that is protected by law and is reimbursable. This can also be an opportunity to participate in lobbying directly at the state level. Students often have the opportunity to participate in grassroots efforts within the state and can see the impact of their work more immediately. The APAGS-ACT Committee also has a State Advocacy Coordinator (SAC) network. SACs represents individual states within the ACT structure. SACs work closely with SPPAs and oversee the activities of the CRs within their state. SACs focus on state-related issues and communicate with students within the state around these issues. They also serve as a conduit for information being communicated from RACs, operating at a regional or federal level.

Regional Associations and Regional Representatives

The ACT Sub-Committee consists of six Regional Advocacy Coordinators (RACs), who manage and recruit the SACs, and the CRs. The RACs oversee the activities of the SACs. (There are approx 8 SAC per RAC.). The RACs are part of the larger ACT committee, which focuses on federal issues impacting psychology and psychology students. RACs meet monthly on conference calls and discuss current legislative issues impacting psychology and mental help. This information is then transmitted through the network. Information from campuses also percolates up through the network and some local issues may be addressed at national level.

National Associations and Divisional Representation

Both the APA and APS have advocacy initiatives and both offer student membership at a significant discount. Within APA, the APAGS committee manages the ACT network, as well as several other groups with advocacy initiatives including the Committee on Ethnic Minority Affairs (CEMA). One can become a member of the APAGS committee by running for an elected position (including the Chair and various members-at-large) or by being appointed to chair a subcommittee.

Historically, APA, as a tax-exempt, 501 (c) (3) organization, has been limited in what it could do politically. With this status, it could not engage in lobbying activities. It has recently taken steps to overcome the limitations on these advocacy efforts due to its tax status. It created a sister organization dubbed the American Psychological Association Practice Organization. The new organization is a tax-exempt, nonprofit companion organization classified as a 501 (c)(6) by the Internal Revenue Service. As such, it is not subject to the three IRS limitations that apply to APA, thus, enhancing the organization's potential to lobby Congress and pursue other professional advocacy activities on behalf of practitioners and researchers.

Another important national organization concerned with advocacy in psychology is the Association for the Advancement of Psychology. The AAP developed the AAP/PLAN (Psychologists for Legislative Action Now), psychology's first successful national political action committee. (PAC) and has important successes in advocating for psychology (see list of advocacy-related accomplishments below). The AAP offers a discounted student membership at www.aapnet.org.

ADVOCACY-RELATED ADVANCES

The success and expansion of our field would not have been possible without advocacy. Without advocacy, psychologists would not be recognized as licensed professionals in all 50 states; psychologists would not be integrated into medicine as they are; healthcare providers would not recognize many of our current mental health diagnoses and, related to this, they would not reimburse for their treatment; psychologists could not sign their own charts and could not treat patients without the supervision of an MD. All of these accomplishments came through advocacy. A list of recent accomplishments made through advocacy and support of advocacy efforts can be found on the AAP website (AAP, n.d.), including:

- Funding for psychology internships through the Medicare GME Program.
- Parity between mental and physical health benefits in private insurance industry health plans.
- A host of patient and provider protections in Medicare and Medicaid.
- Medicare recognition of psychologists as fully independent providers in all settings.
- Removal of Medicare's annual cap on the consumption of Mental health Benefits; thereby encouraging psychological interventions and hopefully minimizing overmedicating in the care of the elderly.
- Increasing clarification of national policy on hospital privilege for psychologists.
- A significant increase in federal support and funding for behavioral research.
- Funding for a DoD Psychopharmacology Demonstration Project.
- Federal funding to help states establish Mental Health Courts.

CONCLUSION

There are some hopeful signs that the trend toward distrust of political advocacy and the move away from civil involvement are now in retreat (Putnam, 2001). Since September 11th, there has been an increase in volunteerism and civic involvement. Graduate students in psychology have volunteered on an impressive variety of fronts and the public roles for psychologists have never been more obvious, roles in important areas relevant to recent events. These include grief counseling, the treatment of anxiety/depressive/sleep and anger disorders, addressing fear/terror generally, talking to children about death/mortality, conflict resolution, understanding and resolving ethnic conflict, human rights, refugee mental health, understanding and opposing racial profiling, prevention of deadly conflict, risk assessment, research in these arenas and many others. We stand at the beginning of the century of psychology. Advocacy and political involvement will help ensure that we are active participants in shaping the future of our profession and the future of our society. With our help, our society can become a psychologically-minded one.

REFERENCES

Association for the Advancement of Psychology. (n.d.). *How AAP membership can benefit you.* Retrieved July 8, 2002, from http://www.aapnet.org/join.html

Buffmire, J. A. (1995). Are politics for you? *Professional Psychology: Research and Practice, 26*, 453–455.

Jennings, T. E. (1996). The developmental dialectic of international human-rights advocacy. *Political Psychology, 17*, 77–95.

Kennemer, W. N. (1995). Psychology and the political process. *Professional Psychology: Research and Practice, 26*, 456–458.

Pfeiffer, S. M. (2002, Spring). Comparison of health care professions political giving performance. *AAP Advance.* Retrieved July 18, 2002, from http://www.aapnet.org/aap_spring_2002.pdf

Putnam, R. D. (2001). *Bowling alone: The collapse and revival of American community.* New York: Simon and Schuster.

Sullivan, M. J., McNamara, K. M., Ybarra, M., & Bulatao, E. Q. (1995). Psychologists as state legislators: Introduction to the special section. *Professional Psychology: Research and Practice, 26*, 445–448.

CHAPTER 19

Public Education of Psychology

An Interview with Philip G. Zimbardo, Ph.D.

PHILIP G. ZIMBARDO

EDITOR' COMMENT: PSYCHOLOGY AND THE MEDIA

By disseminating findings from psychological research and promoting psychological services to the public, the media serves an important function benefiting our society and our field. Psychologists early in their career can serve an important role as consultants to trade media, community media outlets, or even national/international media conglomerates. We asked Dr. Phil Zimbardo to discuss his vision for the role of the media in psychology, his advice for psychologists who are contacted by the media, and also to discuss his own groundbreaking experiences with the media on behalf of psychology over the years.

IMPORTANCE OF MEDIA INVOLVEMENT AMONG PSYCHOLOGISTS

Interviewer (MJP): What do you think is the current public image of psychology as a field?

PGZ: I think that the incident and experiences around September 11th have helped to create a more positive and accurate image of psychology for the public. The public has become more aware of psychologists contributing their services as therapists in New York and Washington and elsewhere. I know the APA website was used very extensively by the general public at this time. The whole concept of posttraumatic stress disorder and the important effects of stress and anxiety in our lives really became salient after 9–11, and I think psychologists have responded expertly and admirably in response to these events.

But, prior to that time, and generally, I think the public has had either a null or somewhat negative image of psychology. I don't think the general public knows the difference between psychiatry and psychology. It has been apparent to me that the media is often unaware of the sub-disciplines within psychology. There is some awareness that psychologists do research

PHILIP G. ZIMBARDO • Department of Psychology, Stanford University, Stanford, CA 94305 and some psychologists do engage in clinical practice, but how the two are related is still often vague. It is rare that the research foundation of practice is apparent to the public. Indeed, it is likely the average person does not know the difference between psychiatrists and clinical psychologists. As a psychologist who has always been concerned with making psychology relevant to the goals of society, it is clear that the media plays a critical role at the interface between what we know, what we do, what we want the public to know, and how to utilize our knowledge and our expertise to help society. So far, this has not really happened in a very productive way. Psychologists and the media could and should have a greater synergy than they currently do.

Interviewer: How does the image of psychology compare with the image of other sciences or related mental health disciplines?

PGZ: I think the public better understands media stories from other sciences such as biology and from medical research, the reason being that newspaper science writers who write about medicine and biology are usually much better trained than the science writers who write about other areas. There are workshops that train journalists in these areas, and those journalists often have had biology or premed courses in college. They want to get the story right. One of the problems with many stories about psychological research is that most reporters don't have a psychology background and they don't get the story right. For example, they don't appreciate what a control group is all about or they will emphasize only one part of a research investigation without understanding its broader context. My feeling is that biology and medicine are better understood and appreciated by the general public than is psychology. I think the media does not clearly differentiate psychology from psychiatry either in terms of practice or in terms of research, or for that matter, from other social sciences. One clear exception can be seen in the articles written by Erika Goode, the New York Times behavioral sciences columnist, who studied for an advanced degree in social psychology at University of California, Santa Cruz. She interviews enough of the right people, does her homework, gets dissenting views as well as supporters of the issue being presented, and crafts it all in an accessible style.

Interviewer: How do you think psychologists' involvement in the media could be helpful to the public.

PGZ: Our field offers much of value that can improve everyday functioning and quality of life, with clear implications for preventive healthcare. Our field could have a dramatic influence on learning and training in the fields of education, law, and business. The media are the gatekeepers between the public and us. It is our job to learn how to open those gates more fully.

In 1969, APA president George Miller startled the American Psychological Association by saying we should give psychology away to the public. It was a startling statement because until that time psychologists gave psychology away to each other. Most psychologists were totally unconcerned about the public. The whole notion of being "relevant" was akin to 'selling out' to the proles. We were saying that we're not pop psychologists, we are serious scientists, and we shun the media since it is part of the commercial establishment. Psychologists did research, we wrote about it in our journals, and we talked to each other. George Miller was an experimental/theoretical psychologist, so coming from him, this statement was very profound. Unfortunately, not as much has been done since then to actually make psychology relevant to the public concerns.

It is a growing trend among psychologists to say that we ought to be able to demonstrate that what we have done makes a difference in people's lives. In more recent years, most funding agencies have asked that researchers indicate how their research could conceivably have societal applications. I think that at a deeper level there are more and more psychologists who believe that research—even basic research—could have meaningful application. Now I should say that one of the reasons psychologists have not been interested in giving psychology away is because many psychologists are very modest, saying: "we're not sure we have anything worthwhile to give away." Other psychologists go on record saying, "we don't know *how* to give psychology away". "We don't know what of all of our psychology people would want." And then the question becomes "what is the process for any psychologist to give psychology away to the public?" And for me, one idea not addressed by George Miller, is a clearer understanding of how we as psychologists can discover how to share information with the public. The media is the secret to how we can give away what we do and know. The media decides which of the information they will pass onto the public, and in what form.

THE FUTURE OF PSYCHOLOGY IN THE MEDIA

Interviewer: What do you think are some of the most important messages that we should be giving away?

PGZ: There are many important messages. My primary APA presidential initiative is to help demonstrate whether and how psychological research has made a significant difference in people's lives. I believe that the answer is of course, "yes—it has in many ways." My presidential initiative has started collecting the database, but we will continue doing so for a number of years. We are starting in the United States and it will hopefully be expanded to many other nations' psychological societies. We have been conducting a survey asking APA members to nominate research that demonstrates a significant impact on individual learning, education, financial behavior, health status, organizational behavior, and more. We are literally identifying hundreds of individual studies or programs of research that demonstrate how psychology has had an impact, and has been translated into public policy, or practice within schools, hospitals, clinics, and organizations. We are just now collecting that information and ideally, we will have a compendium of psychologists' most valuable impacts compiled within a year or two. We will post this list on the APA website to demonstrate that we have made a difference, and we will make this compendium available to the media, to legislatures, and to the general public. It seems to me that this is something that psychology should have done a long time ago to demonstrate that what we do makes a difference in people's lives. APS has also agreed to collaborate with APA in gathering similar data from its members, one of the first collaborative efforts between the two societies.

We are getting some excellent examples of the impact of psychology in making significant changes. For instance, in the area of safety, researchers in the field of perception have made a difference in airline safety by redesigning commercial airline cockpits to correct for a visual illusion that was causing accidents. Other researchers were instrumental in the decision to change the color of emergency vehicles from red to lime green because you can see lime green in dim light better than you can see red. This is basic psychophysics being applied. Another example pertains to social psychologists and psychologists in related subfields working in the area of psychology and law. Here, researchers have demonstrated the conditions under which testimonies can be biased or eyewitness accounts are fallible. Psychologists such as Elizabeth Loftus, Gary Wells, and a number of others have had such a substantial impact on the criminal justice system that former Attorney General Janet Reno arranged to have psychologists work with her staff to develop guidelines on reliable and valid eyewitness testimony. This is an indication that basic research on eyewitness identification by social psychologists has had a direct impact on influencing our legal system.

Another example pertains to research on posttraumatic stress. Terry Keane at the Boston VA is one of the pioneering researchers who have identified, diagnosed, and developed various treatment programs for Posttraumatic Stress Disorder—initially with regard to Vietnam veterans before they realized that this was a general phenomenon. Anyone who's experienced extreme trauma—rape victim, victims of various kinds of natural disasters, victims of terrorist attacks on September 11th—have benefited from this work.

One of the potentially most valuable instances of psychological theory making a difference is the application of Al Bandura's social-cognitive theory of modeling. A Mexican TV producer has developed it in creative ways by weaving different kinds of social models into soap operas. These long-running programs are watched by millions of viewers daily and they see powerful examples of the need for family planning, for raising the status of women through education, for safe sex practices in preventing AIDS, and other vital messages. An international communications agency has extended this approach to develop similar soaps for many other countries worldwide. A critical component of this project is systematic independent evaluation of its effectiveness with solid behavioral outcomes.

Interviewer: Your initiative sounds like an important step towards the giving away of psychology that should be very helpful in educating the public about psychology. Why do you think this has not happened earlier?

PGZ: One problem with the interface between psychology and the public is the ever-present disdain for "pop psychology"—that is, of promoting unscientific psychology for commercial gain. It is important to realize that psychology is unlike any other discipline. Our work in academic psychology spans an enormous range of topics, from the most intricate details of the functioning of the nervous system, witnessed by the current excitement being generated by cognitive neuroscience, all the way to understanding issues such as the cultural construction of the self, conflict and peace, health and spirituality. Psychologists are working at very micro levels of analysis up to the broadest macro level. There is no other academic discipline that has our breadth and range. Moreover, psychology also has an effective, evolving practice component, which is also unique among the behavioral sciences. In addition, we have a built in, intrinsic popular component since we have something to say about virtually every aspect of human nature, how to understand it, and even how to improve it. Because of our breath of focus, and overlap with yoga, meditation, spiritual awareness, religion, and personal effectiveness, we are the core of the "self help" industry. Some for the better of society, some for society's schlock pile. One of the big dangers of psychology, especially among academics and scientists, is that some psychologists have over-popularized it and have pulled it out of the context in which psychology means anything specific to the general public. So we lose our uniqueness and sacrifice what is special, our research foundation, to self-proclaimed gurus peddling contemporary versions of snake oil to the public.

Interviewer: So, it sounds like there might be some ways that our interactions with the media could endanger our reputation or inhibit us from appropriately conveying the kind of work we do as psychologists. Could our involvement with the media also be helpful to the field... how do you think this would happen?

PGZ: My strong sentiment is that we need the media and that the media needs us. Psychology is one of the most interesting fields of intellectual inquiry. Psychologists are doing so much that is exciting and interesting to the general public. The media needs our stories and we need the media to convey them to the public. Without the media, the only outlets for people to learn about psychology are through college and high school courses, or by reading our journals. Magazines, newspapers, TV, radio, and now the Internet are really the major outlets to reach what I'm calling the 'general public,' that is, the less well-educated public and all non-psychologists who are unlikely to read our primary sources of research. If you want to reach teenagers with a message about depression, suicide prevention, or bullying, where else do you go than a public service spot on MTV? We have to become more sophisticated in seeding our important information in media venues most likely to reach the audiences we want to influence.

When I visit congressional offices in Washington during my trips to APA central office, every single office is constantly tuned in to television news; members of congress all have the local newspapers and current magazines available. The point is that legislators have to be tuned into the media. Legislators are the people who vote for funds to support our research, our education, training, and determine how practice dollars will be spent. If our stories get out into the media—such as onto CNN, public television, NPR, and radio talk shows, the New York Times, USA Today—any place where legislators will read or hear about our work, it will help create a positive image of what psychologists do in the minds of those in positions of power. They have the power to help society work better, as well as the power to provide resources to help psychology function more effectively.

Interviewer: Any risks in working with the media?

PGZ: Let's talk about what the media means. At one level, the media is this huge conglomerate. The media is made up of moneymaking corporations—ever larger concentrations of companies dominating multiple media outlets. The bottom line for all of these companies is a profit motive. The media has to present shows on television that will get good ratings, so they can charge more for advertising, which oils the media machine. That's the bottom line. It's the same thing with radio, newspapers, and magazines. If these outlets cover stories that attract more readers or viewers, then the media is going to want more of them. We, as psychologists, have stories to tell that the media will want to report on because people want to see, hear, or read about what other people do, and what they might do differently or better. The popularity of "reality TV" is based on the public's fascination with observing other people behaving in a variety of settings. As an aside, however, there is little reality in these shows since they are so obviously staged, but more importantly, what they lack is some type of psychological analysis of what the behavior means.

Another important aspect of the media is that the decision of what gets accepted, how it gets accepted, and how it gets presented often rests on a single person (e.g., the editor, the production supervisor, or even a higher up). That one person may have a point of view or a particular bias that can affect the story they want to tell, and how they tell it, or reject it. This is one of the dangers of the media. Sometimes a given media source has a prearranged story that they want to get across. They are looking for psychologists that will give them either their expert opinion (without data necessarily) or some supporting data to promote their point of view. This is where psychologists often get trapped—we get misrepresented, misquoted, or quoted out of context because reporters may not be really listening to our whole stories. In some cases, they don't want the whole story; they just want information that will support a particular perspective that they already have in mind. I got trapped once in such a mess, a story I will share with you later on in this interview.

GETTING INVOLVED

Interviewer: How can psychologists get more involved in working with the media?

PGZ: One important problem is that psychologists have very little training in how to deal with the media. Suppose you conduct a study and reveal very interesting findings with important applications. So, what do you do with that? You can write it up for publication, submit it, and it may take a year to two years before it is published—or revise and resubmit endlessly. Mostly other psychologists will read the research. Now if the research is really "hot," that is, the research is touching on some issue of national or regional significance, then you want to make sure that the public is informed about your findings ASAP. What do you do?

One thing you can do is to issue a press release. Not many psychologists know how to write a press release. Some major universities have news services that will do it for you or help you write one. APA also writes press releases each week on articles that it thinks could be of media interest, but again, people don't have to wait for APA. Certainly any researcher should be doing this kind of self-promotion if they really believe the research is important. You can work with the news service of a university, if you have one, or if not, you ought to learn how to write one—one pager leading with the significance and then highlighting the kind of research foundation for the finding you are promoting.

The second thing you can do—we all should be doing more of—is to write op/ed pieces. An op/ed piece in the New York Times, the Washington Post, the Chicago Times, LA Times or Herald Tribune reaches millions of people instantly. You can have more impact with 500 words in one of these media outlets than you can by writing several books. The Science Directorate of the American Psychological Association has a website (www.apa.org/science/editorial.html) with some examples of good op/ed pieces. Early career psychologists can begin by writing op/ed pieces for the local, city, or regional newspaper, or even for a school newspaper if you're an academic.

You can also write a book. A book has the potential to reach many people in the public. Trade paperbacks are like monographs on a single topic, written for the public in an engaging, accessible style. But, if you or your publisher privately arranges a publicity tour for your book, then it has the potential to reach a much wider audience. There are author's agents who can arrange such tours for a fee. For textbooks, publishers hire sales representatives for promotion. But for trade books, you are the sales representative. It is expected that the author will do an author's tour of self-promotion, if the book is judged to be a potential big seller and the author is personable—marketable. Depending on estimates on how well the book will sell, the publisher will organize a tour for you, or will help to support a tour. You might have to hire your own press agent and spend at least a couple of weeks on the road with the media promoting your book. If you are an academic, this is a huge burden, because it is time away from research and teaching. Whereas if you consider yourself primarily as a writer, it is delightful because it is two weeks traveling around the country meeting people, friends, making fans. An ideal author tour might include 7–10 cities, including appearances on television networks or guest spots on AM radio. You might appear on some evening program or a call-in radio and/or television program. Several newspapers and/or magazines might interview you. In some cases, you go to a city, do two or three interviews, go to a new city and be in the Green room by 6 AM the next morning. Your comments on a radio call-in will be very different than when making a brief presentation on morning news show. You cannot have any notes; it must all be well rehearsed. In contrast, newspaper interviews can last an hour or two and be very detailed. But you must keep in mind, that you are selling a product, your book, the topic, and you.

Book writing and book promotional tours are not activities we usually think about as psychologists. But recently, psychologists doing interesting basic research are now repackaging their work as trade books. This is important for summarizing a body of research in a domain that the public and the media will think is interesting. It can also be a lucrative activity. One of the best ways to earn money as a psychologist these days is to be an author or co-author of a trade book or textbook.

One way to get access to publishers for a possible future as a co-author of a text is to volunteer to do text chapter reviewing for the publisher in your domain. And then write brilliant reviews that will catch their attention. That is how I got chosen to replace Floyd Ruch, author of the best selling Psychology and Life introductory psych text, only they asked me to do the review in hopes I might adopt the edition for my course.

Lastly, you can work directly with television. For this approach, it is important that you utilize different kinds of media in your research that can be used on television. Let's say you do an experiment and you have some interesting results. If you called your local TV station to tell them about your research, the very first thing they are going to ask you is if you have any videotape. If you are doing research on topics that might have popular appeal and might lead to media interest, then you must videotape the sessions. Of course, you need to obtain the appropriate consent and human subjects approval to do this. As psychologists, we're trained to focus primarily on results, so when you go to a convention and do a talk we often rush through the procedure and simply describe the findings. The media is interested in the procedure, however, and it is important for them to show this to the public on videotape. Process is as important as Results for visual media.

This is one of the most important things I have learned about interacting with the media. Two examples: Stanley Milgram's research and the Stanford Prison Experiment. The reason those two studies have had enduring value is because they are on video. Milgram was way ahead of his time in the '60s by filming part of his research, and that film is still being shown now—thirty years later. Incidentally, I believe that the flak he got about the ethics of his blind obedience research was due largely to seeing the participants showing so much stress in deciding whether to continue to step up the shock levels. That does not come across in the same dramatic way from just reading his article or book. I did something similar with the Stanford prison study. We videotaped our procedure both as part of our data collection and for future teaching purposes, But because we had this archival material available in a day-by-day chorology of events, the research became more accessible to the media. Over thirty years later (the Stanford prison experiment was conducted in 1971), NBC will show (in 2003) an hour-long documentary on the Stanford Prison Experiment, partly because we have so much video material available to share with them.

Indeed, the Stanford Prison study, in a way, was a forerunner of Reality TV. I have two strong feelings about Reality TV. On the one hand, it's wonderful because it demonstrates that the general public is fascinated with observing human behavior—and that's what we get paid for—that's what psychology is all about. Observing human behavior, trying to make sense of it, trying to explain it, trying to influence it in a positive direction, trying to predict it. Reality TV is popular because it's fascinating for people to simply observe other people in various settings, as I mentioned earlier. On the other hand, Reality TV does not offer any explanation of the behavior—it is raw behavior undigested. What I would want to add is a psychological component. Psychologists have the understanding of non-verbal behavior and of interpersonal dynamics that could help to explain the significance of people's behavior to the public. Second, because of the media ratings, Reality TV has become more and more corrupted—it is hardly reality. It's all staged, and highly edited and hyped to be more appealing to audiences. The enduring popularity of the Milgram study and of the Stanford Prison study was simply having available a film document of what the experience was like from the perspective of the subject. In essence, that is really what Reality TV is all about. That was the gift of Candid Camera, and the genius of Allen Funt, an intuitive social psychologist.

The best of reality television in my biased opinion was a program called "The Human Zoo." It was produced in 2000, in London by Granada Media, London Weekend Television (in conjunction with Discovery Channel). It was a study of the fundamental psychological principles involved when a dozen strangers meet for the first time in a lodge in the lake country of England—a remote area where they lived together for a week. It includes essentially the most basic ordinary psychological and social psychological processes. For instance, people making a first acquaintance, people getting to know one another, people forming impressions of others, making their own impressions on others, forming dyads, forming friendships, organizing into groups, groups dominating one another, etc. What differentiates this from other reality television programs is that a British psychologist and I are commenting from time to time on the process while it is happening. We are making predictions about who will be friends and who will be enemies based on the same evidence the audience has of verbal and non-verbal behavior. And then you can see whether or not we are correct. Throughout the program, there are cutaways from the psychological phenomenon exhibited by the 12 participants to mini experiments and demonstrations that illustrate comparable concepts from a psychological perspective. For instance, we see people making first impressions as they initially meet one another, and then there is a cutaway to a demonstration of research on job interviewers' formations of first impressions within the first 15 seconds of a meeting. Unfortunately, the Discovery Channel decided to show only 2 of the 3 programs. The last program did not air, and the station is not distributing videos. That is part of my frustration with the media; in this case, some stupid executive making the decision that American audiences won't appreciate programs with people who have British accents. Do they not know about the popular British shows on PBS?

Interviewer: What would you say to graduate students or early career psychologists who may be interested in working with the media?

PGZ: Psychologists should always be aware of their reputation within their department and their reputation within the field. And departments vary considerably in terms of their acceptability quotient for media portrayals of research. There are some departments that do not like to see young professors quoted in the media, or promoted in the media; in other departments, it's just the opposite. Certainly universities benefit when, for instance, it is reported that findings come from "a study done by a Yale researcher." This instantly gives Yale credit for important work, and the alumni love to see this. But, there is always tension between colleagues who may be envious of you for the media attention. Also, some colleagues may feel somehow that working with the media is commercializing or popularizing psychology inappropriately. After all, psychology should be a basic scientific enterprise—you do not often see theoretical physicists hocking their wares. Many people believe that media coverage cheapens the research, and if senior colleagues hold this position strongly, then working with the media could be held against you. Indeed, one way I have dealt with this tension was to be sure I always had a sound scientific study to balance against my more popular work, to keep my science colleagues happy and accepting of me.

On the other hand, in terms of promotion of the field, I have always believed from the time I was a little assistant professor without tenure, that media involvement is crucial to help create a positive image of the field to people outside of psychology. If you have something important to say—if you've done something that's meaningful and you want people to know about it—then your colleagues and certainly your administration should be pleased to have you reach out beyond the confines of the traditional academic distribution channels. (If not, send me their names and cousin Gino will pay a friendly visit to them.)

But again, the danger is that no one controls the media. You can't control what the media will say or what the media will do. You can't control it even by giving the media your documentary video—they may elect only to show a minute or two of the video, and perhaps not the most important or cogent part from your perspective. Psychologists are often frustrated because we are used to exercising control over our product—our product is usually an article we're writing, or a book project that allows us to negotiate with the editor before making changes. With the media, once they have the material, they control it—they can change it virtually any way they want. Also if it falls under the heading of "news," then there is no editorial control at all for authors of research.

Interviewer: Given these risks and the loss of control, what advice would you have for early career psychologists who are contacted about their work?

PGZ: Well, you don't want to passively sit and wait for somebody to ask you. There are many sources that can help early career psychologists promote their work. Publishing in *Scientific American* or *Psychology Today* are sources that will help you reach millions with your research. The APA Monitor is another great source. If you have a study that you think is newsworthy and is of interest to psychologists broadly or the public, contact the Monitor staff, and if you can convince them of its value, they may have a staff research reporter do a story on it.

The media may contact an early career psychologist directly, but typically this is because a colleague has mentioned your name. Networking in psychology is very important—early career psychologists should try to know people in different areas of the field. Go to conventions, present posters, give talks, make yourself visible, give constructive feedback to colleagues, give compliments when appropriate, schmooze with your colleagues. But know your limits. You may be contacted for a story that falls outside your area of expertise. Suppose you are contacted by a local reporter to comment on a story pertaining to child molesters or adultery that happens to be in the news at that time. If you are not an expert, indicate that immediately and if possible refer the reporter to colleagues who are. This is important, even if you are asked only for a quote—a single sentence, refuse if you are not comfortable being quoted as The Expert. That is where your colleagues will bristle. Reporters are not really interested in you as an Individual; rather it is you as part of a larger category of relevance to their readers. They will attach your quote to the reputation of your university—for instance, they want to be able to say, "A Stanford professor says..." or a "Psychological researcher believes..."

Overall, if the media contacts you, it is really important to think about the experience as a negotiation. Most young psychologists are extremely flattered that someone from the local newspaper, radio or TV station thinks that what they have to say is important. But you must establish guidelines: What is it exactly that they want from you? What is the theme of the piece? What are they searching for? What's the conclusion? How much time or space do you have? Do they just want a quote? You don't want to talk for an hour when, in fact, they just want a sentence or simple conclusion statement. It's the same thing if you appear on a television program. It's critical to ask how many minutes you will be allotted. It is common for psychologists to plan on communicating several important points, but because they were unaware of the length of the edited interview, they talk too long about only the first point and the others never make the final cut. So you start out by saying, "There are three important features of Z: A, B, and C. A is special because..." That way, it is clear you have a proper overview of what is important, but have had time only to develop point A. Also, be sure to ask about others that have been consulted on this topic, and always suggest other experts, even after you've spoken.

Interviewer: How did you first get involved with working with the media?

PGZ: My very first experience with the media was when I was a graduate student at Yale University. I did a study in 1957 on the effects of caffeine and chlorpromazine on the sexual behavior of the male white rat. I did it with Herbert Barry, a fellow graduate student and we published it in *Science*. I was the senior author and it was a hot topic. Chlorpromazine had just become available, so this was one of the very first studies on this drug that revolutionized treatment of schizophrenia. What we found simply was that chlorpromazine depressed sexual behavior, and caffeine accentuated and enhanced the sexual behavior of the male white rat. Well, we published it and people were mildly interested.

The next week there was an article in Joyce Brothers' column, which said something like 'ladies, if you want to revive your spouse's bedroom vigor, give him an extra cup of coffee.' Our research was dealing with the male white rat and high doses of pure caffeine, and she's making this extension completely out of context. It was actually humorous. Dr. Brothers also reported it on the popular Tonight Show, and I was inundated with reprint requests. It highlights the point that the media are looking for a story. Remember, everyday the media has to fill thousands of pages of newspapers and magazines, and thousands of hours of airtime on radio and television channels. The media is desperate for stories, and we have stories to tell. That was my first experience learning about the media's interest in stories from psychological research, albeit from a somewhat distorted perspective.

I also got involved in news media from other research I had done as a graduate student at Yale, and published in the first volume of Psychology Today. It was an analysis of the psychological tactics used by the police in extracting confessions from suspects—sometimes powerful enough to induce false confessions. I was invited to defend the research at a national law enforcement conference, and it got picked up and distributed by the New York Times. I guess I have tended to work on topics that have broader appeal than some of our more typical psychology subjects, like shyness, evil, cults, violence and madness.

A bizarre incident occurred when I first arrived at Stanford University. I received a call from a New York Times reporter, John Leo (who has since become quite famous), on a deadline for a story on women using profanity. I explained that I did not know anything about this topic. Remember, you should make it clear when you are not an expert. But also remember, that they will never give up if they have to meet a deadline. So, this reporter said that he had a tight deadline the next day, and he needed just one quote. I asked about why he was interested in this story, and he said that his editor was cursed out at a cocktail party and he wanted to know whether it is a general phenomena that women are using more profanity, or whether it was just this woman personally cursing him out. And I said, "well I can't help you." He asked, "are there any psychologists who are studying this?" "Well as far as I know there are no psychologists studying profanity in women," I told him, "there are a lot of areas that psychologists just never study, that they're not interested in." He asked, "Can you think of anything in your experience where you've noticed women using profanity?" "Now that you mention it, yes, I said." Mistake—he sucked me in to the black hole I should not have entered. I told him, "when I was taking an abnormal psychology graduate student course that met at Middletown State Hospital, we visited the back schizophrenic wards. Women patients were typically more expressive than male patients. That is, they often exhibited themselves, cursed, and did other dramatic things, more so than did males." This was 1956, before anti-psychotic medication, and patients' psychoses were much more florid. Now obviously these are not controlled observations, I likely noticed women being more overtly expressive because of the greater deviation from the usual baseline of women not being so publicly demonstrative. Regardless, the reporter thanked me and said a cordial goodbye.

Hold the presses. Next day, the New York Times felt it was fit to report a new trend sweeping America. A front page article exclaimed, something like, "Women are using more obscenities from swanky cocktail party matrons to mental patients on hospital wards—according to psychological researchers"—only ME! The story was distorted to indicate that I had observed *over many years* that female mental patients were very obscene. Notice the changes in timing and lifting of my restricted observations and the special population that I had casually noticed. The story was picked up by news services and spread literally around the globe. I became a very embarrassed world's leading expert on female obscenity, but did turn down talk show offers.

What you may find interesting is that I actually used this anecdote in *Psychology and Life*, the textbook I wrote in 1971, as an instance of how research gets distorted and how an instant authority is created and should not be believed just because the NYT says so. Sometimes all the news is not fit to print, even in the New York Times.

Interviewer: How did you get involved with the Discovering Psychology Series, Candid Camera, and now NBC News?

PGZ: A PBS station in Boston, WGBH-TV, was interested in doing a series on psychology. Some people at the station had taken a few psychology courses, and realized that despite the limited public perception at the time, psychology was about more than the brain and Freud. And so they approached the Annenberg CPB foundation with a proposal to fund a PBS series on psychology. Annenberg officials agreed, stipulating that the series should be geared towards remote learning/adult education. They did a search for a host, who would also be the chief scientific advisor. They wanted someone who had written a textbook, who was doing current research, and had a good media presence. A number of psychologists were "screen tested." I gave some lectures at Swarthmore, attended by WGBH staff, and won the job, undoubtedly on charm points.

I essentially created the series. Originally, it was going to be 13 one-hour programs, and I decided that it would be better to have 26 half-hour programs. I wanted to make sure that we would have something that would be good for PBS viewers, something that would be good for adults and Telecourse learners via videotape, but then also something good for high school and college students to have as an in-class resource. So as not to dominate the 50-minute class hour, I decided the half hour format would serve best. Essentially I laid out what would be a good introductory psychology course, with one program on each of the major topics in psychology. Then I was in the position of selecting the psychologists who would be interviewed, and I shaped each program. In the process, I essentially trained the entire WGBH production staff in basic psychology. For each program I wrote 25–50 pages of background on the topic, including the basic principles, the historical background of each topic, who were the key research contributors, who were the current people who I thought would be the most interesting on camera. Then I would block out the program, deciding on the format and sequence for each episode. I was aided enormously by a team of ten advisors that I selected to represent a broad range of psychology and education. We started filming in 1989 and finished in 1990–1991, and the series has been a huge success. It has aired continuously since 1990. The series has been shown in most colleges, virtually all high schools, and 10 different countries worldwide. They have sold thousands of videos; it is one of the most popular series in the Annenberg program. I have just revised the series in 2001. We have 3 all new programs—cultural psychology and cognitive neuroscience—that did not exist a decade ago, and also applied psychology. For 17 of the original episodes, we have filmed new interviews or revised old material. That project has been my most enduring, and probably most positive impact via the media, because I had a lot of control of the procedure, process, and outcome. I was the chief scientific advisor, as well as co-writer and creator of each series. As the host, I was able to really influence the way that many people teach introductory psychology. Unfortunately, the series never made it to prime time or the basic PBS station. Because it was only a half hour, it was always on the second PBS station, which is really the community college station. It is not reaching the general public as much as it should because it's really a very good series. I should say in passing that I don't receive any royalties or residuals for the Discovering Psychology series. I did it only for my love of psychology and teaching. The new program on cognitive neuroscience just won an Emmy for instructional television, as external justification for my efforts.

Candid Camera, in a sense, was kind of the prototype for Reality TV. The show looked at ordinary people in either natural or contrived situations. Years ago, I wrote to Allen Funt saying I would love to have access to his material in order to create videos for teachers and students of psychology. I wanted to prepare a video for introductory psychology and one for social psychology courses. I worked hard to convince him to work together with me on that project. He initially refused, but I was not deterred. As President of WPA in 1983, I invited him to give a keynote address in San Francisco, which he did brilliantly. Then, I invited him back later on for me to do a "puff piece" interview with him for *Psychology Today* magazine. I wined him and dined him, and we became friends. The key however, was convincing Funt that he was more than an entertainer, he was an educator—that viewers could learn while they laughed. He finally succumbed to this persuasive pressure allowing me to work with him reviewing hundreds of candid camera episodes. We identified 16 programs that I felt were most interesting for introductory psychology teachers and 16 other programs that were interesting for social psychology teachers. McGraw Hill publishes distributes the videos and laser discs, and I wrote a study guide with Allen Funt to accompany the videos. (I do not receive any royalties from the Candid Camera series or study guides either; more doing it for the love of psychology and teaching.)

Another opportunity to work with the media came from the Stanford Prison study. That has been a big media event; the research itself is a dramatic piece. It is really like a Greek drama—what happens when you put good people in an evil place? There is a stage-like setting, costumes, actors, auxiliary actors (i.e., the police, the parents, a public defender, a Catholic priest). There is deep dramatic focus in the story. Do good people win over evil situations or do evil situations corrupt good people?

I am always thinking about how to communicate research findings in my teaching, so during the study, I took video, audio, and slides as the experiment progressed. Afterwards, I prepared a tape narration synchronized with the presentation of 80 slides that I distributed at cost for many years to teachers and community groups. Now that presentation is available on a free website (www.prisonexp.org) along with some video clips from our documentary video. This fine website, created with the assistance of Scott Plous, has had more than 8 million unique page viewers over the last two years. This is astounding to me that my little study should reach so many people so many years after its debut.

Then, working with undergraduates at Stanford, primarily Ken Musen (now a film maker), I created a video of the Stanford Prison study using the original black and white archival footage. We updated this with interviews of some prisoners and guards in 1989. It is titled: "Quiet Rage: The Stanford Prison Experiment." This version has been distributed to colleges, high schools, and criminal justice groups. That video has been influential in a number of ways to help others get a sense of what the experience was like. We distribute it from my office at Stanford, with ordering information on the website (see www.prisonexp.org).

Recently, a German film company produced a film called *Das Experiment*, which was based on the Stanford prison study. It was produced with an outstanding cast and one of the leading directors of Germany. Unfortunately, it is a terrible movie for the image of psychology, and I have debated publicly the screenwriter and lead actor and done interviews deploring it. The first part of the movie documents the procedure used in my research, but then the second part is a fantasy sequence with extreme violence and graphic sex scenes that, of course, had nothing to do with the original experiment. Guards kill prisoners and rape the female psychologist-researcher, and prisoners kill guards! Sadly, the movie ends in a shambles with no debriefing, no explanation of why the study was conducted, and no sense of which part of the movie was real and which part was fiction. All the promotion of the film features references to my study, our web site, and to the research publications with Craig Haney and Curt Banks—but then they say it is a fantasy exercise. It is a sad example of the worse kind of exploitation of psychological research for purely commercial purposes. Recent research in Germany shows that viewer attitudes toward psychology are more negative after watching this awful film. And that is very distressing to me.

Lastly, on the prison study, the BBC recently did a recreation of the study with volunteers for a week that was aired on prime time for over 4 hours. I refused to be a paid consultant on the program because it was now clear the study was unethical and because I felt it would suffer from the Heisenberg effect. A made for prime time TV experiment would alter the behavior being studied by the very act of obviously recording it to get good sound and video close-ups. The participants would be aware at most times of being under surveillance and would want to look good for the home audience when it was all over. And that is indeed what happened. The prisoners wore lapel mikes at all times and often held them while talking to each other. Then there were "confessional" breaks when guards, prisoners and the two British experimenters each spoke at various times to the camera. The essence of my study was creating an intense cauldron of behavioral dynamics that soon lost the sense of being an experiment and became a prison run by psychologists. The BBC experiment was always an "experiment," and always a TV show to the participants, and so lost the essential intensity created in the Stanford Prison Experiment. Interestingly, in that recreation, the prisoners won over the guards—hardly with any external validity to prisons of which I am aware.

Currently, I am the psychological consultant for NBC News. NBC has asked me to help them develop programming ideas that have psychological content, psychological relevance. As I said earlier, one of the programs is going to be an hour-long documentary of the Stanford Prison study in the fall. We are trying to generate other kinds of ideas for how to get good psychology into NBC programming, into the Today Show, to NBC News. Also NBC Dateline creates programs for other networks, like the Discovery Channel. We just did a pilot show for Discovery, called "Only Human", that sadly they did not buy for a season series. In large part they rejected further shows because the host-comedian, whom they chose, got terrible ratings. The concept is a good one, that I hope to push further, a series of interesting or funny skits each based on a psychological theme, like compliance, conformity, the burden of keeping secrets, invasion of other's personal space—but with some psychological analyses after each one, by me or relevant experts. If done right, it can't miss.

Interviewer: You have certainly been our field's leader in helping to educate the public about psychology. Was this initially one of your career goals?

PGZ: When I think back now, my primary experience with the media has really come about mostly through my teaching, but also through my research. In my teaching, I've always used videos, film, audiotapes, newspaper or magazine articles—anything to help me breach the barrier between the classroom and everyday life. The media has always been an integral part of my teaching. As I mentioned earlier, my research tends either toward the dramatic or the appealingly mundane—as with my research on shyness in adults and children. But mainly, the media has always been part of what I teach. In my first edition of *Psychology in Life*, I included a section on how to be a wise consumer of research. Essentially, this is for the average student who is not going to be a psychologist—95% of students who take introductory psychology are not going on to even major in psychology. However, they will be consumers of our research, as physicians, lawyers, business people and legislators, so we want them to know what psychology has to offer. My work educating the public about psychology has been an extension of my commitment to teaching.

Aside from the content of psychology we have another unique message—our experimental research message—our focus on controlled observation, systematic variation, and our sensitivity to human bias. No other discipline has this to the same extent. This makes psychology able to talk to the general public about matters of value to them, and to teach them about dangers in misleading advertising allegedly based on "research shows that..." Thus, we have an important contribution to make—and young psychologists should be taking over from us old farts and leading the way in promoting psychology, to giving it away to the public in the right ways.

In conclusion, I have enjoyed sharing these random reflections of my career as a media maven, or media buff, and hope the basic message gets through to the next generation of psychologists.

As a fitting ending of this interview, I was just notified today that I would receive a special award from the Council of Scientific Society Presidents for my media and textbook work. It is the Carl Sagan Award for Improving the Public Understanding and Appreciation of Science. It puts me in a rather select group of previous winners, among them: Carl Sagan, E. O. Wilson, National Geographic, NOVA-TV, Scientific American and the NYT-Science Times. Wow! Now I will have to redouble my future efforts to live up to such an honor, and hope to be able to do so. Thanks for your attention.

Ciao. Fade to black.

ADDITIONAL RESOURCES

Visit http://www.zimbardo.com.

CHAPTER 20

Strategies for Successful Interactions with the News Media[1]

RHEA K. FARBERMAN

According to the newsletter *Public Relations Tactics* (1996), health information is what news editors and producers want most from public relations professionals and other news sources. Indeed, health news and medical research are among the most widely (and some would say poorly) reported news worldwide.

For psychologists and behavioral researchers, the media reporting of news and current events offer a credible, far-reaching, and inexpensive way to educate large numbers of Americans about psychological findings and knowledge. For the news media, psychologists are interview sources who can help answer the "why" of news events and social trends and can add interest, credibility and a fresh or unique angle to the news. So why is the relationship such a tenuous one?

WHEN JOURNALISM MEETS PSYCHOLOGY

When journalism and psychology meet, two very different worlds are coming together. The foundation of psychology is the careful analysis of research done over time. The foundation of journalism is the clock, or too often the stopwatch; a continuous rush to meet deadlines and beat the competition.

Understanding what is considered news by the gatekeepers of the news process (reporters, editors and producers) is a key factor in successful media relations. What's important to realize is that many of the decisions made during the process by which an event becomes news are subjective. While most editors and producers will tell you that they make decisions about what gets in the paper or on the air based on objective factors such as timeliness, uniqueness, significance, impact on the community, proximity to the audience, drama, and

RHEA K. FARBERMAN • APR, Member and Public Communications Office, American Psychological Association, Washington, DC 20002

[1] This chapter was initially published as Farberman, R. K. (1999). What the media need from news sources. In L. L. Schwartz (Ed.). *Psychology and the media: A second look.* (pp. 8–22) American Psychological Association: Washington, DC. Reprinted with permission of the American Psychological Association.

the availability of good visuals, that person's view of the world also enters into the decision making process.

APA Public Affairs Office

The APA Public Affairs Office and its counterpart in the Practice Directorate work on a daily basis not only to make the news media aware of the knowledge and expertise of psychologists, but also to prepare psychologists to be successful newsmakers. APA's media referral service is an electronic database that records the area of expertise and media experience of approximately 1,500 APA members who have expressed an interest in doing media work. The system works as a match-maker, putting the journalist in touch with the right psychologist, one who can answer questions intelligently and in a speedy fashion. This service lists psychologists with expertise in approximately 150 subject areas from child development to intelligence tests, from eating behavior to sports psychology. In an average year, between 5,000 and 6,000 APA members are referred to journalists for interviews through the referral service.

Interpreting and publicizing the research published in APA journals is another way the organization seeks to educate the media, and through them, the public, about the value and contributions of psychology and psychological research. APA Public Affairs staff review all journal articles for news potential and write press releases based on those judged most likely to attract the interest of editors, reporters, and producers. Between 35 and 40 press releases based on APA journal articles are distributed to the media each year.

During the mid-1990s, APA made a large investment in educating the public about the value of psychological services and undertook similar, but smaller projects, to inform the public about the importance of behavioral research. These investments however, while unprecedented in the over 100 year history of the organization, are dwarfed by the investment other organizations and corporate America make in communicating with the public. For example, the APA public education campaign was funded at the level of one million dollars a year for five years. When Lays wanted to introduce its fat free potato chip to American consumers, it spent over $40 million dollars in a 6 month period on advertising and marketing!

The costs of communicating directly to the public through paid advertising makes news media relations all the more important for psychology. It is important to remember that those professions and organizations which build ongoing relationships with the news media have a voice when important news breaks and when national policies are discussed. Those organizations which remain silent or are not proactive in their communications efforts will be stuck on the sidelines of most news events and public policy debates. The American Medical Association and the American Psychiatric Association are two examples of vocal participants in news media reporting of current events and active players in the Washington public policy arena.

"If you want your views represented, you have to talk to the media," said Roger Allies, a former media adviser to George Bush (Sherman, 1989). The problem with not talking to the news media is that reporters will find other sources to talk to, explains Allies. Those sources may not understand an issue as well as you do and probably will not cast you and your research, university, profession, as you would.

Nearly 20 years ago TV news elder statesmen David Brinkley noted that when a government or industry spokesperson "deals with television, it is not us they are dealing with. They are dealing with the American people through us. They give clear, short answers because they are more effective when they are delivered by us to the American people" (Rafe & Pfister, 1983, p. 56). The news media's ability to be the conduit through which organizations speak to the American public is larger and even more powerful today. A 1996 Harris Poll found that Americans most important source of news, by a 2 to 1 margin, was CNN (Kalish, 1996). And, for the limited number of Americans who get their news from other sources, television news still sets the standard for how news and information is reported.

Most psychologists agree that it is important for organized psychology to build and maintain ongoing relationships with the news media. But, most would also agree that media relations can be a double-edged sword. If you don't know what you're doing you can get hurt.

SPECIAL OPPORTUNITIES AND SPECIAL PROBLEMS

As the news media offers opportunities for psychology and psychologist it also presents special problems. Examples of these special problems are 1) the uninformed reporter, 2) fitting complex research into a sound bite, 3) patient confidentiality, and 4) public education vs. 'on-air' therapy.

The Uninformed Reporter

Typically the reporter assigned to do a story with psychological implications has a limited understanding of psychology and behavioral science. The exception would be a large media outlet with the resources to assign an experienced writer to the psychology beat. Only a few national outlets such as *The New York Times*, have such a reporter. What is more likely is that the reporter who calls the psychologist for comment or explanation of a new piece of research or a news event is a generalist, called a general assignment reporter in the industry.

An investment of time and patience is required when dealing with the inexperienced reporter, but that investment is critical to the quality and accuracy of the final story. A good piece of advice to the news source—the interviewee—one should approach the reporter as one would approach a student. Think of the interview as a teaching opportunity, and as such, communicate to the student (the reporter) in language he or she can understand.

The Foundation for American Communications Media Resource Guide (1990) has the following to say about the importance of providing background material to reporters. The key to background information is the knowledge that the craft of news reporting is very much a story-to-story, day-to-day profession. Unless you are blessed with a reporter covering you regularly, odds are that any reporter covering a story involving you may not know very much about you, the story, and what happened before the reporter was assigned to your story. The protection you need in that situation also happens to be an effective way of providing service to the reporter. Who knows more about you than you do? By compiling basic information, you can make the reporter's job easier. (p. 13)

In other words, by taking the time to educate the reporter and provide him or her with all appropriate background material you are making an investment in more thorough, more accurate news coverage.

Fitting Complex Research into a Sound-Bite

The average news sound-bite today is under 10 seconds in length. But psychological research is complex and there are limitations as to how resulting data should be interpreted and applied. Caveats are important. Simply put, what the researcher sees in his or her research results—one piece of the overall research puzzle that can only be applied within the limits of this particular study, is different from what the reporter wants to find in a research study—the all encompassing headline.

The challenge for the news source, the psychologist, is how to translate the research into a meaningful sound-bite; this is especially true when preparing for interviews with electronic media—radio and television, which often emphasize speed and brevity above in-depth reporting.

One valuable strategy for doing so is for the researcher to ask himself or herself simple questions about the research study. What was the goal of the research? What theory did I set out to prove or disprove? How might the results of this study be applied in the future? Brief but descriptive answers to these questions create a sound-bite that is simple without being simplistic. Also consider the media outlet you are being interviewed by. The type of interview you would do with your community newspaper is different from the one you would do with *National Public Radio* and different again from the one you would do with a network evening magazine like ABC's *20/20*.

Patient Confidentiality

Reporters are also looking to personalize the news and to make it dramatic. Often with issues in clinical psychology, reporters or news producers will ask psychologists to provide names of patients whom the reporter can also interview or who can appear on a broadcast with the mental health provider. These requests create vexing dilemmas for psychologists. Some, indeed many, psychologists feel that their responsibility to uphold patient confidentiality would rule out giving reporters the names of patients, either current or past. Other psychologists see the value, in terms of helping other people with similar issues who are not yet in therapy, of giving the media the opportunity to humanize and personalize the ailment by allowing them to introduce an actual person who is struggling with it or at best who has conquered it. The Division of Media Psychology and APA's Public Information Committee have looked at this issue in depth and found both value and areas of concern. The Division's suggestions for psychologists working with the news media are as follows:

When considering using clients on air, psychologists weigh several issues carefully, and where the needs of the psychologist and patient differ, the patient's welfare always comes first. Among the factors to be considered are: the vulnerability of the patient; whether or not the appearance of the patient would be exploitative; whether the patient is deciding to participate to please the therapist; and whether the appearance is a perceived testimonial or a demonstration of a therapeutic technique. The public education value of the appearance should also be considered(1996, p. 33).

Public Education vs. 'On-Air Therapy'

Experienced media psychologists all recognize that educating the public about psychology and psychological interventions is not therapy nor should it be. The value of media psychology is to inform consumers about how psychology could help them or their loved ones. At its best, media psychology can suggest alternative behaviors, can motivate people to look at a situation with a new perspective or to seek the assistance of a mental health professional for a problem. Media psychology cannot however, in and of itself, solve the complex problems that are part of many people's lives today.

It was precisely the limits of what media psychology can and should do that caused so much disquiet within the profession about the talk show phenomenon of the early to middle 1990s. At that time, talk shows were increasing in number, each trying to outdo the other in terms of the startling personnel or outrageous on-air behavior. The shows were numerous, *Jenny Jones, Ricki Lake, Montel Williams*, to name a few. Each wanted mental health professionals to "perform" as part of the show's formula—conflict for the first 50 minutes, and then a resolution by a therapist during the last two broadcast minutes. Although the shows were successful in being able to attract "therapists" to appear on air, many experienced media psychologists refused to take part.

WHY DO THE NEWS MEDIA DO THE THINGS THEY DO?

What drives the news media? Time, the quest for accuracy and fairness, and competition with other outlets—but mostly time. The only way to really appreciate the time pressures under which journalists work, particularly reporters who work in radio, television and on daily newspapers, is to be aware of them. Reporters writing for daily newspapers typically receive a story assignment in the morning and face a deadline that afternoon. In this time, the reporter has to quickly educate him or herself about the issue, ascertain the facts and get quotes from people involved or other knowledgeable experts to achieve balance between both sides of a story. All this has to be done in anywhere from 4 to 6 hours. Often the news source who returns the reporter's call most promptly or who is most helpful to the reporter's understanding of the issues involved is the person who gets quoted or has the most effect on the story.

Radio journalists face even tighter deadlines, as radio tries to provide listeners with something that newspapers can not: hourly updates on the news. Often a radio station will want to do a news interview with a source immediately, or certainly that same day.

Television deadlines range somewhere between the immediate need of radio and the "this afternoon" deadlines of print reporters. But TV has an added dimension. Whereas the majority of interviews for print and radio journalists are done over the phone, television reporters want to go to the news source's office or to some other appropriate setting to do the interview (and get "pictures" to go along with the story). The TV reporter has to leave the studio and get videotape; that adds time and pressure to the news-gathering process.

Deadlines vary in television. Daily morning or afternoon broadcasts are going to want to do interviews today, or at times do live interviews during the actual broadcast. Other types of television news, like weekly magazine format shows have longer lead times and typically work on a show segment 4 to 6 weeks in advance of its airing.

The need for speed doesn't always allow the media to find the best fit between news source and story. It also doesn't always allow the reporter time to do the necessary homework in order to get grounded in a topic area before conducting an interview. Such situations put both the news outlet and the news source at risk of a story or a quote that is incorrect or out of context or incomplete. The news organization cannot do much to change the nature of the news gathering process and the news cycle. They certainly cannot add hours to the day. News sources can, however, take a few steps to try to be as efficient and effective as possible in spite of the media's time pressures.

HOW TO LEVEL THE PLAYING FIELD

Writing in *Campaign Magazine*, media trainer Karen Kalish called every media interview "a glorious opportunity to get your point across. It's a chance for exposure and free advertising, to inform the public, to clear up misconceptions, and to put your work in the public's mind." (1996, p. 44)

Working with the news media should be on the agenda of every psychologist as psychology and behavioral science fights for appropriate consumer recognition and its fair share of the research pie. But, also compulsory when doing news media interviews is preparation.

The Pre-Interview Phase

From the interviewee's perspective, one of the most important pieces of the interview process is the "interview before the interview." This pre-interview process is when the news source gets to ask the questions. Here's what you will want to know:

1. What news outlet is the reporter calling from. If you're unfamiliar with it, ask more questions. What is its format (newspaper, magazine, radio, TV spot news, TV magazine news, etc., audience, live or on-tape)? Length? Frequency? Other guests?
2. What's the theme of the story, or in what direction does the reporter think the story is moving? What information is the reporter looking to you to provide? If the reporter says "I'm really just beginning to talk to some people about this," it's a golden opportunity for you. It may require a bit more time on your part, but it's an opportunity to really educate the reporter and therefore have more influence on the story than any other news source.
3. Who else has the reporter spoken to, or has plans to speak to? (This information can often give you a clue as to the direction or bias of the story).
4. If you're being asked to appear on a broadcast show pay extra attention to the show's format. What you want to avoid is being asked to participate in what is being set up to be a heated debate; or being asked to solve the complex problems of another guest in the last 30 seconds of the show.

Once you have asked these questions and gotten answers it is time to decide whether you feel you are the right person to do the interview. If the answer is yes, agree on a time that the reporter can call you back or come to your office to do the interview. Keep in mind the reporter's time pressures. The earlier in the process the reporter gets your information and point-of-view the better he or she can synthesize the information into the story in its appropriate context. Remember at this point in the process you also have the right to set some ground rules as to where the interview will take place and how long the interview will last. Being generous with your time in helping a reporter learn about and understand the subject area makes sense, but spending hours with him or her does not. A good length of time for a typical phone interview is 15–20 minutes; for an in-person interview 45 minutes to one hour.

Preparing for the Interview

Having a goal for the interview and knowing the words and phrases you will use to express your knowledge and point-of-view is critical to its success. Preparing brief summaries of your research or clinical work is a good way to help you frame your message, but also gives you a valuable overview you can share with reporters to help them prepare as well.

Before the interview begins, create the three most important message points you want to communicate. Write them out. Practice them. Are they credible, simple without being simplistic, brief and true to your expertise and the psychological literature? It is also important to give some thought to the questions you will likely be asked, and of course, what your answers will be. But don't assume that every question the reporter asks is the right question. Some will be the wrong question based on the reporter's lack of understanding of the subject area or a reporter who is fishing for controversy. It is important to acknowledge a reporter's question but also to correct it if it is based on a false premise. Then bridge away from it if it leads you away from the messages that you want to deliver.

Examples of "bridge" phases are:

- "The real issue is . . . "
- "What's important to remember is . . . "
- "I don't know the answer to that question, but what I do know is . . . "
- "The main point here is . . . "
- "The bottom line here is . . . "

During the Interview

At best, you can control the tempo and pace of the interview by keeping your answers brief and avoiding the temptation to fill all the time with your voice. Silence between questions should not make you nervous; it gives both you and the reporter time to think.

Reporters are fond of asking a few questions at one time and are known to interrupt frequently. When faced with multiple questions and an aggressive reporter, it is important to keep your cool. Break down multi-pronged questions and deal with one issue at a time. When stuck about how to respond or where to go next, remember the message points that you crafted and want to deliver. Returning to your message points will help you get back on track if you feel an interview is going awry.

AFTER THE INTERVIEW

Evaluating Your Performance

We are often our own worst critics, especially when it comes to seeing our image on television or hearing our voice on the radio. However, the best way to evaluate your performance is to ask yourself the question, "Did I deliver my three message points, and did they get into the story in an appropriate context?" The only issues you should concern yourself with in terms of how you look or sound is if your appearance, body language or voice got in the way of the audience hearing your message. Such questions as, "Did I mumble or speak too rapidly?"; "Did I look disinterested or nervous?"; "Was my loud tie a distraction?" are all appropriate questions.

TABLE 1. Strategies for Successful Interactions with the Media

Before You Are Interviewed
- Do your homework.
- Anticipate key questions.
- Prepare key answers; including quotable phrases.
- Prepare and fine tune your three message points.

During the Interview Your Rights Are
- You have the right to determine the approximate length of the interview.
- You have the right to select where you want to be interviewed.
- You can ask in advance for the topics to be covered during the interview. (Occasionally reporters will give you a copy of the questions they would like to ask. But this doesn't happen often and if you do get such a list don't assume that the interview will not stray from that list).
- You have the right to set your own pace in answering questions. Don't let the reporter rush you. Taking time to think before responding to a question is a good idea.
- You should correct false premises and challenge questionable assertions or assumptions.

During the Interview Your Job Is To
- Deliver your message points in brief, understandable, quotable language.
- Speak in plain English and avoid jargon.
- Speak within the range of your knowledge, and don't be afraid to say, "I don't know."
- Be positive, not defensive. Use bridges to move away from topics you do not want to talk about and to your message points.
- Don't let the reporter put words in your mouth or create controversy when none exists.

What To Do When You Are Unhappy With a Story

Very rarely is a news report everything you would have wanted it to be if you had written it yourself. What's important to focus on is the big picture. What broad theme or message is received by the reader or viewer? Remember that it takes many, many impressions over time to influence public opinion. Consider your interview one small piece of that larger effort.

Occasionally news sources feel that they were misquoted by a reporter and want to demand a correction. There are times when it is appropriate to ask for such a correction but there are also times when making such a request can backfire. When a factual error appears in a news story it is fair and appropriate to ask for a correction. Do so firmly, but nicely. Remember that journalists are people, too, and therefore subject to the same issues of ego and anger as everyone else. (What's different, however, is that news people control what will be reported on tomorrow. You do not.) It will also be important to make the correction in future interviews on the subject. Reporters often use old news clips as a way to brief themselves on a topic. If a reporter's question is based on a false premise, tell them so and explain why.

When you feel that the story for which you were a news source has missed a particular context or nuance this is not necessarily the time to demand a correction. One risk of doing so is that you put yourself and your organization at risk of being perceived by the editor or reporter as "protesting too much" and that can beget an embarrassing second day news story, or a less than friendly reporter the next time you are involved in a news event.

CONCLUSION

Working with the news media is an important means by which psychologists and behavioral scientists educate the public about the value of their work. Interviews are the primary means by which news is gathered. The news media and psychologists have important things to offer each other. News media relations is, however, something which should be approached with a degree of caution and lots of preparation. Psychologists who are interested in working with the news media should avail themselves of media training workshops and seminars offered by APA and other entities. As long as marketplace issues impede on the study and application of psychology and human behavior educating the public through the news media about the value of psychology will continue to be an important public relations tool for the discipline.

ADDITIONAL RESOURCES

For more information about APA's referral service or to request a membership application contact the APA Public Affairs Office at 202 336-5700, email: publiccom@apa.org.

REFERENCES

APA Public Information Committee. (1996). *Draft guidelines for psychologists working with the news media.* (8th ed.) American Psychological Association: Washington, D.C.

Foundation for American Communications. (1990). *Media resource guide: How to tell your story.* (5th ed.) Foundation for American Communications: Los Angeles, CA.

Kalish, K. (1996). Meeting the press on your terms. *Campaign Magazine, June*, 44–46.

Public Relations Society of America. (1996). Stories editors are looking for. *Public Relations Tactics, April*, 9.

Rafe, S. C., & Pfister, W. J. (1983). The art of the interview. *VideoPro, August*, 54–58.

Sherman, S. P. (1989). Smart ways to handle the press. *Fortune, June 19*, 69–75.

SECTION V

YOUR CAREER AFTER GRADUATE SCHOOL

CHAPTER 21

Recommendations for a Postdoctoral Fellowship

VALERIE A. SIMON AND ANTHONY SPIRITO

The dissertation or clinical internship is typically the final requirement fulfilled for the psychology doctorate, and its completion is certainly just cause for both celebration and relief. However, completing the doctorate does not necessarily denote the end of "trainee" status. In many of the settings in which psychologists work, a post-doctoral fellowship is increasingly recognized as a desirable, if not necessary, next step prior to employment or licensure as a professional psychologist. Academic institutions and university medical centers increasingly prefer job candidates with advanced postdoctoral training. Such experience may also be required for licensure. Finally, some specialty practice areas within the field (e.g., neuropsychology) now require formal postdoctoral training at an approved program for specialty certification.

The diversification of psychology and the growth of professional practice over the last 50 years have prompted ongoing debate regarding the necessity and definition of postdoctoral training. Supervised experience beyond the doctoral degree prior to psychology licensure was first recommended by the American Psychological Association (APA) in its model acts for licensure (APA Committee on Legislation, 1955, 1967), and today, most state licensing boards mandate some form of supervised, postgraduate experience to qualify for the licensure exam. Yet questions regarding the *definition* of postdoctoral training remain, not only for professional practice, but for academic and research psychology as well. These questions have been the focus of several recent training conferences. For example, the Association of Psychology Postdoctoral and Internship Centers (APPIC) convened a national conference on postdoctoral training in 1992 to develop specific postdoctoral training criteria for students, training programs, and credentialing authorities (Belar et al., 1993; Larsen et al., 1993). In 1994, the American Psychological Association sponsored the National Conference on Postdoctoral Education and Training in Psychology (APA, 1995) to address not only professional practice but teaching and research activities as well. Both associations have developed criteria for formal postdoctoral education and training programs, and APA offers the programs the opportunity

VALERIE SIMON • Brown University School of Medicine, Dept of Psychiatry and Human Behavior, Providence, RI 02912
ANTHONY SPIRITO • Clinical Psychology Training Consortium, Department of Psychiatry and Human Behavior, Brown Medical School, Providence, RI 02912

to become accredited. However, institutions offering postdoctoral training are not required to be accredited. Only a minority of the institutions offering postdoctoral training formally participate in APPIC and fewer are APA approved.

These ongoing conventions and recommendations reflect psychology's increasing focus on postdoctoral training. Leaders in the field are pressing to create more uniform requirements for postdoctoral training, which currently vary greatly between states, and to establish professional organizations, rather than state regulatory groups, as the arbiter of postdoctoral training standards. Although neither postdoctoral training nor the accreditation of postdoctoral training programs has been mandated, these issues remain actively debated by various professional organizations. Supporters of mandated postdoctoral training contend that postdoctoral training benefits not only new psychologists, but also the field as a whole and consumers of psychological services. Detractors assert that the field has unnecessarily expanded its definition of what students need to know to become competent psychologists.

Whatever your position on this issue, it is important when planning your career path to recognize what we believe is a growing reality: the field of psychology, those employing psychologists, and state regulatory agencies maintain that graduate school alone cannot provide the broad range of knowledge and skills required for the modern practice of psychology. Complicating matters is the current state of postdoctoral training, which exists in a variety of institutions offering a range of different experiences, varying in their duration, amount of supervision, and compensation. So, even if you are ready to pursue postdoctoral training, the lack of uniform training standards and variability in positions raise many questions about what kind of position to pursue. The goal of this chapter is to clarify these issues and assist you with two basic tasks: determining whether postdoctoral training is right for you and understanding how to obtain a fellowship that meets your personal and professional needs. With regard to the first task, we will explore advantages and disadvantages of postdoctoral training as well as other considerations in the decision to pursue a postdoctoral position. For those who might wish to seek such training, we will explicate the steps for locating, applying, evaluating, and securing a suitable fellowship. Finally, some thoughts and recommendations about the postdoctoral experience are offered.

TYPES OF POSTDOCTORAL TRAINING

Before evaluating the potential benefits and costs of postdoctoral training, a brief introduction to the range of postdoctoral training opportunities seems warranted. As previously noted, there are no established definitions or requirements to which institutions, mentors, or supervisors must adhere in the training of postdoctoral fellows. Consequently, postdoctoral positions, even within a particular domain (e.g., research vs. clinical/applied) or specialty area (e.g., neuropsychology, health psychology, forensic psychology) are likely to vary greatly along a variety of dimensions, including funding, training focus, structure, and setting. While such variations should not be equated with a corresponding range in quality, understanding the differences will assist you in determining which, if any, type of postdoc will best meet your needs.

Stipends

Stipends considerations are critical, as most recent graduates cannot afford to accept a postdoctoral position that offers no monetary compensation. Such positions do exist, and a few even charge tuition. However, the majority of postdoctoral positions are funded. A 1998 survey of postdoctoral training institutions reported that from November 1995 through October 1996, at least 450 sites provided 1007 funded, full-time slots and 107 funded part-time slots. Only 57 sites offered 489 slots that were unfunded or required tuition payments (Stewart & Stewart, 1998). The amount of funding offered, including both salary and benefits, varies tremendously and often depends on factors particular to the institution, sector (academic vs. industry), geographical area, and funding source of a given position. As of 1997, median salaries for postdoctoral trainees were $25–28,000 for academic settings, $30,000 for industry settings, and $35–40,000 in government settings (Committee on Science, Engineering and Public Policy, 2000).

Training Emphasis

The training emphasis of a postdoctoral position is one of its most salient features and typically a primary criterion for choosing a particular position. Most postdoctoral programs emphasize either research or applied/clinical training. Many offer training in both domains, but fewer integrate research and training activities, and those that do tend to be more highly structured (see below). In evaluating programs, it will be important to examine the relative emphasis placed on research, academic, and applied/clinical training and the fit with your own training goals, as most positions will offer more training in one of these areas.

Although funding and training focus may be persuasive features of a postdoctoral position, other factors, including structure and setting should also be considered. With respect to structure, postdoctoral training programs are frequently distinguished as providing either "formal" or "informal" training. "Informal" training usually occurs when supervision is provided within the context of a traditionally defined job. In contrast to this informal on-the-job training, "formal" postdoctoral training takes place in an organized educational and training program designed for the expressed purpose of developing advanced competencies and expertise (Belar et al., 1987). In defining formal requirements for postdocs related to professional practice, APPIC has designated the following characteristics as essential to the formal programs listed in their directory: 1) the program is coordinated by a designated staff psychologist; 2) the duration of training is at least one year at a minimum of half-time status; 3) training occurs under the supervision of a minimum of two psychologists; 4) at least four hours per week of supervision are required, and at least two of these four hours must be individual supervision of patient care; and 5) direct clinical services must account for a minimum of 25% of the fellow's time commitment.

Looking beyond the clinical focus of some of these characteristics, a more general contrast can be seen in the relative emphasis placed on education and training. This is perhaps the most defining feature of formal postdoctoral programs as compared to the informal, on the job, supervised training that may also be pursued to fulfill licensure or other experiential needs. In weighing the merits of formal versus informal training, the trade-off is typically financial. Formal training programs typically offer lower financial rewards, with an understanding that part of the trainee's compensation is the education gained through structured mentoring and training experiences. Because informal postdoctoral training often happens in the context of supervised employment, these positions may offer more financial incentives but fewer organized educational opportunities, such as seminars and dedicated time for mentoring, supervision, writing, and other professional development activities.

Although survey data suggests that new psychology graduates express a preference for informal over formal postdoctoral training, those who have completed formal programs might be more satisfied with the training they received (France & Wolfe, 2000). In a survey of 117 psychologists who completed formal postdoctoral training, France and Wolfe (2000) found that 68% rated their experience "very valuable", 27% as "valuable", and 5% as "somewhat valuable". None of the psychologists who completed formal programs judged their experience to be "not valuable". In contrast, only 38% of 189 psychologists surveyed who completed informal postdoctoral training rated their experience as "very valuable". Thirty-four percent judged their postdoctoral training as "valuable", 21% as "somewhat valuable, and 8% rated the experience as "not valuable".

Setting

The primary settings offering postdoctoral training in psychology are freestanding hospitals, academic medical centers, and universities, although positions are also available through government agencies and private industries. Differences between the institutional missions of these settings and the type of work they supported might affect whether a particular postdoctoral position is best suited for your training needs. For instance, hospitals and some academic medical centers might be more likely to focus on applied aspects of both research and clinical practice, given their primary mission of service delivery. Accordingly, those whose interests lie in the treatment of particular types of medical or psychiatric disorders might be better suited for this setting than those whose work focuses on basic theory or other issues whose implications for improving health, development, or quality of care may be less direct.

The setting of the postdoc position may also affect the type of training experiences available. Hospitals and academic medical centers might be more likely to offer hands-on and cross-disciplinary training opportunities, such as treatment teams and grand rounds presentations, but may not offer coursework or teaching. Academic medical centers and university psychology departments typically offer more opportunities to teach and mentor, which could be important in obtaining a subsequent university or faculty position. Such institutions may also have more opportunities for learning skills relating to academic jobs, such as grant writing, manuscript review, or presenting research results at conferences. However, a potential drawback to the academic medical center is that postdocs may be assigned to work with a single mentor with little oversight or protection, have little access to university facilities, or be isolated from other postdoctoral trainees.

Postdoctoral positions in industry are usually geared toward creating marketable and profitable products. They typically offer stricter time limits on duration of training, better salaries, employee benefits, well-equipped research facilities, exposure to industrial culture, and the opportunity for teamwork. However, industry positions might also offer fewer teaching opportunities, less choice about one's particular placement, and limited ability to take ownership of projects. The work during the fellowship may have an exclusive focus on marketable results as well as restrictions on information exchange for proprietary reasons.

Lastly, training positions in government facilities typically occur in the context of large national labs that may be unique in scope of research and size of research group. Like academic medical centers, they might offer more interdisciplinary training, more interactions with other divisions and researchers, and participation in joint decision-making. However, government

Table 1. Summary of Differences Across Hospital, Academic Medical Center, University, and Industry Settings for Postdoctoral Training

	Hospital	Academic medical center	University	Industry	Government
Professional practice or applied training	√	√	X	√	X
Ability to accumulate supervised professional practice hours toward licensure	√	√	?	X	X
Participation in decisions regarding training activities	?	√	√	X	X
Cross-disciplinary training and collaboration	√	√	?	?	√
Coursework or teaching opportunities	X	X	√	X	X
Opportunities to mentor or supervise students	X	√	√	X	X
Opportunities to learn and practice grant writing	X	√	√	X	?
Opportunities to participate in peer review of papers submitted for publication	X	√	√	?	√
Opportunities to co-author publications	X	√	√	?	√
Protected time for research activities (data collection, data analyses, writing)	X	√	√	X	?
Opportunities to pursue independent research	X	√	√	X	X
Ownership of projects or data	X	?	√	X	X
Professional level pay scale	X	X	X	√	X
Benefits package (medical, paid vacation)	√	√	√	√	√

√ = likely to be present X = not likely to be present ? = may or may not be present

facilities might offer fewer teaching/mentoring experiences as well as less flexibility in determining the direction of one's work.

A summary of the pros and cons of the various training settings is presented in Table 1. It is important to again note that the variations presented above do not necessarily constitute differences in the quality of the training offered, but differences in the types of opportunities or training activities that may be available. Such differences will arise again later in our discussion, as we discuss how to evaluate potential postdoctoral training opportunities.

Table 2. Potential Advantages of Postdoctoral Training

	Potential advantages of postdoctoral training
Professional Practice Issues	Gain specialty training in an area of psychology or with particular population
	Accumulate hours toward licensure
	Fulfill requirements for specialty area certification (if applicable)
	Increase job marketability
	Supervisors and advisors can facilitate job search
Professional Development as Scientist-Practicioner	Learn new research skills (grant-writing, statistical analyses, paper review, etc.)
	Opportunities to integrate clinical and research skills in applied settings under guidance of experienced mentor
	Protected time for research activities enhances research productivity
	Publish papers
	Initiate program of independent research
	Teaching and mentoring experiences
	Increase job marketability
	Supervisors and advisors can facilitate job search

BENEFITS AND PITFALLS OF POSTDOCTORAL TRAINING

Many professional and personal issues factor into a decision about whether to pursue postdoctoral training, and both types of issues should be seriously considered. Needless to say, the relative import of these issues will vary across individuals, and it will be up to you to determine how much weight to give any one of these factors in your decision-making process.

Potential Benefits of Postdoctoral Training

The overarching benefit of postdoctoral training is the opportunity it provides to develop new or better skills that will advance one's professional goals. This may be accomplished in a variety of ways, including acquiring specialty area training, logging the supervised hours necessary for obtaining licensure, or enhancing professional development as a scientist-practitioner. Although these agendas are not mutually exclusive, they may serve different career objectives. A summary of beneficial functions that postdoctoral training may potentially serve in advancing professional goals is presented in Table 2.

Specialty Training

Postdoctoral training can provide opportunities for advanced clinical or research training in a particular specialty area (e.g., pediatric psychology, neuropsychology, geropsychology, behavioral health, forensic psychology, etc.), with a particular population (e.g., patients with chronic schizophrenia, cancer, substance abuse, etc.), or a certain age group (e.g., infancy, adolescence, older adults, etc). Such specialty training may render individuals more marketable for desired jobs or may even be considered mandatory within some areas of research or practice.

TABLE 3. Specialty and Proficiency Areas Currently Recognized by the Commission for the Recognition of Specialties and Proficiencies in Professional Practice (CRSPPP).

Specialties	Date of recognition
Clinical Neuropsychology	August 1996
Clinical Health Psychology	August 1997
Psychoanalytic Psychology	February 1998
School Psychology	February 1998
Clinical Psychology	August 1998
Clinical Child Psychology	August 1998
Counseling Psychology	February 1999
Industrial-Organizational Psychology	de facto recognition through 2002
Behavioral Psychology	August 2000
Forensic Psychology	August 2001
Proficiencies	**Date of recognition**
Biofeedback: Applied Psychophysiology	August 1997
Clinical Geropsychology	February 1998
Psychopharmacology	August 2001
Treatment of Alcohol and Other Psychoactive Substance Use Disorders	August 2001

For example, a postdoctoral fellow with specialty training in inpatient pediatrics might be preferred over a recent graduate from a more general clinical child internship for a medical center position in pediatric oncology. Similarly, academic institutions may perceive a candidate who utilized postdoctoral training to publish papers and begin an independent program of research to be a surer bet for a faculty position that requires obtaining the support of external grant funding in order to sustain the position and advance academically.

Specialty areas of applied practice are now being organized into formal specialties though a system recently developed by APA under the auspices of the Commission for the Recognition of Specialties and Proficiencies in Professional Psychology (CRSPPP). These specialty distinctions are particularly important for those who might seek postdoctoral training for the express purpose of training in a particular area of research or practice. As specialty areas define themselves, they have begun to require specific types of training experiences for new psychologists seeking recognition or certification in that area. Table 3 lists the specialty and proficiency areas recognized by CRSPPP at the time of this writing. A listing of these areas and their related links may also be found at www.apa.org/crsppp/rsp.html.

Professional Licensure

In addition to providing opportunities for specialized training, postdoctoral positions can provide an opportunity to obtain the supervised postdoctoral clinical hours needed to qualify for the licensing exam. At least 46 states explicitly mandate some form of postdoctoral training before sitting for the licensing exam. However, state requirements vary in the type of required experience, the number of hours that constitute a training year (1500 hours is the mode), the length of time allowed to complete training, and the kinds of activities allowed during training, and the amount of supervision required (1–2 hours per week is typical). Clinicians seeking to work even part-time in professional practice or conduct research with patient populations will likely need to become licensed, and obtaining postdoctoral clinical hours within a formalized training system usually facilitates licensure in that state. Those knowing the state(s) in which they ultimately might wish to practice might want to increase their familiarity with the licensure requirements for those states. Such knowledge might even help to guide decisions about potential internship and postdoctoral training programs. Information about individual state requirements can be obtained by writing to a state's psychology board, which will have copies of relevant statutes, rules, and regulations regarding psychology licensure. Alternatively, *The Handbook for Licensure and Certification Requirements* is published annually by the Association of State and Provincial Psychology Boards (ASPPB) and contains information about specific postdoctoral requirements, such as number of hours and supervision requirements. This and other information concerning professional licensure can also be obtained at the ASPPB web site, www.asppb.org.

Professional Development as Scientist-Practitioner

For those interested in research or academic careers, the postdoc can be an important training ground for professional development as a scientist-practitioner. More formal programs may provide didactics relating to teaching, research, or grant-writing skills. There are often opportunities to work closely with a mentor in a variety of more advanced professional activities, such as writing research papers, developing professional presentations, assisting with the review of papers submitted to journals, and the development of one's own research studies. For those with applied interests, postdoctoral training can provide a level of training in applied settings that is often difficult to obtain in graduate school. The guidance of an experienced mentor can provide invaluable opportunities for integrating research and clinical skills as well as for learning to negotiate the politics and hierarchies involved in doing research in multi-disciplinary settings composed of individuals with divergent professional backgrounds and interests. In addition, if the postdoc is participating in data collection on a new project during the fellowship, that data will be available to analyze during the first few years in a junior faculty position. This opportunity can greatly facilitate academic productivity by providing manuscripts that can be written up for publication while establishing one's own research program at a new site. Finally, postdoctoral training can advance one's research career by providing "protected" research time that may be used to write up the dissertation, other data, and book chapters for publication, develop a grant, or make other types of progress in defining your future program of work.

Potential Drawbacks of Postdoctoral Training

Table 4 summarizes some of the factors that might weigh against the decision to pursue postdoctoral training. One of the biggest struggles encountered in the decision to pursue postdoctoral training is the one between making the transition to becoming a full professional and prolonging one's trainee status (Kaslow, McCarthy, Rogers, & Summerville, 1992). Personal issues, such as finances and relocation, are often an important part of this decision. Postdoctoral training almost certainly entails a continuation of financial sacrifices for another one to two years. You may also need to relocate for a given type of training and then, perhaps, move again in order to obtain a professional position. Other personal issues such as cost of living, dual career demands, family goals, and relationship commitments need to be carefully factored

TABLE 4. Potential Drawbacks of Postdoctoral Training

	Potential drawbacks of postdoctoral training
Personal development issues	Continued financial sacrifices for another one to two years
	Potential need to relocate for postdoctoral training and then again for a professional position.
	Relationship and family obligations: dual career demands, children, childcare, ability of family to relocate, availability of suitable local training.
	Social stressors of relocation
Professional development issues	Prolonging trainee status and delaying entry into professional position
	Balance of available training opportunities with clinical service or other professional demands

into postdoctoral training decisions, as these matters can sometimes outweigh the professional advantages of or perceived need for additional training.

Ultimately, you must decide how each of these factors affects your personal and professional goals. Whatever path you take next will likely entail some level of personal or professional sacrifice. For example, some trainees may be unable to relocate for a postdoctoral specialty training position because of a variety of personal factors such as limitations in the geographic flexibility of a partner's job, the impact of losing extended family supports, financial obligations, or a need for an income that is consistent with their stage of adult development (e.g., purchasing a home). Yet other trainees may decide to pursue advanced training because their partners' careers are relatively mobile, the desired training is available locally, or they are less financially constrained. Potential variations of this scenario are endless, illustrating that the particular sacrifice that any one person is able or willing to make is highly idiosyncratic. Those considering postdoctoral training may wish to rate the relative importance and flexibility of their family, social, relocation, financial, and developmental needs/goals and compare these ratings to the perceived importance of postdoctoral training to their career goals, a subject we turn to next.

IS POSTDOCTORAL TRAINING RIGHT FOR YOU?

The question of whether postdoctoral training is the right thing for any one person depends on their unique constellation of professional and personal goals, needs, and constraints. Therefore, only the person posing the question can rightfully provide an answer. By reading this chapter, however, you will have much relevant information for evaluating your options. We also recommend talking with graduate school or internship mentors, who may offer advice that is more tailored to your particular situation.

In the end, there may be compelling reasons to pursue postdoctoral training. Perhaps the best reason is to learn new skills or obtain specialized training that will enhance your professional goals and make you more marketable in the future. Less ideal, but nonetheless compelling, reasons include the absence of other job offers or the need to obtain another year of supervised experience to qualify for the licensing exam. It would be a poor idea, at least in our opinion, to accept a postdoctoral position based primarily on its availability. At this point, you may feel uncertain about your particular motivations for considering postdoctoral training, and this may indicate some uncertainty about your goals. The first step in the search for a postdoctoral position is to clearly identify your training goals and needs. This assessment should occur well before the application process and include such questions as:

- Are there particular clinical populations with which you wish to gain more experience?
- Are there particular clinical approaches in which you would like more training (e.g., family therapy, neuropsychological assessment, CBT, etc.)?
- Are you looking for opportunities in which to learn more about applied research methods (e.g., cognitive behavioral treatment research, longitudinal research)?
- Do you want opportunities to write and publish so as to become more competitive in the job market?
- Do you want to gain experience in writing grants and learning the "ins and outs" of obtaining external funding?
- Is there a particular clinician or investigator in your area of interest who might serve as a mentor and who might have money to support a postdoctoral fellow?

If you feel strongly positive in your responses to at least one of these questions, you can then consider the other, equally important personal and professional issues raised in the previous sections, such as family, relationship, financial, developmental, and geographical needs, goals, and constraints. If you have not already done so, we recommend returning to Tables 2 and 4 and ranking the relative importance of the potential benefits and pitfalls for your particular situation.

IDENTIFYING THE RIGHT POSTDOCTORAL POSITION FOR YOU

If you have made the decision to pursue postdoctoral training, you must next locate, apply for, and evaluate potential positions. Announcements typically begin to appear in the late fall or early winter months (November through February). By that time, you should already have defined and prioritized your training goals as well as any geographical, institutional, structural, or financial needs and constraints. These considerations will allow you to eliminate positions that do not meet your "must-have" criteria. However, it may not be wise to limit your search beyond the ones that do not fulfill your essential criteria, especially since no single position is likely to meet all of your conditions. We advise you to first establish what issues you cannot compromise on, gather the information necessary to assess whether they meet your most basic demands, and eliminate programs accordingly. You may then wish to consider investigating and even applying to a range of programs that vary in their fit to your other, less critical goals to maximize your range of options.

Locating Potential Positions

There are a variety of ways to locate potential postdoctoral positions. National professional organizations, including the American Psychological Association and the American Psychological Society include monthly advertisements for postdoctoral positions in the APA Monitor and the APS Observer. These ads may be accessed through the actual paper publications (available at most libraries) or the organizations' websites (www.apa.org. and www.psychologicalscience.org). The Association of Psychology Postdoctoral and Internship

Centers (APPIC) also publishes a yearly directory of training institutions whose programs meet the minimum criteria established for APPIC inclusion. There are also other structured and formal training programs that, while not listed in the APPIC directory, may offer comparable experiences. Similarly, publications in your desired area of specialty training may post advertisements. For instance, the Society for Pediatric Psychology, the Behavior Therapist, or APA division newsletters frequently offer such announcements. These resources may be located through university libraries, the professional society itself (many have websites), or faculty and peers who may belong to the organization.

Although published announcements are an excellent reference, many opportunities are never advertised and are made known through word of mouth or electronic announcements on professional list serves. For this reason, direct phone calls or letters to specific persons with whom you might like to work can be a profitable means of identifying potential positions that might not be otherwise known. Similarly, communicating with graduate school and internship advisers about whom they know might also yield additional leads. Several internet groups have also formed for new or soon-to-be new graduates. Some of these member groups offer forums for discussions about professional development and even share announcements for postdoctoral and professional positions. One such group can be joined by sending a blank email to newpsychlist-subscribe@yahoogroups.com. Those wishing only to access posted job announcements can search its archives at http://groups.yahoo.com/group/NewPsychList/messages.

APPLICATION PROCEDURES AND GUIDELINES

Application requirements will vary. Some positions may require only your vitae and letters of recommendation, while others might also ask for a written statement of purpose or job talk. Likewise, interviews can range from informal email and phone correspondence to extensive in-person interviews. We advise you not to make any assumptions about these matters and to ask each institution about specific application procedures early in the process.

Clinical psychologists should note that the application for postdoctoral fellowships is somewhat different than that for predoctoral clinical internships. Postdoc applications, more than internship applications, should be tailored to specific positions and mentors and should emphasize your most relevant experiences. Those reviewing your application will want to know that you understand how the experiences they offer fit with your career goals, are prepared for this next level of specialization, and have valuable skills to offer. These points should be clearly conveyed in your cover letter and you should tailor your vitae accordingly. For instance, those applying for a postdoctoral position emphasizing clinical research might want to elaborate on their research experiences (including publications), including their clinical work as experiences that have informed a research agenda. However, those applying for specialty training in particular areas of clinical practice might want to elaborate on the nature of their clinical experiences and list relevant research training and publications toward the end of the vitae.

Similarly, personal references should be able to speak to your skills that are most relevant for the type of position to which you are applying. You should prepare to have at least three people submit letters of recommendation on your behalf for any position to which you apply. Clinical supervisors and research professors are often asked to write such letters. Although your choice of letter-writers will partly depend on the type of postdoctoral training positions you apply for, you should be sure that whomever you ask would write a very positive recommendation. If you are uncertain, you should reconsider your choice of writers or, in the absence of other alternatives, discuss this concern with your writer directly. Wherever possible, find writers who not only know you, but who are known and trusted by those reviewing your application, as such letters may carry extra weight. It may also be helpful to ask writers to personally address the director or agency in your letter instead of the generic salutation of "to whom it may concern".

Whatever the application process, your job as an applicant is to sell yourself as both a qualified and suitable match for the program as well as a "safe choice" (Koocher, 1997). "Safe choices" are candidates who will not offer undue challenges to the existing training structures or require unusual amounts of time to train. They are not only competent but reliable, interpersonally skilled, collaborative, self-initiating, and professionally consistent as well. According to Koocher (1997), warning signals for selection committees might include comments from supervisors that you were a challenge to supervise; academic transcripts showing several "incompletes", even if they were subsequently completed; requests for special treatment during the application process; and applications that arrive late or at the last minute. Of course, some potential signals may not be correctable (e.g., incompletes), in which case, you may wish to address these matters directly in your application letter or during an interview.

Interviews vary in format, formality, and length, so you should inquire about each position in advance so that you can sufficiently prepare. Whatever the format, interviews provide additional opportunities to convince potential supervisors that you are the person they want to hire. The following suggestions may assist you in presenting yourself as a competent, interested candidate who matches well with the position and program.

- Read the materials sent to you and consider the fit between the position and your career goals so that you may demonstrate your knowledge of the program.
- Be prepared to discuss your work to date in the context of the position you are seeking. For example, if you are seeking training in a new or specialty area, be prepared to discuss ways in which this area is either an extension of your previous work or taught you relevant skills for this new area.
- Prepare a couple of questions that you can ask about the program that were not addressed in the materials sent to you.
- Listen closely to the interviewer and avoid overly personal disclosures.
- As the interview closes, ask whether there are any questions about your application. Instead of arguing with any responses, you may write a thank you note containing a paragraph that corrects any misconceptions or potential shortcomings that were noted.
- Write a thank you note summarizing your interest in the program and its fit with your training goals.

Evaluating Potential Postdoctoral Opportunities

As previously stated, the needs and goals of various postdoctoral training positions may range from well-funded programs at institutions committed to training and high quality services to sites where postdoctoral fellows are little more than inexpensive labor and clinical service is prioritized over training needs. It is your job as the applicant to assess where on this spectrum a potential position falls. The following considerations may be helpful in making this determination:

- Is the position organized around the trainee's or institution's needs?
- What are the clinical demands in terms of billable hours or direct patient care required?
- What is the supervisory structure?
- How satisfied are current postdocs?
- Are there formal didactics in place?
- How many hours are dedicated to individual and group supervision?
- Are there a sufficient number of clinical hours built in to meet licensure requirements?
- How much time is protected for research activities?
- What is the number of licensed psychologists available for training and supervision?
- What is the stipend?
- Is medical insurance offered and at what charge to the postdoc? Are spouses and children eligible for coverage?
- How much time is allowed for vacation, sick leave, and professional leave?

Information relevant to these questions may be obtained in a variety of ways. Read all program brochures and descriptions carefully, attending to the stated training goals and agency mission (Koocher, 1997). Take note of whether the program and agency promote themselves as a training site or talk about their educational mission. Review all listings of supervisory staff, their interests, and career paths to assess their fit to your particular training interests and needs. For example, a program staffed by well-published, faculty appointed psychologists will probably offer different training than a staff of experienced direct-service providers. Although one is not necessarily better than the other, one may provide a better fit to your training needs.

Evaluating Potential Postdoctoral Mentors

Most postdoctoral fellows work with a mentor who takes primary responsibility for the postdoc's training program and with whom the postdoc works most closely. Choosing a mentor can be an important part of the decision process. Both the mentor's prestige and mentoring abilities should be considered in balance. Ideally, you should select a mentor who is an expert and productive in your area of interest. It is desirable to arrange a personal meeting with a prospective mentor, or at least a series of phone conversations. Talking with current or former postdocs who have worked with that person and organization can also be quite helpful. Your communications with potential mentors and other informants should answer most, if not all, of the following questions.

- What are the mentor's expectations of the postdoc?
- Will the mentor or the postdoc determine the content of the training program?
- How many postdocs has this mentor had? What positions did they obtain after the postdoc?
- What do former and current trainees of this mentor think about their experience?
- Will the mentor have sufficient time for mentoring or will it be necessary to seek out other mentors?
- How many others (grad students, staff, postdocs) now work for this mentor?
- How many papers are being published? Where are they being published?
- What are the mentor and institution's policies on travel to professional meetings? (e.g., Is the trip only paid for by the institution if you present a paper? If so, how many trips are covered?)
- What is the mentor's policy on authorship and ownership of ideas?

- Is there time and opportunity to develop skills in grant writing, teaching, oral presentations, manuscript preparation, manuscript review?
- Can you expect to collect data or be a part of data analyses or manuscript preparation after completion of the postdoc?
- How are issues of authorship negotiated for projects where data collection extends beyond the postdoc's tenure?
- How long is financial support guaranteed? On what does renewal depend?
- Can you count on assistance with locating and obtaining your next position?

The Final Decision

If you are considering several postdoctoral options, your final decision may not be an easy one. Revisiting your prioritized list of benefits and drawbacks in light of the specific positions you are considering may be of assistance, though you may find that some of your priorities have changed. Before making your final decisions, you should gather enough information to adequately assess what you and your potential mentor(s) each expect from one another and the experience of working together. You should have a rough "roadmap" of expectations and goals that seem appropriate to your position and overall career objectives. Once you accept a position, use this roadmap as the basis for outlining a more specific training and work program with your new mentor/supervisor.

Once You Have Accepted a Position

After accepting a position, you should expect to receive an appointment letter stating the basic contractual framework for your appointment, including your title, the sponsoring institution or department, the beginning and ending dates, stipend level, and benefits received.

WHAT TO EXPECT DURING YOUR POSTDOCTORAL FELLOWSHIP

Although postdoctoral positions vary widely along a number of different dimensions, there are some underlying similarities in the experiences encountered and the responsibilities taken on. The primary intention of the postdoctoral experience should be to provide a period of apprenticeship for the purpose of gaining professional skills that advance one's professional career. Because the primary function of the postdoctoral fellowship is educational, you have the right to expect mentoring that includes oversight, feedback, consultation, and periodic evaluations. Ideally, you will have ample opportunity to learn relevant skills that will further your career. The mentoring relationship can be important to helping you understand the context of your work and the requirements of your chosen career path. However, both the postdoc and mentor share the responsibility for making this relationship work through frequent and clear communication.

In order to maximize the training experience, new postdocs should arrange to meet with their mentors early on to further clarify the "training roadmap" discussed during the application and interview process. The postdoc and mentor should come to some agreement about the work products or experiences that will further your training goals, the timeline for these accomplishments, the extent of collaboration between fellow and mentor; the form that collaboration will take, and the type and frequency of supervision. You and your mentor should jointly appraise this roadmap, especially your professional goals, once or twice yearly for the purpose of evaluating your performance and updating your goals as you develop in your position.

For many, the postdoctoral training period serves as a developmental transition period from "professional adolescence" to "professional young adulthood" in which the developmental task is to create a more coherent and integrated sense of professional self that is separate from one's mentors and supervisors (Kaslow et al., 1992). Early in this process, postdoctoral trainees must create and define their roles within their new position and fulfill their new responsibilities with increased autonomy. Those in more structured programs may focus more on their responsibilities while those in less structured programs may expend more effort in defining their experience. According to Kaslow (1992), the most common difficulties encountered by postdocs at this early stage are associated with role functioning in multidisciplinary settings and negotiating autonomy and status issues.

In the middle phases of postdoctoral training, professional identity solidifies and commitment to one's work deepens. Having resolved concerns about where they fit in, postdocs at this phase begin to carve out their own unique role in their setting. More aware of their professional strengths and weaknesses, postdocs often begin to pursue their professional goals more actively and with greater commitment. The end of postdoctoral training signals a move toward greater independence and the termination associated with both the postdoc and the end of one's formal training may give rise to a new set of professional concerns. Concerned mentors can be useful in supporting the postdoc both in finding the next position and in supporting the postdoc through this termination process.

REFERENCES

Belar, C. D., Bieliauskas, L. A., Klepac, R. R., Larsen, K. G., Stigall, T. T., & Zimet, C. N. (1993). National conference on postdoctoral training in professional psychology. *American Psychologist, 48*, 1284–1289.

Committee on Science, Engineering, and Public Policy (COSEPUP). (2000). *Enhancing the postdoctoral experience for scientists and engineers: A guide for postdoctoral scholars, advisors, institutions, funding organizations, and disciplinary societies.* Washington, DC: National Academy Press.

France, C. M., & Wolfe, E. M. (2000). Issues related to postdoctoral education and training in professional psychology: Results of an opinion survey. *Professional Psychology, Research and Practice, 31*, 429–441.

Kaslow, N., McCarthy, S. M., Rogers, J. H., & Summerville, M. B. (1992). Psychology postdoctoral training: A developmental perspective. *Professional Psychology, Research and Practice, 23*, 369–375.

Koocher, G. (1997). Progress notes. *Newsletter of the Society of Pediatric Psychology, 21*, 6–7.

Larsen, K. G., Belar, C. D., Bieliauskas, L. A., Klepac, R. R., Stigall, T. T., & Zimet, C. N. (Eds.) (1993). *Proceedings: National conference on postdoctoral training in professional psychology.* Washington, D.C.: Association of Psychology Postdoctoral and Internship Centers.

Lopez, S. J., & Prosser, E. C., (2000). Becoming an adaptive new professional: Going beyond Plante's principles. *Professional Psychology, Research and Practice, 31*, 461–462.

Plante, T. G. (1996). Ten principles of success for psychology trainees embarking on their careers. *Professional Psychology, Research and Practice, 27*, 304–307.

Stewart, A. E., & Stewart, E. A. (1998). Trends in postdoctoral education: Requirements for licensure and training opportunities. *Professional Psychology, Research and Practice, 29*, 273–283.

CHAPTER 22

Applying for NIH Grants

PAUL A. PILKONIS AND JILL M. CYRANOWSKI

INTRODUCTION: THE "RIGHT (ATTITUDINAL) STUFF"

Applying for grants from the National Institutes of Health (NIH) is a difficult process, so why do we put ourselves through this particular test? The most compelling reason for many investigators is the autonomy provided by successful pursuit of federal funding. The budget and duration of NIH grants are often more generous than those from other sources, giving investigators sufficient support to pursue the scientific questions of greatest interest to them and to focus their professional efforts primarily in this direction (by "buying out" their time from alternative demands). There may also be systemic pressures to solicit external funding, as investigators are expected to subsidize both their own salaries and the costs of their laboratories, especially in academic medical centers. In addition, the validation, recognition, and prestige associated with receiving an NIH grant can be important incentives. Nonetheless, before plunging into the arduous world of grantsmanship at the federal level, be sure to ask yourself, "Why me?," and be confident that your answer is convincing enough to sustain you through the inevitable ups-and-downs you are guaranteed to experience.

Stamina—staying the course through the process of developing, submitting, and amending grant applications—is a crucial ingredient in success. We believe that stamina is best developed and maintained by viewing science as a collaborative process and by establishing a rich network of professional associations with which to sustain your work. This attitude and behavior require a commitment to "peer review" in the broadest sense—take every opportunity to read the grant applications and summary statements (i.e., grant reviews) of others, and share your own writing with as many people as will read it. Relationship-building of this kind needs to be done, not only with local peers, but also with scientific collaborators and consultants at a national level and with personnel at funding agencies (never underestimate the importance of a good program officer).

PAUL A. PILKONIS AND JILL M. CYRANOWSKI • Department of Psychiatry, Western Psychiatric Institute and Clinic, University of Pittsburgh Medical Center, Pittsburgh, PA 15213

GETTING STARTED

One of the first choices you will confront is whether to proceed down the path of investigator-initiated research awards (R-series grants) judged primarily on their scientific merit or whether to pursue career development awards (K-series grants) that are evaluated as training mechanisms including both career development and research plans.

With R-series awards, the start-up sequence can include:

- Behavioral Science Track Awards for Rapid Transition (B/START) grants
- R03 small grants
- R21 exploratory/developmental grants

Please note that different NIH institutes and centers may have different policies, guidelines, and priorities for different funding mechanisms. Given our own backgrounds in clinical psychology, we use the National Institute of Mental Health (NIMH) as an example throughout this chapter, but be prepared to find differences among the NIH institutes. There is no substitute for repeated information-gathering, much of which can be done electronically (see the Appendix for the most important web addresses relevant to this chapter).

The B/START grant (a component of the R03 small grant mechanism) was developed to facilitate the rapid entry of new investigators into the field of behavioral science research. This mechanism supports small-scale pilot projects, with a budget of up to $50,000 for one year. Advantages to this mechanism include an abbreviated application (i.e., the research plan may not exceed 7 pages) and a rapid review and funding timeline (reviews are done by mail and funding can be awarded within 6 months of the receipt of the application). B/START applications, however, can be resubmitted only once.

A related mechanism that may serve as a helpful stepping stone to the new investigator is the R03 award. The R03 Small Grants Program provides funding of up to $50,000 per year for up to two years (with no option to renew the grant beyond that period). Advantages of this mechanism include an abbreviated application (i.e., the research plan may not exceed 10 pages) and the fact that, like the B/START, priority is given to new investigators. R03 applications, however, are subject to the same review and funding timeline as other NIH grants. Thus, the potential for multiple cycles of review (with each cycle requiring about 9 months) may delay the process of pilot data collection and postpone application for a more substantially funded grant.

Another mechanism that can serve as an entry into the NIH funding system is the Exploratory/Developmental Grant (R21) intended to encourage innovation and research with a high potential impact. For this purpose, extensive preliminary data are not expected, but applications must make clear that the proposed research is sound and that the investigators and available resources are appropriate to the task. Under the general program announcement (PA) for the R21 mechanism, applicants may request direct costs of up to $100,000 per year for up to two years. Some specific uses of the R21 mechanism, however, are more generous. For example, the PA for R21s in the area of mental health intervention research allows up to $125,000 per year for as many as three years. R21 proposals require the entire 25-page application, and they are subject to the full 9-month review and funding cycle. Competitive renewals are not allowed.

It is possible, of course, to plunge in directly with an application for a standard investigator-initiated research grant, the R01. You will be identified as a new investigator if you have not had previous R01 support (a designation intended to provide the review committee with additional perspective on the application), but you will still have the onus of convincing the review committee that you possess the background and experience necessary to carry out a large-scale, independent program of research. Determination of your ability to carry out the proposed research will be made largely on the basis of your training, publication record, support and collaboration from other co-investigators and consultants, and pilot work as presented in the preliminary studies section of the research plan.

With K-series awards, the start-up sequence includes the:

- K01 Mentored Research Scientist Development Award
- K08 Mentored Clinical Scientist Development Award
- K23 Mentored Patient-Oriented Research Career Development Award

Entry-level career development awards are evaluated as training mechanisms. Applications require not only a research plan but also a training plan for career development activities under the tutelage of a research mentor, local collaborators, and external consultants. For the new PhD, the K01 (for basic science) and the K23 (for clinical research) are the usual entry-level vehicles. For applicants with more clinically oriented training (MDs and some PhDs), the K08 may be a more appropriate mechanism (see the Appendix).

PROS AND CONS OF CAREER DEVELOPMENT VERSUS RESEARCH AWARDS

Advantages of a Career Development Award

At some institutes, a K-award can now fund up to 100% of your salary for up to 5 years, a more generous and more stable arrangement than the typical R01, which may fund 25–40% of the principal investigator's (PI) salary for a period of 3–5 years (see Table 1 for a summary of the advantages and disadvantages of career development versus research awards). This level of support allows new investigators to concentrate their time and energy on research efforts without the distractions of seeking additional sources of support or fulfilling extensive clinical or teaching responsibilities. Other advantages include the explicit opportunities for training in your developing area of research. This mechanism can provide the funds and, perhaps more importantly, the time needed to take additional coursework, engage in directed readings, learn from consultants, and travel to research sites and professional meetings to learn new methodologies, all in a personally relevant, "problem-based" way. Because of the training plans included in these awards, the expectation regarding the amount of research to be done as part of a K-award is more modest than that for an R01. Thus, this mechanism may be particularly suited to the needs of the junior investigator who has limited pilot data and who would like to collect more extensive pilot data or receive specialized training to support a subsequent, larger scale project supported by an R01.

Other advantages include the higher success rates for K-awards (often in the range of 35–45%) versus research grants (now in the range of 20–25%). Receipt of an initial K-award also provides professional recognition for a career trajectory reflecting serious commitment to life as a biomedical researcher, and it can facilitate access to mid-career (K02, K24) and senior (K05) awards. Thus, the career development funding stream has the potential for a 20-year sequence of support (5 years at the initial level, 10 at the mid-career level, and 5 at the senior level).

TABLE 1. Pros and Cons of Career Development (K) Awards versus Research (R) Awards

		K-Awards	R-Awards
Advantages of K-Awards:	• PI salary support	Up to 100%	25–40%
	• Success rate	High (35–45%)	Moderate (20–25%)
	• Qualifications of investigator	More modest investigator qualifications; includes explicit training plan to be carried out under tutelage of research mentor and consultants	More stringent investigator qualifications to support performance as independent PI, including more extensive publication record
	• Research approach	More modest; may include collection of pilot data to support future R01	More rigorous expectations regarding pilot data and research plan
Advantages of R-Awards:	• Research budget	Limited to $25–50,000 per year; can limit type of research to be supported	More expansive, dictated by scientific needs of project
	• Transferability	Difficult to transfer because of reliance on training environment and proximity to research mentors	Relatively less difficult to transfer to another institution
	• Social role	Continuation of perceived role as "trainee"	PI acquires new role as independent researcher

Disadvantages of a Career Development Award

Some applicants are put off by the prospect of never-ending training and are eager to leave behind the role of "student." The importance of such factors requires some reflection about whether you are, in fact, avoiding necessary developmental challenges or whether you are being astute in considering all possible mechanisms for promoting your research career. In addition, K-awards lack some flexibility. In their earliest phases, they are not easily transferable since they rely heavily on an institutional research and training environment, including proximity to a primary mentor and other local consultants. This constraint may complicate your professional and personal life, especially if there are joint career issues that must be negotiated with a partner.

Advantages of a Research Award

Although the size of small and developmental research grants may be limited (in the range of $50,000 to $125,000 annually), the major advantage of the conventional R01 award is the lack of constraint on the size of the budget—the costs should be dictated by the needs of the science (although prior permission is required for any budget in which direct costs exceed $500,000 in any single year). By contrast, career development awards (which are generous in terms of salary support) provide limited research funds, usually in the range of $25,000 to $50,000 per year. Although these research funds are in addition to your salary support as PI, this limited level of research support may not allow for larger scale or more expensive projects, including some types of intervention research where costs for staff, patients, and therapists quickly mount.

Disadvantages of a Research Award

New investigators applying for an R01 award must demonstrate to a review committee that they have the background and skills to undertake, manage, and complete an independent research project. Evidence of these competencies may include the availability of pilot data, a "track record" of publication in your area of research, and a thorough, well-conceived, and convincingly argued plan of research. Applications for R01 funding are evaluated rather exclusively on their scientific merit, and both the standards used to evaluate merit and the much larger pool of R01 applications (versus career development applications) ensures a lower success rate.

CRAFTING AN APPLICATION

A critical step in writing your grant is the first: choosing a topic (cf. Watson, 1993; Kahn, 1994). This initial decision includes identifying a well-specified research question and selecting appropriate methods for addressing it. There are a number of issues to consider when choosing a topic. What are the research questions that you find most intriguing? What excites you about your field? What types of research methods do you most enjoy using? What work can you see yourself doing in a consistent and self-sustaining way for the next 5 years? How will the work of the next 5 years contribute to your professional and personal development? What is a strategic way of "individuating" yourself within the area that you have chosen, that is, what distinctive aspects of the work set you aside from other investigators working in the same area and how can you emphasize these aspects?

Although questions regarding the intrinsic rewards you receive from your research work are important to keep you motivated throughout the ups-and-downs of a research career, it is naïve to think that these should be the only considerations guiding your decisions. Other factors to consider when selecting an appropriate research topic and methodology are more practical. Which research questions are realistic to address and answer over the next 5 years (especially within the constraints of what may ultimately be a rather modest budget)? A common mistake of junior investigators is a lack of perspective regarding feasibility, that is, biting off more than you can chew with unrealistically broad or complex study aims. Keep your specific aims focused, and make it clear how you will provide unambiguous tests of your hypotheses in which something important will be learned from both the positive and negative outcomes that you document. Although your intellectual curiosity may be limitless and your aspirations high, remember that any single grant represents just one step in a lifelong career of research.

A related issue in creating a persuasive application is that of narrative coherence. You must develop a "story" that is interesting but also straightforward for the reader. Keep things as simple as possible within the context of the scientific work that you are proposing, but also consider how you can motivate genuine curiosity and interest on the part of others who may not share the same investment that you do in the details of the work. What is the general rationale for the project and why should it be compelling to other scientists? Never underestimate the general intelligence of the members of your audience, but never overestimate their specific knowledge about the area that you are investigating. In crafting your story, keep in mind the evaluative criteria used by NIH review committees: significance, approach, innovation, qualifications of the investigator, and adequacy of the environment in which the work will be conducted. An application does not need to be outstanding in every one of these areas in order to succeed, but each criterion will be addressed. For advice on scientific writing skills in general and the important relationship between substance and structure in your writing, see Gopen and Swan (1990).

Another important pragmatic consideration when selecting a topic of research is identifying a problem that is consistent with current NIH funding priorities. Negotiating the maze that is the organizational structure of NIH may seem a daunting task for an investigator new to the system, but the first step is to subscribe to the electronic Table of Contents of the NIH Guide to Grants and Contracts published each week. The Guide provides informational notices, requests for applications, and program announcements. To subscribe, send email to the NIH LISTSERV at listserv@list.nih.gov and in the first line of the text (not the subject line), provide the message "subscribe NIHTOC-L your name," where your name is the name you wish to use.

Requests for applications (RFAs) offer special opportunities for support of newly identified research priorities within NIH. They are often one-time solicitations for applications to be funded with monies earmarked for a particular area of research, and the number of applications submitted for any particular RFA is typically smaller than the number entering the general R01 stream. Applications in response to RFAs also typically receive reviews by ad hoc committees separate from the usual review process. Although the deadlines for RFAs may be short, they provide an excellent opportunity if your research matches well with the request. Program announcements (PAs) also describe new research priorities, but they are less compelling than RFAs because they are not associated with set-asides of research funding. They encourage applications at the regular submission deadlines (February 1, June 1, and October 1 for most applications), and they are usually issued for a period of three years.

NIH is organized into institutes and centers, and a first step is to identify which of these is most likely to fund research in your field. Institutes are usually organized hierarchically into divisions, branches, and programs responsible for different parts of the institute's research portfolio (see the Appendix). Ask your colleagues and mentors about the institutes and programs that are currently funding their research projects. Each of the institutes has its own web page, and from there, you can link to strategic plans, reports of research priorities, and archives of RFAs and PAs that represent the specific expression of these priorities. Remember also that the titles, principal investigators, and abstracts for all NIH-funded research are available electronically through the Computer Retrieval of Information on Scientific Projects (CRISP), a searchable database that will allow you to find everything currently being funded in your area. Once you have identified a research problem and an NIH program that is supporting work in that area, the next step is to make direct contact with the program officer who is responsible for such work. Again, prevail upon mentors and other colleagues to provide an introduction, which is preferable to a "cold call." Develop a relationship with this person, who, more likely than not, will welcome your approach. Remember that it is in the best interest of program officers to cultivate new investigators in the area for which they are responsible.

Collecting Pilot Data

Make the effort to collect pilot data for inclusion in the preliminary studies section of your grant application. Having good pilot data serves a variety of purposes. First, it demonstrates your capability as an investigator, i.e., that you can actually plan and implement the type of research proposed in your grant. This issue of general competence is closely linked to that of feasibility. Pilot data also indicate that the subject population and research methodology that you have chosen are feasible, i.e., that you are able to recruit the types of subjects that you want to study and that your research methods produce acceptable data. Ideally, pilot data also provide preliminary support for your study aims and hypotheses and allow initial estimates of effect sizes, which can inform power analyses. These issues of competence and feasibility are serious considerations for a review committee when deciding whether to support a new investigator—with no previous track record of NIH research—who may now receive a rather large sum of money. We focus in this chapter on funding from NIH, but for the purpose of collecting pilot data, you may want to consider other sources. Internal funding from your own university may be an option. Explore other non-federal sources, including private foundations. One of the best sources for information about private foundations is the Foundation Center, which has five locations across the country and a network of cooperating collections (see the Appendix).

The Actual Application

Public Health Service (PHS) form 398 is used for new and competing continuation grant applications to NIH. The form is available electronically in both portable document and rich text formats (PDF and RTF), with the latter compatible with most word processing software. It is difficult, of course, to predict the future, but now that grant application kits are available electronically, it is only a matter of time before electronic submission of applications follows. PHS 398 can be confusing for novices, so don't hesitate to ask for clarification and advice about completing it from mentors, experienced colleagues, and support staff from your own office of grants administration. Also take every opportunity to examine grant applications, both successful and unsuccessful, that colleagues are willing to share with you in order to begin to form your own opinions about what goes into a good application.

We do not have the space here to review all parts of the application in detail, but we do provide some initial pointers. The first is to develop an NIH dossier for yourself that you update on a regular basis like your curriculum vita. Certain standard parts of the application lend themselves to such treatment, e.g., the biographical sketch, with sections for academic positions and honors, peer-reviewed publications, and ongoing or completed research support (federal and non-federal) in the previous three years; and the resources page, where you can document the facilities available in your laboratory, department, and university that support your research work. This practice will serve your own purposes and will make it convenient to share your biographical sketch with others as opportunities arise to collaborate as a co-investigator or consultant.

Inform yourself about the alternative formats for budgets. The majority of applications (requiring budgets of less than $250,000 in direct costs in any single year) use the modular budget format in which requests for support are made in increments (or modules) of $25,000. A standard budget page is available for this purpose, and it consists primarily of the overall budget figures requested in each year of the project (in multiples of $25,000) and a list of study personnel, with brief descriptions of their level of effort and roles in the project. Given the brevity of the budget page, review committees now have rather limited information about the details of how you plan to spend your money; nonetheless, they can recommend changes in the budget (usually decreases), and these must also occur in modules of $25,000.

Larger budgets (with any single year in excess of $250,000) require the traditional and more detailed budget pages. The greatest detail must be provided for the first year of the project, with expenses itemized into standard categories; projections for the later years of the project must also be done, using the same categories. Justifications are then provided for all parts of the budget, and this text is not constrained by page limits. Use the budget justifications to convey to the reader that you have thought carefully about the roles of all key personnel and about the details of procedures. A "vivid" account of how you will implement the project gives readers greater confidence in your commitment to the work and in the preparation you have already embarked upon. Be sure to consult with your local research administrators about the budget and accounting requirements in your own setting. Note that the final budget includes "indirect" costs, i.e., administrative overhead to your institution that typically ranges from 40–70% of the "direct" costs that support the actual scientific work. This indirect cost rate is negotiated by your institution for all federally sponsored research and is independent of any individual project. Even if you submit a modular budget to NIH, you may also be required to submit a more detailed, line-item budget to your university office of research accounting. See Miller and Westerberg (1998) for some strategies on developing a budget. See also Dickert and Grady (1999) for a discussion of the ethical implications of different approaches to reimbursing research subjects.

Increased attention is being paid to issues regarding the use of human subjects and the inclusion of both genders, children, and members of minority groups in research supported by NIH, a trend that is likely to continue. Note, for example, that a data and safety monitoring plan is now required for all clinical trials (phases I, II, or III). NIH reporting requirements for ethnicity and race have also been changed to conform to the 1997 Office of Management and Budget (OMB) criteria. These criteria include two ethnic categories (Hispanic or Latino, and Not Hispanic or Latino) and five racial categories (American Indian or Alaska Native, Asian, Black or African American, Native Hawaiian or Other Pacific Islander, and White). Relying on self-report, investigators are now asked to use two separate questions, with ethnicity information collected first, followed by the option to select as many racial categories as apply. The general point is that you must acquaint yourself with the current standards and be prepared to stay up-to-date as these standards evolve. Staying up-to-date will require your ongoing participation in activities to enhance your education in the responsible conduct of research, so investigate opportunities for such education at your own university and nationally.

THE REVIEW PROCESS

Be aware that there are two levels of review for grant applications. The majority of reviews are done on an NIH-wide basis through the Center for Scientific Review (CSR; see the Appendix). Thus, the typical review committee will see applications with a variety of kinds of science (within its own broad charter) relevant to different diseases and the interests of different NIH institutes. Some initiatives, however, will be reviewed in-house at the separate institutes, which maintain their own internal review mechanisms. Responses to RFAs, for example, are likely to remain in-house, and in some institutes, career development awards are reserved for internal review. The general point is that you need to be informed about exactly where and by whom your application will be reviewed. Check with program staff.

Since the majority of applications go to CSR, let us review briefly what happens with them following submission. First, your application will join thousands of others to be logged into an NIH database. Next, a referral officer will review the contents, focusing on the title and abstract, to determine which NIH institute or center would be most likely to fund the research and which Integrated Review Group (IRG) would be most appropriate to assess the scientific merit of the application. IRGs are groups of review committees (also known as study sections) that evaluate similar areas of science. Once an IRG is identified, an assignment to a specific review committee is made. Assignments to institute and to review committee are critical decisions for the fate of your application. For this reason, it is extremely important that you do your homework regarding the research portfolios of different institutes that may be interested in your work and the charter and composition of the different review committees that may be evaluating your application. The mandate and roster of each review committee are public information and most easily available on the world wide web. Once you have identified a review committee that is most appropriate to judge the topic and methods of your proposed research, you can suggest an assignment to this group (and to the appropriate NIH institute) in a cover letter submitted with your grant application. In our experience, NIH referral officers are responsive to such suggestions.

Once your application has received assignments to NIH institute and study section, it is given a unique grant number. Shortly thereafter, you will receive a notice documenting this information and providing you with the name and contact information for the Scientific Review Administrator (SRA) who organizes the work of the review committee (e.g., distributing applications; assigning specific reviewers; coordinating dates and sites for the 3 review committee meetings each year). There is a lengthy interval between the time you submit your application and the time it is actually reviewed; for example, applications received on June 1 are typically reviewed in October or November. For this reason, many study sections will accept supplementary materials in the 3 to 4 weeks prior to review. For example, if you have collected additional pilot data since submitting your application, you may want to provide a brief report about these research activities and results. Such supplemental materials should be brief (e.g., 1–2 pages). To determine whether and when you might submit a supplement, contact your SRA.

Approximately 6 weeks prior to the review meeting, members of the study section receive copies of all of the applications being reviewed in that cycle. Typically, three members (designated as primary, secondary, and tertiary) are assigned to each application, based on the fit between their research expertise and the content of the grant. They are asked to provide written critiques of the application, organized according to the NIH review criteria: significance, approach, innovation, investigator, and research environment (see Table 2 for more detail about the criteria and how best to address them). If sufficient expertise is not available from the standing membership of the committee, the SRA can invite ad hoc reviewers to participate. As the meeting approaches, the SRA will solicit feedback about which grants are ranked in the bottom half of the current group and eligible for "streamlining." A final consensus about streamlining is usually made at the beginning of each review meeting, and these applications are neither discussed further nor scored at the actual meeting. The rationale for streamlining is to allow greater time for discussion about those applications perceived to be ready for support and thus to maximize the value of the review for both applicants and NIH program staff. Streamlined applications do, however, receive the written critiques done by reviewers.

In contrast, applications ranked in the top half of the group are discussed at the review meeting. The primary reviewer begins the discussion, with the secondary and tertiary reviewers contributing to the commentary with their additional concerns and emphases. A general discussion follows, with an attempt to reach consensus about the scoring range in which the application falls. After this consensus is articulated, all members are asked to provide a personal (and private) priority score for the application, using an effective range from 1.0 to 3.0, where 1.0–1.5 is "outstanding;" 1.5–2.0, "excellent;" 2.0–2.5, "very good;" and 2.5–3.0, "good." The full rating scale ranges from 1.0 to 5.0, but it is understood that the streamlined applications not scored would have fallen into the range from 3.0–5.0, i.e., satisfactory to fair to poor. These

TABLE 2. NIH Review Criteria

Evaluative criterion	Relevant questions	Tips
Significance	Does this research address an important problem? How will this research advance the field? How might this research advance public health?	• Highlight relevant "gaps" in current knowledge base and how they hinder progress in the field. • Highlight the prevalence and costs of the problem of interest, including economic, social, and personal costs. • Discuss scientific and clinical implications of proposed work.
Approach	Are the concepts, design, methods, and analyses integrated and well-developed? Do these directly address the study aims? Are potential problem areas and limitations acknowledged and alternate approaches considered?	• Be sure to develop a coherent "story" that is consistent throughout the application. Avoid too many diversions or "subplots." • Be sure your study aims are directly addressed in your design and analyses. Clearly label which analyses will test each aim and hypothesis. • Discuss alternate methods or designs that might have been used to address your study aims. Demonstrate that you considered these alternatives, and discuss why you made the choices you did.
Innovation	Are the study aims original and innovative? Does the research employ novel concepts, approaches, or methods? Are new methodologies or technologies developed?	• Highlight how your research differs from the existing literature. • Highlight any potential areas of novelty or innovation, while at the same time emphasizing that these novel approaches will be embedded within sound scientific methodologies.
Investigator	Is the PI appropriately trained and experienced to carry out the proposed research?	• Articulate how your previous research experience will guide your current work. • Highlight relevant work you have published. • For those areas of research in which your own background is limited, enlist and discuss the expertise of co-investigators, consultants, or mentors.
Environment	Are the scientific environment and available resources adequate to support the proposed research? Will the institution support this research?	• Emphasize unique resources at your institution, such as consultants, research and clinical facilities, and currently funded projects and research centers. • Build a local research network, and highlight previous collaborative projects in your application. • Include letters of support from co-investigators, consultants, and other collaborators.

priority scores are averaged, multiplied by 100 to produce whole numbers from 100 to 500, and percentiled, using the entire pool of scores from the current and previous two rounds of review. Within a week or two of the review meeting, you will be informed about whether your application was scored, and if so, what the priority score and percentile are. The written critiques are organized into "summary statements" (still called "pink sheets" by some investigators because of the color of the paper originally used in the NIH peer review process). Approximately 6 to 8 weeks later, you will receive the summary statement, including a brief account of the committee discussion as well as the written comments provided by separate reviewers.

The summary statement is crucial, because the issues and concerns included in these evaluations must be addressed directly in the revision of the grant. Amended applications are allowed three pages for an introduction that documents the responses and changes made to the application based on the prior review. Be prepared to resubmit any application you send to NIH. It is the rare application that is funded on the first submission, and under the current rules, two resubmissions are allowed. As a young investigator, do not be daunted by the prospect of having to go back twice as you "cut your teeth" on the application and review process. With a sufficient blend of promising ideas, good mentoring, access to models of polished grantsmanship, stamina, and emotion regulation skills, you are bound to succeed.

ADDITIONAL RESOURCES

Structure of the National Institutes of Health (NIH)

- Institutes, Centers, and Offices: http://www.nih.gov/icd/
- Center for Scientific Review (CSR): http://www.csr.nih.gov/default.htm

General Information on Grants

- NIH grant application forms: http://grants.nih.gov/grants/forms.htm
- Computer Retrieval of Information on Scientific Projects (CRISP) for information on all funded grants: https://www-commons.cit.nih.gov/crisp/
- Success rates and other award data: http://grants.nih.gov/grants/award/award.htm

Research (R-Series) Awards

- Behavioral Science Track Awards for Rapid Transition (B/START) Grants: http://grants.nih.gov/grants/guide/pa-files/PAR-00-119.html
- NIMH Small Grants Program: http://grants.nih.gov/grants/guide/pa-files/PAR-99-140.html
- NIMH Exploratory/Developmental Grant (R21) Program: http://grants.nih.gov/grants/guide/pa-files/PA-00-073.html
- NIMH Exploratory/Developmental Grants for Mental Health Intervention Research: http://grants.nih.gov/grants/guide/pa-files/PA-99-134.html

Career Development (K-Series) Awards

- General information on career development awards, including the "career award wizard": http://grants.nih.gov/training/careerdevelopmentawards.htm

Support from Private Foundations

- The Foundation Center: http://fdncenter.org/sitemap.html

REFERENCES

Dickert, N., & Grady, C. (1999). What's the price of a research subject?: Approaches to payment for research participation. *New England Journal of Medicine, 341*, 198–203.

Gopen, G. D., & Swan, J. A. (1990). The science of scientific writing. *American Scientist, 78*, 550–558.

Kahn, C. R. (1994). Picking a research problem: The critical decision. *New England Journal of Medicine, 330*, 1530–1533.

Miller, W. R., & Westerberg, V. S. (1998). A case-based approach for estimating costs in psychosocial research. *Psychological Science, 9*, 419–422.

Watson, J. D. (1993). Succeeding in science: Some rules of thumb. *Science, 261*, 1812–1813.

CHAPTER 23

The Job Search

Robert J. Sternberg

Just a few years ago, one could obtain almost any product or service one could imagine through the Internet. One could buy pets or pet food, order food to be delivered to one's house, buy clothing from an astonishing array of manufacturers, and much, much more. Today, some of these Internet services remain, but many others are gone. Radio and television advertisements for Internet sites, so common even a year or two ago, are sparser. No doubt there are many lessons to be learned from this Internet meltdown, but certainly one of the most powerful is that, before investing in the creation of a product or service, one needs to ensure a market will be there, ready to buy.

This lesson is perhaps the fundamental lesson that aspiring psychologists need to keep in mind, whether they plan to pursue an academic job, a practice job, or any other kind of job: You need to establish a market for your skills. It is for this reason that I recommend to my own students that they start thinking about job prospects pretty much from the very beginning of their graduate-school career. Graduate school training is qualitatively different from undergraduate school training, because it is preprofessional in character. It is designed, of course, to enrich students' knowledge and understanding of psychology; but most of all, it is designed to prepare students for a career. Because a career largely begins with one's first job, getting that job can be one of the most important steps a psychologist ever takes. And because one's first job often contributes substantially toward shaping both one's professional possibilities and even the future jobs one may obtain, it is important to devote substantial resources to getting the best job one can.

WHAT IS THE "BEST JOB"?

Before talking about how to get the "best job," it is important to talk about just what the "best job" is. People have different priorities in searching for jobs. Among the characteristics they look for are (a) geographic location, (b) prestige, (c) salary, (d) benefits, (e) teaching load, (f) research opportunities, (g) congeniality of colleagues, (h) opportunities for advancement, (i) levels and kinds of expectations of employer, and (j) general working conditions, such as the condition of the building or office where one will spend much of one's time. In my experience,

Robert J. Sternberg • Department of Psychology, Yale University, New Haven, CT 06520 however, by far the most important consideration in targeting that first job is "fit"—the extent to which the institution or people with whom you will work match your own system of values, motivations, and expectations. The more their expectations are congruent with what you wish to offer, on average, the happier you will be.

I have seen students take jobs that, on paper, looked wonderful, only to find that, when they arrived, what they had to offer was a poor fit to what the institution wanted to gain from them. So in my experience, the most important question to ask is the same as that you would ask in any kind of marriage, that of compatibility. If you and the institution in which you go to work are not compatible, you may find that little else matters: You will be miserable despite everything else. For example, you could be the best teacher in the world, but if you take a job at an institution that values research, but, at best, pays lip service to teaching, you may find all of your best-developed skills unappreciated by the people in your environment. Or you might be a wonderful researcher, but if you are required to teach four classes a semester, you can expect to have relatively little time to exercise those wonderful research skills.

THE VARIETY OF JOBS

A doctorate in psychology can lead you to a wide range of jobs (Sternberg, 1997). Among these jobs are (a) teaching and research in a college or university psychology department, (b) teaching and research in a university school of education, (c) teaching and research in a university business school, (c) psychotherapy administered in private practice, (d) counseling in a clinic or private practice, (e) outreach through community services, (f) psychotherapy administered in a hospital setting, (f) government service, (g) service in a school setting, (h) service as an industrial/organizational psychologist, (i) work in a consulting firm, and (j) work in the military. Of course, this is not a complete list. What it shows, however, is the wide range of careers available to people who specialize in psychology.

PREPARING FROM "DAY 1"

You may not literally start preparing for your job search on Day 1 of graduate school, but the sooner you do so, the better. By the time you are nearing the end of graduate school, you should already have set much of the scaffolding in place upon which you will construct your job search. What kinds of preparations do you need to be making:

- *Courses.* There are many reasons to take courses. For example, you may wish to learn how a particular professor sees the world, or you may wish to acquire specific statistical, laboratory, or therapy techniques. In a clinical program, your courses may be largely prescribed. But whatever program you are in, be sure to take courses that you will need to get employed in the kind of position you will seek. The appropriate courses will differ as a function of the kind of job you want, so you need to consult with your advisor, other faculty, and advanced students regarding what courses will serve you best.
- *Research.* Most graduate programs have a major research component (although some PsyD programs may not particularly emphasize research). Doing research that will distinguish you from others applying for similar jobs can be one of the best ways to prepare yourself for the job search.

- *Service.* Many graduate students do not think of service to their advisor's lab group, or the department, or the university, as an important aspect of graduate training. Indeed, it probably is not the most important. But when it comes to hiring people, many institutions would rather have someone who will be willing to help others than someone who cares only about him or herself. Showing you are willing to contribute to others is an important step in getting yourself hired. At the same time, you do not want to drown yourself in service activities so that you have little time for everything else.
- *Letters of recommendation.* You probably will need three or even possibly four letters of recommendation. You therefore have to start thinking early about ensuring that at least three, and possibly four, individuals (usually, faculty members) know you and your work well. One of these recommenders will almost certainly have to be your main advisor. Another might be a secondary dissertation advisor, and a third, someone for whom you have been a teaching assistant. Or, if you are going into practice, you will probably want to have a clinical supervisor write you a letter. Do *not* wait until near the end of your graduate career to start thinking about recommenders. It will be too late. Start thinking about them early, and then get to know them sooner rather than later.

PREPARING YOUR MATERIALS

Different institutions require different kinds of materials. But, on average, there is a core of stuff that most institutions require, regardless of the kind of job for which you apply.

The Vita

The vita, also called the "curriculum vitae," is a summary of your main accomplishments. Often, it is the document that hiring institutions look at first. If your vita does not fit the profile of the person or person they wish to hire, they may look no further. Hence, a strong vita is essential to your success.

The most basic elements of a vita are your (a) name, (b) contact information (postal address, phone number, e-mail address, fax if you have one), (c) present status, (d) degrees (including anticipated ones), listing what they are and where they are from, (e) job experience, including consulting (f) honors and awards, if any, (g) publications, if any, (h) teaching experience, if any, (i) clinical experience, if any, (j) reviewing you have done for journals, if any, (k) teaching and research interests. Many people also list family information (such as whether they have a spouse and/or children) and date of birth, although this information is optional. Although people sometimes list social-security numbers, I would not advise it, given the problems that can arise from theft of such numbers.

When you list publications, you should list both published and in-press articles. If an article is submitted for publication you may wish to list it, but do not say to where it has been submitted, as you may later be embarrassed if the article is rejected. Make sure that anything you list you can produce. Listing a paper that you cannot provide on demand marks you as deceptive. And listing things on your vita that are not true (e.g., phony degrees, papers as accepted that are not accepted, and so forth) can be grounds for you to be terminated from a job if the falsifications later are discovered. Hence, put yourself in the most favorable light, but *never* fabricate.

A strong vita is an important basis for getting a job. Hence, you should start building up the vita as soon as possible. Keep in mind the categories above, and try to fill them in. But remember that quality will usually be more important than quantity. A few good publications often are worth more than a smattering of not so good ones. Hiring institutions look at the quality of the journal in which the articles are published, and are likely to be less impressed with publications that appear in weak or non-peer-reviewed journals.

The Personal Statement

Although some job candidates integrate the personal statement with the vita, I usually recommend keeping them separate, as they serve somewhat different functions. For academic jobs, one might even wish to have separate teaching and research statements. For clinical jobs, one may wish to prepare a statement regarding one's clinical experience and aspirations. The statement is important, because it helps define who you are both as a professional and as a person. A good statement tells a story. It might tell about how your teaching or research interests developed, or it might tell how your various projects tie together. It is worth putting a lot of time into the statement, and getting feedback on it from multiple faculty members and other colleagues.

Whereas a strong statement can generate interest in you, a weak statement can kill it. Statements may be weak for several reasons. The most foolish thing you can do probably is not to proofread what you write. Who wants to hire someone who turns in a statement with spelling, grammatical, or capitalization errors? An unfocused statement is also not likely to help you. Hiring institutions like to see focus, clarity, and coherence, not a stream-of-consciousness approach that seems incoherent to the reader, however coherent it may seem to you. Also, do not just say what you are interested in. Say what you have done about your interests.

When and if you write a teaching statement, keep in mind not only your own interests, but also, the needs of the institution. Almost all teaching institutions expect new faculty to teach some service courses, such as Introductory Psychology or Introductory Statistics. You are also more desirable to an institution if you can teach lower division courses. So when writing about your teaching plans, be sure to list lower division (basic) courses as well as more specialized seminars.

When and if you write a research statement, keep in mind that a major factor in hiring for a research-oriented institution is that you will have a research program that will keep you busy for the next several years. So be sure to spell out in some detail not just what you have done, but also, what you plan to do. It also helps if you can show how the research you are doing does indeed form a coherent program rather than consisting of isolated bits with little relation to each other.

Letters of Recommendation

Letters of recommendation are required for almost all jobs. You cannot directly control what your recommenders say, of course. What you can do, however, is to choose your recommenders carefully. Choose people who know you well and who, to the best of your knowledge, have a positive view of you—the more positive, the better, of course. In the real world, it also matters who the recommenders are. Chances are that a recommendation from a person of distinction will carry more weight than a recommendation from someone who is unknown or, worse, who has a bad reputation. Sometimes, in choosing recommenders, you have to trade off how well known the person is with what you think the person will say. But given the choice between a more well-known recommender and a better letter, I would advise you to go for what you believe will be the better letter.

Most important is that the person really knows you. No one is impressed to read a letter, even from a well-known person, when it is obvious that the person writing the letter has only the foggiest idea of who the person is for whom he or she is writing the letter of recommendation. Also, people who knew you a long time ago but have not kept up with you tend to be poor choices as recommenders. It usually is obvious from their letters, even if they do not explicitly say so, that their knowledge of you is not up-to-date.

Sometimes job applicants wonder whether they should include "political letters." Such letters might be from actual politicians (e.g., a Senator or a member of the House of Representatives), or might be from people who are supposedly "connected," such as a member of a Board of Trustees or a major donor. In my experience, such letters are much more likely to backfire than to have a positive effect. Unless you absolutely know that such a letter will be received warmly, do not arrange to have it sent. It sends a message about the kind of person you are, and probably not the message you want to send.

Publications

For academic and even many nonacademic jobs, you may be asked to provide sample publications. If you do not have any, of course, publications are not at issue. If you do, be sure to include them with appropriate citations. If you have the luxury of having produced a number of publications, you may wish to select only those you and your advisors consider to represent your best work. You can also send in-press and submitted or even to-be-submitted papers with your credentials. But do not send anything that seems half-baked.

FINDING OUT ABOUT JOB OPENINGS

How do you even find what jobs are available in the first place? In my experience, there are several major options:

- *APA Monitor on Psychology.* This monthly magazine, published by the American Psychological Association, publishes a list of almost every job opening in psychology in the United States, and some abroad. It lists jobs by universities within states.
- *APS Observer.* This monthly magazine, published by the American Psychological Society, contains a somewhat more limited selection of jobs. It specializes in academic jobs.
- *Chronicle of Higher Education.* This weekly newspaper contains a number of academic jobs but is especially useful in finding administrative jobs.
- *Electronic Bulletin Boards.* There are many electronic bulletin boards that post job listings. For example, many of the divisions of the American Psychological Association have listserves that post selected jobs.
- *Newsletters of Specialized Organizations.* Many specialized organizations have newsletters that occasionally post jobs. You should therefore look at newsletters of special interest organizations that are relevant to your own professional interests.

- *Letters and Phone Calls to Advisors.* Sometimes, faculty members receive letters or phone calls advising them of the availability of jobs. Thus it is always a good idea to check with faculty members regarding possible job listings.
- *Word of Mouth at Meetings and Elsewhere.* Sometimes news about jobs is passed by word of mouth. For this reason, networking can be an excellent way of finding out about jobs. Think about all the possible contacts you have, and use them. Talking to others on the job market or individuals who work for organizations that you might be interested in working for may inform you about jobs that are not yet posted, or even that will not be posted.
- *Creating Jobs.* It doesn't happen much, but it happens. Three times in my life I had an idea for a job, and spoke to high-levels managers in the relevant organizations about what I thought I could do for them. In two cases, the jobs were summer jobs, and in one case, a part-time job. In all three cases, it worked: A job was created for me. You cannot count on jobs being made to order for you, but you never know until you try.

KINDS OF JOBS

A degree in psychology opens up many different kinds of jobs—so many, it is not possible to list all of them in one short book chapter. Different kinds of careers require different kinds of preparation, so the earlier you can decide on the kind of career you are interested in pursuing, the better off you are likely to be in preparing yourself appropriately. For example, if you wish to become a practicing psychologist, you will need to prepare for an internship. If you wish to prepare for an assistant professorship, you will need to get your publication record in order. You also may wish to consider a postdoctoral fellowship before going on the market for assistant professorships.

In my opinion, the best thing you can do to prepare is to be flexible. Many graduate students do not know exactly what they want to do when they start. Therefore, acquiring a broad range of skills will serve you well later on. For example, courses on statistics or on research methods will probably serve you well in almost any career. Many psychologists, even those in practice, teach at least part-time, so gaining teaching experience also will be useful for a wide variety of jobs. Acquiring experiences that will be useful in a variety of jobs can enable you to delay a bit your zeroing in on exactly what kind of job you want.

A good source of information on different kinds of jobs is *Career Paths in Psychology* (Sternberg, 1997), which describes 14 different kinds of careers, including (a) what the career is, (b) how to prepare for the career, (c) typical activities people pursue while they engage in the career, (d) the approximate range of financial compensation for people in the job, (e) the advantages and disadvantages to the career perceived by people in the job, (f) personal and professional attributes desirable for success in the career, and (g) opportunities for employment and advancement in the career[1]. The book covers academic careers (in a psychology department, a school of education, and a business school); careers in clinical, counseling, and community psychology, both within and outside hospitals; careers in diverse organizations (government, schools, organizations, consulting); and careers in diverse areas of psychology (human factors, military, and health). The book also contains references suggesting other places one can seek information about careers.

[1] Royalties for the book go the Society of General Psychology (Division 1 of the American Psychological Association).

THE JOB INTERVIEW

Regardless of the type of job you pursue, one of the most important events in getting a job is the job interview. If you are fortunate enough to be called for a job interview, the chances are that your performance in the interview will determine, to a large extent, whether you become merely one of a number of candidates who are interviewed or, instead, the candidate who is (first) offered the job. Thus, you wish to prepare assiduously for the job interview.

The Job Talk

The job interview may have many elements, but the central element almost always is the job talk. There is no one formula for a successful job talk, but there are elements that are common to many successful job talks.

- *The job talk is a performance.* Remember that when you speak you are performing. Good performances always require a great deal of preparation. If you give the talk off the cuff, it will show. And you most likely will not get the job. Some professionals appear very spontaneous. In fact, it is their enormous amount of practice that enables them to *appear* to be spontaneous.
- *Keep your audience in mind.* You may know the meanings of all the jargon-words you use in the talk. Typically, though, the audience for a talk is quite broad, including many people who have only a vague knowledge of the area in which you work. Therefore, prepare for a general audience. Usually, the audience will have good background in general psychology, but not necessarily in your specialty. On the one hand, you don't want to insult the audience by being too elementary. But you are much more likely to lose the audience than to insult it. Therefore, explain all terms that are not generally known and make sure the talk is comprehensible to almost everyone.
- *Motivate the talk.* Don't expect your audience to know why your work is interesting or important. You need to motivate your talk up front by explaining why you are doing what you are doing and why anyone in his or her right mind should want to learn about it! Starting off your talk with a concrete example of the phenomenon about which you will be talking often helps. Often, speakers get or lose their audience in the first minute or so. Therefore, start strong.
- *Be clear on what question or questions you are addressing.* Always be clear about what question or questions you are addressing. If you are not, your audience is likely to be confused about what you are trying to do, and why.
- *Rehearse, rehearse, rehearse.* I generally encourage job candidates to give the job talk at least three times before presenting it for real. Virtually no one gives their best presentation the first time they present. The more similar your audience is to the audience to which you will present your job talk, the better. Often, lab groups scheduled research meetings provide a forum for practice talks.
- *Time yourself.* It is embarrassing to finish a job talk with too much time to spare. You look under-prepared. It is no better to have much too much material, and either to stop in the middle of the talk or to start rushing at the end. Rushing does not work. And remember to allow time for interruptions.
- *Organize.* A good talk is like a story, with a beginning, a middle, and an end (at least, the end up to wherever you are in the story). Say what you are going to say, say it, and

then, at the end, say it again. Make sure that anyone in the audience can follow your talk. Disorganized talks often bespeak disorganized minds, and given the choice, most institutions would prefer to hire people who think in an organized way.

- *Be enthusiastic.* Enthusiasm often is contagious. If you are enthusiastic about your work, others may well be. But if you sound bored, others are likely to be bored, no matter how intrinsically interesting the work may be.
- *Cite relevant work, especially of people in the audience.* Audiences expect you to be aware of the relevant literature in your field, and of the intellectual antecedents of the work you have done. Therefore, be sure to cite near the beginning of the talk past work that led up to yours. If someone in the audience has done work that is relevant, it is essential that you cite that work. It makes no sense to insult someone who might have a potential say in your being hired!
- *Be prepared for questions.* Sometimes, job candidates give a good talk, only to blow their chances of getting the job during the question period. By rehearsing your talk, you can get a sense of what kinds of questions you are likely to get. Have answers prepared to the tough ones. But there may always be questions that are unexpected. Therefore, you need to be prepared for the unexpected. It is very rare that a question demolishes a talk. (It has happened to me once in my career, and it was truly a drag.) Chances are no one will demolish you. But some people may try. Never respond defensively; it makes you, not the questioner, look bad. But do not feel like you have to agree with everything everyone says, just because you are on a job interview. People who capitulate too easily appear to lack spine. Give an honest, constructive response. If you just cannot answer a question, tell the truth. People usually can tell if you are faking it. You may be able to think of an answer later, and then to respond. I often start off my talks by saying that, during the talk, I welcome questions of clarification, but prefer that questions that go beyond clarification wait until the end. If people ask whatever comes to mind during the talk, the risk is that you will finish very little of what you prepared, no matter how well you timed the talk in advance.
- *Never demean or insult a questioner or give a flip answer.* Inevitably, you will sometimes receive questions that undermine your faith in humankind. How could anyone ask a question that stupid? Never, ever demean or insult a questioner. There are several reasons for this. First, you probably do not know who the questioner is. I'm sorry to say that when I applied for my first job, I got a question from a member of the audience—who looked like a graduate student—that I thought was quite silly. I gave a flip answer. Unfortunately, the questioner was a senior faculty member in the area to which I was applying for a job. I didn't get the job. Second, what for you may seem like a stupid question may not seem to be a stupid question to the questioner or others in the audience. A flip or insulting answer may therefore be viewed as quite inappropriate. Third, you portray yourself in an unflattering light when you react in a flip or insulting way.
- *Do not be a slave to your audiovisuals.* Over the course of a career, almost everything that can go wrong, will. There will be overhead projectors, slide machines, or Powerpoint projectors that do not work. There will be problems with lighting and microphones. There will be rooms that are too small or too large. You need to be prepared for all eventualities. I usually try to make sure I have backup. So if Powerpoint does not work, I have transparencies or slides in reserve. Or I have a handout. Or I can manage with no audiovisuals at all. One would like to believe that major screw-ups never happen during

job talks because the talks are so important. But they happen with some frequency. You can lose valuable time if you are not prepared. So be ready for the unexpected and don't be totally reliant on one source of audiovisual aids.

- *Get the level of detail right.* The right level of detail for a talk is a sometimes hard-to-find middle ground. When you go into great levels of detail about your participants, materials, procedures, and so forth, you bore people; but when you give insufficient details, you lose them. In a talk, it is important to distinguish the forest from the trees, but to make sure that you tell enough about the trees so that people can understand the nature of forest.
- *Have a clear take-home message.* Make sure that, at the end of the talk, people leave with a clear take-home message regarding what you tried to show, what you did show, what it means, and why they should care.

The Conversations

Although the center of the job interview is the job talk, another important aspect of it is the series of informal conversations one typically has with potential future colleagues, such as faculty members or practicing psychologists, sometimes with graduate students, and sometimes, with administrators outside the unit in which one is to work. These conversations, almost as much as a job interview, can make or break a job offer. Therefore, keep in mind some important tips about the conversations:

- *Find out about your potential future colleagues in advance.* People almost inevitably are flattered when you know about them and their work; some people, especially more senior ones, may be insulted when you do not. Before you to go the interview, learn as much as you can about the people you are likely to talk to, and then show your knowledge (unobtrusively) in your conversations with them.
- *Show your interest in the work of the people with whom you speak.* One of the worst but most frequent errors of job candidates is to appear self-preoccupied and interested only in their own work. Egocentric people make bad colleagues, and are not prime candidates to be hired. By showing an interest in the work of others and in what you can contribute to it, you not only paint a flattering portrait of yourself, but you also open yourself up to learning experiences you might otherwise never have.
- *Show your interest in the institution.* You want to show that you know the institution to which you are applying, and that you would be thrilled to receive a job offer. Communicating the message that you do not really want to go to a place is a pretty good way of not getting a job: No institution wants to be turned down!
- *Be modest but not self-effacing.* No one likes a show-off. So maintaining an appropriate level of modesty helps show that you have a perspective on yourself and your work. But do not belittle yourself: If you do not have confidence in yourself, you may find that others will not either.
- *Disagree if you must, but don't lose your cool.* Most likely, one or more of your conversational partners will challenge some of your work, especially if you talk to people after the job talk. Conversations during job interviews are terrible places to lose your temper. You do not have to be disingenuous and pretend to agree with others when you do not.
- *Be yourself.* People can tell when you are faking it.

THE PERSPECTIVES OF THE SEARCH COMMITTEE

It would be nice if there were secrets that would crack open the deliberation process of the search committee. There are no such secrets, because different search committees value different things. Moreover, hiring decisions typically go to a faculty vote, at which point anything can happen. However, I think the main issues are these, with different weights for different search committees.

- *General fit to department.* Departments want someone who will fit in—who shares their values, who meets their teaching and research needs, who will be a good colleague. A candidate could be strong on many dimensions, but if the individual does not seem to fit with the department, the candidate is likely not to get hired. If you want to know what people are looking for, you might try simply asking them what is important to them. If what they value is not what you value, you probably are in the wrong place!
- *Specific fit to job.* Beyond general fit, departments typically have a search image in mind. It might be limited to an area (such as social psychology) or even to a particular specialty within an area (such as social cognition). If you do not do what the department is looking for, you have a tougher sell ahead of you.
- *Potential for research.* Especially at the entry levels of the academic job market, you are selling not so much who you have been but who you will be. You need to convince the committee that you are someone with a wonderful future in front of you.
- *Teaching.* Departments vary greatly in how much they value teaching, but almost all departments want someone who is at least a good teacher, if not necessarily a great one. Typically, your job talk and letters of reference are the main information departments get regarding your teaching.
- *Willingness to give as well as to take.* It is surprising how many candidates appear to be focused only on themselves and their own research. Showing interest in the work of others and in other people, more generally, can make a big difference to a final outcome.

QUESTIONS TO ASK ON A JOB INTERVIEW

The questions you ask on a job interview will vary with the issues that concern you. You should consult the department's web site for general information. However, here are some questions that candidates often ask. (see Table 1). Often, the most appropriate person to ask is the Chair, although it sometimes is interesting to obtain a variety of perspectives.

NEGOTIATIONS

If you are fortunate enough to get a job offer, there is room for negotiation! Here are the things that are most commonly negotiated:

- *Salary.* At the junior level, there is often some but not much room for negotiation. Sometimes having a competitive offer helps. But you should be very low-key in such negotiations.

TABLE 1. Sample Questions to ask on a Job Interview[2]

General Questions

- What is the size of the department?
- What is the structure of the department (different tracks, disciplines, etc.)?
- What is the number of faculty at each rank?
- What are the department's future expansion (or contraction) plans?
- What is the department's standing within the university?
- How are graduate students matched with faculty?
- How are graduate admissions handled, in general?
- How long does it typically take for graduate students to finish the program?
- Does the graduate program have both masters and doctoral students, or just one or the other?
- For clinical psychologists, what is the relative emphasis on research versus clinical work?
- What is the relationship between subdisciplines or areas within the department?
- What is the relationship between psychology and other departments?
- Are any of the faculty in private practice? Are there any guidelines with respect to private practice or consulting?

Responsibilities

- What is the teaching load?
- Is there any reduction in teaching load during the first year?
- Is there any reduction in teaching load for departmental service? For grants?
- Can you buy out of teaching with grants?
- Is summer teaching expected?
- What is the proportion of junior faculty that is tenured?
- What are the expectations for tenure?
- What are the expectations with regard to committee work?

Resources

- How much lab space can you expect? Where will it be?
- How are research assistants and teaching assistants assigned?
- How are resources like secretaries, photocopying, postage, long-distance calling, and parking handled?
- What kinds of computer equipment and support can one expect?
- What library services are available?
- What kinds of mentorship are available for junior faculty?

Benefits

- What kinds of travel funds are available from the department?
- What kinds of medical, dental, and retirement plans are offered by the university?
- Are there opportunities for summer funding?
- What is a typical starting salary?

Grants/Research

- What are university's expectations with regard to obtaining outside grant funding?
- What kinds of internal grant funding are available?
- What kinds of participant populations are available? Is there a subject pool?
- Is there an office of sponsored research in the university or college?
- How much time is typically available for research?
- What is the quality of the students, and might they reasonable become involved in research?

Location

- What are the real-estate opportunities available?
- What is the cost of living?
- Is there any university assistance with mortgages?

Faculty Relations

- Are relations between junior faculty and senior faculty cordial?
- Is collaboration among faculty encouraged (or discouraged)?
- Why do people decide to come to the university? Why do some people not decide to come?

[2] Questions provided by Mitch Prinstein

- *Start-up funds.* Many universities will give start-up funds. You should find out the range of start-up funds available, if any are available at all. Then you may wish to prepare a budget.
- *Employment opportunities for significant others.* Many, but not all universities are willing to help find employment for significant others.
- *Lab space.* Many universities will provide lab space if you wish it.
- *Teaching load.* Some universities will negotiate a reduced teaching load in the first year. But they will generally not make a special arrangement beyond that.

CONCLUSIONS

You cannot guarantee yourself the job you want, or even a good job. But there is a lot you can do to improve your chances of getting the job you want. Preparing early for your eventual foray into the job market will improve your chances of effectively marketing yourself. By following the suggestions in this chapter, you will find yourself a step ahead in getting your ideal job. But if you do not get that job, all is not lost. Many people start off with jobs that were not what they hoped for, and either find that they are much happier than they expected they would be, or that, within a few years, they can move to a job that represents a better match to what they want. So, if you are patient, chances are quite good that sooner or later, you will end up in a position that makes you happy.

REFERENCE

Sternberg, R. J. (Ed.) (1997). *Career paths in psychology: Where your degree can take you.* Washington, DC: American Psychological Association.

CHAPTER 24

Contemporary Employment in Psychology and Future Trends

KATHLEEN BARKER AND JESSICA KOHOUT

How are new psychology doctorates faring when seeking their first professional position? What are the criteria by which applicants are judged? Is there any point to trying to get a job in academe? Are practice jobs easier to come by? What about consulting? In this chapter, we will use a number of data sources to answer questions like these regarding employment in psychology. Using data from the biennial APA Doctorate Employment Surveys, as well as data from the National Science Foundation and the National Survey of Postsecondary Faculty (NSOPF) conducted by the U.S. Department of Education, we will sketch a picture of the current employment situation for doctoral-level psychologists in the United States. Data will be presented on employment settings, salaries, perceptions of the marketplace, time to employment and any changes in these over time.

It is also our intent to discuss employment prospects for future psychologists. We will present data on prospects in the more "traditional" careers one would find in psychology: academe and practice. Discussions of the current issues and future employment trends in these more traditional options will be followed by information on what might be called innovative careers and the pros and cons of nontraditional careers. This latter piece will be less grounded in data and will be more speculative.

For the most part the data contained in the accompanying tables and graphs describe doctoral-level psychologists. The titles of these pieces will indicate whether we are discussing all doctoral-level psychologists, only PhDs, or more generally, doctoral-level faculty in higher education, regardless of field. This variability is a function of the fact that we must rely on different sources of information and that the sources gather, analyze and present their data differently.

KATHLEEN BARKER • Department of Psychology, Medgar Evers College of The City University of New York, Brooklyn, NY 11225
JESSICA L. KOHOUT • Research Office, American Psychological Association, Washington, DC, 20002

EMPLOYMENT SETTINGS FOR NEW PSYCHOLOGY DOCTORATES

Where Are New Doctorates Going?

APA's survey of 1999 doctorate recipients in psychology revealed that the leading single category of primary full-time employment settings among 1999 new doctorates was business (e.g., National Head Start Association, IBM, trial consultant, the GAP, church's national office) and government (e.g., CDC, Department of Education, state health department, school system district office, county mental health services), representing almost 19% of new doctorates. This was followed by university settings (18%), other human service settings (counseling centers, specialized health services, rehabilitation facilities, outpatient clinics and the like) (14%), hospitals at just under 13%, and managed care at almost 12%. Schools and other educational settings claimed a little less than 9%, and independent practice was at 6%. Four-year colleges claimed 4% of new doctorates, medical schools got 3% and fewer than 2% were located in other academic settings.

In summary, just over one fourth (26%) of new doctorates were employed in higher education and almost 9% were employed in schools or other educational settings. Organized health care settings[1], including hospitals, managed care, and other human service settings accounted for another 38%, while business, government and other settings accounted for almost 19%. Independent practice was the smallest category of employment at 6%.

EXAMINING EMPLOYMENT SETTING BY SUBFIELD. Which settings hold the most promise when seeking employment? Not surprisingly, the employment settings for new doctorates differ by whether a doctorate is in one of two broad areas: health provider and research. Over two thirds of new doctorates were granted in the health service provider subfields with 31% of new doctorates in research subfields. Graduates in the health service provider subfields were employed primarily in organized health care settings (52%). Ten percent were in schools and other educational settings, and 15% were in higher education. Twelve percent of health service graduates were located in business and government settings, and 8% in independent practices. The remaining few percent were found in other academic settings. Graduates in the research fields were found most frequently in higher education settings (54%) and in business, government and other settings (34%). Far fewer were found in organized health care settings (6%), or in schools (5%).

Time to Employment

Seven percent of 1999 psychology doctorates were in their current job when they began their programs. Almost one fourth found their current position before completing their doctoral program. Fully 41% had had found their current position within three months of completing work on the doctorate. Sixteen percent took up to half a year and almost 10% took more than 6 months. The data placed almost three fourths of new doctorates in their current jobs within three months of earning the doctorate. The shift that has occurred in the past decade has been a

[1] Organized health care settings are those practice settings usually located in some organizational or business structure and in which the psychological practitioner is an employee of the organization. Examples include hospitals, clinics, CMHCs and so on. This is in contrast to the independent practice, either as a solo or group arrangement, of psychology, which is not considered as an organized health care setting.

decline in the proportion of new doctorates that found work prior to receiving the doctorate and a concomitant increase in the proportion taking three months to find their current positions. There were differences by subfield such that new psychology doctorates in teaching and research positions were more likely than those in health service positions to have the time to find a job last more than 6 months. It is important to remember that some of these graduates may not have been actively seeking work but may have been completing postdoctorates during this time.

Unemployment and Self-Employment

Data from the 1999 Survey of Doctorate Recipients (NSF, in press) reported the employment settings for the 93,137 psychologists in the United States. According to the NSF survey, less than 10% were not working.

Among those working in business and industry settings, as health care providers or researchers, half of new doctorates were self employed and the other half were employed by a firm. The vast majority of those who were self employed (77%) were not incorporated, while 23% had taken steps to incorporate their businesses. It is evident from the patterns of degree subfield found in these data that not all the psychologists who were self employed were in health service provider subfields. This indicates that self-employment has become a viable option for psychologists regardless of subfield background, an important shift for professionals in psychology. Psychologists are demonstrating a higher rate of self-employment (including those who are not incorporated and incorporated) than the rate of 10.5% observed for all U.S. professionals in 1996 (Manser & Picott, 1999). In fact, according to Department of Labor estimates, more than 4 out of 10 psychologists are self employed, about 6 times the average for professional workers (U.S. Department of Labor, 2002).

Almost 61% of the doctoral-level psychologists employed in business (not self employed) were located in for-profit settings, while the remaining 39% was to be found in nonprofit settings. Obviously psychologists are finding a place in the business world. In recent years, the numbers of psychologists in for-profit settings or self-employment has exceeded those in university settings (see Figure 1).

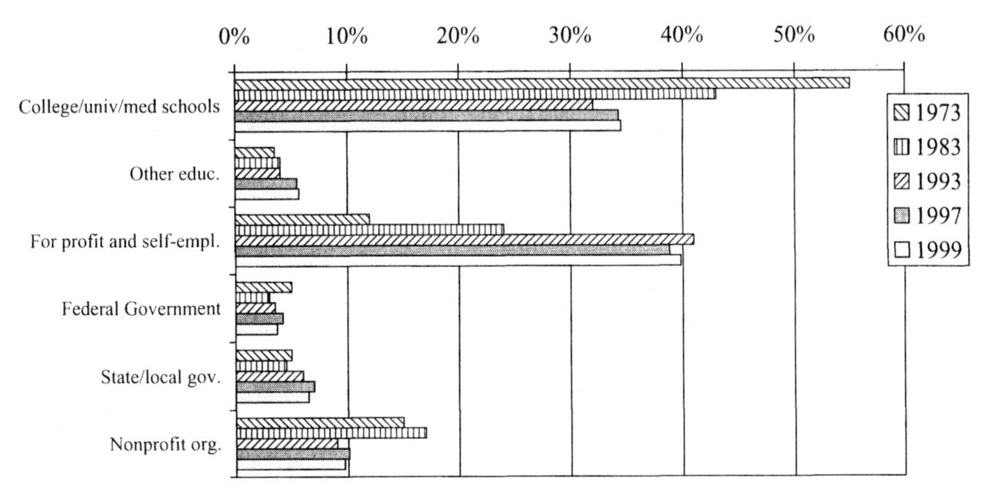

FIGURE 1. Changes in Employment Settings for PhD Psychologists: 1973, 1983, 1993, 1997, 1999
SOURCE: Survey of Doctorate Recipients, selected years. National Science Foundation. Compiled by APA Research Office, March 2001.

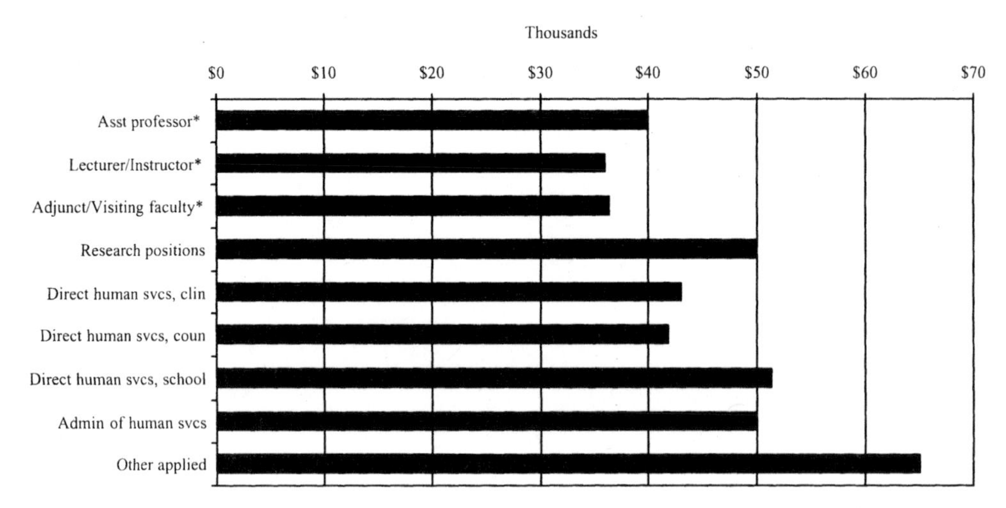

FIGURE 2. Median Starting Salaries for Full-time Employment Positions: 1999 Doctorates Recipients in Psychology
SOURCE: 1999 Doctorate Employment Survey. Compiled by the APA Research Office, March 2001. *Salaries are reported for a 9–10-month academic year. To calculate 11–12 month equivalent, multiply by 11/9.

The second largest subgroup (405) of psychologists in the current marketplace are located in educational institutions, including universities, four-year colleges, and other types of educational settings. Fully 83% of these were working in universities and four-year colleges. Graduates in the traditional academic research subfields were more apt to be located in an academic setting than was the case for the psychologists with degrees in the health service provider subfields, industrial-organizational or general psychology.

Just over one tenth of the doctoral psychologists in the United States in 1999 were employed in government, and almost two thirds of these worked at the state rather than at the federal level (see Figure 1).

Salaries

Psychologists' salaries have traditionally been lower than those reported by PhDs in the other science and engineering fields according to the NSF Surveys of Doctorate Recipients, and although they have shown gains in the past decade, when adjusted for inflation, the salaries remain lower than many other fields. However, past data indicate that students enter psychology for more than financial benefit. Salary data are available on the Internet through the aforementioned NSF and NORC sites (http://www.nsf.gov/sbe/srs, http://www.norc.uchicago.edu, and http://research.apa.org. The first two sites report largely on PhD salaries while the last site (APA) includes all type of doctorates in its data gathering exercises.

We do find that there were differences in median salaries by subfield and setting (see Figures 2 and 3)[2]. Median salaries for established psychologists tended to be highest in settings

[2] Median salaries are used for ease of comparison. They represent the midpoint in a distribution, the point at which half the scores are above and half below. They are less subject to the influence of extreme salaries than are means and thus give a truer picture of the salaries available Ranges are not used as they would focus again on the extreme scores and make comparisons difficult. In fact, medians, means, and ranges are available on the web sites noted in the chapter.

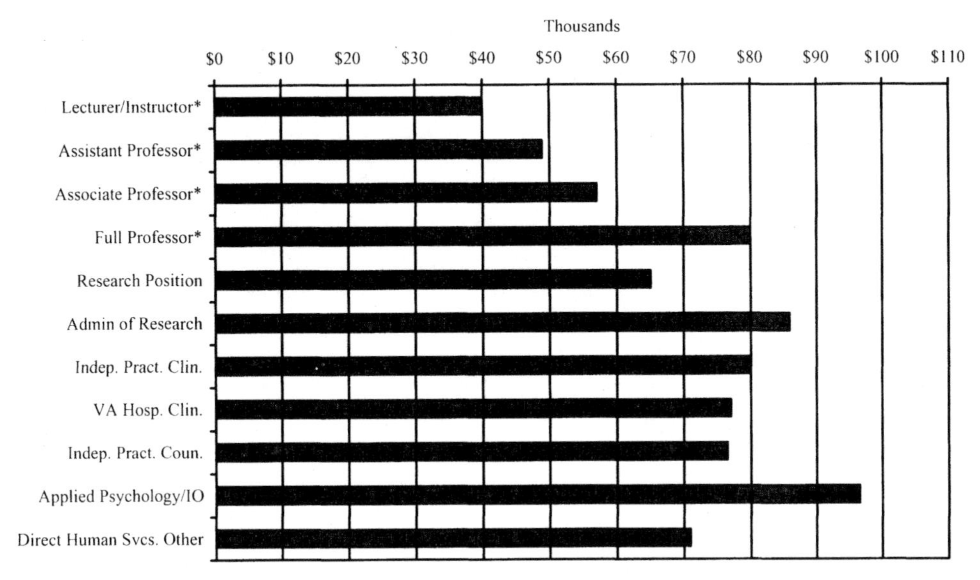

FIGURE 3. Median Full-time Salaries of Doctoral-level Psychologists by Employment Position: 2001
SOURCE: APA Research Office. 2001–2002 Faculty Salaries in Graduate Departments of Psychology. 2001 Salaries in Psychology. APA. *Faculty salaries are reported for a 9–10 month academic year. To calculate 11–12 month equivalent, multiply by 11/9.

where there was greater individual control over pay, such as practice settings. These settings would pay less well for psychologists just starting out who do not yet have the experience or credentials that would allow them to practice independently. Salaries also tended to be higher among psychologists in business and in applied settings, especially for those in administrative positions. On the other hand, they were lower for those in organized health care settings, particularly settings such as community mental health centers and clinics. Salaries of psychologists in government settings tended to be relatively high because government pay scales recognize and compensate for higher education and experience. Further—government pay scales tend to be public information and therefore are somewhat standardized. Among new psychologists, those in school psychology fared quite well. This is a function of the strong niche that school psychology has in the schools and in school system district offices. Academic salaries have not kept pace with inflation and they will differ with level of program, experience, type of institution and so on. It remains important for psychologists entering academe to be aware of shifts in academic employment in the direction of contracts and away from tenure-based systems. These shifts and others require keen negotiating skills.

Perceptions of the Marketplace

What did new doctorates think of the marketplace? Results from the 1999 Doctorate Employment Survey indicated that perceptions continued to improve from the early 1990s. Forty-seven percent of the respondents reported a good or excellent perception of the job market, and although this is an increase from 1995, it is still less than the 52% who responded positively in 1989. It may be that the decrease in perceptions in the early 1990s was the consequence of a combination of a sagging economy that coincided with the beginning of structural shifts in both practice and academe. The result was greater uncertainty for psychologists regardless of setting and training. The "improvement" in perceptions may be due more to perceived improvements in the general economy than to any improvement in the actual practice or academic milieus for psychologists. Both academe and practice still appear to be changing in response to external factors. Not surprisingly, perceptions varied by employment status, with those employed full-time were more apt to respond positively.

Moving from the categories of full-time to postdoctoral to part-time to unemployed/seeking employment, perceptions of the job market became less positive. The group that was voluntarily unemployed—not working and not looking for employment—responded similarly to those who were employed full-time. Fully half of those employed full-time responded positively about the marketplace compared to 40% of those working part time, 43% of those in postdoctoral positions, and 17% of those who reported being unemployed and seeking employment. One might interpret these data to indicate that half of the new doctorates in full-time jobs did not have confidence in the marketplace. Thus, they did not think that the marketplace provided mobility in moving from their current job to another while the other half did. Clearly, subfield specialty, employment setting, and even region of the country have an impact on perceptions of mobility in the marketplace.

WOULD YOU DO IT AGAIN? In general, most recent doctorates said that they would choose psychology again (80%), with almost 87% stating that they would choose the same subfield again. Some of the responses are affected by the small number of respondents but it is possible to see that 93% of clinical graduates compared to 76% of counseling graduates and 69% of new doctorates in experimental said they would choose the same subfield. The logical follow-up to these two items was to ask whether they would choose the same doctoral program. Again although most new doctorates responded in the affirmative, some of the graduates in the research fields exhibited a certain amount of ambivalence. Only 62% of cognitive, 60% of experimental, and 64% each of industrial organizational and neuroscience doctorates responded affirmatively, that they would choose the same training program again. None of the health service provider subfields was as low as any of these.

PSYCHOLOGISTS IN ACADEME

As the new doctorate survey showed, over a quarter of new doctorates were employed in higher education. In this section we consider a traditional source of employment for PhD's, the university and college setting. We examine those individuals who are primarily working as faculty.

Data from the NSOPF (National Study of Postsecondary Faculty) offer information on general trends in faculty hires across disciplines. The NSOPF is a nationally representative sample of instructional faculty and staff and non-instructional faculty at two-year and above, non-proprietary or public postsecondary institutions in the 50 states and the District of Columbia. The sample of faculty is achieved through stratified sampling of postsecondary institutions. These institutions provide lists of faculty who are subsequently surveyed. The NSOPF 1993 and 1999 surveys were distributed to different sample faculty during the fall of 1992 and 1998 (U.S. Department of Education, National Center for Education Statistics 1996, 2001). These successive studies have provided a snapshot of short-term changes in instructional staffing. As it is important for psychologists to understand their own academic situation within a general context, we offer a brief review of findings on academic employment more generally.

How Are All Faculty Faring in Higher Education?

Employment trends in the U.S. point toward an increasing proportion of faculty employed in nonstandard instructional arrangements, such as in temporary or part-time adjunct positions (Barker, 1998; Barker, 2002) (see Table 1). Across disciplines, the past 20 years has revealed substantial growth in the proportion of part-time and non-tenure eligible faculty (U.S. Department of Education, National Center for Education Statistics, 1995). Although there was an overall increase of 47% of all faculty between 1975 and 1995, there were substantial reductions in the number of full-time new hires and non-tenured faculty on track during this same time period (see Table 1). Data suggest that these trends apply equally to members of majority groups (i.e., White males), as well as members of groups who have been traditionally consigned to the margins of academe (i.e., female faculty and racial/ethnic minority faculty).

The recent trends are most dramatic for changes in non-tenure track appointments as compared to part-time employment. In 1992, part-time faculty accounted for 41.6% of all faculty with responsibility for teaching some courses and by 1998 they had increased by only 1% to 42.6% with full-time faculty accounting for the remainder, 57.4%. Yet, between 1992 and 1999, the proportion of faculty who were tenured or on the tenure track declined from 70% to 67.6% while those who were temporary increased from 30% to 32.4%.

Whenever the issue of part-time faculty is discussed, a myth is invariably raised: women prefer part-time jobs. Let's take an empirical look at this myth. Table 2 displays several of these trends by gender. Indeed, male faculty are much more likely to be working full-time while women's part-time employment appears to be more regularized. Since part-time faculty positions are rarely tenure track, however, this type of employment is often not prized by many aspirants in the higher education labor market. When considering the long-term costs of part-time jobs—little if any benefits, no pension, no promotion ladder, and many positions lacking a long-term promise of stability—part-time work may fit a particular short-term need but may be problematic over the long term for individuals seeking a traditional academic career. One of the myths associated with part-time employment is that it is "preferred" to full-time employment. However, most part-time psychology faculty with doctorates do not prefer their part-time employment (62%). Indeed, one research study showed that evaluators were less likely to evaluate a faculty candidate positively when candidates had more than 5 years of part-time experience (Barker, 1998) and qualitative research indicated that adjunct faculty were aware of this bias (Barker, 1995). Alternatively, if you are self-employed in private practice or

TABLE 1. Number of Faculty According to Employment Status in Higher Education Institutions, 1975 and 1995

	1975	1995	Change from 1975 to 1995
Total faculty	633,210	931,706	47%
Part-time faculty	199,139	380,884	91%
Full-time faculty	434,071	550,822	27%
Non-Tenure Eligible Faculty	81,010	155,641	92%
Full-time new hires	37,302	30,785	−17%
Nontenured Faculty on Track	126,465	110,311	−12.8

Source: U.S. Department of Education, National Center for Education Statistics. E.D. TABS: *Fall Staff in Postsecondary Institutions*, 1995, NCES 98-228, by Stephen Roey and Rebecca Rak. Project Officers, Rosa Fernandez and Sam Barbett (Washington, D.C.: 1998).

TABLE 2. Gender Composition of Regular and Temporary Instruction Staff by Part-Time vs. Full-Time Work Status, All Disciplines: NSOPF 1993, 1999

	Regular %	Temporary %	*n*	*N*
1993				850,090
Female Faculty	70.8	29.2	322,230	
Part-Time	48.0	52.0	161,710	
Full-Time	93.7	6.3	160,510	
Male Faculty	75.5	24.5	527,860	
Part-Time	43.6	56.4	201,130	
Full-Time	95.1	4.9	326,720	
1999				953,310
Female Faculty	66.0	34.0	393,570	
Part-Time	40.4	59.6	197,810	
Full-Time	91.9	8.1	195,760	
Male Faculty	71.5	28.5	559,740	
Part-Time	36.4	63.6	214,610	
Full-Time	93.3	6.7	345,130	

Sources: NCES 1993, 1999 NSOPF. Excludes faculty who reported an "acting" status. Percentages may not add to 100% due to rounding; weighted sample N's may not always total exactly also due to rounding.

employed full-time in the corporate or government sectors, teaching as an adjunct can bring many personal rewards (and a few headaches too).

In summarizing the important points in this section, the emergence of nonstandard work in academe (i.e., work that substantially departs from traditional notions of permanent or full-time employment, including part-time jobs, temporary part-time jobs, and temporary full-time jobs) now accounts for a substantial proportion of academic positions and is slowly rising. Currently, more than half of all jobs in academe are nonstandard. A temporary academic job is a semester-to-semester arrangement with no promise of an on-going relationship with a teaching institution. Under these arrangements, for example, individuals can be hired on a semester-to-semester or annual basis or for a specific project. An example of the latter are instructors hired to create multi-media courses that they do not teach or distance-learning materials. In both cases, instructors could be hired on a limited contractual basis.

Now that a basic picture of instructional employment in higher education has been rendered, we turn our attention to faculty in psychology.

How Are Psychologists Faring in Higher Education?

Just as employment trends in the U.S. point toward an increasing proportion of workers employed in nonstandard arrangements, such as in temporary or part-time jobs (Barker & Christensen, 1998a, b; duRivage, 1992; Hudson, 1999; Kalleberg, et al., 1997), the proportion of new psychology doctorates working full-time has declined steadily since the mid '80's from 80% to 67% by 1999 (Kohout & Wicherski, 1991; Kohout & Wicherski, in press; Wicherski & Kohout, 1999). Over the same period the proportion working part time has increased slightly from 7% to 10% and those in postdoctorates have increased from 10 to 17%. National Science

Foundation data that examine the employment of scientists also point to an increase in the proportion of new psychology PhDs pursuing postdoctoral study in the past decade (from almost 14% with definite postdoctorate positions in 1990 to 22% with postdoctorates in 2000) (Thurgood & Weinman, 1991; Hoffer et al., 2001). This substantial change in employment plans among new doctorates may be interpreted as pointing to a need for new doctorates to acquire greater expertise. It may also, however, indicate a competitive post-degree job environment in which more new doctorates are taking postdoctoral training positions in lieu of full-time employment.

Just how well is psychology doing? Is there a growth in the number of faculty hired? Or a decline? This is important because teaching at the B.A. level (or at the community college or "feeder college" level) accounts for a significant proportion of employment for psychology PhDs. Counter to the general instructional trends noted in the foregoing section, between 1992 and 1998 the total number of faculty with a degree in psychology and whose primary responsibility was teaching increased from 18,730 to 19,320[3]. The proportion of those faculty in nonstandard teaching arrangements marginally increased from 52.6% to 54.4%. The number of teaching faculty with doctorates increased slightly from 11,810 in 1992 and 12,130 in 1998. Thus, only half of the increase of jobs in psychology was for those with a doctorate. Obtaining the doctorate, however, greatly reduced the chance of psychology faculty working in nonstandard jobs. Slightly less than 38% were in nonstandard jobs in 1992; some increase was observed in 1998 when the nonstandard figure increased to 39.4%. Thus, we observed that half of the jobs created for psychology faculty were for those with a doctorate. The doctorate also enhanced the chance of getting a better (e.g. standard or regular) job in academe but did not totally eliminate the possibility of nonstandard employment.

Race and gender continue to be of enduring importance for those learning, teaching, and managing in higher education. When considering gender, women with psychology doctorates were as likely to be employed in nonstandard jobs (48.5%) as in standard jobs (51.5%). Men with doctorates were more likely to be employed in standard employment (66.3%) than nonstandard employment (33.6%). Unfortunately, the NSOPF does not capture psychologist's subfield of training so that we were unable to more carefully examine this phenomenon of underemployment in nonstandard jobs. We can examine, however, the distribution of faculty with doctorates in psychology across institution type and this is portrayed in Figure 4.

Since the 1970s, researchers, policymakers, and educators have commented on the slow pace toward achieving gender and racial/ethnic diversity in higher education, including faculty composition (Allen, et al., 2002; Altbach, 1991; Altbach, Lomotey, & Rivers, 2002; Lomotey, 1997; Solmon, Solmon, & Schiff, 2002). The distribution of psychology faculty by race/ethnic group is displayed in Figure 5. This Figure indicates about 11.5% minority representation among psychology faculty with doctorates in psychology. APA data from the annual Faculty Salary Survey are generally consistent with these results, indicating that minority representation among full-time faculty has increased gradually from 5% in 1981–82 to 10% by 2000–2001 (Wicherski, Randall, & Kohout, 2002). Clearly, psychology faculty continue to display a lack of diversity among its ranks in terms of race and ethnicity, a legacy, in part, of the doctoral application and recruitment process.

[3] If the faculty who classify themselves as "acting" are included in the analysis, the figures for both years are constant: slightly less than 20,000. However, the "acting" category obscures the actual work status of faculty. NSOPF treats acting faculty as "temporary" but a substantial minority are actually tenured. Therefore, all the analyses reported in this chapter have dropped the "acting" faculty. Also, these analyses do not include faculty whose primary responsibilities are not teaching or individuals with psychology degrees who are not teaching psychology.

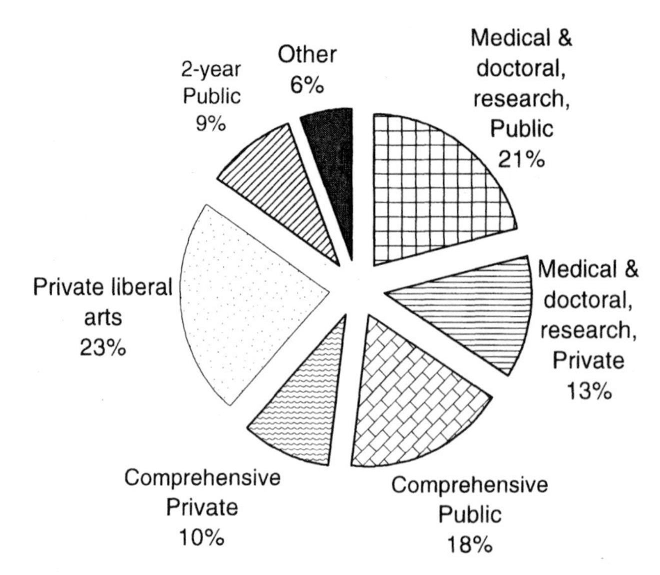

FIGURE 4. **Distribution of Psychology Faculty with Doctorates in Psychology by Type of Higher Education Institution (N = 12,130)**
SOURCE: NCES 1999 NSOPF. Psychology faculty whose primary responsibility is teaching, who have earned a doctorate in psychology, and who teach psychology courses are included. Table excludes psychology faculty who reported an "acting" status. Percentages may not add to 100% due to rounding.

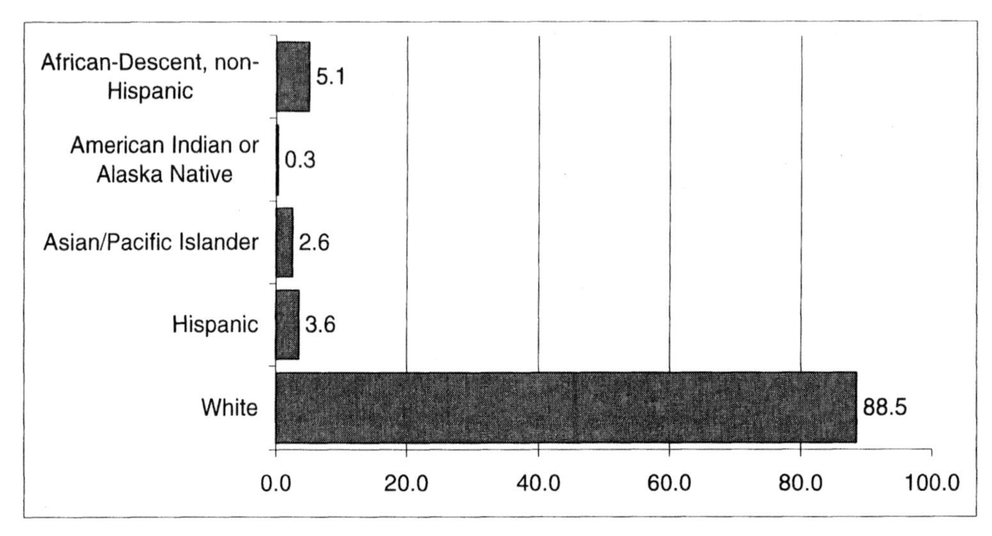

FIGURE 5. **Distribution of Psychology Instructional Faculty with Doctorates in Psychology by Ethnicity and Race, Fall, 1998 ($N = 12{,}130$)**
SOURCE: NCES 1999 NSOPF. Psychology faculty whose primary responsibility is teaching, who have earned a doctorate in psychology, and who teach psychology courses are included. Table excludes psychology faculty who reported an "acting" status. Percentages may not add to 100% due to rounding.

HOW ARE NEW DOCTORATES FARING WITHIN THE LAST FIVE YEARS? THE ISSUE OF WORK STATUS. While a picture of all psychologists in academe is interesting, it is also important to consider recent trends. One way to look at employment trends is to look at what is called the "new entries' in the labor market or new PhD's. When considering rank, of those with a psychology PhD degree minted within the last 5 years as of the fall of 1998, 3.4% reported a rank of full professor, 3.1% reported an associate rank, 41% reported being at the assistant professor level, and 58%, mostly part-time, reported a rank of instructor, lecturer or other. In this newly minted subsample, full-time faculty were younger (average age = 34.8 years) than part-time regular faculty (44.3), full-time temporary faculty (38.5) or part-time temporary faculty (37.7).

What is the quality of the jobs new PhDs are obtaining? In 1998, "new entries" in academe reported an average of 3.5 prior jobs in higher education and a significantly higher chance of being in a nonstandard job than a standard job. Temporary full-time faculty reported the least amount of higher education experience (1.8 prior jobs) than all other groups. Furthermore, most in nonstandard arrangements reported that they would prefer a standard (i.e., full-time, permanent) appointment. For instance, of those in part-time employment, whether long term or short term, only 19% preferred that arrangement, with about 60% reporting that a desired full-time job was not available. Slightly more than 61% of these faculty reported that they had a second salaried position.

An important lesson from the data points to the importance of experience—prior positions in higher education—if a full-time regular position is desired. The data confirm research findings for at least one specific subfield of psychology, social psychology, reported by Sheehan and Haselhorst (1999). They found that prior positions in higher education are substantially visible to faculty selection committees when considering applicants for assistant professorships in psychology but teaching experience is but one variable. Table 3 summarizes the characteristics of the resulting pool of applicants from recruiting for an applied social psychology position at one University in the late 1990s. As Sheehan and Haselhorst point out, although the sample is not representative of all applicants or even all social psychology applicants, it does provide a sobering view of the quantity (total applicant N = 137) and quality of applicants for an academic position. Sheehan and Haselhorst note that these data provide

> [J]ob seekers something to compare themselves with; [and] it should also help those entering doctoral programs [to] set goals that will help them be more competitive in the search for a position in academia. (Sheehan & Haselhorst, 1999, p. 29)

HOW ARE PSYCHOLOGISTS FARING IN TENURE COMPARED WITH OTHER DISCIPLINES? When considering the lucrative careers a PhD recipient can pursue, one might ask why do psychologists pursue a job in higher education? The most succinct answer might be stability. Tenure is the sought after prize of many higher education aspirants and the reason many individuals work the long-hours-for-less-pay than they would receive in nonacademic jobs. But tenure is under attack and it is eroded by the rise of nonstandard jobs. How is psychology faring in this area? Of all psychology PhDs teaching in higher education, 37.4% were tenured, 19.1% were on-track and the rest, 43.5%, were in positions or institutions that did not offer tenure. Faculty in standard academic jobs were overwhelmingly more likely to be tenured or on-track for tenure (90.3%) than individuals who were in nonstandard jobs (4.8%). Nonstandard employment was overwhelmingly associated with those positions, and to a lesser degree those institutions, which did not offer tenure. Tenure was an *unavailable* option for just over 92% of PhDs in *nonstandard* jobs. When considering gender and tenure together, men

TABLE 3. Summary of Candidate Teaching and Research Experience from Pool of Applicants for an Applied Social Psychology Assistant Professor Position N = 137 (adapted from Sheehan & Haselhorst, 1999)[1]

Teaching Experience Characteristic (SD)	%	Research Experience Characteristic (SD)	%
Percent who taught a course	98	Research assistant experience	58
Percent who had taught social psychology	84	*Average number of juried publications (5.9)	4
*Average number of different courses taught (3.6)	4	Average number of juried publications with applicant as first author (3.9)	2
*Average total number of courses taught (5.5)	5	*Percent with at least one publication in an American Psychological Association journal	42
Percent who provided sample teaching evaluations	80	Average number of book chapters (2.1)	1
Percent who had teaching assistant experience	80	Percent who had been a principal investigator on a funded grant	22
Percent who had supervised student research	28	Average grant amount	$24,000
Percent who had taken a class on university level teaching	11	Average number of juried presentations (8.1)	9
Percent who had advising experience	18	*Average number of non-juried publications (1)	0.23
		Average number of non-juried presentations (2.9)	1.3

[1] Items with an asterisk indicate a characteristic that the final selected candidate met or exceeded.

appear to be more likely to be tenured, a historical effect of discrimination. However, when examining men and women on-track for tenure, typically representing new doctorates in psychology, equal proportions of men (19.2%) and women (19.1%) are on track (see Table 4). Thus, good jobs appear to be equally going to men and women. But it is important to look even further at the data and indeed, the outcome is not as simple. Nearly half of all female psychology PhD instructors (49.5%) are employed in institutions that offer tenure but not to

TABLE 4. Tenure Status and Gender: Faculty Teaching in Psychology by Standard/Nonstandard Work Status, NSOPF, 1999

	Tenure Status and Gender					
	Tenured Female %	Tenured Male %	On track, Female %	On track, Male %	Not on track, Female %	Not on track, Male %
Total	11.1	26.3	7.4	11.7	20.4	23.1
Standard	17.8	42.3	11.4	18.8	3.9	5.9
Nonstandard	0.8	1.7	1.4	0.9	45.7	49.6

Source: 1999 NSOPF. Psychology faculty whose primary responsibility is teaching, who have an earned doctorate in psychology, and who teach psychology courses are included. Table excludes psychology faculty who reported an "acting" status. Percentages may not add to 100% due to rounding; weighted sample N's may not always total exactly also due to rounding.

them in their jobs, compared with less than a third of their male peers (30.4%). Clearly, parity for men and women has been achieved in the number offered tenure tracks but women are much more likely than men to be relegated to non-tenure eligible jobs in institutions that offer tenure. Although this may be partly a function of women's greater representation in and pursuit of part-time employment, these findings make it imperative for new doctorates, especially women, to ascertain whether the job they are seeking is "on-track."

Because tenure is typically prized by faculty, it demands careful consideration, especially since observers have noted the decline of tenure in higher education and the rise of non-tenure eligible jobs (Baldwin & Chronister, 2001; Barker, 2002). When job candidates visit campuses in application for full-time jobs, institutional faculty and staff may point to their department and proclaim the wonderful success of new faculty in acquiring tenure. Aside from the obvious (the nontenured and 'discouraged' former faculty are not available for interviews), it is worth examining not only how psychology is doing in terms of tenure but also how psychology compares with other fields. We next analyzed the data to answer these questions.

Psychology PhDs who stood for tenure accounted for 33.6% of all faculty tenured during the 1990s. The years 1982–1990 appeared particularly harsh, with only 20.5% of all psychology faculty being tenured during that time period, in part, because academia experienced low hiring rates (the so-called "lost generation"). Yet, an analysis of these tenure cohorts does not show how the field as a whole is faring with regard to those faculty who have successfully acquired tenure. An analysis of the proportion of faculty tenured in 1992 and 1998 and comparisons with other academic disciplines, is provided in Table 5. The proportion of faculty who were tenured in 1998 declined dramatically. In addition, slightly more individuals were on tenure track than in 1992. This could bode well or not. There is no way of knowing how many academic jobs are "disposable" with departments regularly not giving tenure and therefore recruiting new tenure-track faculty on a rotating basis. The only way to determine this is through carefully researching each institution to which you are invited for a campus visit.

As a discipline, psychology also appeared to experience a rise in the number of tenure ineligible positions from 1992 (39.9%) to 1998 (44.5%). Poor tenure records are not just a function of the scholarly and teaching record of a particular faculty member. Failure to tenure also indicts the recruitment, selection, and/or mentoring processes of the department and institution. When a poor "fit" occurs due to a poorly executed search, departments may rectify it by a failure to grant tenure.

It is in your own best interests to know as much as you can about tenure at a prospective department and institution. As a shrinking number of faculty are actually tenured, and as tenure ineligible jobs rise, job candidates should be very astute in evaluating a potential employer's proclivities toward tenure. While this was always true in the past, it has become very important in an environment in which standards for tenure are increasingly ratcheted up (Burgan, 1997) while the number of tenure-track jobs decline.

WORK LIFE CHARACTERISTICS OF PSYCHOLOGY FACULTY. Full-time psychology faculty work a long week. The average total hours worked per week among full-time psychology faculty is 53.5 hours per week. Faculty reported spending, on average, 63% of their time on teaching, though wide fluctuations exist based on the nature of the institution and teaching load. Faculty reported a lower preference for time spent on teaching. Faculty also preferred to spend more of their time on research (26.2%) than they actually reported spending (15.1%). Of those working full-time, full professors reported publishing more sole and multi-authored articles in the last two years (6.1) than either associate (2.8) or assistant (3.2) professors but full professors were also more variable in their production than either of the

TABLE 5. Tenure Trends in the 1990s: Changes in the Proportion of Faculty Tenured by Academic Discipline: NSOPF 1993, 1999

Instructional Area of Teaching	1992 %	1998 %	Percent Change in Tenured %
First-professional health sciences	50.31	62.52	12.21
Nursing	40.82	49.91	9.09
Communications	44.96	53	8.04
Mathematics	56.46	63.59	7.13
Economics	62.99	68.78	5.79
Engineering	54.58	59.34	4.76
Fine arts	48.83	52.77	3.94
Business	51.51	54.29	2.78
Occupationally specific programs	54.29	56.29	2
Political science	60.84	62.5	1.66
Physical sciences	60.81	57.55	−3.26
Sociology	53.48	49.96	−3.52
English and literature	51.83	47.23	−4.6
Biological sciences	57.11	51.65	−5.46
Agriculture and home economics	79.71	73.41	−6.3
History	58.82	52.09	−6.73
Foreign languages	53.35	46.6	−6.75
Teacher education	44.58	35.81	−8.77
Psychology	**43.45**	**34.14**	**−9.31**
Computer sciences	55.43	44.98	−10.45
Other health sciences	47.35	36.04	−11.31
Philosophy and religion	58.14	45.93	−12.21

Source: 1999 NSOPF. Psychology faculty whose primary responsibility is teaching, who have an earned doctorate in psychology, and who teach psychology courses are included in the row "Psychology". Table excludes psychology faculty who reported an "acting" status. Percentages may not add to 100% due to rounding; weighted sample N's may not always total exactly also due to rounding.

other two faculty ranks. All groups had a comparable number of presentations over the last two years.

PERCEPTIONS OF THEIR JOBS AND CAREER. Of full-time psychology faculty with PhDs in 1998, the overwhelming majority reported they were "very" or "somewhat" satisfied with their instructional duties (92%), overall job (88.5%), and with advancement opportunities (81%). They were less frequently satisfied with their salary (51.1%) and benefits (58.7%). Nearly 80% of all full-time psychology faculty thought their workload had increased over time and 34.6% thought research was rewarded more than teaching.

When interviewing for employment in academe, it is useful to carefully query about the number of adjunct faculty teaching courses and their proportion to full-time faculty. Part-time faculty are rarely paid for advising and most do not sit on committees. This increases the workload for full-time faculty, and may impact negatively on attempts to gain tenure due to the time demands placed on junior faculty.

WOULD YOU CHOOSE AN ACADEMIC CAREER AGAIN? Considering the personal and financial investment that is made to acquire a doctorate, and the long career progression from assistant to full professor, how do psychology faculty with PhDs respond to questions regarding their choice of career? When asked in 1998 if they would choose an academic career again, almost 10% of full-time psychology faculty reported they would not, a clear minority. Another way of evaluating this response is to ask individuals about whether they had plans to exit academe for a non-postsecondary position, either full-time or part-time. After eliminating individuals who planned to retire over the next 5 years, a slightly greater number of psychology faculty voiced disenchantment with academe. Almost 14% stated that they were "somewhat likely" to "very likely" to accept a full-time non-postsecondary job over the next 3 years. Almost 4% indicated the same for a part-time non-postsecondary job. Part-time psychology faculty were much more likely to state they had plans to leave academe: 42.2% reported that it was "somewhat likely" to "very likely" they would leave their jobs for a full-time non-postsecondary job while 19% reported similar thoughts about leaving for a part-time non-postsecondary job. Clearly, dissatisfaction among doctorate-holding psychology faculty is greater for those working in part-time variants of academic work. When considering the absence of benefits and stability, the low status associated with many part-time positions, and the fact that many part-timers want full-time work, this finding is not surprising.

An overview of the institution of higher education is beyond the scope of this chapter. This section should make it clear, however, that higher education is a complex set of "small worlds" (Clark, 1997) that is in a rapid cycle of transformation. If you are considering pursuing an academic career, you should become aware of the importance of each element of your application package for every position for which you apply (see Sheehan & Haselhorst, 1999; Sheehan, McDevitt, & Ross, 1998). Your advisor is also critical in your job search process. However, we cannot overemphasize how important it is to learn about some of the structural or societal level issues (recessions, emergence of new sub-fields, retirement rates, etc.) that are affecting or will affect contemporary higher education as you make your decision to enter academe or even apply for particular jobs. Indeed, your advisor may not be aware of many of these as he or she did not face these issues when they were "coming up." Appreciation of these contemporary issues will serve you well in your first position as you are expected to be more than just the new member of the psychology department; you are also expected to be a good colleague who is familiar with the practices and concerns of a "knowledge worker" in higher education.

PSYCHOLOGISTS AS HEALTH SERVICE PROVIDERS

Both the survey of recent doctorates conducted by APA, and the National Science Foundation's survey of recent doctorates offers data on the work of psychologists in the provision of health services. Earlier discussion highlighted the growth in the number of health service provider doctorates being awarded in the past several decades. Over 2/3s of new psychology doctorates in 1999 were in the health service provider subfields (Kohout & Wicherski, 2003); and just over 48% of all PhD psychologists in the United States in 1999 were in clinical and counseling psychology. Recent decades have witnessed a concurrent growth in the number of doctoral programs whose primary function was the education of health service provider psychologists. Where have these professionals found work?

The APA data indicated that just over 40% of 1999 psychology doctorates were employed or working in organized health care settings or in an independent practice setting. The NSF data (Hoffer et al., 2001) placed almost half of all the employed PhD-level psychologists in business settings (e.g. private practices, both incorporated and not, legal firms, retailers, trial services, nonprofit organizations, research, and software firms). Fewer than 62% of these psychologists were in clinical and counseling psychology. More specifically, the largest proportions of psychologists in both of these subfields were to be found in unincorporated self-employment arrangements (i.e., unincorporated private practices). In fact, in 1999, there were more clinical PhD psychologists who were in self-employed business arrangements than were in all educational settings (Hoffer, et al., 2001). These data serve to illustrate the strong direct service thrust in psychology today.

For the remainder of this section on the health service provider side of psychology we have used data from the APA Directory survey, from the state licensing boards, as well as the APA data sets on new doctorates, and the NSF data sets on new PhDs and the PhD population.

How Have Health Service Providers Overall Fared in the United States?

As we did for those employed in academe, we have examined national employment trends for practitioners across disciplines. Health service providers (and mental health providers, particularly) have grown in number and variety across the past decade. Using data from past editions of the Mental Health United States publication (Center for Mental Health Services, SAMHSA, DHHS) and from current collaborative efforts among representatives from psychology, school psychology, psychiatry, social work, clinical nursing, counseling, marriage and family therapy, psychosocial rehabilitation, and clinical sociology; we have seen that in most fields, the provider pools have grown. In several cases the growth has been tremendous, in others it has been more modest, and in still others (e.g., nursing), there have been notable declines. It is true that psychologists will not compete directly with representatives from each of these fields but competition for clients/resources is likely with professionals from several of these fields, including those psychological personnel trained at the master's level. With increasing recognition of the behavioral bases of many physical ailments, and an increasing acceptance of the legitimacy of mental health services, competition becomes even more likely as health service provider psychologists expand the scope of their practices and the settings in which they work.

A second major force that has had an impact on any of these fields judged eligible for reimbursement via health care plans is cost containment—the major mission of managed care that has come to permeate the health care system in the United States in the past two decades. In the next section we review data specific to the practice of psychology but it can safely be said that managed care has raised concerns among practitioners about the power that a third party wields over clinical decision making, with the potential for harm to the client and possible ethical violations particularly with respect to privacy and confidentiality. Across all fields, the *independent* provision of health services has become more difficult as health care organizations and insurance companies have imposed regulations and cost containment strategies on providers, greatly reducing professional autonomy. Similarly, this loss of autonomy and power, which diminishes the quality of professional work life, has occurred in higher education as tenure has been eroded, instability regularized, and faculty temporized. Increasingly, the delivery of services, be they psychotherapeutic services or teaching, has come to be housed in encounters as opposed to relationships (Gutek, 1995). Traditionally, in relationships, services were provided directly by individual practitioners to clients or customers with whom the provider had developed relationships. Services were not filtered through an organizational middleman. Increasingly, these services are provided in encounters in which the customer or clients may interact with many different, yet ostensibly similarly qualified, providers. In one sense, the provider loses some measure of control over the service being provided, and can be viewed more as an agent of the organization.

What Are the Professional and Demographic Characteristics of Practitioners?

In 2000, seventy four percent of new PhDs in clinical psychology were women as were 67% of new PhDs in counseling, school and marriage and family counseling. Minority representation among new PhDs in clinical psychology was 19% and 20% in counseling psychology, school psychology and marriage and family counseling. With the exception of developmental psychology, these percentages are as good as or better than the representation of women and minorities in most of the other psychology subfields (Hoffer et al., 2001).

In 1999, approximately 48% of clinically trained psychologists were women, an increase from 38% ten years ago. About 8.3% of clinically trained women psychologists in the United States were minorities and 6.2% of clinically trained men were minorities in 1999. Among the other health service provider fields, social work, psychiatric nursing, counseling, marriage and family therapy, psychosocial rehabilitation and school psychology had a higher proportional representation of women compared to men. Marriage and family therapy and school psychology did not have as high a minority representation as did psychology.

Just over three fourths of clinically active psychologists were working full-time in 1999, and just over 50% of these were employed in one position only. Not surprisingly, when we consider primary employment setting, the largest single proportion of clinically active psychologists was employed in independent practice, with 38% in individual practice settings, and another 10% in group practices. Twenty one percent were located in educational settings, and 17% of these were in higher education. Eleven percent were working in hospitals, while 8% were in clinics. Eleven percent were in other settings. When looking at secondary employment settings, we found that 43% of clinically active psychologists were located in independent practice settings (private and group), 23% were in educational settings and 13% were to be found in hospitals or clinics and 19% were in other settings. Fully 90% of the clinically trained psychologists were involved in some type of patient care and direct services, almost 20% was conducting some research, and another 40% was teaching. Furthermore, 39% reported having administrative duties while 43% reported other activities. Although the health service provider in psychology is involved in an array of tasks, the primary role remains one of health service provision.

How Are Psychologists Faring in Health Services Provision?

As we saw in the previous section, psychologists and other health service providers have faced significant challenges to their autonomy. Yet, their numbers have continued to grow. Estimates of the number of doctoral-level licensed psychologists have risen from 44,600 in the mid 1980s (Stapp, Tucker, & VandenBos, 1985) to at least 88,000 in 2002 (West et al., 2001). As the numbers have increased so too the involvement in direct service provision. Health service providers in psychology are found across the range of mental health settings, from veteran's hospitals to community clinics, general hospitals, and of course independent practices. Roles also have expanded and diversified to include prevention, community intervention, and assessment of service delivery systems, client advocacy, corporate training and employee assistance programs.

Several articles from the late 1990s looked directly at the impact of managed care on psychology and they offer valuable insights. In the introduction to their trio of articles, Benedict and Phelps (1998) stated that managed care has had a dramatically negative impact on psychological practice. The concerns include external controls (loss of autonomy), ethical dilemmas such as maintaining confidentiality and privacy, and that the professions' existing ethics codes do not provide adequate guidance. The incomes reported by practitioners have also been impacted negatively. Finally, the authors mention that in spite of these negative impacts it does seem that most psychologists do continue to practice in independent settings and that they continue to offer a similar combination of services as in the past. Although the data support the conclusion that practitioners continue to practice in independent settings, we also observed in the NSF data that a significant proportion are no longer in self-employment but are in for-profit business settings. A 1995 survey of APA's 47, 119 practitioner members yielded almost 15,000 responses (Phelps, Eisman, & Kohout, 1998). The survey found that over half the respondents worked in independent practice settings, while another 12% were in academic settings, 8% in government, 14% in medical and 13% in other settings, including business. Psychotherapy was the primary activity for all except those in academic settings.

When the psychologists were asked about the impact of managed care on their practices, 79% of respondents rated the effect as negative. The impact did vary by setting with those engaged in independent practice and medical settings affected most severely, with those in academic settings and government less apt to report negative consequences. However, it is the case that the single largest proportion in each employment setting did report negative impacts. Professional concerns with respect to the impacts of managed care were most pronounced among independent practitioners; specifically, they mentioned managed care changing clinical practice, excessive pre-certification requirements, declines in income and perceived ethical dilemmas posed by managed care. Practitioners in academic settings were more apt to note a concern over a reduced job market for graduates and those in government settings emphasized psychologists losing clients, market share or positions to less trained providers.

Interestingly, despite recommendations for psychologists to diversify, data have not suggested that practice-oriented psychologists' are increasing their involvement in research, teaching or consultation. A study conducted in 1996 on New Jersey psychologists (Rothbaum, Bernstein, Haller, Phelps, & Kohout, 1998) looked at the impact of managed care on psychological practices and patients well-being. They found that the higher the involvement in managed care the more likely practitioners were to report an increase in caseload and paperwork, a decrease in the average number of sessions, changes in morale and professional identity, changes in approach to therapy, and pressures to change the quality of care and to compromise their ethical principles. Murphy, DeBernardo, and Shoemaker's (1998) results from a survey sent to a sample of members of APA's Division of Independent Practice reported similar findings. The respondents did report that managed care had had significant perceived impacts on their practices, yet they did not report making changes to their patterns of practice. There was some movement to joining larger practices or hospital staffs. The results also pointed to a concern over ethics and the perception of a lack of guidance regarding ethical dilemmas.

In summarizing the findings on health providers, we find that like academics, psychologists who are health providers are working under new constraints. New opportunities, such as for-profit ventures, are evident but psychologists are not "diversifying" their portfolio of experience as much as they perhaps should be in order to be competitive. The veritable explosion in the number of psychologists, and the pipeline of new PhDs from graduate schools, assure that competition will be present for the long-term.

CAREER TRENDS FOR THE FUTURE

Almost twenty years ago the APA Committee on Employment and Human Resources noted that American society was changing and that psychology was being affected by these changes (Howard, et al., 1986). Between the 1960s and 1980s, this seminal article portended the "maturing of the baby boom" generation, the rapid expansion of the college age population and the subsequent explosion of participation in higher education; the movement of women into the labor force, and an "increasing concern with the self."

In 2002, we see that some of these trends have continued, others have waned, and new ones have come along. The baby boomers are now aging and of course their numbers are unprecedented. Technological change, particularly that related to computers and the Internet, continues unabated. Psychology has remained a popular field. Women have expanded their presence in psychology and have changed the face of psychology. Large numbers of Asian and Hispanic immigrants have come to the United States and psychology has had some luck in attracting Hispanics to the field. In the late part of the 20th Century, the numbers of practitioners in psychology grew at an unprecedented rate in response to societal and legislative changes, and ran headlong into the brick wall of managed care, while the move toward obtaining prescription privileges for psychologists has gained ground. Universities and colleges managed their rising costs, in many instances, through the use of a just-in-time-workforce—part-time and temporary faculty. The widely anticipated job market growth for faculty in the late 1990s was not realized and the faculty remain a largely white professional class.

Yet, retirements among academic baby-boomers will be forthcoming. The next 10 to 15 years, when a relatively large cohort of academics plans to retire, will reveal whether higher education will look more like U.S. society. It will also be a point at which the managers of higher education and their trustees decide whether to fight for and maintain today's level of full-time jobs with the potential for tenure or continue a slide into more nonstandard lines for faculty. Will retiring faculty be replaced by a more transient faculty work force? Or will the succeeding generation enjoy the autonomy and satisfaction associated with an earlier cohort of faculty? Below, we consider what these larger societal and economic trends portend for employment in psychology in the future.

Academe

When one of us entered graduate school in social-personality psychology in 1981 at City University of New York, a prominent faculty member repeatedly warned: "You will never work in academia—there are no jobs!" Sure enough, most of those graduating from the program in the late 1980s to early 1990s did not even pursue academic jobs, although some did (including the first author who, in fact, has had a few). The discussion in the foregoing section demonstrated that the quality of worklife in the academy—workload and stability—has declined while weekly hours of work are high. Salaries and benefits have not kept pace with non-academic compensation. The forecast becomes even more complex if we consider the yet unknown role of technology (e.g., distance education), Universities that cross state lines (e.g., University of Phoenix), the rise in non-tenure eligible jobs, and the emergence of new disciplinary fields. Yet, the allure of tenure (or, more accurately, the "marriage" to colleagues and institution) beckons many. By the year 2008, fully 22.4% of the psychology doctoral faculty respondents in the NSOPF 1998 survey year predicted they would retire. Therefore, it might be concluded that employment prospects in academe are rosy. That would be premature. At one public university, five neuropsychology faculty were replaced with one full-time tenure-eligible line and all other courses were covered by newly hired adjuncts. Clearly, the abuse of part-time faculty in many doctoral student- and PhD-rich geographic areas has abetted the decline in tenure eligible jobs. What is more certain is that faculty in all fields need to address the erosion of good jobs in their own workplace: jobs that ensure intellectual generativity for future generations of academic workers, tenure which protects academic freedom and judgment, and a work life that provides a certain trade-off of income for a deeply satisfying personal autonomy.

Given the dissatisfaction of many faculty with salaries, and the fact that most faculty prize autonomy and freedom and do not want to trade their position for a 5-day a week higher-paying administrator's title, has meant that many faculty supplement their income with consulting or other work. Individuals, therefore, should think carefully about the professional time commitment that academic work entails—its high workload and work hours—and the possibility that additional work may be needed to supplement income in some cases.

For many, teaching is rewarding work. Technology will result in as yet unimagined opportunities for those with more of an entrepreneurial approach to their academic careers. Finally, some sectors, such as community colleges, will be recruiting to replace about 30% of nearly 100,000 community-college faculty members who will retire or leave within the next 2 years, according to the American Association of Community Colleges. In fact, some states have pushed to end the reliance on part-time faculty. A 1998 California law mandates a 75–25 percent ratio of full-time to part-time faculty.

Industry

We are discussing future trends for industry right after our discussion of academe and we're doing that on purpose. Perhaps you do not want to live in outer-suburbia or you have your heart set on being in a major league university but you do not think you have "superstar" appeal. Then, there are those academic salaries that you've been warned about and all that publishing. Or, you simply may enjoy working in a "real world" setting applying yourself to the solution of "real world" problems and questions. In a recent article, Robert Sternberg was quoted about the influx of psychologists into nonacademic careers:

> It's partly a result of changes in the economy, but also there was a time when, if you went nonacademic, there was a sense that you failed. It was like, 'what a loser you are.... There are some people who still feel that way, but not everyone. There's a sense that people should find a job that's right for them, rather than satisfy some preconceived notion of what's prestigious. (Smallwood, 2001, p. A10)

Traditionally, jobs in industry were restricted to some policy areas in government, market research and advertising, statistical and quantitative areas, and the training and human resource development functions within large firms. Those opportunities do still exist today but the rise of the human-computer and human-software interface has opened up new applications for psychologists. In fact, psychology is superbly poised to train a new field of specialists: interactive designers. Interactive designers are not programmers or visual designers. Rather, interactive designers conceptualize a variety of applications—how they look and "feel" to a user as they design the way users and programs interact in a dynamic sense regarding the form and content of digital information. Other examples that come to mind include, increasing the efficiency of corporate web-sites, designing equipment such as jet cockpits, conducting research for pharmaceutical corporations, improving standardized tests, helping patients adapt to and use medical aids and prostheses, assisting private schools with organizational and management issues (Smallwood, 2001). Many of these can be carried out by a consulting arrangement as well. Backgrounds in human factors, cognition, social psychology, perception and sensation, to name a few, have clear applications in these areas.

Consulting

Hellkamp and his co-authors conducted a study of consultation among psychologists in the subfields of clinical, counseling, industrial/organizational, and school psychology (Hellkamp, Zins, Ferguson, & Hodge, 1998). They concluded that graduate education and training in the 21st century needs to focus on the role of consulting but that market forces will determine its importance to each subfield. A large subgroup reported that they did not have any formal training in consultation. Of those who did have formal training, the experiences varied with 31% reporting workshop training, 42.5% reporting practicum experience, and nearly half reporting that they had taken courses. Clinical psychologists reported the most dissatisfaction with their courses in the area. This may be due to, as Maddi (1997) and Somerville (1998) observed, the belief that skills associated with clinical populations are transferable across normal populations and organizations and that this belief often goes unchallenged. Most surveyed consultants did not publish extensively, although when they did, they were prolific. Most were not involved in grants. Interestingly, Hellkamp and co-authors asked respondents if they read journals devoted to consulting and 30% answered no.

A consulting practice is not for everyone. To rely on a consulting income alone requires adaptation to an absence of benefits and regularized pay. Others note that the transition from academia to business is often rocky enough to end the attempt (Somerville, 1998). Yet, the financial rewards can be great in some instances and the autonomy associated with consulting is a bug easily caught. Opportunities for psychologists over the past 25 years have developed as different trends in business and organizations emerged. Whatever your specialty or sub-field, you should be alert to changes in government policy that would invent a need for your expertise. Developing knowledge of government agencies at the federal and state level is essential to uncovering how laws and regulations may provide opportunities. For instance, after the Three-Mile Island near-nuclear accident in 1979, psychologists were recruited to develop better control panels, train supervisors in observing human reliability, develop screening measures for the industry, measure reaction time during simulations, and predict human response during evacuations. A range of psychological expertise was needed. Post 9–11, a similar scenario may develop regarding terrorism. Being alert to government actions, developing industries, and technological advances will locate you at the center, rather than the margins, of a new consulting enterprise.

Practice

As we have noted throughout the preceding sections, the past several decades have been ones of change for psychology and certainly those psychologists engaged in health service provision have not been exempt. It is safe to say that psychological practice has seen some of the greatest changes among all the various roles that psychologists can fill. Opportunities expanded in response to legislative and societal changes, and their numbers burgeoned. Concerns for soaring medical costs resulted in the managed care crunch that began in the mid 1980s, concurrent with rising competition from providers in other fields. What areas then still need to be addressed and where are the opportunities that remain largely untapped?

Despite this growth in the number of trained psychologists, services do continue to be inaccessible in many areas of the country and certain target populations continue to face shortages. These populations include rural residents, seriously emotionally disturbed children and adolescents, adults with serious mental disorders, and the elderly. A recent e-mail survey of a small sample of APA health service provider members reported the prevailing client type to be an adult, with more than 40% and up to 50% of the respondents stating that fewer than 10 (including none) of the patients they saw were elderly adults, adolescents or children (APA Research Office, 2002). It may be the case that these populations remain underserved because they do not have or are not given access to health service provider psychologists. It is also likely that if these populations present higher than normal problems with reimbursement, providers may not as readily accept them.

One of the most positive shifts in the practice of psychology has been the broadening reconceptualization of psychologists who practice as *health service providers*, not only professionals who address mental health issues, but as professionals who are eminently equipped to work alongside specialists from other disciplines to address a wide range of health and behavioral problems. Many of the leading causes of death in the United States today have their roots in maladaptive behavior. Many medical procedures can be made less traumatic for the patient and family with the intervention of psychologists and it is the case that practitioners have helped individuals cope with the consequences of large-scale natural or man-made disasters, made all the more imminent through today's technology. A corollary to this shift is the interest, if not actual need, to work with other professions to realize one's promise as a health service provider. Finally, the movement to an interdisciplinary health service provider role is aided by a focus on prevention as well as treatment. These three emphases offer many opportunities that are not encompassed within the more traditional framework of the provider focusing on treating mental health. Expanding the definition of practice also makes possible the expansion of where the work occurs, so we see practitioners moving into settings other than independent practice or organized health care.

Two areas that can often polarize discussion among practitioners include prescription privileges and the importance of outcome or efficacy measures. Organized psychology is supporting legislation that would extend prescription privileges to psychologists with specialized training and preparation. By 2002, 12 states had introduced legislation that, if passed, would allow psychologists to prescribe medications. Ideally this would help to extend services to currently underserved communities and populations. New Mexico passed its bill and it became law on July 1, 2002. Demonstrations of effectiveness appear to be an offshoot of the managed care movement but also have appeared (in a different form, of course) as courses of action that are desirable for graduate programs to pursue. Both represent opportunities for practitioners who might be interested in pursuing prescription privileges or getting involved in the construction of systems of measuring efficacy.

Ongoing changes in federal regulations are moving toward requiring compliance with specific billing and reporting procedures for those seeking reimbursement, much of these will be electronic, and compliance will be mandatory. Involvement in explaining these and other systems to psychologists and in designing aids specific to psychology represent emerging areas of work.

In sum, it appears that the outlook for employment in psychology is positive. In large part this is a function of the very breadth and diversity of the field. It may seem difficult at times to *keep* such diversity under one "roof" and that was not a topic of this chapter. The breadth is strength and a reason that the field continues to be relevant to the world today.

REFERENCES

Allen, W. R., Epps, E. G., Guillory, E. A., Suh, S. A., Bonous-Hammarth, M., & Stassen, M. L. A. (2002). Outsiders within: Race, gender and faculty status in U.S. higher education. In Smith, W. A., Altbach, P. G., & Lomotey, K. (Eds.), *The Racial Crisis in American Higher Education: Continuing Challenges in the Twenty-First Century* (pp. 189–220). Albany, NY: State University of New York Press.

Altbach, P. G. (1991). The racial dilemma in American higher education. In P. G. Altbach, & K. Lomotey (Eds.), *The racial crisis in American higher education* (pp. 3–17). Albany, New York: State University of New York Press.

Altbach, P. G., Lomotey, K., & Rivers, S. (2002). Race in higher education: The continuing crisis. In Smith, W. A., Altbach, P. G., & Lomotey, K. (Eds.). *The Racial Crisis in American Higher Education: Continuing Challenges in the Twenty-First Century* (pp. 23–42). Albany, NY: State University of New York Press.

Baldwin, R., & Chronister, J. (2001). *Teaching without tenure: Policies and practices for a new era.* Baltimore, MD: Johns Hopkins University Press.

Barker, K. (1995). Contingent work: Research issues and the lens of moral exclusion. In L. Tetrick, & J. Barling (Eds.), *Changing employment relations: Behavioral and social perspectives* (pp. 31–60). Washington, DC: American Psychological Association.

Barker, K. (1998). Toiling for piece-rates and accumulating deficits: Contingent work in higher education. In K. Barker, & K. Christensen (Eds.), *Contingent work: American employment relations in transition* (pp. 195–220). Ithaca, NY: ILR/Cornell University Press.

Barker, K. (2002). Standard and nonstandard employment in higher education: Findings from the 1990s. *Changing Career Paths in Science and Engineering. Report by the Commission on Professionals in Science and Technology.* Retrieved April, 2002 from, http://www.cpst.org/Changing.pdf

Barker, K., & Christensen, K. (1998a). Introduction. In K. Barker, & K. Christensen (Eds.), *Contingent work: American employment relations in transition* (pp. 1–18). Ithaca, NY: ILR/Cornell University Press.

Barker, K., & Christensen, K. (1998b). Charting future research. In K. Barker, & K. Christensen (Eds.), *Contingent work: American employment relations in transition* (pp. 306–320). Ithaca, NY: ILR/Cornell University Press.

Benedict, J. G., & Phelps, R. (1998). Introduction: Psychology's view of managed care. *Professional Psychology: Research and Practice, 29*(1), 29–30.

Bureau of Labor Statistics, U. S. Department of Labor, 2002. Occupational Outlook Handbook. Washington, DC: Author.

Burgan, M. (1997). Ratcheting up. *Academe, 83*(3), 5.

Clark, B. R. (1997). Small worlds, different worlds: The uniquenesses and troubles of American academic professions. *Daedalus, 126*, 21–42.

duRivage, V. L. (1992). New policies for the part-time and contingent workforce. In V. L. duRivage (Ed.), *New policies for the part-time and contingent workforce* (pp. 89–122). Armonk, NY: M. E. Sharpe.

Gutek, B. A. (1995). *The dynamics of service: Reflections on the changing nature of customer provider interactions.* San Francisco: Jossey-Bass Publishers.

Hellkamp, D. T., Zins, J. E., Ferguson, K., & Hodge, M. (1998). Training practices in consultation: A national survey of clinical, counseling, industrial/organizational, and school psychology faculty. *Consulting Psychology Journal: Practice and Research, 50*, 228–236.

Henderson, P. H., Clarke, J. E., & Reynolds, M. A., (1996). *Summary report, 1995: doctorate recipients from United States universities.* Washington, DC: National Academy Press.

Hoffer, T., Dugoni, B., Sanderson, A., Sederstrom, S., Ghadialy, R., & Rocque, P. (2001): Doctorate recipients from United States universities: Summary report 2000:. Chicago: National Opinion Research Council (NORC).

Howard, A., Pion, G. M., Gottfredson, G. F., Flattau, P. E., Oskamp, S., Pfafflin, S. M., Bray, D. W., & Burstein, A. G. (1986). The changing face of American psychology: A report from the committee on employment and human resources. *American Psychologist, 41*, 1311–1327.

Hudson, K. (1999). *No shortage of nonstandard jobs: Nearly 30% of workers employed in part-time, temping, and other alternative arrangements.* Briefing Paper. Washington, DC: Economic Policy Institute. Retrieved on June 10, 2001 from http://www.epinet.org/briefingpapers/hudson/hudson.pdf

Kalleberg, A. L., Rasell, E., Hudson, K., Webster, D., Reskin, B. F., Cassirer, N., & Appelbaum, E. (1997). *Nonstandard work, substandard jobs: Flexible work arrangements in the U.S.* Washington, DC: Economic Policy Institute.

Kohout, J., & Wicherski, M. (1991). *1989 Doctorate employment survey.* Washington, DC: American Psychological Association.

Kohout, J., & Wicherski, M. (2003). *1999 Doctorate employment survey.* Washington, DC: American Psychological Association.

Lomotey, K. (1997). Introduction. In K. Lomotey, (Ed.), *Sailing against the wind: African Americans and women in U.S. education* (pp. 3–14). Albany, New York: State University of New York Press.

Maddi, S. R. (1997). Strengths and weaknesses of organization consulting form a clinical psychology background. *Consulting Psychology Journal: Practice and Research, 49*, 207–219.

Manser, M. E., & Picott, G. (1999, April). The role of self-employment in U. S. and Canadian job growth. *Monthly Labor Review*, 10–25.

Murphy, M. J., DeBernardo, C. R., & Shoemaker, W. E. (1998). *Professional Psychology: Research and Practice, 29*(1), 43–51.

National Science Foundation. (1991). *Academic science and engineering: Graduate enrollment and support: 1989.* (NSF 90–324). Washington, DC. Author.

National Science Foundation, Division of Science Resources Studies (in press). *Characteristics of doctoral scientists and engineers in the United States: 1999.* Arlington, VA: National Science Foundation.

NSF/NIH/NEH/USDOE/USDA. (1998). *Survey of earned doctorates, prepublication tables from the summary report 1997, doctorate recipients from United States universities.* Chicago: National Opinion Research Center.

Phelps, R., Eisman, E. J., & Kohout, J. (1998). Psychological practice and managed care: Results of the CAPP practitioner survey. *Professional Psychology: Research and Practice, 29*(1), 31–36.

Research Office. (2002). Summary of results of e-mail survey of health service provider members. Unpublished report. Washington, DC: American Psychological Association.

Rothbaum, P. A., Bernstein, D. M., Haller, O., Phelps, R., & Kohout, J. (1998). New Jersey psychologists' report on managed mental health care. *Professional Psychology: Research and Practice, 29*(1), 37–42.

Sheehan, E. P., & Haselhorst, H. (1999). A profile of applicants for an academic position in social psychology. *Journal of Social Behavior and Personality, 14*, 23–30.

Sheehan, E. P., McDevitt, T., & Ross, H. (1998). Looking for a job as a psychology professor? Factors affecting applicant success. *Teaching of Psychology, 25*, 8–11.

Smallwood, S. (2001, January 12). Star graduates turn down faculty jobs, finding better pay and less stress in industry. *The Chronicle of Higher Education*, p. A10.

Solmon, L. C., Solmon, M. S., & Schiff, T. W. (2002). The changing demographics: Problems and opportunities. In Smith, W. A., Altbach, P. G., & Lomotey, K. (Eds.). *The racial crisis in american higher education: Continuing challenges in the twenty-first century* (pp. 43–76). Albany, NY: State University of New York Press.

Somerville, K. (1998). Where is the business of business psychology headed? *Consulting Psychology Journal: Practice and Research, 50*, 237–241.

Stapp, J., Tucker, A. M., & VandenBos, G. R. (1985). Census of psychological personnel: 1983. *American Psychologist, 40*, 1317–1351.

U.S. Department of Education, National Center for Education Statistics. (1995). *E.D. TABS: Fall Staff in Postsecondary Institutions, 1995*, (Rep. NCES 98-228). Washington D.C.: Government Printing Office.

U.S. Department of Education, National Center for Education Statistics. (1996). *1993 National study of postsecondary faculty (NSOPF-93), CD-ROM Public Use Faculty and Institution Files.* (Rep. No. NCES 99-288). Washington, DC: Government Printing Office.

U.S. Department of Education, National Center for Education Statistics (2001). *1999 National study of postsecondary faculty (NSOPF-99).* CD-ROM Public Use Faculty and Institution Files. Washington, DC: Government Printing Office.

U.S. Department of Education, National Center for Education Statistics (2001). *1999 National study of postsecondary faculty (NSOPF-99).* (Rep. No. NCES 2001-152). Washington, DC: U.S. Department of Education, Office of Educational Research and Improvement.

Wicherski, M., & Kohout, J. (1999). *1997 Doctorate employment survey.* Washington, DC: American Psychological Association.

Wicherski, M., Randall, G., & Kohout, J. (2002). *2001–2002 Faculty salaries in graduate departments of psychology.* Washington, DC: American Psychological Association.

Index